Berlin Fellowship:

East German Perspectives and Missional Encounter

1961 – 1989

Berlin Fellowship:

Oost-Duitse perspectieven en missionaire ontmoeting

1961-1989

met een samenvatting in het Nederlands
und mit einer Zusammenfassung in deutscher Sprache

Proefschrift

ter verkrijging van de graad van doctor in de godgeleerdheid aan de Protestantse Theologische Universiteit te Amsterdam - Groningen, op gezag van de rector, prof.dr. F.G. Immink, ingevolge het besluit van het college voor promoties in het openbaar te verdedigen te Amsterdam op woensdag 19 juni 2013 des middags te 1.45 uur

door

Jane Frances Holslag

geboren op 7 mei 1948
te Denver Colorado, USA

Promotoren: Prof.dr. M.M. Jansen
Prof.dr. H. Noordegraaf

Dit proefschrift werd (mede) mogelijk gemaakt met financiële steun van The Diaspora Foundation, California USA.

CIP KONINKLIJKE BIBLIOTHEEK, DEN HAAG
ISBN 978-3-643-90387-7

Jane Holslag

Berlin Fellowship

*Contact*Zone

Explorations in
Intercultural Theology

edited by

Prof. Dr. Volker Küster

(Johannes Gutenberg-Universität Mainz)

Volume 14

LIT

Jane Holslag

BERLIN FELLOWSHIP

East German Perspectives and Missional Encounter
1961 – 1989

LIT

The cover design makes use of Lee Chul-Soo, *Malttugi* (by courtesy of the artist) and François Goddart, *African Crucifix* (by courtesy of Vivant Univers, Namur, Belgium)

This publication is sponsored by The Diaspora Foundation, Pasadena, CA

This book is printed on acid-free paper.

Bibliographic information published by the Deutsche Nationalbibliothek
The Deutsche Nationalbibliothek lists this publication in the Deutsche Nationalbibliografie; detailed bibliographic data are available in the Internet at http://dnb.d-nb.de.

ISBN 978-3-643-90387-7

A catalogue record for this book is available from the British Library

Klosbachstr. 107
CH-8032 Zürich
Tel. +41 (0) 44-251 75 05
Fax +41 (0) 44-251 75 06
E-Mail: zuerich@lit-verlag.ch
http://www.lit-verlag.ch

LIT VERLAG Dr. W. Hopf
Berlin 2013
Fresnostr. 2
D-48159 Münster
Tel. +49 (0) 2 51-62 03 20
Fax +49 (0) 2 51-23 19 72
E-Mail: lit@lit-verlag.de
http://www.lit-verlag.de

Distribution:
In Germany: LIT Verlag Fresnostr. 2, D-48159 Münster
Tel. +49 (0) 2 51-620 32 22, Fax +49 (0) 2 51-922 60 99, E-mail: vertrieb@lit-verlag.de
In Austria: Medienlogistik Pichler-ÖBZ, e-mail: mlo@medien-logistik.at
In Switzerland: B + M Buch- und Medienvertrieb, e-mail: order@buch-medien.ch
In the UK: Global Book Marketing, e-mail: mo@centralbooks.com
In North America: International Specialized Book Services, e-mail: orders@isbs.com
e-books are available at www.litwebshop.de

Contents

Foreword

The Berlin Fellowship program was initiated in 1961 as a ministry of American Christians visiting East German congregations. Prior to this, as a university student activity of a Presbyterian church in southern California, it had its roots in post-war international youth reconciliation projects in many parts of Europe. With the building of the Berlin Wall in 1961, this program narrowed its focus on Berlin and in cooperation with the Evangelical Church of Berlin-Brandenburg (West) began a ministry of regular visits, initially to East Berlin and eventually to the entire German Democratic Republic. Twice a year, beginning in 1967, groups of American Presbyterians (2 - 12 lay and clergy) traveled to West Berlin and into East Germany for a 12-day visit with six to eight congregations. The eastern hosts from all corners of the country welcomed a small team of three to four people for an evening, a day, or a weekend visit. As the years went by, the trip took on a pattern of two weekends spent in different congregations, with the weekdays usually being spent with several congregations just for a day or two.

Typically, the Americans did not speak German, nor the Germans much English, so most communication was done through an interpreter, often the team leader. The visits consisted of shared meals, walks, sightseeing, organized meetings with youth, young adults, children's groups, church leaders. Sometimes a visit would include participation with the host congregation in a Kirchentag (regional or national church congress), a parish festival, or a Sunday worship service. Conversation was central to all meetings and occasions, with topics ranging widely from thematic biblical discussions and other church-related matters to political or social issues of the day (from both countries), along with personal and family matters. Each year, the composition of the teams was different, with teams visiting both old and new congregations; only a few Americans participated more than one or two times. Though sometimes misunderstood as 'short-term mission' by the Americans, this program wasn't evangelistic or a work-service trip but rather a form of diaconal and ecumenical interpersonal or intercultural exchange and support.

Though Berlin Fellowship was sponsored and in large part financed by the Evangelical Church of Berlin-Brandenburg (West), East German church bishops throughout the country were aware and informed of the visits. However, it remained an unofficial church-related activity, in both East Germany and the United States. Americans traveled as tourists (registered by the police) and stayed in Inter-Hotels. From as early as 1969 / 70, the state authorities (Ministry for State Security, *MfS* or *Stasi*) were aware of and closely watching this twice yearly visitation program, as well as the monthly East Berlin "Fellowship" gathering of those interested in conversation and contact, and a yearly "East Committee" meeting of regional hosts for planning team visits. Besides hosting American teams in his own congregation, the *Stasi's* main information source for 20 years was a trusted member of the both the "Fellowship" in East Berlin and the East Committee.

After the Wall opened in November 1989, some of the eastern congregations were interested in reverse visits to the U.S., and several congregational partnerships grew from these contacts. The eastern Berlin "Fellowship" group continued to meet as did the East Committee until 1996 when the entire program was formally celebrated and closed.

Acknowledgements

This chapter of my life began in 1980 during my first Berlin Fellowship trip to the German Democratic Republic. It was on that initial visit that I began to learn to listen to the voice of the "other," and what I heard and what then happened in a place of fellowship and encounter I did not anticipate. More than thirty years later, I dedicate this work to the many Christian brothers and sisters in East Germany who opened their homes, their congregations, and themselves to *koinonia* with Christians from the United States, *koinonia* in ways no one expected. Their voices are hopefully well-represented in the interviews, which I trust still speak today.

I am most grateful to God for ten years of gracious financial support and encouragement from the Diaspora Foundation in southern California. I am also thankful for all friends, east and west, whose Berlin Fellowship experiences led them to cheer me on through this process, and for the special friends in California, Berlin, Lithuania, Lebanon, Qatar, and in the Netherlands who granted me and this project space, not just in their homes but also their hearts.

I extend deep gratitude lastly, to my supervisors, Dr. Mechteld Jansen and Dr. Herman Noordegraf. They have been an inspiritation and, like beacons, have shown the way with kindness and scholarly wisdom, with open and honest critique and with what I found to be an abiding spirit of integrity and love for both the academy and God's mission and the church.

Chapter One

Research Question, Background Information, and Study Methodology

1. The Main Research Question and Statement of the Problem

Is fellowship encounter a missional experience? This research question is historically and contextually bound to the specific time period of a visitation program participated in by American and East German Christians between 1961 and 1989. This study is primarily missiological and seeks to explore how the "recipients" or "partners" in East Germany perceived, remember and evaluate a mission-like or missional activity known as Berlin Fellowship. Fellowship and missional are the two operational terms which warrant attention and brief definition at the outset of this introduction.

The term 'missional' entered North American theological vocabulary and missiological discussion in the 1990's, primarily through publications and conferences of the Gospel and our Culture Network.[1] The word is still in formation, but for the purposes of this research, I will use it in reference to the evolving discussion of Church as mission. Rather than doing mission, as one of its many activities (i.e. worship, teaching, service, proclamation), the Church is "missional" as it realizes and embraces its very nature (cf. Hendrik Kraemer, "The Church is Mission").[2] Discussions precede David Bosch's examination of the topic of mission in *Transforming Mission*, but his *and* Lesslie Newbigin's contributions to missional church thinking and theology point to God as already being in mission toward people and toward his creation (*Missio Dei*). As such then, the Church is participating in what God is already about, the healing and transformation of God's world. The term missional is not a new

---

[1] GOCN, http://www.gocn.org/(accessed August 2005).

[2] Hendrik Kraemer, *Religion and the Christian Faith*, Philadelphia 1956, 29.

definition of the Church but rather a call for it to realize anew its identity and purpose in God's work of redemption, reconciliation and transformation; it is called anew to witness to the world of God's healing purposes and intentions for it.[3] The Church's witness is manifest in all that it does and is all dimensions of its life and service are missional witness[4] and more importantly, for this discussion, that witness is even within, among, and to the Christian community itself. For this research study, I am using the word missional and not missionary, for in American English, this term can have very distinct, dated and limited usage. For example, traditionally, it is implicit that missionaries are sent out by a mission agency or a denomination to bring the Gospel to those who haven't heard it. Being missional, on the other hand, is witnessing to and participating in God's redemptive and transforming mission already operative the world. Being missional constitutes who the Church is and what the Church does as the body of believers. This missional body is realizing its identity when assembled for worship or witnessing through proclamation and service, when ministering to any in need or gathered and united in fellowship.

This second key term, fellowship or *koinonia* offers a much longer history of usage rooted in biblical Greek. Fellowship is but one translation of this Greek word. In the New Testament, *koinonia* may be defined in English with several words: communion, participation, fellowship or sharing (i.e. having a share in the gospel, fellowship with Christ, sharing in the Spirit, partnership or participation with one another for witness and service).[5] Regardless of which English word is used, *koinonia* is at root an essential component in the nature and mission of the Church, witnessing to the restored relationship with God, given and mediated through Christ and maintained by the Spirit. It then further signifies Christian experience through relationship in community with each other. This relationship is not just a spiritual reality, for it also manifests itself as engagement and encounter with other believers. For the participants within the body of believers, *Koinonia* enables and includes sharing of worldly goods, encouragement, and witnessing to God's love for one another. Though varied in biblical usage, in this research I am using the word fel-

[3] Darrell Guder, Worthy Living: Work and Witness from the Perspective of Missional Church Theology, in: *Word and World*, 25:4; Fall 2005, 424 - 426.
[4] *Mission and Evangelism in Unity Today*, WCC, CWME Preparatory Paper, 2000, A9, http://www.oikoumene.org/en/resources/documents/wcc-commissions/mission-and-evangelism/cwme-world-conference-athens-2005/preparatory-paper-n-1-mission-and-evangelism-in-unity-today.html (accessed August 2009).
[5] Günter Gassman and Thomas Best, Koinonia in Scripture: Survey of Biblical Texts, in: *On the Way to Fuller Koinonia*, 1994, 61.

lowship as referring to the community in Christ given through the Spirit, which shares in and actively engages in a common life or in a shared encounter, however short or long. This fellowship in the Gospel may entail communing as the body of Christ at table, in the Sacraments or worship, in conversation or study (see Chapter 2 for discussion). This research then asks, is this shared experience of fellowship a place, a happening, an encounter of a missional nature? Do such encounters of "life together" even in a limited, existential period of time count as missional experience?

Though the vocabulary of the question postdates the time period, the question standswas the Berlin Fellowship experience a missionally-stamped encounter for the Germans? How so? Do the memories and recalled experience of this encounter reveal *koinonia* as a valid locale of missional activity? Will these recollections shed light on how fellowship, evidencing how *missio Dei* functions? Along with other classic signs of the Church proclamation, worship, witness, and diaconal service (all more easily mission-connected), is fellowship missional?

The history of this unofficial yet church-sanctioned and sponsored visitation program of American Christians to East German Protestant congregations is partially recorded with story and documentation from the western side of the experience. There is no eastern participants' documentation elucidating or testifying to the encounters. There is sufficient eastern documentation (state security files, some private photos, calendar notes, correspondence) that testifies to the program's existence but not to the individual experiences. This mission-like program, which was initiated by American Presbyterians and was greeted by the German church leadership in Berlin, resembled ecumenical visitation actions of the time and had a foundational missional component of visiting the sister or brother in prison, cf. Matt. 25:36. It took the shape of and was labeled "short-term mission" by U.S. citizens who participated.

Berlin Fellowship's origins are rooted in post-war international student efforts at reconciliation between former allied and German enemies. After the Wall was erected, though the enemy status remained, the program was housed in West Berlin and focused on solidarity, mutual fellowship and encouragement through visitation. East German congregations were the "recipients" who chose, for more than 20 years, to host the visitors in their homes and congregations repeatedly. Their memories and interpretations of the visits warrant examination, as valid and necessary additions to existing documentation. Additionally, this research will contribute to the growing body of missiological research in the field of church partnerships.

Recently assembled information, in the form of interviews, along with this research comprise key components in this discussion and in the larger story. These gathered memories and recollections of eastern participants constitute an important component of East German and Presbyterian Church mission history. Moreover, such information attests to the experience of being the "visited" and is a word from those who were not just recipients but full participants and conversation partners in an experience of Christian fellowship, across cultural, ideological, and language barriers.

2. Directly Related Resource Literature

Several factors are noteworthy at the outset of this literature review pertaining to both this section of directly related literature and that which follows. Research of such a specific chapter of church and mission history pertaining to the German Democratic Republic (GDR) would ideally be conducted accessing literature in as many languages as possible; this review is limited to German and English language sources. The exact research question and time period both contribute to the complex nature of the study, resulting in a somewhat limited number of directly-related literature resources, as indicated in the following:
(1) Between the end of World War II and 1989 there were many congregational German-German partnerships, Dutch-German partnerships, official international and ecumenical church visitations in East Germany as well as regional level partnerships (i.e. Berlin Brandenburg (east and west) and the United Church of Christ (U.S.A.)[6];Herrnhuter Brüdergemeine and sister congregations around the world;[7] partnership between the churches (*Landeskirchen*) of Thuringia and Württemberg[8], among others. However, the specific kind of quiet visitation at the congregational level conducted by the Berlin Fellowship for over 20 years appears to have been unique. I am unaware of any other ongoing, organized, regular visitation or church-related program of individual us Christians to a wide variety of congregations in the GDR during this time period.

---

[6]http://globalministries.org/get-involved/church-to-church-partnerships/GLobal-Church-Partnerships.pdf (accessed September 2009).
[7] Hedwig Richter, *Pietismus im Sozialismus, Die Herrnhuter Brüdergemeine in der DDR*, Göttingen 2009.
[8] Karoline Rittberger-Klas, *Kirchenpartnerschaften im geteilten Deutschland, Am Beispiel der Landeskirchen Württemberg und Thüringen*, Göttingen 2006.

(2) University and public library shelves are filled with published studies of the East German communist dictatorship and its system, politics, leaders, eras, economy, secret police, state church policy, and the Protestant church's role and activities during the entire existence of the country (1949-1989). Contributing to a plethora of analyzed and published resources are sociology, psychology, and political science studies of community life, private life, the work world, opposition groups, the women's movement, the "Wende" (1988/90 and the opening of the Wall), Protestant peace initiatives and groups, the conciliar process, youth work all aiding in the understanding about the key elements and influences on the setting and context during the target years of this study. However, very few of these sources actually offer theological or missiological analysis of, reflection upon, or insight into the personal or daily life experience of individual Christians or of congregational life in the GDR.[9]
(3) After the first individual contacts in the early and mid 1960, American team visits went beyond the city limits of East Berlin to the entire GDR (Brandenburg, Saxony, Thuringia, Saxony-Anhalt and Mecklenburg). Berlin Fellowship's western records indicate more than 100 different congregations in all five regions were visited. However, record of Berlin Fellowship activity is documented nowhere in official eastern church files (at the congregational, district or synod levels), though there is a faint trail of notes in pastors' calendars, eastern related correspondence, private copies of secret police files and personal photos.[10] The program is only noted in a few officials western consistorial or church headquarter records, either in former West Berlin or in the U.S.[11]
(4) State documentation in the Ministry for State Security's files (*Ministerium für Staatssicherheit, MfS, Stasi*) includes extensive reports on all aspects of the program and its key personalities in two main operative procedure files (*operativer Vorgang, OV*) and three similar files accessed.[12] Reports focused on the program aspects of the monthly meeting

[9] The Enquete-Kommission's ‚Aufarbeitung von Geschichte und Folgen de SED-Diktatur in Deutschland' two-volume set on the Church in the GDR, entitled *Rolle und Selbstverständnis der Kirchen in den Verschiedenen Phasen der SED-Diktatur*, is as one source of such information offering manuscripts of hearings from the early 1990's. Pastors, theologians, and Christians from all walks of life and various experts "tell their story."
[10] See Chapter 3, Introduction.
[11] Correspondence records primarily indicate reimbursement requests and responses between the West Berlin Zinzendorf congregation and the West Berlin Consistory, Zinzendorf Collection.
[12] Federal Commissioner for the Stasi Files (*Bundesbeauftragter für die Stasi Unterlagen*): MfS BV/Gera, Abt. XX, Reg.-Nr. X547/71, Archiv-Nr. 1456-78; MfS BV/Berlin, Abt. XX, Reg.-Nr .XVI644-73/84, Archiv-Nr. 1486/84; MfS BV/Berlin Abt. XX, Reg.-Nr. X/476/84, MfS AKG0342; MfS BV/Berlin Abt. XX, Reg.-Nr. 20954/92, BE 54; MfS BV/Berlin Abt. XX, Reg.-Nr. 20955/92, BE55.

of interested East Berliners with West Berlin Pastor Ted Schapp and his co - worker Bärbel Eccardt, on the yearly East Committee planning meeting (leading eastern representatives from the different regions), on spring and fall U.S. visitation trips, and on assorted personal conversations. None of these examined records contains any theological observations or analyses, although they provide an rather detailed picture of the *MfS* and its methods of information gathering.

Further, the German Democratic Republic's system of rule included municipal, county, regional and national level government officials whose job descriptions included church matters (*Kirchenfragen*). It might be assumed that those officials would have known of or been interested in such an American visitation program. For any of those offices to have been put on alert for such visitors, the Central Committee of the Socialist Unity Party or the State Secretary's Office for Church Questions would have had to have been aware of Berlin Fellowship's presence and activities. Normally foreign visitors to the GDR who identified themselves as church-related (groups or individuals) applied directly through this office for permission to enter the country, making their affiliation, travel plans, host congregation or event known. If such groups applied through the border authorities or police with stated church connections, their applications were also passed to the State Secretary's office. In the case of Berlin Fellowship, the applications for entry[13] were never filed with this office but rather through the central travel bureau in Berlin.[14] These applications never indicated purpose for travel as church-related business. Moreover, Berlin Fellowship team members entered the country on individual visas as tourists, overnighted in inter-hotels (as required by law), and if registration with the local police was necessary, this was attended to by team leaders in the locality. Upon advice from the West Berlin consistory, these precautions were standard operating procedure and were adopted in order specifically not to draw attention of the state authorities.[15] No examined documentation (1969 - 1989) from the German Federal Archive's files from the office of the State Secretary for Church Questions contained reference to Berlin Fellowship.

---

[13] Copy of an application for entering the country (*Antrag auf Einreise*) for Nina Dulabaum traveling in the GDR, 26.4.88-9.5.88, Zinzendorf Collection.

[14] Siegfried Suckgut, *Die DDR im Blick der Stasi 1976: Die geheimen Berichte an die SED-Führung,* BStU: http://www.bstu.bund.de/DE/Wissen/MfS-Dokumente/DDR-Blick-Stasi/_node.-html. In 1975 and the first half year of 1976, 23,6 million persons from socialist and non-socialist countries and West Berlin entered the country for a visit or as tourists.

[15] Notes from telephone conversation with Ralph Hamburger, August 8, 2012.

Because government municipal, county, and district officials had responsibilities to ensure state church policy (*Kirchenpolitik*) be carried out, it might seem they would have interest in such visitors. However, their responsibilities were to see that the official church policy of the state was understood, affirmed, and adhered to by the bishops, superintendents, and pastors under their supervision. These officials were not necessarily policing the activities in every parish, unless for instance, politically hot issues or topics were being preached on, advertised in church display cases, or reported to their offices. Furthermore, examined files from five administrative government archives (responsible for church questions) at the district, county, and city levels. Archives produced no evidence indicating knowledge of Berlin Fellowship or associated key names (cf. Archiv Landesarchiv Berlin, Land Brandenburg Archiv-District Potsdam, Schwerin Landeshauptarchiv-Mecklenburg, Schwerin Stadtarchiv, and Hauptstadtarchiv Dresden - Sachsen).[16]

3. Related Resource Literature

There being no comparable or directly related resource literature doesn't preclude studies of a similar nature offering interesting and informative related material, especially in church partnerships. These studies offer limited examples of participants' voices, and several note the need for further study in this aspect of partnerships.

German church archives (parish, district, and national) contain various kinds of records attesting to partnerships between church districts, congregations, youth and student groups, and diaconal services in both east and west. More importantly, there are a number of published and researched works about these relationships, with several being pertinent to this study and the voice of the partner. Each mentions congregational level visitation and regular contact, with reference to personal interaction and encounter. Each contributes substantial information about partnerships between East German and either Dutch or West German congregations and in varying degrees, give voice to the eastern partners.

---

[16] Rittberger-Klas, *Kirchenpartnerschaften*, 22. In the opening section of this author's research on a decades-long German church-to-church partnership, she notes that looking for files containing the theme of church partnerships in state archives is, even as in church archives, like looking for a needle in a haystack. In relation to this, a former officer from the State Secretary for Church Questions' office informed me that in the case of Berlin Fellowship, such a search would be less than likely to produce data. Notes taken in personal conversation with Horst Dohle, July 3; 2012.

Stückwerk, Partnerschaften zwischen den Evangelischen Kirchengemeinden Elias-Berlin(Ost) und Iserlohn (Westfalen) in politischen Spannungsfeld der Jahre 1978-1998[17], is a chronological scrapbook-like array of letters, stories, narrative recollections, photos, examples of publications during 1989, program itineraries and other memorabilia of the 20-year long partnership between two congregations, one in Berlin and the other in western German region of Westphalia.

Beatrice deGraaf's study *Über die Mauer, Die DDR, die niederländischen Kirchen und die Friedensbewegung*[18] focuses primarily on the Dutch church and political interests in the East German church life and the peace movement of the late 70's and 80's. Church to church partnerships, of which there were 200 by 1985, played key roles in the contacts. DeGraaf reports that both the Dutch and the German congregations found having contacts more important than political purposes or aims.[19] "The East German guest families were looking for attention/acceptance, solidarity, Christian connections and a window to the west."[20]

Karoline Rittberger-Klas' thorough examination of the East-West partnership between Thuringia and Württemberg, *Kirchenpartnerschaften im Geteilten Deutschland. Am Beispiel der Landeskirchen Württemberg und Thüringen*, contains a number of clear citations with individual voices noting the benefits and advantages of such partnerships. The author's scholarly goal, however, is not to examine the individual memories or perceptions of either partner but rather to examine the development of this partnership on the regional level over the course of 40 years. Although it began in 1949 primarily as a relief action sending packages (foodstuffs, books, medicines, textiles) and was then called a *Patentschaft* (relation of God-parent to baptized child or infant), the *Partnerschaft* (partnership) label was adopted in the early 70's. Besides the official institutional cooperation with material and financial support supplied by the West German churches, the personal "partnerships from family to family and individual to individual" counted as one "pillar" of the church to church relationship over the years.[21] "At least as important as the material aid was the personal sharing and exchange through letters and visits which gave the Thuringian congregation the feeling of not hav-

---

[17] Georg Katzorke and Klaus Görig, Wolfgang Lindenberg, Ingrid Kaden, *Stückwerke, Partnerschaft zwischen den evangelischen Kirchengemeinden Elias-Berlin(Ost) und Iserlohn(Westfalen) in politischen Spannungsfeld der Jahre 1978-199,* Iserlohn 2002.

[18] Beatrice de Graaf, *Über die Mauer, Die DDR, die niederländischen Kirchen und die Friedensbewegun,* Münster 2007.

[19] De Graaf, *Über die Mauer*, 249.

[20] Op.cit., 291.

[21] Rittberger-Klas, *Kirchenpartnerschaften,* 139.

ing been forgotten and the Württemberg congregation knowledge of the conditions in church and private life in the GDR [...] The exchange with partners from the west was understood as a window to the world for the Christians in the GDR, it gave them the feeling of not being forgotten, not being written off, of not being completely cut off."[22]

In *Pietismus im Sozialismus Die Herrnhuter Brüdergemeine in der DDR*, Hedwig Richter examines a long history of Moravian Church brotherly/sisterly partner relations between the East German Herrnhut parish and congregations in West Germany and West Berlin, the CSSR (Czechoslovakian Socialist Soviet Republic) and above all, in this study, the U.S. Moravians. As the title indicates, she does examine the faith understanding of this unique pietistic tradition, ecumenical contacts, and the role these contacts played in helping this Moravian world center in Herrnhut and its congregation to persist in Christian community throughout the entire 40 years in the GDR. The western support for the Brüdergemeine in the GDR was generous and especially strong in the 50's and 60's, but Richter emphasizes that the exchange at synods, conferences, and during visits should not be underestimated.[23] "The foreign visitors gave to the GRD Hernnhuters a glimpse of the world, that was strange at least to the youngest generation [...]"[24]

Two other studies provide further glimpses into partnership relations and ecumenical contacts. Katharina Kunter's *Erfüllte Hoffungen und zerbrochene Träume, Evangelische Kirchen in Deutschland im Spannungsfeld von Demokratie und Sozialismus* (1980 - 1993) is an examination of the East German engagement with the "Conciliar Process for Justice, Peace, and the Integrity of Creation." This movement, launched in 1983 at the World Council of Churches meeting in Vancouver was embraced by the East German delegation.[25] The movement, which gathered momentum in the 80's was one which many lay people were drawn to, affording them ecumenical contacts and a chance for public political engagement and dialogue. Three assemblies in 1988-89 addressed the conciliar process by bringing many the chance to have their voices heard and be listened to:" to be open for mutuality, that means ready to listen to each other, to understand each other and to learn from one another. That

---

[22] Op.cit., 141f. and 253.

[23] Hedwig Richter, Wir spürten den Herzschlag brüderlicher Liebe, von transnationalen Austausch der Herrnhuter Brüdergemeine im Kalten Krieg, in: *Umworbener Klassenfeind, das Verhältnis der DDR zu den USA*, Uta. A. Balbier und Christianne Rösch (eds.), Berlin 2006, 97-122.

[24] Op.cit., 219.

[25] Heino Falcke, *Vom Gebot Christi, daß die Kirche uns die Waffen aus der Hand nimmt und den Krieg verbietet. Zum konziliaren Weg des Friedens. Ein Beitrag aus der DDR*; Stuttgart 1986.

is what being in connection and friendship are all about.“ [26] Focusing on the more formal partner relations between the Evangelical Church in Germany(*EKD*) and the Federation of Churches in the GDR (*BEK*), Anke Silomon's *Anspruch und Wirklichkeit der "besonderen Gemeinschaft": Der Ost - West Dialog der deutschen evangelischen Kirchen 1969 - 1991*[27] rehearses in detail many conversations and meetings with the partners, though they are more centered around the maintenance of high-level church to church contacts.

Such specific GDR partnership studies are supplemented by projects in oral history, like that conducted in 1987 by Lutz Niethammer, Alexander von Pluto, and Dorothee Wierling in *Die Volkseigene Erfahrung*[28] and by a growing body of memoirs, autobiographies, biographies, collections of sermons, internet sites, and educational materials all of which do contribute to a substantial body of church-related works in this period of history. This book provides 30 biographical reflections on life in the GDR from various perspectives of workers, intellectuals, and professionals. This collection of anonymous interviews affords personal insights into life and the situation in the GDR, including recollections from one Protestant pastor and one Roman Catholic priest. The date of collection, 1987, and the unusual fact that a western researcher was given permission to conduct such a wide variety of interviews at this juncture in time, is noteworthy.

Further reference to participant reflections on congregational level partnerships can be found in a 1996 research project on the partnership relations between four West German Lutheran congregations and four congregations in Africa. This study by Lothar Bauerochse alludes now and again to the African partners' reactions, thoughts, and concerns. Bauerochse states at the outset of his study that foundational research from the side of the African church is long overdue and should be done by the Africans themselves.[29] Bauerochse concedes that his emphasis is on the German side of the German-African relationships. A second similar recent research project examining sister-church relationships offers a bit more "air time" to the voices of partner / recipients in North Ameri-

---

[26] Katharina Kunter, *Erfüllte Hoffnungen und zerbrochene Träume: evangelische Kirchen in Deutschland im Spannungsfeld von Demokratie und Sozialismus (1980-1993*, Göttingen 2006, 98.
[27] Anke Silimon, *Anspruch und Wirklichkeit der »besonderen Gemeinschaft«*; Göttingen 2006.
[28] Lutz Niethammer and Alexander von Plato, Dorothee Wierling, *Die Volkseigene Erfahrung, Eine Archäologie des Lebens in der Industrieprovinz der DDR*, Berlin 1991.
[29] Lothar Bauerochse, *Miteinander leben lernen. Zwischenkirchliche Partnerschaften als ökumenischen Lerngemeinschaften*, Erlangen 1996, 16.

can-initiated partnerships but the author concedes she has not ably included those voices.[30]

In spite of less attention being given to the perspective and voice of the "other" partners in most of these studies, those related to the church in the GDR in the time period under scrutiny are valuable resources. Depending on era and region, they illumine the complex contextual and historical setting, one that was quite varied. These studies are a clear reminder of the organizational, personal, and faithful attention given partners and partnerships over many years and are a testimony to the decade-long actions of committed western partner parishes and churches. These works, along with other publications (a growing body of autobiographical, theological, and educational literature) further add to the documented picture of the life lived daily by active Christians in the GDR. Biographical reviews,[31] collections of dedicatory essays,[32] memoirs,[33] autobiographies,[34] theological and historical essays,[35] websites,[36] and reflections by and about pastors,[37] bishops,[38] their children[39], along with educational curriculum and related material[40] all offer glimpses and insights into the specific and varied era and circumstances in the years 1961 - 1989.

4. My Role, Involvement, and Contribution to Research in the Field

In 1980, I was selected to participate as a team member with the Berlin Fellowship, and I made my first trip to Berlin and East Germany. This

[30] Janet Kragt Bakker, *Encountering the Church in the Global South: Sister Congregation Relationships and Their Impact on Parishoners in Select Washington, D.C. Churches, A Dissertation,,* Washington, D.C., 2010 and Samuel Broomfield Reeves, *Congregation-to-Congregation Relationship : a Case Study of the Partnership between a Liberian Church and a North American Church*, Dallas 2004.

[31] Johannes Hempel, *Erfahrungen und Bewahrungen Ein biographischer Rückblick im Gespräch mit Udo Hahn*, Leipzig 2004.

[32] Joachim Heise and Johannes Gruhn (eds), *Horizont und Mitte, Albrecht Schönherr Pfarrer und Bischof in zwei Diktaturen, Zum 100. Geburtstag*, Berlin 2011.

[33] Theo Lehmann, *Freiheit wird dann sein, Aus meinem Leben*, Neukirchen-Vluyn 2005.

[34] Werner Krusche, *Ich werde nie mehr Geige spielen können. Erinnerungen*, Stuttgart 2007.

[35] Heino Falcke, *Wo bleibt die Freiheit? Christ sein in Zeiten der Wende*, Freiburg 2009.

[36] http://www.wolf-kroetke.de/links.html (accessed July 2012)

[37] Klaus-Peter Hertzsch, *Laß uns vorwärts in die Weite Sehn, Texte zu meiner Biographie*, Stuttgart 2004.

[38] Hagen Findeis and Detlef Pollack, *Selbstbewahrung oder Selbstverlust. Bischöfe und Repräsentanten der evangelischen Kirchen über ihr Leben in Der DDR*, Berlin 1999.

[39] Bettina Ernst-Bertram, Jens Planer-Friedrich, *Pfarrerkinder in der DDR*, Berlin 2008.

[40] *Zeitreise DDR, Elf Beiträge zur DDR-Geschichte*, Leipzig 2010. 11 film CDs and accompanying material.

visit was life changing in ways I never expected, and I returned for team visitations in 1982, 1984 and 1986. In 1987 - 1988 I lived and worked in Berlin for the regional church of Berlin-Brandenburg (West) as a fraternal/sororal minister. My pastoral work in the Zinzendorf congregation was limited, for I worked primarily with Berlin Fellowship, Reverend Ted Schapp, Frau Bärbel Eccardt, and the eastern leaders. After fifteen months, I returned to my associate pastorate in a Presbyterian congregation in southern California. In 1990, I was commissioned by the Presbyterian Church U.S.A. as a mission worker in Berlin for my denomination to encourage and establish mission "partner" relations with Reformed congregations in the newly opened countries of the former Warsaw Pact and to work with Berlin Fellowship in a new chapter of its post-Wall, post-Iron Curtain life.

After November 1989, the eastern Germans were anxious to finally travel to U.S. congregations and to see for themselves what life for Christians in the U.S. was like. In June 1996, after four reverse trips to the U.S. and the establishment of a few congregation-to-congregation partnerships, Berlin Fellowship corporately celebrated its life and history; 120 + former participants from the U.S. and eastern Germany gathered for three days and concluded the ministry program. This closing celebration entitled 'Hallelujah, Amen!' took place in the same church-run diaconal home and retreat center in eastern Berlin, which was the same locale for pastors' conferences visited by American visitors in the 1960's. For further information, see Chapter 3.

In 1996, the program ended, and volumes of the notes, records, letters, and reports from West Berlin and from the California files were boxed and stored in basements and closets. The U.S. documentation from the 1950's and 1960's was donated to the archives at Fuller Theological Seminary (Pasadena, CA) and the Presbyterian Historical Society (Philadelphia, PA) received the material from the 1970's and 1980's, but German records remained in personal storage, awaiting an archive home. It was apparent the material needed to be archived. Not until 2003, as I sorted through the West Berlin Zinzendorf church office files in preparation for archiving, did I come to recognize that there was no record, at least not on paper, of the "eastern" perspective or side of the Berlin Fellowship story in this collection of western records.

From 1961 - 1989 those official church office records were housed in the Zinzendorf parish in West Berlin by Bärbel Eccardt. A substantial collection, it contains periodic record of West Berlin consistory correspondence (original and copies) regarding funding, as well as a large chronological collection of GDR hotel vouchers, exchange receipts, entry application forms, restaurant, post receipts, team reports, observation notes, notes from planning trips, team itineraries and reports all directly related to Berlin Fellowship. Although the archived files from West Berlin consistory officers responsible might contain copies of these same correspondence and reports, no western consistory files were consulted for this study.

In efforts to keep a low profile and to avoid risk, few eastern pastors have records of their congregations' involvement in Berlin Fellowship. Few entered dates for team visits in their calendars; the name of the organization did not appear on any reminder post cards,[41] nor was it supposed to be uttered in public places. Eastern participants were not to write their guests. Printed materials or announcements typical to congregational events were not produced for Berlin Fellowship visits. The context in the GDR in these years dictated a high degree of caution and wariness, and there was a certain fear of discovery and eventual repercussion, although nothing illegal or criminal was happening. In spite of these precautions, there is a small body of eastern documentation available, mostly in private holdings and further referenced in Chapter 3.

Before I could choose an archive for the assembled western records and papers, it seemed the other half of the story was calling to be written down, in spite of there being very little eastern German participant documentation. Thus, I set out to research the eastern perspectives via interviews in hopes of collecting and compiling recalled information for the archives. This project began under the tutelage of two professors, both of whom were unable to see the project beyond its first three years of part-time research. In the process of the first years of collecting data, I became convinced that this information is not only essential for the story of Berlin Fellowship, for church annals and future research, but that it also may offer foundational insight of a missiological nature into the effects of fellowship in mission/missional programs on recipients. I am seeking to validate and draw attention in this dissertation to this kind of missiological inquiry and qualitative research.

Though I initially assumed records about missional or diaconal efforts to the former Warsaw Pact countries and Soviet Republics exist, there seems to be very little evidence of scholarly, evaluative, literary or historical material by the visited, the ministered to, the recipients of gifts, medicine, Bibles, and the myriad of other items sent and smuggled. Moreover, there appear to be no formal studies of the recipients' or partners' impressions, memories, reflections, or evaluations of those times,

[41] Private collection, Günter Mieth, Detmold.

events and visitors. This research offers to initiate a new aspect to this field of mission studies, particularly related to central and Eastern Europe and the former republics of the Soviet Union.

5. Main Concepts

In this study, there are a number of seminal concepts underlying the discussion. Some of these key concepts are usual vocabulary in typical theological discussions:

Fellowship/*koinonia*, church/*ecclesia*, kingdom/reign of God, mission/*missio Dei*/missional, reconciliation, Trinity, and Christology. Other related vocabulary is more closely tied to the field of missiology: context, contextual and intercultural theology, partnership intercontextuality, and interculturation. Chapter 2 addresses definitions and relevance of these and other theological terms and concepts, as they pertain to the research question, data analysis methods, and findings.

Because this study focuses on the eastern German perspectives with participant interview material comprising the target data, several issues related to qualitative research should be noted. First, background matters related to oral history, narrative and storytelling don't play a major role in this research. Interviewees do lapse into storytelling or anecdotal recollection but only occasionally. At the outset of the project, the interview questions were not designed to gather facts already documented in western materials, nor were they necessarily seeking personal biographical reflection, theological analysis, or specific information about the social or political context. When the interviews were conducted, I was gathering "perspectives" from eastern participants on what happened and what they thought about it. Memory and recollection issues about data in this regard are of secondary relevance. The interviewees were asked to talk about their experiences as they remembered them. In the course of the interviews, they did remember and recount feelings, faces, names, events, and specific occurrences, noting periodically quite openly, what they did not remember. Some also took care to reflect and analyze, often theologically, though this was not solicited.

Secondly, qualitative research is subjective and tightly bound to the interviewing process, interview coding and data analysis. In this study, these research matters meld into the missiological findings, and a surprising body of quotations emerges from the interview transcripts. Chapter 4 addresses the particulars of qualitative data collection, methodology of analysis and its significance for the research question.

6. Methodology of the Study

Three of four chapters of this study result from gathering information from various forms of narrative documentation.

(1) For the story and background of Berlin Fellowship, I read the West Berlin congregational records and archived U.S. related files (correspondence, reports, office notes, etc.) outlining, analyzing, condensing and summarizing the material. At the time I worked through these files, I paid particular attention to comments or reports which clearly rehearse the eastern voices or perspectives; these voices are contained in direct or indirect citations from documentation in 1961-1970. In addition, Walter James' *Tumbling Walls*[42] contributes a foundational narrative rehearsal of the background of the Berlin Fellowship.

(2) The second written resource examined was a body of varied official state records. These records were located in different government archives, and each set of records was from three separate branches of government offices of the GDR: the party apparatus and state/local/municipal government administrative offices; the office of the State Secretary for Church Questions (a federal level office with district branch offices); the Ministry for State Security (*MfS*). Of these government branches, the only archival collection which includes reports and files about Berlin Fellowship activities and its key personages is that of the *MfS*, known also as the *Stasi*. This information is mainly comprised of the unofficial informer's findings (*inoffizielle Mitarbeiter, IM)* and of supervisory administrative action plans and summarizing reports. Reports delivered by the unofficial informer and the administrative reports both reflect a specific style of observation and evaluation typical to this branch of the government. The *MfS* was quite successful in identifying the goals and purpose of the Berlin Fellowship program early on, gaining the trust of its western leaders, and effectively infiltrating the eastern side of the organization with an unofficial informer. Not surprisingly, the *MfS* reports do not capture or address any theological aspects or substance of the program, nor do they examine the effect of the visits on the eastern participants. The object of the *MfS* operation was information gathering with the suspicion of illegal activity (espionage).

I examined the *MfS* files, using a form of rhetorical analysis to look especially for eastern perspectives. Moreover, I examined and read both *MfS* and state administrative files and documents for specific mention of individuals, activities, evaluation, or judgments regarding Berlin Fellow-

---

[42] Walter James, *Tumbling Walls*, LaJolla, California 1990.

ship (or American visitors to church congregations or districts). The *MfS* files, the primary source of documentation for this research, are composed in a repetitive style and format with a specific vocabulary. Most repetition results from copying of earlier reportsverbatim, edited or rewritten. Although much information is collected, little of national political interest to the *MfS* is uncovered. The unofficial informer reports are business-like, lacking adjectives, emotional responses, or critical comments. However, several thousand pages of *MfS* documentation comprise these files, repeatedly noting that nothing noteworthy merits being recorded. Unlike many who suffered at the hand of the *MfS* methods or whose lives were marred by their insidious methods, except in a few recognizable instances, the effect on Berlin Fellowship individuals and reports of the program's activity seem inconsequential. Appendix 1 presents an overview of the Ministry for State Security and further information about the origins, development and organization of this branch of the GDR government system. The appendix focuses on the *Stasi* department for church affairs as it relates to this research.

In addition to the *MfS* files, I researched files in five federal state archives, looking at agendas, minutes, and protocols from council meetings at district, county, and city levels (*Rat des Bezirkes, des Kreises, der Stadt*). Those potentially pertinent files were primarily records from the office or officer responsible for church questions/matters. On the national level at the Federal Archive in Berlin (*Bundesarchiv*), I examined records from police offices (border and customs matters), the central travel bureau, and those of the State Secretary for Church Questions (*Staatssekretär für Kirchenfragen, Abteilung DDR: Inneres / Kirchenfragen*). All examined federal level administrative records contain no Berlin Fellowship related information for analysis.

(3) Most importantly, eastern participant interviews constitute the target data and third part of this study. Over the course of two years, forty-one interviews were conducted in German, digitally-recorded, transcribed by native-speakers, and analyzed with the help of a computer software program (ATLAS ti.5). All interviewees signed release forms allowing their transcripts to be cited or used for further research. As the interviewer seeking eastern recollections and evaluative remembrances, I primarily asked personal history-giving questions, asking why a person participated, what Berlin Fellowship was, and what he or she remembered. In order to evaluate the transcripts, I created a possible list of code categories (based on the discussion in Chapter

(4) These categories were either confirmed or dismissed by categories that "emerged" from the transcript texts. Both of these code lists were

subject to my coding methods. The final list of code categories was confirmed and limited by density (number of times a word or phrase occurred).

The original question list was used as a guideline and conversation enhancer. These interview questions were, as mentioned, initially designed to gather memories and impressions and at the time were based on an assumption that I was doing a form of oral history project, not necessarily a missiological or qualitative research analysis. This disparity might have affected the findings, but I believe the interview contents are, nonetheless, a more than sufficient resource for probing the main research question.

The transcribed interviews are full of individual and theological reflections, memories, feelings, opinions, and in a few cases, specific anecdotes and stories recalled by the interviewees. This variety offers a full range of recollections and perspectives with personal and evaluative comments about the participant experience, both affirming and critical. The reliability of this information is dependent upon the interviewees' strength of memory and articulation ability, as well the effect of an elapsed 15 - 25 years. In addition, this study does not include any interviews with one-time only participants, who may have been antagonistic, dissatisfied, or disinterested participants. Certainly, these voices merit further research.

Using a computer program, I gleaned data from the transcribed manuscripts (average 38 minutes in length). This collection of personal, reflective, and theological recollections adds to the story of Berlin Fellowship, supplementing and contrasting the West Berlin, the American and the *MfS* data. With this corpus of first-hand recollections, I began with an open-coding framework. As I coded, I tried to let the story tell itself, allowing words, anecdotes, and memories to address the research question and main concepts, directly or indirectly. Then, making what I understand to be grounded theory assumptions, I inductively built a list of concepts and themes related to the main research question, keeping the key concepts (missional, fellowship, church, reconciliation, and recognition) in mind. The main research question and key vocabulary served as the searchlights for developing this system of open coding and evaluating the resulting "groundedness" of certain codes and code relationships. The resultant constructed theory is a brand of a "hybrid" analysis, a crossbreed between grounded theory, responsive interview coding, and narrative comparison.

Structure of the research

Preceded by a foreword which briefly rehearses the background of Berlin Fellowship, this study's introductory chapter begins with an overview of the problem, research question, and key terms. It then reviews directly related resources and other resource literature, main concepts, methodology, and structure. Chapter 2 examines key terms and vocabulary in depth and other important concepts as they relate to the research question. Chapter 3 begins by presenting the story of Berlin Fellowship's origins, 1951 - 1961. Then the remaining years are divided into eras. This chapter relates the evolution of this visitation program, its development, activities, and expansion from 1961 - 1989. Nested in an overview of the larger contextual setting (social and political issues of the eras), this narrative is accompanied by synopses of MfS activity and findings. Chapter 4 is an analysis of eastern participant interviews and the key research findings. The final chapter's discussion returns to the main research problem in light of a number of open questions raised in analysis and consideration of the research findings. Lastly, this study calls for much-needed further research on both the missional function of fellowship and the yet-to-be examined voices of the partners or recipients in *all* form of missional engagement.

Resources Used

This study relies on theological and missiological literature, participant interviews (methodological resources and training), and historical documentation (including secondary resource literature). The main research question is illumined by the eastern participant interview perspective, through reflections and observations.

To begin the study, I examined all available western (West Berlin and U.S.) archival documentation. Secondly, the Ministry for State Security's archive provided thousands of pages of information related to Berlin Fellowship (see Appendix I for *MfS* and Berlin Fellowship background). Concurrent to interviewing and *MfS* file research, I read and consulted a number of books, journals, news articles, and periodicals for historical, social, political, and church-related contextual information. Most of these sources addressed the Protestant church and its relationship to the state or to the *MfS*. These sources were gleaned for information about the years of the study, developments in church-state relations, and information about local congregational matters and daily life. I also studied theological and missiological publications; both journals and books were consulted, primarily combing foundational works in missiology, mission theology, and "missional church" developments, reviewing standard works in mission history, ecclesiology and contextual theology. Looking at subjects like reconciliation, the Trinity, fellowship, Christology, ecumenism, ecclesiology, and church partnerships (including current research studies), I sought to re-acquaint myself with basic concepts and developments in these fields, including developments in field of missiological research over the last 70 years.

The target data and main thrust of this study are the transcribed participant interviews. To prepare for the interviews, I attended an oral history seminar at the Overseas Missionary Study Center in Connecticut, read a number of books on qualitative analysis, and trained in Hannover, Germany to use the software program. For supplementary and contextual information, a number of extra interviews were conducted with retired western Berlin consistory officials, with the three target subjects of *MfS* files (all western voices) Ted Schapp, Ralph Zorn, Bärbel Eccardt. I also interviewed one former East German church general superintendent, a former eastern theological educator, and one former eastern consistory church officer. These interviewees were either involved with Berlin Fellowship or familiar with it, and moreover, knew the church situation most intimately. I further interviewed two former leading *Stasi* officers directly related to the Berlin Fellowship files as well as the primary legal counsel for the Office of the Secretary for Church Questions. In the course of the years of research and writing, I called on many of those interviewed and other church leaders, bishops, and historians (Rudolf Mau, Friedrich Winter, Jürgen Henkys, Günter Krusche, Johannes Althausen, Johannes Hempel, Joachim Heise, and Horst Dohle) and attended one conference in Thuringia addressing Stasi involvement in the Thuringia Church.[43]

The current research study is primarily theological and missiological. The literature review and documentation investigation provide empirical data and a foundational context for the discussion of interview findings. Though both historical and sociological research is involved, the research question is directed at the Church's self-understanding and mission practice. In that light, though I am not a historian or a sociologist, I have sought to provide the reader with a broad sweep of contextual and historical background related to a very complex social, cultural, religious and political setting in the GDR. The interview process and analysis could be expected to afford much more complex sociological findings. However, to the best of my ability I have sought to use the fundamental methods of

---

[43] epd Dokumentation, Nr. 16, 17 April 1, 2007, *Stasi-Aufarbeitung in der Thüringer Landeskirche, Dokumentation einer Tagung in der Evangelischen Akademie Thüringen*, Gutmannshausen 29. September bis 1. Oktober 2006.

information gathering through interviews for the purposes of rhetorical analysis and theological reflection with integrity and good will. I believe the results serve the following discussion and purposes of this research well.

Chapter Two

Foundational Vocabulary: Fellowship and Missional a meeting of old and new, constants in context?

"Is fellowship encounter a missional experience?" This question implies understanding of two foundational terms or concepts commonly used in the academy as well as in the Church fellowship and missional. In fact, these two terms as distinctly Christian vocabulary are seminal to the missiological and theological discussion in this research.

At the outset of the 21st century and in many corners of the "Christian world," however, the term fellowship rings much more familiar than the term missional. The newer English word, *missional* has come to identify the church's nature and activity, under the larger contextual umbrella of the "mission of God" (*misso Dei*). Until the middle of the 20th century, a rather usual and perhaps even traditional understanding of mission was sending missionaries out to "bring the gospel" to the unchurched, non-Christian world. This definition, though still widely held and used, has been changed markedly by the discussion of *missio Dei*. "In the new image mission is not primarily an activity of the church, but an attribute of God [...] Mission is thereby seen as a movement from God to the world; the church is viewed as the instrument for that mission."[1] The church, in all aspects of its life, is then witness to God's love manifest in Jesus Christ. In the late 1990's as part of this change, the adjective "missional" emerged in North America as a new label or tag descriptor for the self-understanding of the Church's very life (essence and activity) as well as for the individual congregation's engagement in "mission." [2]

---

[1] David Bosch, *Transforming Mission*, Maryknoll, N.Y. 1992, 390 ff. Bosch draws his argument together citing Barth and the influence of the IMC Willingen Conference in 1953, among others, and quotes Aagard, 1973:11-15.

[2] As early as 1994 James Brownson published an article, Speaking the Truth in Love, in the *International Review of Mission*, and the term also began to appear in the publications from the Gospel and Our Culture Network in North America. Darrell Guder, the editor of *Missional Church, A*

While missional is unquestionably a newer term and still in process of being defined, since the first century, the word fellowship has been standard vocabulary in talking about what Christians "do." In theological and ecclesiological discussions, it is often listed as one of several traditional characteristics describing the nature of the church (proclamation/*kerygma*, worship/*leiturgia*, service/*diakonia*, testimony/*martyria* and fellowship/*koinonia*). In daily parlance, fellowship reflects or describes an often-named, usual and identifying activity of the Church universal and the local congregation participation, communion, or sharing. On the local community level it would refer to conversation or sharing in life experience, in learning situations, in study or prayer groups, in family or house church meetings. Though the theological reference is also often understood as the communication between the Father, the Son, and the Holy Spirit (the fellowship of the three persons in the Trinity), most North American Christians sitting in the pew would understand and use fellowship in reference to what *they* do. This word usage then ranges from coffee hour to Bible study groups, to what happens when Christians gather for worship, service, common meals, encouragement, and fun. However the term fellowship is understood, if missional used as a descriptor of what Christians do while "being church," then fellowship is unlikely to be labeled mission or a missional activity.

It was recognized by the German and U.S. founders of Berlin Fellowship that this program, a Christian to Christian "fellowship/*koinonia*" experience, was considerably more than a chat over coffee. As a visitation across borders, it was an activity of the church being the church in an ecumenical sense, the gathered body of believers participating in and sharing their common faith. In fact, the growth of the ecumenical movement following World War II (WWII) was instrumental in preparation for the launching of the early phases of the program.

During the early years 1961 - 1967, as this visitation program came into being, there was regular discussion and question in the U.S. about the sense and direction of this ecumenical project, the expense, the purpose of the visits and reasons for continuing. The Berlin Fellowship archives reveal that in the GDR there was at the same time a moderate-sized circle of East German church leaders, lay and clergy, who em-

---

Vision for the Sending of the Church in North America, states in a personal letter, August 2009, "We hoped to be able to define the discussion by claiming that 'missional' referred to the fundamentally and pervasively missionary purpose and character of the church founded by the apostles. We were fleshing out Vatican II's statement, 'the pilgrim church is missionary by its very nature." Guder states that the work of *definition* continues and that they are "just beginning to flesh out all that this means."

braced the effort, entering into planning and evaluation meetings for the American visits. However, on neither side of the ocean, did there seem to have been questions about whether this was mission or missional, ecclesial or ecumenical. Berlin Fellowship "happened" or some might say it evolved or unfolded, growing out of the times. See Chapter 3 for further background.

The contemporary, apparent and perhaps superficial disconnect between missional and fellowship in today's vocabulary pulls at the imagination and begs examination of both words. Furthermore, the examined missiological, theological, and ecclesiological research discussions to which fellowship, missional and related terms might belong have proven to be almost barren regarding the fellowship aspect of church life and of missional engagement. The welcome exception to this is found in various publications from the World Council of Churches and the Faith and Order Commission, which have focused their attention on fellowship during the last 15 - 20 years. More importantly, in light of the relative dearth of missiological research particularly reflecting recipients' viewpoints, experiences, recollections, and assessments of mission activity aimed at them, this dissertation shall probe how fellowship, shared and reciprocated, is indeed an overlooked aspect of missional and missiological self-understanding.

What constitutes the parameters of meaning for these key terms, fellowship and missional? Once defined, can both terms and related concepts provide a framework or grid for filtering, understanding and evaluating the eastern participants' perspectives of the Berlin Fellowship visitation program? Was this visitation program, a non-mission but mission-like activity of the church (terminology pre-Bosch) or was it rather a missional endeavor or experience (2012 vocabulary)? From the perspective of the recipients, the participating eastern German Christians, what can this kind of fellowship experience reveal about the nature of such missional activity? What made this intercultural crossing of borders (all manner of borders) a unique missional endeavor and one meriting examination? Is Church being Church across borders different or more than ecumenical exchange?

The key concepts necessary for this discussion, integrated in the *missio Dei* realm of reflection, include reconciliation, recognition, contextualization, intercontextualization, interculturalization, crossing borders, and hermeneutics (remembering, telling, interpreting and listening to the story). This interwoven family of words and accompanying theological concepts illumine the rehearsal of the narrative about the origins, development and context of Berlin Fellowship in Chapter 3 and the German participants' oral interview analyses from Chapter 4. All of these terms are important, need defining, and are integral to the missional and fellowship discussion of the entire research data.

1. Fellowship

Since the primary activity of the Berlin Fellowship visitation program was fellowship in and between Christians, the nature of fellowship, as foundationally defined by the New Testament, shall be considered first. Reports produced in recent years by the World Council of Churches fill in aspects of definition that provide further dimension and theological context. Finally, Dietrich Bonhoeffer's *Life Together* then affords significant additional definition and perspective.

Biblical perspectives

General use and understanding of fellowship (Greek *koinonia*) in the Bible is shaped primarily by Paul's use of the noun and related words, and is most usually defined as communion, participation, fellowship, sharing. As noted in *The Nature and Mission of the Church* (Faith and Order Paper No. 198, WCC, 8 - 10), the term has fallen out of vogue in some periods of church history, but fellowship has been reclaimed today as a key to understanding the Church's nature and mission. Fundamental in both Old and New Testaments is the covenant relationship between God and the chosen people and their related communion or fellowship with him (cf. Ex. 19:4 - 6). This purposed covenant relationship in turn enables communion among and between people and with the created order. Sin distorts, however, and bends and breaks the relationship, destroying the fellowship (Gen. 3-4, Rom.1:18ff.). God's persistent faithfulness demonstrated in Jesus Christ restores brokenness on all sides and fellowship in all manner is renewed.

Key to this discussion of fellowship is what the participants hold in common, as shared, participated in, or somehow acted upon. However, it is not so much a question of holding but rather that of being held, and this shared state of being held has to do primarily with the person in whom the fellowship is found or through whom fellowship is, by grace, enabled. In Galatians, Paul speaks of the relationship of the believers to their Lord as being "in Christ" and of Christ being in the believer, through the Holy Spirit.

Paul addresses this directly and repeatedly throughout his epistles, stating it is because of Christ and "in Christ" that fellowship happens, can be realized, and is made possible (2 Cor. 5.17). That is, in fellowship with and united to Christ all who are in Christ belong to the new community. It is not something produced but rather received and shared. It is in and through Christ's death and resurrection and by the power of the Holy Spirit that Christians may enter into fellowship with God and one another.[3] Both sacraments are fundamental to Paul's understanding of *koinonia*, as seen particularly in 1 Cor. 10:16. Paul here identifies the bread broken as the participation and sharing, the *koinonia* in the body of Christ and the cup of blessing as participation or *koinonia* in the blood of Christ. In celebration of the Eucharist, the "body of Christ" refers to Jesus' body on the cross and his blood, that which was poured out at his death. However, Paul is not only referring to the body of Christ but also to the body of believers, the community.[4] Likewise, the sacrament of baptism results in a relationship with Christ and in a shared relationship with the community (45). This new community is a spiritual reality but a physical one as well; it is a community of real, live people bound in fellowship to God and to each other.

How this sharing is described and manifests itself is varied in New Testament usage, from references to partnership in work (2 Cor. 8:4,23) to table fellowship (Acts 2:42 ff) to sharing in the sufferings of Christ (Phil. 3:10) as well as in his glory (Eph.2:5 - 6, Rom.8:17). This participation and shared status in the gospel is both an individual and a corporate act[i.e. collections brought to Jerusalem]. Christians are called into fellowship firstly with Christ (1 Cor.1:9), but this engaged participation with the Son is, as well, participation and sharing with other followers, in any number of active ways (45). One example of this is found in Philippians where Paul thanks God for the believers who share "in the gospel from the first day until now" (1:5). That is, the Philippians shared "in the message about Christ that Paul preached, by believing, so that a local 'fellowship in the Gospel' resulted" (45). Later in this epistle Paul refers to the Philippians sharing the gospel with others (4:15 - 16), that is directly sharing from their resources of money and persons. "Koinonia thus involves sharing in the gospel for salvation and sharing it with others in mission" (45).

---

[3] World Council of Churches, *The Nature and Mission of the Church. A Stage on the Way to a Common Statement, Faith and Order Paper 198,* Geneva 2005, A II 29, http://www.oikoumene.org (accessed November 2009).

[4] Thomas F. Best and Gunther Gassmann (eds.), *On the Way to Fuller Koinonia. Official Report of the Fifth World Conference on Faith and Order*, Geneva 1994, 43.

"Fellowship with Christ means fellowship with other Christians in a partnership of faith and service." [5] Fellowship manifests itself in sharing of material wealth (Gal.2:9, Rom. 15:27) as well as partnering with those publicly abused, persecuted, or treated poorly (Hebrews 10:33). Furthermore, Pauline thought reiterates that the law of fellowship dictates that individual sufferings are the burden of the entire community (Col.1: 24, 2 Cor. 1: 5, 7).[6]

It should be noted at this juncture in the discussion that the original offer from the Presbyterians to the German church came in the face of the burdens the Christians of the newly divided German nation were carrying, especially those in the divided city of Berlin, and this offer was positively responded to. In 1959 Bishop Otto Dibelius said, "They [East Germans] need to know there are Christians in other parts of the world who know about them and who do really care about them, who still claim them as part of the worldwide community of believers."[7] Long before Berlin Fellowship began sending teams, Christmas packages were sent from the United States to families in both parts of the divided city of Berlin. In response and gratitude, Alfred Schroeder, youth pastor for the whole of Berlin, wrote in English, "I wish we could do more from our side in order to show you how thankful we are for this christian belonging together."[8]

The activity of fellowship as portrayed in the first chapter of 1 John (four occurrences of *koinonia*) describes this belonging together in a concrete way, as an encounter, specifically an experience or encounter with what is "heard, seen, touched" (1 John 1:1 - 3), and then it is testified to and announced. In the encounter with the living Christ, the author makes it clear *something* has happened in terms of personal experience. "What we have heard, what we have seen with our eyes, what we have looked at and what we have touched with our hands, concerning the word of life" is a revelation of life, in some very specific way "this life was revealed, and we have seen it." John then states further that in declaration of the experience, fellowship occurs, is made possible, and this fellowship is firstly with the Father and the Son (1 Jn. 1:3). Moreover, "we declare to you what we have seen and heard *so that* you may have fellowship with U.S." (1:3). The very message being shared about the experience seems then in the very act of sharing, to unite all participants. Or perhaps the

[5] Friedrich G.Kittel and Gerhard Friedrichs (eds.), *Theological Dictionary of the New Testament, Abridged in One Volume by Geoffrey Bromiley*, Grand Rapids, Michigan 2003, 449.
[6] Ibid.
[7] James, *Tumbling Walls*, 140-41.
[8] Letter from Alfred Schroeder to Walt James, December 23 1959, Hamburger Collection.

proclamation is simply a reminder to all of the fact of their communion, their fellowship. Regardless, the use of fellowship here, as well that found in Paul's letters (i.e. Gal. 2:9), is the active recognition of and sharing together "being in Christ." 1 John goes further, however, for the announcement itself is both a recognition of the validity of the experience described (touch, seen, heard) and a recognition of the "other," of that recipient of the message, of that partner in the conversation. The "other" then in the listening is reminded of the reconciling act of Christ uniting believers to God the Father *and* to other believers, be they speakers or listeners. Together they all participate in the common act of sharing the message a message encountered in the dialogue, that is, in the telling *and* listening.

In these opening verses of 1 John this shared fellowship is further described as a matter of "walking in the light," having been cleansed from sin by Jesus Christ" if we walk in the light as he himself is in the light, we have fellowship with one another" (1:6-7). Jesus Christ has made this *koinonia* possible, and by walking in his light, the followers together find each other and only so because of the light to which they have all responded.

What did this *koinonia* "walking in the light" of Christ look like in the early church? The brief description of the first body of believers gathered after Pentecost in Acts 2 provides a paradigmatic description of some of the fellowship activities of early Christians. "They devoted themselves to the apostles' teaching and fellowship, to the breaking of bread (common meal and the sacrament) and the prayers" (2:42). Further sharing included having all things in common, selling private goods and distributing the proceeds to those in need, spending time together in the temple, eating together, praising God, and having goodwill for all (2:43-47). The picture here is one of people *in relationship*, in a dynamic of giving and receiving, a loving and interactive fellowship which implies friendly, open and trusting communication, mutual understanding, and willing acts of kindness, concern, interest and mutual support. This description of the communion occasioned by common faith and discipline (certainly experimental and nascent in these early chapters in Acts) remains an ideal for those in the Church to this day. This understanding has been instrumental and foundational for the World Council of Churches, the Lutheran World Federation, the World Alliance of Reformed Churches and other ecumenical, ecclesial and mission bodies.

KOINONIA a brief review of ecumenical happenings

It is indeed ironic that in the very years when the politics of a divided Germany separated Christians, the ecumenical movement was being launched and gaining a foothold in many portions of the larger Church world. The Cold War dividing line, as symbolized in 1948 by the Iron Curtain and after 1961 by the Berlin Wall, was a harsh border and a stark reminder that any and all western contact, conversation and support was unwelcome and viewed with a high degree of suspicion in the GDR (see Chapter 3). In spite of this dividing wall, members of two church bodies, the Evangelical Church of Berlin-Brandenburg (West) and the Presbyterian Church from the United States made a modest effort at being "ecumenical"via fellowship, encouragement and conversation. In fact, it was thanks to the programmatic efforts of and encouragement of the Brethren Service commission, the newly founded World Council of Churches (WCC) and CIMADE (Comité Inter-Mouvements Auprès Des Evacués) that the early deputation work teams of college students from the 1st Presbyterian Church of Hollywood went to Europe in 1950. These teams acted as forerunners for the Berlin Fellowship program in the early 1960's.

The ecumenical movement's history, growth, and ongoing developments, on the other hand, played only an indirect role in the actual Berlin Fellowship activities after 1961. However, in this light, it is interesting to note that coincident to Berlin Fellowship's pre-history ecumenical work trip actions (1950 - 1961), World Council of Churches and Faith & Order were hard at work, clarifying and defining their identified goal the unity of the Church. The WCC determined at its founding in 1948 to deepen the understanding of this goal and to seek ways to realize it.[9]

The Faith and Order Commission, as well as the World Council of Churches, has repeatedly focused on unity and communion (also to be understood as *koinonia*) with varying degrees of intensity over the course of the last 60 years. Even as early as 1927, at the First World Conference, Lausanne, Switzerland, the Faith and Order Movement identified the unity of the Church as "the very reason for its existence."[10] Their call to this day to continue to seek that which is a given, unity in Christ, is resultant from clear understanding of and commitment to being made one in Christ, the gift of *koinonia*. Continuing to emphasize the mutuality of call, *Called to be the One Church* (adopted by the WCC Assembly in 2006, Porto Allegro, Brazil) reminds member churches that they "...have

[9] *Nature and Mission*, paragraph 1.
[10] Ibid.

not always acknowledged their *mutual responsibility* to one another, and have not always recognized the need to give account to one another of their faith, life, and witness." The assembly further reiterated the importance of the ecumenical journey and invited churches to renewed conversation on the "quality and degree of their fellowship and communion."[11] As recently as October 2009, the Faith and Order Plenary commission meeting in Crete again called for churches to renew their commitment to seek this unity.

Fellowship or *koinonia* has thus been noticeably used to identify world-wide Church relations as an accompanying sign or descriptor of Church self-understanding, as foundational to dialogue, to sharing, to solidarity, to continuing awareness, recognition, and embrace of shared unity.[12] However, three particular studies offer some specific insights and comments about *koinonia*, especially pertinent as they relate to the Berlin Fellowship and its activities. These declarations represent discussions and developments in the 1980's, the 1990's and the first decade of the new millennium.

(1) *Baptism, Eucharist, and Ministry* (BEM, World Council of Churches, 1982), as indicated by the title, focuses on the sacraments and the work of the Church universal, the worldwide body of believers (*oikumene* referring to the world). This study paper defines and identifies the nature of the sacraments and the call to ministry and service, reminding member churches of their common bond. Pertinent to the case of Berlin Fellowship, the following references illumine some aspects of this bond or communion:

- "Through baptism, Christians are brought into union with Christ, with each other and with the Church of every time and place [...] Therefore, our one baptism into Christ constitutes a call to the churches to overcome their divisions and visibly manifest their fellowship."[13]
- "Within a fellowship of witness and service, Christians discover the full significance of the one baptism as the gift of God to all God's people"(paragraph 3).
- "The Eucharistic communion with Christ who nourishes the life of the Church is at the same time communion within the body of Christ which is the Church. The sharing in one bread and the common cup in a given place demonstrates and affects the

[11] World Council of Churches, *Called to be the One Church (as adopted by the Assembly). An invitation to the churches to renew their commitment to the search for unity and to deepen their dialogue*, Geneva February 23, 2006, http://www.oikoumene.org (accessed January 2010).
[12] World Council of Churches, *The Unity of the Church: Gift and Calling – The Canberra Statement*, February 2, 1991, http://www. oikoumene.org (accessed March 2012).
[13] World Council of Churches, *Baptism, Eucharist and Ministry Faith and Order Paper No. 111*, Geneva 1982, para. 2, http://www.oikoumene.org (accessed May 2009).

oneness of the sharers with Christ and with their fellow sharers in all time and places" (paragraph 12).

Each of these selections of text refers to some aspects of the experience of fellowship. The union in Christ through baptism and affirmed at the Lord's Table is almost so much an assumption as to be overlooked, but this was the initial base understanding for the Hollywood deputation teams in the 1950's, as well as the basis for the unity embraced by the early Berlin Fellowship team visits, guest and hosts alike. Fellowship is not an end in itself, but it is a gift of union with Christ and with one another, which breaks down divisions, and is visible in witness and service and encounter. Moreover, this fellowship is a place of discovery and learning for all involved.

Further clarification and reference to sacraments, ministry and mission indicates:

> "The very celebration of the Eucharist is an instance of the Church's participation in God's mission to the world. This participation takes everyday form of proclamation of the Gospel, service of the neighbor, and faithful presence to the world (paragraph 13)."
> "The Church is called to proclaim and prefigure the Kingdom of God [...] In Jesus the Kingdom of God has come among U.S. [...] Living in this communion with God, all members of the Church are called to confess their faith and to give account of their hope. They are to identify with the joys and sufferings of all people as they seek to witness in caring love [...] This mission needs to be carried out in varying political, social, and cultural contexts (paragraph 16)."

Most interesting in these statements is the reference to God's mission to the world. Here, a new aspect of fellowship (already established in baptism and Eucharist) is named; not only are proclamation and service essential but also "faithful presence." Fellowship certainly doesn't exclude engaging conversation, mutual enjoyment, shared insights, but the act of fellowship in the community in daily terms is defined as telling and listening to the good news, taking care to note the needs of the neighbor(getting to know the neighbor), and being faithfully present in all manner . When fellowship happens, it is indeed a gift (as seen in the sacraments), but it is, as well, certainly manifest in these kinds of very intentional, concrete, daily, and identifiable activities and encounters, with God and with the sister or brother in faith.

How the Kingdom of God makes itself known is defined in the Church and in its life engagements. This Church is, as the BEM paper states, clearly a pre-figuring, a hint or a glimpse of that Kingdom. Members of the Church in confessing their faith, give account of their hope, identify with the joys and sufferings of all people, witnessing in caring love. "In order to fulfill its mission faithfully, (members) will seek relevant forms of witness and service in each situation" (paragraph 16). Though mission and witness are most often considered something done for the sake of outsiders, those yet to hear the good news, there is an amazing relevance within the walls of the Church as well; faithful service and witness among and between Christians and congregations in a ministry of presence, is foundational to fellowship, encouragement and upbuilding. This "place" (as referred to above) happened to be in a particular social, political and cultural context, the GDR, and the neighbor was both a former enemy (WWII) and a current enemy (Cold War).

On a final note, in BEM, a statement made in reference to the role and ministry of women (ever as much an issue then as today, in some corners) reads, "Where Christ is present, human barriers are being broken" (paragraph 20). Though the context of this statement in this 1982 paper is very specific, it has wider applications. Because of Christ's presence, the nature of fellowship and the experience of the Berlin Fellowship participants indeed were if not boundary-breaking then boundary-crossing. This topic will be further and later addressed in this research.

In the years following the BEM document and through the 1990's, *koinonia* and fellowship began to appear as key words in major reports and study papers.[14] The Canberra Statement, *The Unity of the Church, Gift and Calling* labels *koinonia* a calling and a gift, expressed in a common confession of faith, in a common sacramental life, in a common life where members and ministries are recognized and reconciled, and in a common mission witnessing to all of God's grace.[15] Echoing the biblical description of the early Church in *Acts*, the ecumenical movement's progress is described; churches walk together in mutual understanding, common suffering and common prayer, shared witness and service, and they draw close to one another.[16] This drawing close happens when people are in each other's presence, when they engage in mutual recognition of each other and each other's lives, ministries, needs and challenges. As an aspect of *koinonia*, recognition is indeed key to realized and participated-in ecumenical encounter.

---

[14] At the 7th assembly of the WCC in Canberra 1991 and at the 1993 5th World Conference on Faith and Order in Santiago de Compostela, statements and messages contained familiar reminders of the key role *koinonia* plays in the ecumenical journey.

[15] *Unity of the Church* 1991, 2.1.

[16] Op. cit., 1.3.

In the world conference in Santiago de Compostela, the message *On the Way to Fuller Koinonia* states the "koinonia we seek and which we have experienced is more than words. It springs from the Word of Life, 'what we have seen with our eyes, what we have touched with our hands.'(1 John 1:1)." [17] I believe this then identifies the very real but "hard to put words around" experience of encounter and live engagement with another person, in Christ. To illustrate the point, local ecumenical projects and base communities are named, people-to-people ventures. "The koinonia which we share is nothing less than the reconciling presence of the love of God [...] This koinonia comes to U.S. as a gift we can only accept in gratitude. Gratitude, however, is not passivity. Our koinonia is in the Holy Spirit which moves us to action."[18] In the case of Berlin Fellowship, both hosts and guests were severely restricted in ways to live out, even to fully express the significance of their shared encounters. However, both sides in this existential and momentary quasi-partnership were unwilling to deny the surprising validity of the experience and thus the action was to continue for more than 20 years. Why? It would seem for the sake of the fellowship itself.
(2) *On the Way to Fuller Koinonia*, a 1994 publication of the World Council of Churches contains a chapter on biblical witness to *koinonia* which concludes with several noteworthy exegetical observations:[19]

- *Koinonia* is spoken of as a matter of faith, life and witness, faith totally tied to God's fidelity, and life is tied to Jesus (life now and life in the ultimate kingdom to come). The present life is with one another in community, in solidarity, in suffering, including the sharing of self as well as finances for the needy.
- *Koinonia* is about humans having a share in the gospel, fellowship with Christ, fellowship in the Spirit, partnership in the church for mission and service. *Koinonia* may be not be equated with the definition of *ekklesia*/church or with the life of the Trinity.
- Though references in Paul are sufficient to say there is a theology of *koinonia*, very little in either Old or New Testament theologies are found regarding this.
- *Koinonia* is not an interim step on the way to being church nor is it a name for the *ekklesia* itself. It is "instead an early and important aspect of the church and its unity, in faith, witness and life, including baptism and the Lord's Supper."
- Whether there was fellowship between early church groups poses a question the New Testament story is not concerned with. It begs supposition. Most likely, *koi-*

---

[17] World Council of Churches, *On the Way to Fuller Koinonia, Message of the World Conference, Message of the World Conference*, Geneva 1993, para. 4. http://www.oikoumene.org (accessed May 2009).
[18] Ibid.
[19] Best and Gassmann, *Fuller Koinonia*, 61-64.

nonia worked on the local, community level, sharing what was held in common, the "Christ-event as the way to God."

- *Koinonia*, a non-existent term in the Hebrew scriptures, is never used by Jesus, and is part of the 'new creation' (2 Cor. 5:17), but *its usage in the NT letters offers the church today a perspective and perhaps even a new understanding of the nature and mission of the church.*
- *Koinonia* reflects a clear crossing of boundaries and "involved for New Testament Christians the expression of a world of shared gospel experiences and associations in Christ and the Spirit but presented in the vocabulary and ideas of Greek thought. Thus, the Greek term was brought into the service of the gospel. The gospel, in turn, reshaped the social categories of that world and its world, with new emphases on solidarity with suffering, the poor and human needs."

This crossing of boundaries may be in ecclesial friendship, on a ecumenical or on a world-level scale, but it may also be in occasions of Christians meeting Christians in all manner of hospitable sharing, in spite of barriers and borders.

(3) *The Nature and the Mission of the Church, A Stage on the Way to a Common Statement* (Faith and Order Paper 198, WCC, Geneva) was published in 2005, and is but one study in a long series of publications addressing the essence and identity of the Church. Its opening chapter, "The Church of the Triune God," examines the church as *koinonia* or communion. Though *koinonia* can't and shouldn't be equated with the church in terms of definition, *koinonia* is "reclaimed as a key to understanding the nature and mission of the Church."[20] Although there is no direct reference in the Old Testament to *koinonia*, the covenant relationship between God and the chosen people is named in this study as an example. God's persistent faithfulness in ever and again restoring the fellowship between God, humans and the created order is a reference point for other biblical terminology which metaphorically describe the relationship; i.e. vine, bride of Christ, the holy city.[21]

This Faith and Order paper rehearses the already-named signs of new life in *koinonia* or communion but unlike some earlier documents, concludes with, "The communion of the Church consists not of independent individuals but of persons in community, all of whom contribute to its flourishing. The Church exists for the glory and praise of God, to serve the reconciliation of humankind [...] The Church as communion, is instrumental to God's ultimate purpose (cf. Roms.8:9-21; Col. 1:18 - 20)."[22]

---

[20] *Nature and Mission*, paragraph 24.
[21] Op. cit., paragraph 27.
[22] Op. cit., paragraphs 32, 33.

For most Christians, the existential experience of this communion, this fellowship takes place in a congregation, in a local community of believers where a "life together" is shared, over the course of months or years, sometimes even over the course of a lifetime. This participatory communion is actively shared and participated in and often embraces mission in one form or another. As this Faith & Order paper asserts, the purpose of this communion is to serve the reconciliation of humankind because of its head, Jesus Christ, in whom all things hold together and by whom all things are reconciled (Col. 1). In the course of church history, intentional community has often been sought out or constructed and then either studied or written about, as exemplified by the fellowship of theological students at Finkenwalde with Dietrich Bonhoeffer.

Dietrich Bonhoeffer Life Together

Dietrich Bonhoeffer's *Life Together*[23] is a description of and theological reflection on the Christian community Bonhoeffer and other young theologians engaged in for a brief period of time at Finkenwalde. I have chosen this particular description of Christian community because it affords a brief but incisive glance at some key aspects of Bonhoeffer's anthropological and Christological understanding and reflections upon the nature of fellowship.[24]

Beginning with a statement that the Scriptures provide for "life together under the Word,"[25] Bonhoeffer's opening chapter paints a multi-dimensional picture of the lived experience of fellowship. Acknowledging that Christians, like Christ, aren't called to a cloistered existence but rather are called to live in the midst of the world and even "in the thick of foes,"[26] Bonhoeffer opens his work by stating that living in visible fellowship with other Christians is a blessing and a gift but not necessarily a given. For the imprisoned, the sick, those who are lonely or living apart from the community, visible fellowship is a blessing. "The physical presence of other Christians is a source of incomparable joy and strength to the believer."[27] "The believer lauds the Creator, the Redeemer, God, Fa-

[23] Dietrich Bonhoeffer, *Life Together*, San Francisco 1954.

[24] Bonhoeffer's understanding of community and his "theology of sociality" is launched in *Sanctorum Communio* (cf. Clifford Green, *Bonhoeffer, A Theology of Sociality,* Grand Rapids Michigan 1999), which offers a more rigorous and thorough philosophical and theological examination of the topic. Others of his writings amend and compliment the key points highlighted in *Life Together*.

[25] Bonhoeffer, *Life Together*, 17, "das gemeinsames Leben unter dem Wort."

[26] Ibid., "mitten unter die Feinde."

[27] Op. cit., 19, "Die leibliche Gegenwart anderer Christen ist dem Gläubigen eine Quelle unvergleichlicher Freude und Stärkung."

ther, Son and Holy Spirit, for the bodily presence of a brother,"[28] for that very person is a "physical sign of the gracious presence of the triune God. Visitor and visited in loneliness recognize in each other the Christ who is present in the body. They receive and meet each other as one meets the Lord." Knowing that such fellowship is a gift, which "may any day be taken from us" Bonhoeffer reckons with the fact "that the time that still separates us from utter loneliness may be brief indeed."[29] In fact, he boldly asserts, "Christianity means community through Jesus Christ and in Jesus Christ. No Christian community is more or less than this. Whether it be a brief, single encounter or the daily fellowship of years, Christian community is only this. We belong to one another only through and in Jesus Christ."[30]

The activities of such community are integrally tied to the bodily presence of the "other", the brother or sister in faith. Echoing 1 John, Bonhoeffer mentions one of those activities, meeting or encountering the living Word of God, as mediated by another person. "When one person is struck by the Word, he speaks it to others."[31] Christians need other Christians to speak God's Word to them and especially in times of discouragement and loneliness, for alone no one is able to help herself. "The Christ in his own heart is weaker than the Christ in the word of his brother; his own heart is uncertain, his brother's is sure."

In this statement is the essence and goal of Christian community or fellowship: meeting one another as "bringers of the message of salvation."[32]

This encounter is only possible by reconciliation through Jesus Christ, says Bonhoeffer, for, "he is our peace." (Eph. 2:14) Reconciliation occurs between humankind and God, but this reconciliation also unites believer to believer, and the resultant fellowship "consists solely in

---

[28]Op. cit., 20, "ein leibliches Gnadenzeichen der Gegenwart des dreieinigen Gottes. Besucher und Besuchter erkennen in der Einsamkeit aneinander und begegnen einander, wie man dem Herrn begegnet."

[29] Ibid., "das uns täglich genommen werden kann, dass es nur eine kurze Zeit sein mag, die uns noch von der tiefsten Einsamkeit trennt."

[30]Op. cit., 21, "Christliche Gemeinschaft heißt Gemeinschaft durch Jesus Christus und in Jesus Christus. Es gibt keine christliche Gemeinschaft, die mehr, und keine, die weniger wäre als dieses. Von der kurzen einmaligen Begegnung bis zur langjährigen täglichen Gemeinschaft ist christliche Gemeinschaft nur dieses. Wir gehören einander allen durch und in Jesus Christus."

[31]Op. cit., 22, "Wo einer von ihm getroffen ist, da sagt er es dem andern."

[32]Op. cit., 23, "Der Christus im eigenen Herzen ist schwächer als der Christus im Worte des Bruders; jener ist ungewiss, dieser ist gewiss [...] sie begegnen einander als Bringer der Heilsbotschaft."

what Christ has done to both [...]"[33] It is at this point that Bonhoeffer states that *fellowship*/community (*christliche Gemeinschaft*) is not an idea but a divine reality In answer to those who might want more or those with a wishful idea of religious community and fellowship, he concludes his opening chapter by reiterating that daily fellowship, daily Christian community is bound by faith, not by experience, that fellowship is founded in Jesus Christ, and that "participation" in Christ is what constitutes genuine community.[34] Continuing the discussion in the following chapters, "The Day with Others," "Ministry" and "Confession and Communion", it becomes apparent that the theology concerning this divine reality, this genuine community, must be manifest in the *lived* and practiced community. The group of young theologians gathered around this professor and pastor are the context for the rest of the discussion. Bonhoeffer then outlines more closely the activities of a community that spends extended time together, ordered by the rhythm of the day (Scripture, song, prayer, table fellowship), with service in and among the community. He particularly draws attention to the role of confession as the breakthrough to genuine fellowship in the Lord's Supper. Addressing the hard edge of real life together, day in and day out, Bonhoeffer reminds the reader that "pious fellowship permits no one to be a sinner."[35] However, it is confession of sin one to another, in which a breakthrough to community takes place. Berlin Fellowship's short visits, though a breakthrough of some sort, were both limited and momentary and far too seldom for such intimate experiences.

These varied and complimentary definitions of *koinonia* or Christian community from *Life Together,* from the New Testament, and from WCC / Faith and Order studies afford general parameters for an overview of daily Christian fellowship. The comparison of Berlin Fellowship, however, to life of a single congregation or of church partnerships over time, is limited.

For the purposes of this thesis, the more pressing concern and question is, can then Christian fellowship actually be realized in a cross-cultural or intercultural, one-time meeting or encounter? Can this communion, participation, sharing which the Church proclaims as characteristic of its nature and an essential part of its very life be realized in a brief conversation, in a few hours of dialogue or discussion, or in a day spent with other Christians, especially when those "others" are strangers, for-

---

[33] Op. cit., 25 "Unsere Gemeinschaft besteht allein in dem, was Christus an uns beiden getan hat."
[34] Op. cit., 26f.
[35] Op.cit., 110, "Die fromme Gemeinschaft erlaubt es ja keinem, Sünder zu sein."

merly unknown to each other? Moreover, is such possible when the participants have been labeled former or current enemies? Does this definition and do the general parameters of fellowship activities function with people across borders from another culture and language, another political or economic system, or even an enemy political system? How can any of those factors which plainly separate individuals otherwise be overcome in the context of Christian fellowship, especially in the "brief encounter" form, where no guarantee of a second meeting or a continuation of the conversation by correspondence can be entertained?

It is just that "overcoming" even in its existential form that demands attention, for it is within the walls of Christian fellowship, certainly within the walls of the Church (*ekklesia*), that overcoming is enabled and can happen. My discussion thus far points to the centrality of Jesus Christ; for it is "in Christ" that *koinonia* is found, experienced and lived out. However, it is also clear that *koinonia* is integral to a foundational definition and essence of the Trinity. Even though the New Testament does not directly mention the fellowship of the Godhead, reference to the Spirit in both the Old Testament (*ruah*) and to the Holy Spirit (*pneuma*) in the New Testament is abundant. The history of theological and classical doctrines of the community of the Father, Son, and Holy Spirit is nearly two thousand years old beginning with Tertullian in the 3rd century. Over the course of time Trinitarian doctrines have provided suitable paradigms for the *sharing* and *participation* in church life and identity and equally as important, in mission. Moreover, because the Trinity is a relational and dialogical foundation and model for communication, relationship, and community[36], the Trinitarian construct serves as a paradigm of mutuality in which fellowship occurs.[37] The benediction, "The grace of the Lord Jesus Christ, the love of God, and the fellowship of the Holy Spirit be with you all" underscores the role the Spirit plays in connecting and making it possible for those who stand alongside each other in fellowship to be *mutually* accessible, as well as united by the grace of the Lord Jesus Christ and the love of God.

Both Trinitarian and Christological frameworks umbrella and embrace the experience of fellowship and the discussion of related topics: reconciliation (*katallasso*, to reconcile), church-to-church partnerships, and matters key to this study, like crossing borders, telling and listening to the story, and the Church being "missional."

---

[36] Miroslav Volf, *After Our Likeness, the Church as the Image of the Trinity*, Grand Rapids 1998, Chapter V.

[37] Stephen B. Bevans, and Roger Schroeder, *Constants in Context: A Theology of Mission for Today*, Maryknoll, N.Y. 2004, 292.

Insofar as Berlin Fellowship was both at its inception and throughout its short life an action of reconciliation and an ecumenical engagement, the topic of partnership will be addressed, but partnership in an organizational sense played no formal role because of the time and context. Although the Presbyterian Church (as represented by the Synod of Southern California and Hawaii) and the Evangelical Church of Berlin-Brandenburg (West) were conscious and supportive of the program, formal or even intentional partnership between the individual team members from the USA and scattered congregations in the entire GDR was hardly thinkable at the time. The GDR and the Western allies, the USA included, were on opposite sides of the Cold War world, standing watchtower to watchtower along the inner-German border.

However, in spite of these separations, the East German hosts' and the us travelers' repeated conversations and encounters mirror an unusual kind of engagement and commitment to an existential and momentary fellowship experience and some form of partnership and life together. The following examination of the nature of this one-time engagement, a reconciliatory and border-crossing encounter, as well as a brief look at the phenomena of church-to-church partnerships, contribute to the discussion.

2. Recognition, reconciliation, and partnerships

Post WWII years witnessed many attempts to re-build not just war-torn countries and societies but to address the root issues of the enmity and strife, the suspicion and nationalism, which led to the destruction. Many of these efforts at reconciliation (*Aktion Sühnezeichen* in Germany being one of the better known groups) sought to find a new way of relating, opening what had been thus far century-long closed doors between cultures and nations. Ambitious efforts like the United Nations, NATO, and the World Council of Churches all recognized the disastrous consequences the affairs the first half of the 20th century had wrought. Placing hope in the hard work of encounter, dialogue, recognition, and acknowledgement of the others' rights and sovereignty, nations, national groups, and the Church (mostly Protestant bodies) began efforts in conferences and in dialogue and learning from each other to find new ways on many levels to cooperate. There was a desire to mutually benefit from joint efforts at solving common problems, and to discover avenues for productive and peaceful meeting and continuing dialogue. Berlin Fellowship, a miniscule and modest effort at this very thing, had its roots in these post-war years and began as an action of reconciliation.

Recognition and Reconciliation

If the first steps to any act of reconciliation are noting the break, acknowledging the breach and at the same time acknowledging the other, the "action" begins in that multifaceted moment of recognition. Though there are certainly other factors to consider, for the purposes of this brief discussion, I begin with the Bible, seeking definition and example specifically from one key Pauline passage in 2 Corinthians.

Speaking to the church at Corinth (2 Cor. 5:16ff.), Paul identifies God's having reconciled humankind to himself through Jesus Christ. This is the launching pad for his hearers' "ministry of reconciliation" in and among themselves as well as with those around them, Jews and Gentiles alike. Paul is the primary user of the term reconciliation, and this term is a basic concept in his theological argument.[38] The verb *katalasso* and related words occur only eight times in the New Testament (Romans 5:10 - 11, 11:15, 1 Cor. 7:11, Col. 1:21 - 22 and Eph. 2:16) and refer in general terms to restoration of a relationship once hostile or broken.

Reconciliation with God is a gift from God (Romans 5:11) as is the ministry of reconciliation (2 Cor. 5: 18), a ministry of being entrusted with a message that any and all in Christ are new creations, with their sins not counted against them. What has been thus far separated and divided is made whole. In Old Testament terms, the covenant is restored. Paul then asserts that the task of those reconciled with God is to become ambassadors on God's behalf, God making his appeal for reconciliation through them, the messengers, who act as Christ's ambassadors. An ambassador carries oral messages to and from his or her government but most importantly, not as a diplomatic mailbag, rather as a personal representative of that government, the very embodiment of the one who sends, bearing the words of the sender.[39]

This passage with its ambassador metaphor opens with the curious phrase, "From now on, we regard no one from a human point of view even though we once knew Christ this way" something has happened to change the viewpoint, the perspective. As Paul continues to argue, the reason for the change in vision is that anyone in Christ is a new creation in this case both the one "regarding" as certainly as the one being "re-

---

[38] Colin Brown, *The New International Dictionary of New Testament Theology*, Grand Rapids, Michigan 1978, 167.

[39] David Bosch, A *Spirituality of the Road*, Eugene, Oregon 2000, 43.

garded." The "other" and that in the other which has been tainted or broken or even falsely understood is no longer a consideration, for in Christ, the vision, the encounter, and the conversation is new; the creation in the other person and his/her identity is made new, as is the creation in the one viewing. This then opens the door for mutuality, for relationship, for participation, for communication with the other; moreover it creates a place for genuine and trusting dialogue, fellowship, and community.

This definite theological and Christological posture and ensuing discussion is not limited to Pauline thinking, for in other realms of modern, post-modern philosophical thought and discussion, (i.e. the "politics of recognition" and Charles Taylor's contributions), it is said that in dialogue and in relationship, *identity* is forged and constituted. Identity is formed, by acknowledgement given and received; humans are shaped by the recognition or by the misrecognition of others and equally granted dignity and worth as humans in relationship, in a life-long dialogical process. [40] It seems that Taylor's philosophical stance, stands in agreement with the well-researched sociological and psychological facts about human development. Pauline theology hardly differs, though the key enabling factor in overtly Christian thinking is divine and radical intervention in the process that interactive, dialogical invasion, and central reconciling role of Jesus Christ in the equation.

"But now in Christ Jesus you who once were far off have been brought near by the blood of Christ. For he is our peace; in his flesh he has made both groups into one and has broken down the dividing wall, that is, the hostility between us"(Eph. 2.14). Granted, the original audiences for these words were Gentiles and Jews trying to find a way to live together in belief and community, but Paul's thought continues, "so he came and proclaimed peace to you who were far off and peace to those who were near; for through him both of us have access in one Spirit to the Father [...] You are no longer strangers [...] but members of the household of God [...] joined together and built together into a spiritual dwelling place for God" (Eph. 2. 17-22). The facts Paul emphasizes here are that strangers now belong in the family (household of God), and the family is not a construct of their imaginations but rather the very dwelling place for God. They are being bound to each other, finding themselves no longer strangers but rather partners, with God and with each other.

Reconciliation then begins with God's double recognition of the breach *and* the partner, the "other" in the relationship. That recognition is

[40] Charles Taylor, *Multiculturalism: Examining the Politics of Recognition*, Princeton, NJ 1994.

made manifest in the person of Jesus Christ, in his incarnation, his teaching, sacrifice, death and resurrection. Having been "recognized" and restored to relationship with God, the strangers (those who stood separated) are no longer strange or separated but now members of the household and co-reconcilers with the others who have been thus far outside or separated.

In the case of the Berlin Fellowship, the boundaries and the breach were clear, for the political and historical reality and divisions of the Cold War world were not invisible. As regular and repeated participation in a visitation program developed, former enemies or strangers, who were Christians reconciled in Christ, came to greet each other as brother or sister in the household of God. Being present with and for one another, the others (in both directions) were recognized or became more clearly identified, not as the enemy or even as stranger but as the fellow Christian. Participants who were other became the sister or brother whose world though culturally, politically, and geographically distant actually seemed closer. They were somehow in the same world, in and because of Christ. These former strangers came to anticipate the yearly visits and the embraces that punctuated meeting completely new people or renewing acquaintances, as well as emotional leave-takings and farewells.

Though it was but one way of communicating, the embrace, or the American hug became a regular experience for Berlin Fellowship participants, regardless of host or guest status, regardless of German or American background. This casual and very un-German manner of greeting and bidding farewell is interestingly enough a helpful metaphor for some final thoughts on reconciliation. In Miroslav Volf's theological exploration of identity, otherness and reconciliation, *Exclusion and Embrace*, though addressed from a different context, this topic of reconciliation is illumined by Volf's exploration of the metaphor of a hug.

In short, his "drama of embrace" entails an integrated and continual movement. It begins with the opening of the arms, as a "code of desire" for the other (and I would add overt recognition of the other). This opening of arms is a sign that I am dissatisfied alone or self-enclosed; "I want the other to be part of who I am and I want to be part of the other." This action entails making space in oneself for the other to come in and moving out of oneself to enter the other's space, created and open and waiting. This act is an invitation, a "soft knock" on the other's door, says Volf. There follows an act of waiting, waiting for the other to respond. Here the self waits at the boundary of the other, until that person's arms open as well. Waiting is necessary and a sign of anticipated reciprocal action. In Act Three of this drama of embrace, the goal is reached, and "each is holding and being held by the other, both active and passive. In an embrace, a host is a guest and a guest is a host. Though one may receive or give more than the other, each must enter the space of the other, feel the presence of the other in the self and make its own presence felt. Without such reciprocity, there is no embrace." Finally, the arms must open again, for the moment of embrace is not a welding together but a reciprocal holding and releasing of the self and the other, in full and on-going recognition.[41]

As intriguing as this metaphor for reconciliation might seem, there is a catch, and that catch comes in the middle of Act Three as Volf describes it, in that a "soft touch" is necessary. A "bear hug" negates and perverts, destroying boundaries of those involved and swallowing the other and potentially the self as well. This sounds very much like the kind of tension encountered in cross-cultural interchange and communication. In the guise of having understood the other, understanding based on one's own terms, it is easy to falsely assume mutuality and commonality because of the embrace. This is a usual but not easily identified phenomenon in cross-cultural encounters, especially of a brief nature. However, in order to preserve "alterity," the otherness of the other, Volf claims it is necessary "to acquire the ability to *not* to understand the other"[42] (emphasis mine). That is to say, there must be room in both the embrace and in both partners, for the boundaries to nonetheless exist, though they *appear* to be broken or crossed. The boundaries persist in unanswered questions, as on-going cultural differences and in unknowing about a future encounter, as the embrace is ended.

Partnerships, for better or worse

Coincident to the modest Berlin Fellowship efforts at dialogue and a loosely defined form of cooperative participation and partnership on the local and one-time meeting level of the early developmental years (1960's and early 1970's), major international efforts at partnership and engagement in the mission world of the WCC and its partner organizations, assemblies and commissions were happening on a regular basis. The International Missionary Conference in Edinburgh 1910 called for cooperation between mission agencies, and it called upon those agencies to develop relations of partnership with the local or national churches. Over the course of the next 100 years, "partnership" became standard

---

[41] Miroslav Volf, *Exclusion and Embrace, a Theological Exploration of Identity, Otherness and Reconciliation*, Nashville 1996, 140-147.

[42] Op. cit., 143.

vocabulary in international mission circles, with varying degrees of intensity reflected in the rhetoric of many assemblies and conferences. With unification of the International Missionary Council and the World Council of Churches in 1961, partnership was redefined and thrust to the forefront with changes in the mutuality in sending and receiving missionaries, in unequal power relationships being addressed, and with churches realizing and embracing their own identity. This topic persists to the present; the 1986 "Guidelines for the Ecumenical Sharing of Resources," stressed "opening to one another as friends in mutual trust and accountability, sharing with one another our needs and problems in relationships where there are no absolute donors or absolute recipients."[43] In 1989, at the San Antonio Commission on World Mission and Evangelism (CWME) conference, "Your Will be Done: Mission in Christ's Way," encouraged "exchange visits", stating that "the purpose of international relationships would be to help churches share joys and sorrow, talents and needs. Relationships should be characterized by: mutual acceptance as partners, recognition of cultural diversity as an enrichment, joint planning and implementation of policies."[44] Furthermore, renewed missionary relations were to be typified by "commitment to acting together wherever a common approach is required [...] transparency in relations and the sharing of responsibilities [...] reciprocity in decision making."[45]

In the years surrounding the fall of the Berlin Wall and the independence movements in the Warsaw Pact countries as well as in the Soviet Union, regional consultations in mission (CWME, 1988 - 1992) addressed key issues. Among those were: mutuality and reciprocity, mission still meaning crossing geographical frontiers, ecumenical team visits, mutual visits which provide exposure to each other's reality and "enable examination of one's reality through a partner's eyes," decisions for action made jointly, exchange of ideas and resources, cultural diversity, removing donor/receiver attitudes, sharing theological insights, openness, transparency, solidarities in struggle, and partnership in God's mission.[46]

These are all characteristics of partnership and though not exhaustive, they are admirable and worthy goals for any international relationship and might likely have been considered by Berlin Fellowship participants as key to their understanding of this ministry and mission. However, can there really be partnership in a relationship between unequals? In

---

[43] John Brown, International Relationships in Mission, a study project, in: *International Review of Mission*, 86 (342), 1992, 207-273, 223.

[44] Ibid.

[45] Ibid.

[46] Brown, International Relationships, 224.

the case of Berlin Fellowship, the East Germans had no hope or opportunity for reverse visits, which along with other differences, certainly calls equality into question. On the other hand, equality may not necessarily only be defined or restricted to one aspect of the joint venture of fellowship, freedom to travel; mutuality, ownership, commitment, solidarity, transparency, and reciprocity are all potentially valid determinants of how one partner might view his role, her status, their equality.

Asking just this question, Kai M. Funkschmidt examines various mission structures and how they facilitate overcoming unequal or unjust relationships or how they make overcoming impossible.[47] Looking at three separate acclaimed ecumenical partnership models (Communauté Évangélique d'Action Apostolique, Council for World Mission, United Evangelical Mission), this author underlines the complexity of ecumenical partner relationships due to money, language, the organization's self-understanding, composition and history. Most interesting and germane is reference to lay people at the grassroots being excluded or side-lined in mission efforts because of organizational structures, church politics, and bureaucracy. Naming several ways to avoid that, Funkschmidt refers to the "twinning" partnership idea, which enables direct long-term partnerships between congregations or districts in two different regions. These relationships might include mutual visits, letter exchange, intercession, partnership Sunday services, and financial sharing.[48] Labeling this as a democratic or bi-lateral alternative, he refers to the extensive study of just such partnerships between German and African congregations discussed in *Miteinander Leben Lernen. Zwischenkirchliche Partnerschaften als Ökumenische Lerngemeinschaften/Learning to Live Together: Interchurch Partnerships as Ecumenical Communities of Learning*, by Lothar Bauerochse.

Bauerochse's study of "ecumenical communities of learning" highlights the strengths and weaknesses of longer-standing formal church-to-church partnerships (on local, mid-governing and national levels). Though Berlin Fellowship cannot be compared to any similar kind of formal twinning or sustained partner relationship, the comments and observations made by participants, and repeated assessments about the meaning and significance of the relationships and encounters echo with assessment and reflection of Berlin Fellowship participants. Bauerochse's study reveals weaknesses in the relationships over the years, dif-

---

[47] Kai Michael Funkschmidt, Partnership Between Unequals—Mission Impossible? Mission structures revisited, in: *International Review of Mission*, 91 no. 362, Jl 2002, 395-413.
[48] Op. cit., 410.

ficulties with language and communication, the one-sidedness of German-initiated actions (creating dependencies), markedly different expectations from partners in both directions, and the dependence on individuals or very small groups in the German congregations and primarily church leaders in Africa. However, there are repeated and consistent comments throughout this 300+ page book which underscore that the personal contact and friendship and the meetings themselves, between Germans and Africans, are very important if not paramount. "As a rule, partnerships come into being from personal connections or contacts."[49] It seems the partnerships are thus shaped by personal influence and interests of the founding person or group, and in most cases, the founders are not just initiators but remain active and influential over many years.[50]

An abbreviated report on the African comments about the partnerships noted, "Partnerships, in this context, meant the possibility of boundary-crossing and reconciling Christian fellowship."[51] It is regularly noted at the parish and not just on the leadership level that fellowship is one of the most important aspects of the partnerships, and the references are about what happens when a delegation comes to visit. "That people from Europe would make the effort to travel a long and troublesome distance, that they aren't put off by dusty streets nor sparsely and simply inhabited areas [...] all to visit their African partners, that is what makes the partnership so valuable."[52] Discussing the different motives and experiences, the author notes, "The immediate and close encounter and fellowship with the guests can generate much enthusiasm and becomes then motivation for more intense commitment in the partnership."[53]

Though the German partners wished for more correspondence contact, for the Africans, the partnership meant something quite different. For them it was the "visit" or the "trip." The meaning of the partnership, the meetings, and the relationships are thus described: "Personal inner sympathy, thoughts, prayers, feelings are all included [...] the ultimate

---

[49] Lothar Bauerochse, *Miteinander leben lernen. Zwischenkirchliche Partnerschaften als ökumenische Lerngemeinschaften*, Erlangen 1996, 193, "Partnerschaften entstehen in der Regel von persönlichen Verbindungen oder Kontakten."

[50] Op. cit., 194.

[51] Op. cit., 235, "Partnerschaften bedeuteten in diesem Kontext die Ermöglichung von grenzüberschreitender und versöhnender Christliche Gemeinschaft."

[52] Op. cit., 236 "Allein, dass sich Menschen aus Europa auf einen weiten und mühsamen Weg machen, dass sie weder staubige Strassen noch ungewohnte und einfache Lebensbedingungen scheuen, um ihre afrikanischen Partner zu besuchen, das macht die Partnerschaften für viele so wertvoll."

[53] Op. cit., 248 "Die unmittelbare und nahe Begegnung und Gemeinschaft mit den Gästen kann dann viel Begeisterung auslösen und zum Anstoß für ein intensiveres Engagement in der Partnerschaft werden."

meaning was the relationship between people. Discussion full of whatever content played no role." In this context, Bauerochse notes how even after fourteen years of no contact, two women fell into each other's arms, seeing themselves as friends over the time and distance, even though they had had no regular exchange or contact.[54]

Though both partners have different expectations and assessments of success in the partnerships, there is a joint and shared desire to be together and to be in contact, and when the actual meetings happen, the visits themselves become the key event for both sides, generating new enthusiasm for the partnership (253f.).[55] In a more systematic evaluation, programmatic goals do not seem to be as important as the meetings with people. In spite of major differences in the worldviews, for example, the Germans wanted to do something about the poverty they encountered, while the Africans simply embraced the partnerships as they were, for they had had no other similar or comparable experiences. In spite of the partnerships seeming to have had little if any effect in the life of the larger congregation or the church districts, it is reiterated that those most greatly affected were the individuals (281).[56] Bauerochse labels this a weakness. However, is there any other level on which meaning is embraced? In light of the African comments recorded and discussed, it is clear that the personal nature of relationships plays a great role and lends value to the partnership and engenders motivation and commitment.

Finally, Bauerochse's study asks questions about both groups' mission and partnership understanding, and though "mission" and "ecumenical" were viewed differently by the partners, they both saw the meetings and the relationships as a chance to experience unity. The study ends on two notes, one that reinforces the acceptance of the "other" as advantageous and good, while also acknowledging that the "other" can easily be regarded as a "subject" *or* as someone just like me; in both cases, this is a warning of the ever-present precarious nature of partnerships.[57]

Secondly, though this very thorough and detailed report on partner church relationships between four German and four African church districts and their congregations offers key insights into twinning and the importance of personal relationships, there are several scattered side comments I found enlightening. At one point, looking more closely at the

---

[54] Op. cit., 253 " Innere Anteilnahme, Gedanken und Gefühle sind ebenso eingeschlossen [...] Von geradezu schließlicher Bedeutung, die zwischenmenschliche Beziehung. Inhaltliche Diskussionen spielen keine Rolle."

[55] Op. cit., 253f.

[56] Op. cit., 281.

[57] Bauerochse, *Miteinander*, section 4.2 Die Fremden Partner.

African understanding of the partnership, Bauerochse remarks that in English, the word friendship or fellowship was used more often than partnership, seeming to correspond to the "spiritual" aspect of the relationship. In German, *zusammenkommen* (to come together) or *sich verbinden* (to unite) were also used but rarely. Further analysis of descriptions of the relationships revealed the "not readily dissolved connection of the partner" and the capacity of the partners to help each other, get more done together than they would each do alone.[58] For the African partners, friendship and family-like connections meant caring for one another, helping one another, sharing of goods, sharing in sorrow and joy and celebrating together.[59]

As revealing as these statements are, there was relatively little direct information or citation from the African side of the partnerships. Bauerochse states that the foundational research from the African partners is both long overdue and should be done by them. To date, I have found no evidence of further research from the African side. Other comments scattered throughout the study draw attention to the fact that the African partners do indeed have a voice, but Bauerochse concedes that it is not reflected in this particular study as completely as it should be.

This dilemma of "partner silence" is slowly being addressed in the emerging body of research and data about the sister-church movement or "twinning relationships," especially as they have developed since the 1980's.[60] In many cases, studies primarily consider the effects and transformations for the American or western partners, noting the importance of strangers meeting on common ground, of friendship developing, of people being given new vision and being drawn out of themselves, among others. A 2010 dissertation by Janet Kragt Bakker at the Catholic University of America is an incredibly thorough examination of twelve church-to-church partnerships representing several denominations and very differentiated twinning relationships from around the global south. The focus of the study is interview data collected from American participants. The findings do allude briefly to results for the partners; however, Bakker concedes from the outset of her study that the voice of the part-

[58] Op. cit., 430.

[59] Ibid.

[60] cf. Karoline Rittberger-Klas, *Kirchenpartnerschaften Im Geteilten Deutschland. Am Beispiel Der Landeskirchen Württemberg Und Thüringen*; Anke Silomon, Harry Oelke, and Siegfried Hermle, *Anspruch Und Wirklichkeit der »besonderen Gemeinschaft«*; Richter, Hedwig, *Pietismus im Sozialismus: Die Herrnhuter Brüdergemeine in der DDR;* id., Wir spürten den Herzschlag brüderlicher Liebe, Vom transnationalen Austausch der Herrnhuter Brüdergemeine im Kalten Krieg in: *Umworbener Klassenfeind: das Verhältnis der DDR zu den USA*, Berlin 2006, Uta A. Balbier and Christiane Rösch (eds.), Berlin 2006.

ners will only be represented by second-hand reporting.[61] There seem to be very few missional studies or research projects (if any) focused on the "voice" of the partners, much less *from* the voice of partners.

In a similar vein, but more closely related to partnership and the geography of the Cold War, is a 2004 study *Über die Mauer, die DDR, die niederländischen Kirchen und die Friedensbewegung* by Beatrice deGraaf. In this rather overwhelming and thorough analysis of the East German and Dutch congregation partnerships in the 1980's, deGraaf states she wants to examine the theological and religious motivations of East German and Dutch churches and church organizations in light of the arms race. DeGraaf primarily considers issues of protest against the USSR and USA stationing rockets in both Germany's, as well as the common wish for a just and peaceful world. She examines in great detail the Dutch interest in the GDR and its churches, the political developments between 1945 and 1989, the effects of "Ostpolitik" and the peace and opposition movements in both countries, as well as development and crises in Dutch-German partnerships over the decades. This research makes for very interesting reading and focuses primarily on the sweep of context and history, highlighting the partnerships, key meetings, activities, and ever-present complex of the MfS (*Ministerium für Staatssicherheit*), the *Stasi*, but de Graaf's work reveals only few or extended details about the yearly, regular, faithful congregation-to-congregation visitations and eventual reverse visitations.

When those relationships are mentioned or alluded to, the commentaries echo much of what Bauerochse's study reveals. Person-to-person conversation, shared worship and meals, visits in homes, time spent with one another all are named by many interviewees as the point.

At least in part, the openness for and willingness to allow the contact with Christians from the Netherlands (congregations, church delegations, peace activists) served to heighten the international legitimacy of the German Democratic Republic; though it also served that state's propaganda ends within the country.[62] Some of the motivation for contact came from Dutch political sympathizers who wanted to be part of the learning process of a church living in a "political Diaspora but emerging from a people's church situation" (70). Language facility, geographic proximity, and the fact that the church in the GDR also had a large Protestant representation were further motivations; in addition, it was the

[61] Janet Kragt Bakker, *Encountering the Church*, Washington, D.C. 2004.

[62] De Graaf, *Über die Mauer*, 55.

only country in the communist bloc with a majority Protestant church (70).

While Dutch-East German official church-to-church contacts were established soon after the war, the parish-to-parish contacts began to take root in the early 1970's, and by 1989 there were 400 such partnerships (288). Initially, motivation came from within peace working groups in the Netherlands, and contacts began to be established. Though supported by both the Germans and the Dutch, the active Dutch visitors were soon given guidelines for behavior when traveling, the most important of which was to listen, without constantly showing sympathy or compassion (149). Though officially sanctioned, many of the parish partnerships "happened" spontaneously and informally, and the rapid growth in the number necessitated some coordination from both sides in higher church offices (149). The motivations and interest at the congregational level were a bit different for each side, but they had several things in common: both wanted to know about being Christian in another social and political system, and both were looking for encouragement and new points of orientation in a modern, secular/non-churched society (150). For some, motivation stemmed from the peace movement in the Netherlands, and without wanting to criticize the GDR, the Dutch were looking for brothers and sisters in faith who were also interested in peace activism (151). As long as the church contacts and visits, their participants and church workers didn't criticize the GDR regime, there weren't too many problems, but as deGraaf explains, that was not necessarily always the case. By the middle of the 1980's, the contacts in the more politically involved circles had become problematic for the GDR, both for the government and for the Federation of Protestant Churches. However, it was the parish-to-parish contacts which were foremost in the minds of the participants. "For the Dutch and East German congregations, contacts were more important than radical political goals." [63] It was more important that contacts be maintained, and less 'dangerous' themes occupy parish visits (249).

The parish visits continued through the 1980's, and they were organized on the *Prinzip Diakonat*, meaning the Dutch participants understood their task as being church to visit brothers and sisters on the other side of the wall. Contacts were then focused on worship services, common hymn singing, Bible discussions and studies, and conversation about matters of faith and personal cares (289). DeGraaf also names other con-

[63] Op. cit., 249, "Für die niederländischen und ostdeutschen Gemeinden waren Kontakte wichtiger als radikale politische Zielzetzungen."

versation topics, gleaned from interviews: reconciliation with the Federal Republic, dismantling of the picture of the enemy (*Feindbilder abbauen*), cooperative peace work, deepening and spreading of faith, and encouragement of the believers in the GDR. She continues, "It was, above all, the close friendships which held the partnerships together."[64] Concluding the only extended discussion of parish cooperation and partnerships in this study, deGraaf states that parish contacts were boundary-crossing but not boundary-breaking. The Dutch had a sympathy for their East German brothers and sisters in faith, but at the same time they were also curious about and had respect for the "church in socialism." The East German host families were looking for attention or notice (*Beachtung*), deGraaf says, solidarity, Christian connections and a window to the west. DeGraaf concludes that the parish contacts were a carefully protected *Niche*, from which the congregations benefited and which the East German government tolerated.[65]

In the case of both the deGraaf study and that of Bauerochse, the rough edges as well as the benefits of the partnerships are described. In both cases, however, the voices of the other partner are primarily reported and not directly quoted. Admittedly, these observations and opinions take a back seat to the findings of the more vocal and verbal and researching partners. In both studies, the other partner's descriptions of boundary-crossing experiences are not highlighted or more than alluded to.

A similar treatment is evidenced in another report of a partnership between a parish in East Berlin and one in Iserlohn, in the Federal Republic of Germany. Entitled *Patchwork, Partnership between the Evangelical Elias Parish in East Berlin and Iserlohn in Westfalen during the Political Tensions of 1978 - 1989*[66], this detailed, carefully assembled, and noteworthy collection of written data attests to the 20-year partnership between two German congregations. It is replete with reports, letters, examples of visitation programs, posters, newspaper articles, and photographs; however, the "voice" of the eastern partner in the years 1978-89 is much softer and harder to hear that that of the western partner.

In yet another publication, a reflection upon East-West German partnerships, Dietrich Mendt, theologian from Saxony, reports in 1996,

---

[64] Ibid., "Es waren vor allem die geschlossenen Freundschaften, die die Partnerschaften zusammenhielten."

[65] Op. cit., 291.

[66] Katzorke, *Stückwerke.*

> The cooperative work with them (West German partners) had several aspects for us. It was a great encouragement and strengthening of faith because they were people from another country with a totally different political basis, with a successful economy, with a factual, well-founded but also ideological anti-communist posture. They were an encouragement not only with their counsel, their prayer, their message, but also in material ways. They brought us books, which for them were dangerous, both to have and to transport. They brought us medicine for our children's' whooping cough, but also coffee, fabric, phonograph records, necessary and not so necessary things, which we, with our small church salaries could not afford [...]
> But I've just recently figured it out, that our admiration was also guilty of producing in us a state of inertia, of stand-still, where in awe and gratitude, one was stuck, which actually build a border between us in conversation, from both sides. To carry together, that was endearing and welcome! And for us (East Germans) that meant, letting yourself be carried. But there was then no room for a critical accompaniment, that we also very much needed. From our side, we hardly had space to be interested in the West German church relationships or to ask critical questions of them.[67]

In naming inertia or a kind of numbness in both partners (*Erstarrung*), Mendt, in this post-1989 reflection, puts his finger not only on what built walls for both sides but also on that which deGraaf might mean regarding boundaries being crossed but not actually being broken. He notes that "carrying together" (*mittragen*) was community-building, resulting in mutuality, and that was good. However, for the East Germans, it often meant allowing themselves to be carried, which rules out having a voice, a critical voice being able to truly be a partner in a two-way conversation, from which all might benefit. Mendt's final words of explanation that the easterners were thus numbed and silenced is a reminder that critical accompaniment (which is disallowed by being carried

---

[67] Dietrich Mendt, Christen in Ost und West, Partnerschaften im geteilten und im vereignigten Deutschland in: *Zeichen der Zeit, 2-96*, 62-63. "Die Zusammenarbeit mit ihnen hatte für uns verschiedene Aspekte. Sie war eine große Ermutigung und Glaubensstärkung. Menschen aus einem anderen Land mit einer völlig andrer politischen Grundeinstellung, mit einer erfolgreichen Wirtschaft, mit einem sachlich begründeten, aber auch ideologisch zu sehenden Antikommunismus, nicht nur mit ihrem Rat, ihrem Gebet, ihrer Verkündigung, sondern auch materiell. Sie brachten uns Bücher, deren Besitz und schon deren Transport gefährlich war, sie brachten uns die Medikamente für den Keuchhusten unserer Kinder, aber auch Kaffee, Textilien, Schallplatten, benötigte und weniger benötigte Dinge, die wir uns bei den niedrigen Gehältern in unserer Kirche nicht leisten konnten. Aber heute habe ich begriffen, dass diese Bewunderung auch schuld war an einer gewissen Erstarrung, in der man bewundernd verheilt und die dem Gespräch zwischen uns Grenzen setzte, von beiden Seiten. Mit-Tragen, das war das Nahe liegende und Willkommene! Und für uns heiß es: Sich tragen lassen! Da blieb kaum Raum für eine wirklich kritische Begleitung, die wir auch nötig gehabt hätten. Und da blieb auf unsere Seite kaum Raum für ein wirkliches Interesse an westdeutschen kirchlichen Verhältnissen und für kritische Rückfragen in umgekehrter Richtung."

or when one partner "has all the say") enlivens dialogue and encounter; critical accompaniment can indeed deepen the experience of fellowship and open the way for learning, insight and boundary crossing for both partners.

The boundary, the border between the two Germany's, was a unique intercultural or intra-cultural place, and over the years an intercontextual locale as well, which didn't in all cases at all times result in jointly embraced partnership.[68] The complexities of German-German partnerships, though examined on several levels in a number of studies, will not be directly addressed in this research. It would be a worthy study to consider the role the border played in the various phases of the German-German partnerships or any other partnerships on the congregational level but again and importantly, as told through the voices, memories, and opinions of both partners.

In this research, in order to further understand similar encounters, their benefits *and* their limitations, this border, as a place of intercultural or intercontextual interchange must be considered. It is indeed the essence of interculturality and intercontextuality which affects the nature and the boundaries of partnerships, cross-cultural dialogue, and certainly even one-time encounters, like those in this research.

Recognized and reconciled but not necessarily fully understanding the place of missional encounter

These limited findings from *partnership studies* as well as Miroslav Volf's metaphor for embrace offer a suitable launching pad for brief reflection about interculturality and intercontextuality. How a cross-cultural or intercultural encounter is experienced and interpreted by either partner reflects differences. Each partner brings their own culture and context to the encounter and to the assessment. Both have and experience boundaries because of the differences. Embracing and being embraced is equally so, culturally and contextually stamped by the individual participants' backgrounds, among other factors. Berlin Fellowship was no exception.

The developments in mission studies and in the field of missiology, emerging "missional theology," and related *missio Dei* discussions since Bosch offer a stark reminder that cross-cultural encounters (old terminology) act to highlight how unique and particular dialogue partner-contexts

[68] Rittberger-Klas, *Kirchenpartnerschaften*, 317f., "Die Kirchenpartnerschaften verliefen in ihrer vierzigjahren Geschichte unter den Bedingungen der deutschen Teilung weder problemlos, noch waren sie unumstritten […]"

really are, and even how contextually bound Christians are, not just to their tradition of faith but to their country, culture, and political systems. The ecumenical movement has contributed to the growing awareness of our globalized world and has highlighted the need for the Christian community to embrace "wholesome intercontextual, cross-cultural relations that take seriously the significance of plurality and promote community across differences."[69]

This intercontextual and intercultural challenge (community across differences) is not a new one and has biblical roots as early in Israel's history as Abraham's call. The call to Abraham became a call to a people and an affirmation of that people's identity; the people were to be blessed, in order to be a blessing beyond themselves to all the "families of the earth." God's call to Abraham affirms the identity and purpose of this particular people but only in relation to and for the sake of the others. "The call of Abraham is a call to refuse to let one's identity be absolutized and one's borders closed."[70] This discussion immediately draws to mind, as well, the Pentecost meeting of cultures, languages and peoples, where the interculturality and intercontextuality of the occasion appear a barrier beyond the pale. However, on that occasion the Spirit of God breaks through and rather than ignoring the differences and borders, acknowledges them, propelling a diverse and divided gathering into a community, ever as diverse but no longer defined by the division of contextual and cultural background.

As was the case with Berlin Fellowship, the participants were not only bound to and in a very real way defined by their own contexts (contextuality), the encounters propelled them into being intercontextual (newly related to a situation and to others beyond their borders because of their Christian faith). The very reason for the meetings and ongoing visits had its origins and was centered in that which they shared, the Christian faith.[71] To say it another way, participants were certainly bound to and defined by their background cultures, but in so far as they bumped up against each other and were "together" because of their Christian faith, they experienced a form of interculturality, even in an existential or momentary sense.

---

[69] Christopher Duraisingh,, Mission towards reconciled and inter-contextual communities, in: *International Review of Mission* , 91.363, 2002, 483-499, 484.

[70] Ibid.

[71] Berlin Fellowship 'pre-history' had its roots in ecumenical work projects in post-WW2 Europe. These friendships resulted years later in an offer from Presbyterians in southern California to visit and an invitation from the German church in Berlin to return for further cooperative mission service (see chapter 3).

Andrew Walls contends that it is just this being together of very different kinds of persons, this encounter, time spent with the other, which launched the Church. As the early apostles found they were needing to separate from the Jewish practices of piety so familiar to them and find new ways of practicing faith, they moved out of traditional Jewish territory and its observant Jewish society and into Hellenistic pagan society, where they encountered Greeks, Gentiles who had converted to the new Christian belief but whose culture and context were markedly different than their Jewish counterparts.[72]

Discussing not just the history of the origins of the church but its very essence, Walls refers to this as the Ephesian Moment: "In union with him (Christ), you too are being built together with all the others into a place where God lives through his Spirit." (Good News Translation, Eph. 2:22) Drawing attention to one specific place, table fellowship, both an important part of early church life, as well as a sign of religious, cultural and ethnic division up to this point, Walls notes that the nascent Ephesian church could have had two cultures represented in the church, separated by the meal table, but that did not happen (76). Separation isn't in the Ephesians' author's mind, for the metaphor is that of the diverse parts of the body being joined and knit together, building itself up in love (4:16), "in Christ," so as to reach full stature; this is an overwhelming affirmation that the "very height of Christ's full stature is reached only by the coming together of the different cultural entities into the body of Christ" (77). The experienced interculturality and intercontextuality then in the Ephesians' setting is mediated by knowing Christ, which "arises from the coming together of the fragmented understanding that occurs within the diverse culture specific segments of humanity where he becomes known" (78).

Is this then *the* very "place" where God lives through his Spirit, the place where he becomes known, in spite of fragmented understanding or incorrect or mistaken perceptions of the other? Is this then a place or potentially so, where boundaries and barriers are certainly being crossed and perhaps even broken? For the purposes of this research, at this point, the questions remain unanswered, but they stand as an echo of the main research question of this dissertation.

---

[72] Andrew Walls, *The Cross-Cultural Process, The Cross-cultural Process in Christian History: Studies in the Transmission and Appropriation of Faith*, Maryknoll, New York 2002, 72-81.

3. Mission or *missio Dei*? The Place Where God is Moving and at Work

The often assumed and most likely "place" where God might be encountered, where he lives and makes himself known has been seen traditionally to be *within* the four walls of the local congregation's sanctuary. Mission and making God known, has then fallen to those sent out from that place. Since the first century, the church has been in mission, sending missionaries, with God and the Gospel in their back pockets, to evangelize and expand the Christian faith.[73] This understanding still prevails, for "not insignificantly, the Latin root of mission implies 'sending,' and the term has thus been commonly associated with those who venture beyond the boundaries of the faith community."[74]

David Bosch, in *Transforming Mission*, reconfigures this understanding of being sent, however, and offers a new paradigm: "In the new image mission is not primarily an activity of the church, but an attribute of God [...] Mission is thereby seen as a movement from God to the world, and the church is viewed as the instrument for that mission."[75] "To participate in mission is to participate in the movement of God's love toward people."[76]

Bosch has been attributed to re-launching this discussion which began after World War II at the International Missionary Conference in Willingen, Germany (1952), and it appears to be only the very edge of the ongoing discussion[77] and debate. Retooling of the definition of *missio Dei (*God's mission) continues[78] with queries related to mission theology's path and developments,[79] questions about application and use of the term, *missio Dei*, asking whether it is not rather a mission movement *to* God as opposed to God's mission[80] or whether it isn't "mission having a

---

[73] Michael Barram, The Bible, Mission, and Social Location: Toward a Missional Hermeneutic, in: *Interpretation* 61, 1, Jan 2007, 42 - 58.
[74] Ibid.
[75] Bosch, *Transforming Mission*, 390.
[76] Ibid.
[77] Jacques Matthey, God's Mission Today: Summary and Conclusions, in: *International Review of Mission* 92.367, 2003, 579–587.
[78] Tormod Engelsviken, MISSIO DEI: The Understanding and Misunderstanding of the Theological Concept in European Churches and Missiology in: *International Review of Mission*, 92.367, 2003, 481 - 497.
[79] Wilhelm Richebächer, MISSIO DEI: The Basis of Mission Theology or a Wrong Path? in *International Review of Mission*, 92.367, 2003, 588 – 605.
[80] J.Jayakiran Sebastian, Interrogating *missio Dei*: From the mission of God towards appreciating our mission to God in India today, www.edinburgh.2010.org (accessed May, 2011).

church" as opposed to the other way around.[81] Bosch's initial shift in definition and description was one of the first and essential steps. Such additional suggestions more recently for new parameters and paradigms are examining missiological thinking and challenging it to broadened and ever more multifaceted views of *missio Dei*, mission and missional activity, mission and theology, and missional theology.[82] This ongoing and timely discussion has expanded the notion of mission, which is no longer limited to the activity of the Church or of the local congregation; however, at the same time and most importantly , mission is absolutely foundational and "constitutive" of the church[83] and remains a mandate for the third millennium.[84] In a holistic manner, Bosch's notion definitely undoes the reductionist definition of mission and broadens the horizons of discussion immensely. It should be remembered "that the Church exists not for itself and not for its members but as a sign and agent and foretaste of the kingdom of God."[85]

Moreover, this sign, agent, and foretaste (Lesslie Newbigin) has a key role and does act as a pointer to the "Kingdom of God beyond its present horizon; as an instrument God uses the church for his work of healing and liberation and as a first fruit, the church has a real taste now of the renewal God intends for all."[86] God and God's Church are in the business of "reaching out" to the whole of the created order, and it is indeed the Church which is the primary recipient and partner, having been reached out to and in turn, being agents through which God reaches out. The WCC CWME paper entitled *Mission and Evangelism in Unity Today* offers wording specifically describing the actions of that sign and agent: "Mission carries a holistic understanding: the proclamation and sharing of the good news of the gospel by word *(kerygma)*, deed (*diakonia*), prayer and worship (*leiturgia*) and the everyday witness of the Christian life *(martyria)*; teaching as building up and strengthening people in their relationship with God and each other; and healing as wholeness and rec-

---

[81] Stephen Bevans, The Mission Has A Church, Perspectives of a Roman Catholic Theologian, www.edinburgh2010.org (accessed November, 2011).

[82] Darrell Guder, From Mission and Theology to Missional Theology, in: *The Princeton Seminary Bulletin* 24.1, 2003, 36 – 54. See also Guder, Missional Church, Forschungsbericht über eine missiologische debate in den USA, in: *Theologische Zeitschrift*, 2-66, 2010, 185 - 198.

[83] *Mission and Evangelism in Unity Today*, WCC, CWME Preparatory Paper.

[84] Eberhard Jüngel, To Tell the World About God : The Task for the Mission of the Church on the Threshold of the Third Millennium, in: *International Review of Mission,* 89.353, 2000, 203 – 215.

[85] Lesslie Newbigin, *The Gospel in a Pluralist Society*, Grand Rapids, MI 1989, 136.

[86] Michael Goheen, The Future of Mission in the World Council of Churches, in: *Mission Studies* 21.1, 2004, 97-111, 104f.

onciliation into *koinonia* communion with God, communion with people, and communion with creation as a whole."[87]

Insofar, as mission's expanded definition launched by Bosch and followers is based on a Trinitarian model (God the Father sending the Son, and the Father and the Son sending the Spirit), *missio Dei* does offer a deeper understanding and a new perspective of God's movement in and for that whole world, and as importantly, in and for the whole Church as well. The familiar self-understanding of the "church in mission" has changed and expanded. The Church is now the sent, rather than solely being the sender, and rather than participating on behalf of God, it participates in and with God in God's mission and in so doing, lives out its mission. "Mission is the basic and most urgent task of the church [...] because to be Christian is to become part of God's life and God's vision for the world."[88] This way of perceiving mission engagement, reflected in the internal community in the Trinity, is also a new perspective on ecclesial self-understanding and thus a new way of understanding ecumenical engagement and dialogue. In a volume dedicated to mission as prophetic dialogue (discussion to follow), echoing Bosch(above), citing *Ad Gentes*, and referring to the Trinity, Stephen B. Bevans and Roger P. Schroeder assert that God is a verb, "a Movement, an Embrace, a Flow more personal than we can ever imagine who is always and everywhere present in God's creation. God in God's deepest identity is a relationship, a communion [...]."[89] They continue, all Christians, as participants in that communion, are "called to minister in ordinary and extraordinary ways in their daily lives, both within the church and in the world."[90] If one takes the statement "the church is mission"[91] seriously, and if this mission is *missio Dei* (the movement of God's love toward people[92] and God as a verb), then activities like those of Berlin Fellowship are but one of the ways of *missio Dei* Bible studies, common meals, worship, prayer, and sharing, through conversation and dialogue *in* Christian fellowship.

In a discussion of the Willingen conference and mission's anchor in the triune God, Theo Sundermeier suggests further that *missio Dei* may be manifest as a process of four dimensions. The process has an "inside" in which something like a "universe" is interwoven with other people. It

---

[87] Mission and Evangelism, WCC, 7a.
[88] Stephen B. Bevans and Roger P. Schroeder, *Constants in Context*, Maryknoll, N.Y. 2004, 303.
[89] Stephen B. Bevans and Roger P. Schroeder, *Prophetic Dialogue, Reflections on Christian Mission Today*, Maryknoll, N.Y. 2011, 9-10.
[90] Op.cit., 16.
[91] Kraemer, *Religion*, 29.
[92] Bosch, *Mission*, 390

has an "outside," characterized by paths, which are places or spaces which people go through or are influenced by, and the experience itself shapes the people involved.[93] Sundermeier describes these dimensions as characterized by mystery, freedom, pluralism and what he labels "dense hope."

The "inside" of Christian mission he contends is then mystery but not hidden, for it becomes interpreted text and no secret; the message is born in a person, responding to God and allowing himself to be recognized in the triune God. "The mystery of mission goes down in history and can be narrated. It is meant to be told; it seeks public attention. It becomes an 'open secret.'"[94] A second dimension, freedom, is clearly manifest in God freely coming to coming to the human person whom he loves, respecting the dignity of that person, creating and receiving trust, and listening and granting space to the one to whom he has come. Mission then is coming to, in friendship as God has come. A relationship or friendship may result, and this relationship is dialogical, freely flowing back and forth, "a mutual opening, from the longing to learn from and be enriched by the other."[95] Because mission propels one across boundaries toward the stranger, toward the other, one is changed by the encounter and by the differences. Being brought into relationship doesn't erase the differences, but they cease to be experienced as divisive. "Foreignness can be overcome, understanding becomes possible, familiarity can grow, and commonalities take root. Strangers can become friends."[96] The final dimension Sundermeier suggests has to do with the kingdom of God in the present time yet as a foretaste of the future, shining as it does, interrupting time and making itself known in the forgiveness of sins, the healing of disease, the reintegration into the community, and the call to discipleship, in rebirth, as festive joy. The kingdom is then "in the midst" of (Luke 17:21) and in the fellowship with the risen Christ, as close as the brother or sister.

Sundermeier's definition of Christian mission's center lies in the fact that the center's origins lie outside itself and stem from mystery the mystery of God's coming into the world in Jesus. Mission proceeds to be an opening up to that mystery, which creates a space of freedom enabling people to come closer and into dialogue, and there they meet, with all

---

[93] Theo Sundermeier, *Missio Dei* Today: On the Identity of Christian Mission, in: *International Review of Mission*, 92.367, 2003, 560-578, 561.

[94] Op. cit., 562.

[95] Op. cit., 565, Sundermeier quoting U. Schoen, *Dialog, Lexikon, missionstheologischer Grundbegriffe*, Berlin 1987, 5.

[96] Op. cit., 567.

their differences, nonetheless able to see and recognize each other. In recognizing the other and being recognized, a meeting takes place, and perhaps afterwards, this encounter can be called a sign of the kingdom itself.[97] The way of God (*missio Dei*) is to come to and to meet, to speak and to listen, and to engage in dialogue.

"missio Dei"- Tthe way of God through prophetic dialogue
In Stephen B. Bevans and Roger P. Schroeder's initial volume, *Constants in Context, A Theology of Mission Today, 2004*, it is suggested that a theology of mission is characterized by dialogue, prophetic dialogue[98], and it is exactly *in* the church or through the church's witness that mission as prophetic dialogue is both housed and occurs. These authors, taking the label from their own Roman Catholic congregation, the Society of the Divine Word, equate "prophetic dialogue" with the interior life of God ("communion of gift and reception, identity and openness to the other, communion in relationship and communion in mission" (348). The church then, called into mission "must be a community that not only gives of itself in service to the world and to the peoples of the world's cultures but learns from its involvement and expands its imagination of the depths of God's unfathomable riches [...] Mission, as participation in the mission of the triune God, can only proceed in dialogue and can only be carried out in humility" (348). Drawing further on *Service of Documentation and Study on Global Mission* (SEDOS), pontifical and World Council of Churches developments and related documents since the 1980's, Bevans and Schroeder note that mission is indeed multi-dimensional and includes witness, proclamation, inculturation, and reconciliation as some of the key components. These four are most pertinent to this research, but the actual list is longer (353).

Some of these aspects have been discussed in the previous sections of this chapter (fellowship, reconciliation, and intercontextualization/inculturation) and are indeed essential underpinnings for dialogue and essential to the discussion of the research question. Bevans and Schroeder, however, offer some important added detail in definition that might illumine Berlin Fellowship's very limited and specific activities and help in reflection later in this research.

As defined by the 6th General Assembly of the World Council of Churches, *witness* is "those acts and words by which a Christian or com-

---

[97] Op. cit., 572f.
[98] Bevans and Schroder, *Constants*, 348. See also *Prophetic Dialogue, Reflections on Christian Mission Today*, Maryknoll, N.Y. 2011.

munity gives testimony to Christ and invites others to make their response to him" (353). These authors choose to focus on lifestyle and presence in their discussion and refer to "individuals of faith living their lives in the light of that faith" (353). This witness, then, may be manifest in and through the life a local community, which Newbigin would call the "hermeneutic of the gospel,"[99] and it was just such individuals and local communities in the GDR whose lives were lived in faith which made for quiet but profound witness to their neighbors, colleagues, and families, but also to visiting North American Christians. This way of life lived in Christian authenticity, with its celebrations (sacraments) and its practices of reconciliation and hospitality has been embraced by many in the "missional church movement" (discussion to follow). Witness also has an institutional and public nature, and church-run hospitals, nursing homes, and orphanages were among the diaconal services in the GDR which witnessed to the society at large and to the visiting Americans, for whom the diaconate in these forms was a new or unknown concept. Lastly, "common witness" takes on singular importance in acts of mutual encouragement, common prayer and conversation, recognition of those "in need," those suffering isolation, imprisonment, or rejection. As such, the visits to the Christian communities in the GDR by other Christians were a form of ministry of presence to those "locked in." [100] "As a person or a Christian community lives in contact with another religion or another context, is open to it and learns from it indeed, is in some sense evangelized by it ('mission in reverse'[101]), a tremendous witness is given [...] Christians witness to the fact that community is more than a support group or a place for personal growth but rather is a communion in which individuals can find their deepest human identity" (356). Concluding this section, these authors concede that the church has witnessed imperfectly, but it has witnessed, and they affirm the ecclesial nature of witness in Christian mission (357). Therein is perhaps something thus-far unnoticed or not yet closely analyzed in missiological research, and that is the witness in and among the members of the body of Christ; by definition given above and earlier in this research study, this aspect should most certainly also be included in the larger discussion and definition of missional activity and missionality.

Moreover, witness is not simply to an idea but to a particular person, "the name, the teaching, the life, the promises, the Kingdom, and the

[99] Lesslie Newbigin, *The Gospel in a Pluralist Society*, Grand Rapids, Michigan 1989, 222f.
[100] Matthew 25:35-45.
[101] Bevans and Schroeder, *Constants*, 356.

mystery of Jesus of Nazareth, the Son of God" (22) and in a particular context, setting, time and place. Though proclamation is often defined as an invitation to join the community of followers and as such is explicitly about Jesus Christ, his life, death and resurrection, it is as well noted at the CWME conference in San Antonio that proclamation is invitational and accompanied by "signs," as well as stamped by an attitude of listening (360). Insofar as Berlin Fellowship engaged in dialogue, perhaps prophetic dialogue (see following), and in that the conversation focused on matters of faith and practice, the visits then acted as "signs" of solidarity to both host and guest. The conversations and dialogue were both witness and proclamation, both essential to God's mission being lived out within the body of Christ and among its members, in a unique form of prophetic dialogue. This prophetic dialogue attests to what Jesus Christ is doing in individual lives, in the life of the community, and in the larger and surrounding world.

The hallmarks of inculturation, intercontextualization and reconciliation in mission discussed earlier are added keystones for Bevans and Schroeder's definition of prophetic dialogue. Genuine dialogue within a specific context involves listening and discerning, and as Schroeder describes, it involves, "entering someone else's garden" (387). This can only take place it would seem because "the faith of Christ is infinitely translatable [...] and creates a 'place to feel at home'" (387). Authentic engagement, however, may not look or feel like an idealized picture of "home" necessarily, for it involves the dialogue partners, both host and guest, being open to transformation, and being ready to change. As example, the "outsiders" or visitors might let go of superiority, of illusions that they understand a culture or that theirs is the true understanding of the Christian faith, while "insiders" are given the task to speak out; the complexities of the ensuing dialogue may potentially take on prophetic significance for both participants. Berlin Fellowship participants, both East Germans and Americans often describe their feelings of "having been spoken to" and "listened to" in spite of barriers of understanding, having learned from the other, and having a new understanding of the Church (and themselves) and this experience is then seen as witness for or evidence to God's using the encounters for encouragement and building of faith.

The "praxis" of reconciliation (2 Cor. 5:9) has also been addressed, but reconciliation *within* the church itself and among Christians is a key facet of mission as prophetic dialogue as defined by Bevans and Schroeder. Reconciliation being practiced via dialogue in the late 20th century includes accompaniment, incarnation and solidarity (389). With

God working as the mediator, it can happen within the church itself, as evidenced by recent decades in the ecumenical movement. This is witness to God's work in the community in places of safety, truth, care, concern, prayer, genuine participation and solidarity, as hospitality is extended among believers, and fellowship is experienced (393). These descriptors and similar words are characteristic of Berlin Fellowship experiences and often are alluded to in the remembrances of what happened.

Concluding their discussion of mission as prophetic dialogue in *Constants in Context*, Bevans and Schroeder speak of mission in two directions, one to the world and one to the church itself, based on a threefold-structure of word (kerygma), action (diakonia) and being (koinonia or martyria). The testimony to the church itself about its own being, in fellowship, may also be understood as a form of witness to the world. Because mission is God's work, the church lives out its missionary and missional nature, as God's sign and instrument of reconciliation in preaching, witnessing and serving the reign of God (395).

"missio Dei" The Missional Church movement's contribution

This synthetic paradigm of prophetic dialogue (word, action and being/witness) is a provocative model for defining or identifying an aspect of the church's role in *missio Dei,* and this model of dialogue complements much of what mission theology in the last two decades has focused on. This discussion and self-examination has been at the center of the missional church movement.

The missional church movement is calling for an ecclesial re-embracing of a "missional" posture (Guder, Hunsberger, van Gelder). That is, a newly embraced self-understanding of participating in God's mission is being owned and explored in congregations (primarily in the U.S. and Great Britain) which are discovering that they are in and surrounded by "places" God is at work and to which God is calling. Those places are in neighborhood soup kitchens and food pantries, in the literacy programs at the local library, and in simultaneous outreach, evangelism and service to the local community. More traditionally stamped congregational mission efforts (overseas or local) are included. To some degree, a part of this movement was labeled earlier the "social gospel" and the discussion today is housed, in part, under the roof of the Gospel and Our Culture Network.[102] In recent years this movement in "missional" church thinking, writing, and theological research has expanded and asked the question, "What would a missiological ecclesiology for the

[102] www.gocn.org

church in North America look like if we were to take the missionary context (post-Christendom) we are now in seriously?" Although the question and much of the missional church discussion is not directly pertinent to this research, some key parameters for the definition of "missional," and "missional activities" as activities of the gathered body of believers are.

The operative term missional is a term used to summarize the implications of Vatican II's *Ad Gentes* statement, "The church on earth is by its very nature missionary, since according to the plan of the Father, it has its origin in the mission of the Son, and of the Holy Spirit."[103] This statement and much of the critique of ecclesiology and its legacy of silence about mission in Western thinking up through the time of Karl Barth are in response to the limited understanding which reduced the Kingdom of God to the building up of the Church. Much twentieth century criticism of the church has resulted because of this misreading of the task and the context. Though it may have once thought so, the church certainly no longer finds itself at home in "Christendom,"[104]so this context must be reexamined. God's love for the created order goes far beyond the boundaries of the Church. God's offer of salvation extends to the entire world; the role the church plays and its task in that extension is being expressed and described in a new way. "The church does not do mission, it is mission. By its very calling and nature, it exists as God's sent people (*mission* = sending). Its worship, its proclamation, its life as a distinctive community, and its concrete demonstration of God's love in acts of prophetic and sacrificial service are all witness to the good news."[105] The church's very essence is then missional. "By adding the suffix 'al' to the word 'mission,' we hoped to foster an understanding of the church as fundamentally and comprehensively defined by its calling and sending, its purpose to serve God's healing purposes *for* all the world as God's witnessing people *to* all the world."[106] This task has been and is yet often divided into the categories of missions = overseas and evangelism = at home, in both cases performed by the called and appointed missionaries and the evangelists. Missional re-orientation calls for a conversion of the church to a missionary self-understanding and a missionary vocation, one which means the entire community witnesses and serves as the "hermeneutic of the gospel" (Lesslie Newbigin) to the world. To be

[103] Darrell Guder, Walking Worthily: Missional Leadership after Christendom, in: *The Princeton Seminary Bulletin*, 28.3, 2008, 251-291, 252.
[104] Op. cit., 253f.
[105] Guder, Darrell, Missional Theology for a Missionary Church, in: *Journal for Preachers*, 22.1, 1998, 3-11, 5.
[106] Guder, Walking Worthily, 252.

missional, the vocation of the church as community is to be the agent of God's mission to the world, a vehicle for reconciliation and healing, transformation and renewal.

It is the nature of the "call," or the vocation then which becomes tricky and even problematic in the current research discussion. This stems from the nature of the activity, visitation, and the vocation of witness was, in the case of Berlin Fellowship, from "church to church" and "from Christian to Christian." This could, in essence, be understood as a perpetuation of an inward ecclesial "feathering of the nest," albeit with the good intentions of ecumenical engagement. Though the very essence of fellowship encountered and hospitality offered and experienced may be understood on a one-dimensional plain, these practices certainly reflect the very nature of God. They may be identified with God's purposes intercontextually and with God's multi-dimensional purposes for humankind, which are restorative, reconciling, healing, and re-creative.[107] If the local church body or its members were in any way affected, restored, encouraged, or re-motivated to live out their faith walks differently because of a Berlin Fellowship encounter, then was not the call to and participation in this form of "missional" engagement affirmed? Granted, missional definition and terminology post-date the entire time period under investigation (1961-1989) and in many ways might be deemed inappropriate or misnomers. However, I wonder if in the interview material there is not evidence to underscore or point to this aspect of this missionality. Would such a community (existential and short-lived as each encounter was) have understood itself, if asked, to be not just in the world for the hours they spent together but in some way for the world as well? Did the participants really think the meetings were ends in themselves, even the Eastern Germans whose options for "mission" or outreach were severely limited? To what degree, if even measurable, did the Berlin Fellowship encounters, act as mini-models for how intercontextual community might work, at least within the confines of the body of Christ? Were these encounters places of prophetic embrace, dialogue, or transformation?

Perhaps an aspect of Karl Barth's ecclesiology of the community (Church Dogmatics, IV.3.2) lends itself to further understanding this missional and gathered community of the Berlin Fellowship moment. Firstly, the missional community is certainly *not* the gospel nor is it the kingdom of God; it does not believe in itself but believes itself to be what God calls it and enables it to be that is, to profess Christ and in gratitude

---

[107] Personal letter from Darrell Guder, August 18, 2009.

be totally dependent upon God for its future.[108] To what degree were the Berlin Fellowship community experiences parabolic missional community gatherings? If as Guder relying on Barth, proposes, the missional community is a parable in the New Testament sense, then it reminds the watching world (and I would add, the world inside the parable itself) what the kingdom of God is like. In pictures and explanations it tells the story of the deeds of him who calls all people out of darkness, to recognize one another in the light of the One who brought them together. Just as the gospel event happens parabolically and provisionally in the church and in church life, its witnesses can only partially and parabolically describe the event. Nonetheless, the event or events hint at and maybe even disclose the coming and very near kingdom.[109] Parables throughout the New Testament almost always point beyond themselves.

The question then naturally follows, what do those interpreting their experience say about it in retrospect, viewed as parabolic or not? How are these interpretations affected by memory, and are they affected by the fact that the "story" may have not been told for a long time or never at all?

These and similar questions turn the discussion to the hermeneutical nature of the entire endeavor, beginning with what happened in the Berlin Fellowship meetings in East German homes and congregations, in hundreds of one-time encounters. If the gathering focused on a biblical text and theme, did this focus remain a part of the recollection or act to interpret the encounter? How did both guest and host understand and interpret what was happening while it was happening? What impressions were left behind and why? What about the experience and the interpretations of the experience made both guest and host seek to repeat such, in some cases many times? In spite of the fact that American recollections and interpretations are predominately from the actual time period (archival material), how do new perspectives from eastern participants' recollections twenty or more years later contribute to the understanding, assessment, and interpretation of the encounters? Can some form of a "missional hermeneutic" offer a framework from which to more fully interpret the Berlin Fellowship experience and especially the eastern perspectives for this research, thus complimenting or illumining the western narratives, memories and interpreted recollections of the event?

---

[108] Guder, Walking Worthily, 268.
[109] Ibid.

4. A Missional Hermeneutic?

How do we remember, recall, understand and interpret what we think we experienced and why do we remember that experience? Do those memories offer only a picture of a past experience of the moment (labeled fellowship) or do the memories also reflect a truth or a reality that includes the moment but simultaneously points beyond it to something else, the work of God, *missio Dei*, God's spirit providing the context and at the same time, participating and operative in the intercontextual, intercultural encounters? What text or story serves as focal point for the encounter and is that part of the memory? Furthermore, was the trigger for remembering a special biblical text or can there not also be a metanarrative for a missional hermeneutic framework of understanding and interpretation? Was there a central text in Berlin Fellowship meetings? As the determining or defining characteristic of missionality, did this biblical text serve as the literal gathering point or was the text's place or role in the gathered community the accepted biblical metanarrative, itself intuited as the mutually embraced and assumed reason for meeting? Is this shared metanarrative an initial point of cohesion but also an equally valid "place" of meeting and dialogue?

These questions are but the tip of the iceberg in unpacking this aspect of the central question of the research: is fellowship encounter a missional experience? This question demands not only an assessment of the nature of actual fellowship experience, but it also demands a definition of "a missional hermeneutic." In addition, the multi-layered nature of the analysis of interview texts should fit into this "missional hermeneutic." The following aspects of the data gathered through oral interviews highlight the complexity of the task.

In the case of Berlin Fellowship, there is no obvious or direct link (and only limited documented references) between the gathered memories and biblical texts around which group discussions periodically occurred. Thus, the interpretive task in this research primarily focuses on identifying and defining how missional the eastern participants' articulated memories and interpretations of their Berlin Fellowship *koinonia* experiences may be labeled today. Though specific texts are rarely named and only in western documents, it was indeed under the umbrella of the biblical story and metanarrative that conversations at least began, *koinonia* happened, and dialogue was pursued. This research must then be alert for reference to that larger text, the biblical metanarrative, noting if and how it is identified or referred to in the oral recollections. This is the first step of the hermeneutical task.

Secondly, the coding and analysis of those allusions or references is yet another interpretive layer. This research's definition of missional, as well as the definition of fellowship, offer basic vocabulary and a thematic framework for selection and ordering of recollections and stories about the original Berlin Fellowship encounters, their intercultural and inter-contextual nature, and what they meant to the eastern participant-interviewees. However, many questions surround the task: Do the recollections and descriptive narratives reveal a core missional essence experienced in most fellowship encounters? In addition, is there an existential and articulated recollection of "missionality" not directly related to a biblical text but to the assumed larger common metanarrative (i.e. salvation history, the basic tenets of the Christian faith as found in the Apostles' Creed, the words of institution at the Lord's Supper, or the words of the Lord's Prayer)?

There is also a possible third layer of the interpretive task to be reckoned with. What evidence is there, in the interview texts, of any kind of missional self-awareness, new theological or ecclesiological learning or articulated understanding regarding commonalities or differences between guests and hosts? That is, did the Germans in some way view this as "missional" or more traditionally as an "ecumenical" activity? What seems to have been their own estimation of the encounter experience in relation to "missionality?"

Lastly, the interview manuscript analysis itself (see Chapter 4) qualifies as another layer of interpretation, with the selected interviews serving as the "text." These four hermeneutical levels are formidable and pose an interpretive challenge, one which may or may not be met by the current research.

A missional hermeneutic for Berlin Fellowship – a definition in process

The term missional hermeneutic usually refers in a general sense to a missional understanding of the biblical text and metanarrative[110] within a community setting, often assuming diverse backgrounds in the readers. "A missional hermeneutic presupposes one God, one scripture, and one sacred story. At the same time, however, this sacred story does not serve to promote or sanction a monocultural religious perspective, but rather a multicultural one. God's presence is irreducibly multicultural."[111] The

---

[110] George Hunsberger, Proposals for a Missional Hermeneutic: Mapping the Conversation, January 28, 2009, http://www.gocn.org/resources/articles/proposals-missional-hermeneutic-mapping-conversation (accessed December 2010).

[111] James V. Brownson, Speaking the Truth in Love, Elements of a Missional Hermeneutic, in: *International Review of Mission*, 83, no. 330, JL 1994, 479-504, 486.

social location for understanding the text is of considerable importance, with the community of faith serving as both a sent community and as the locale for the discussion. The Bible is at its heart the key missional document.[112] As an overview, these thoughts are a starting point for definition.

Moreover, a missional hermeneutic usually asks questions of how biblical texts function missionally, in the original setting and today, along with underscoring an assumption that "God's saving power comes to each culture in both affirmation and critique."[113] James Brownson asserts that along with this affirmation and critique, the Christian experience, and I would add this experience in the context of the biblical story, "deepens the awareness that one participates with all of humanity in a multicultural worship of God that transcends any particular context,"[114] creating a dual identity. This identity means that one is a member of a particular community, yet at the same time a member of a diverse and much larger human community. This interplay between these two sources of Christian identity constitutes part of a basic understanding of a missional hermeneutic.[115]

James Brownson, some years later, contends that this hermeneutic indeed *needs* cross-cultural encounter as its space or place of happening; furthermore, this hermeneutic must take the "reality of difference with utmost seriousness." Referring to Lesslie Newbigin and George Hunsberger on Newbigin, Brownson states that "we all should hear the gospel at least when we hear it as most transformational from someone who is deeply 'other,' from someone who is *not like us*."[116] With the New Testament as evidence, he posits,

> [...] there is something about the gospel which only discloses its deepest and truest transforming power when it crosses cultural boundaries; when speaker and hearer, in the midst of deep and abiding difference, find a still deeper unity with each other in Jesus Christ [...] the only way our apparently fundamental difference and aloneness can be overcome can only be learned [is] when we hear the gospel from someone who is different from us in deep and abiding ways. In this way, the hermeneutical task and the goal toward which the gospel itself is directed are finally the same goal: the reconciliation of all things. This reconcilia-

---

[112] Michael Barram, The Bible, Mission, and Social Location: Toward a Missional Hermeneutic, in: *Interpretation*, January 2007, 42-58, 43.
[113] Brownson, Speaking, 486.
[114] Op. cit., 487.
[115] Ibid.
[116] James V. Brownson, "A Response at SBL to Hunsberger's "Proposals" Essay, http://www.gocn.org/resources/articles/response-sbl-hunsbergers-proposals-essay (accessed July 2011).

> tion happens, however, not in our constructed narratives, but only in Jesus Christ [...] A missional hermeneutic thus must continually break itself open again to the reconciling work of God in Christ, lest any of our constructed narratives displace the true reconciler.[117]

Brownson continues discussing the heart of the missional hermeneutic which he says is not a claim about God, even that God is on a mission and the church is invited to catch the tailwind; nor is it a claim about a biblical narrative or about the purpose of biblical narratives to equip the church for mission. A missional hermeneutic is not about the "transformative vision of the context in which the gospel message is heard nor the centrality of the gospel as the interpretive matrix, but the heart of a missional hermeneutic is about Christ, Christ is all and in all (Col. 3:11)."[118]

Using Colossian 3:11 as but one centering text, differences remain and may not have to be overcome, for in Christ the gospel "holds out a vision for a deeper and transformed vision of what it means to be human. That image is the body of Christ, in which difference is not erased [...for there is] a vision of reconciliation without uniformity." This missional hermeneutic, Brownson continues, will

> [...] underscore the critical link between interpretation and the various practices of cross-cultural encounter and friendship, without which missional interpretation will remain abstract and ungrounded [...] will lift up the parabolic dimension of Scripture, which opens us up to a God who continually draws us out of our comfort zones and into mission [...] will lift up a theological anthropology that cultivates a vision of reconciliation indispensable to a full humanity....giving vision to the vision of bridging the difference and overcoming indifference [...] and focus upon the significance of cross-cultural encounters within the biblical text and thus invite the exploration of the missional encounter of the people of God with their surroundings.[119]

Berlin Fellowship encounters may qualify as mini-laboratory settings for an incarnated form of this hermeneutic. Brownson suggests that "the shared identity the Bible imparts to the community cannot be fully grasped and embodied, apart from the actual *practice* of participating in God's mission to the world."[120] A Berlin Fellowship encounter would qualify as just such practice. He further asserts, though cultural identity won't be erased, it is transformed "in pervasive ways, so that the quality and character of the life of the people of God becomes, in itself, an em-

---

[117] Ibid.
[118] Ibid.
[119] Ibid.
[120] Hunsberger, Proposals.

bodiment of the good news they are called to proclaim."[121] Both of these statements would affirm the potential validity of a experiential and somehow incarnated hermeneutic framework. Practice in participating in God's mission happens somewhere, in a locale, among and between people; there is a place of occurrence and a place of interpretation. This place of interpretation and how it functions is key.

Citing Pablo Richard, George Hunsberger offers further thoughts about the "place" of interpretation or the notion of what he labels hermeneutical spaces. The two traditional spaces, the *academic space* and the *institution of the liturgy of the Church* are supplemented by reading the Bible in community, and that is to say, the community's locatedness as a sent community might be the "very heart of the missional hermeneutic."[122] If the Bible's grand metanarrative is equally foundational to a gathered community's self-understanding (as in a typical Berlin Fellowship meeting), it is plausible that metanarrative also qualifies, if not as the heart, at least as the impulse for missional engagement and thus the place from which a missional hermeneutic originates. The Berlin Fellowship eastern recollections may be an interpretive framework for a story, or they may be but one more example of historical recounting and research in the field of missiology, church history or ecumenical studies. These recollections and critique might also, however, constitute example of a twist to the missional hermeneutic construct thus far overlooked. Why a twist? These collected memories are not those of the "doers" or primary initiators of the encounters but rather those of those on the "receiving" end for they are the recollections of the "other," who is the partner in the conversation.

Interview coding criteria and analysis

This discussion of a missional hermeneutic can only be continued after interview manuscript analysis and findings have been discussed. Missional or missionality are clearly the operative terms. However, insofar as neither this concept or its related vocabulary nor the word fellowship were intentionally suggested or considered in the interviews, the task of interview coding and analysis becomes a matter of prescriptive and descriptive or emergent coding work. The task is prescriptive in that I look for evidence in the interview manuscripts of post-event vocabulary (missional labels for instance) as well as traditional and classical notions related to both missional and fellowship matters (key vocabulary words or

[121] Ibid.
[122] Ibid.

concepts which repeat see Appendix 3). The task is as well, descriptive or emergent, in that I seek to let the texts of the interviews themselves evidence 'from below' commonalities or characteristics of missionality or fellowship and related vocabulary not necessarily falling into the prescribed categories. That is, as the interviewees describe and evaluate recalled experiences, the evidence gathered from the interview "text" is categorized in two ways: prescriptive (mirroring fellowship- and missional-related concepts) and emergent (descriptive of common emergent threads of either vocabulary or thoughts not anticipated by prescriptive labels). In either case, the task is subjective and qualitative, bound finally by this researcher's facility at reading, listening, coding, analyzing and interpreting interviews all personally conducted in German five years previous.

One final word concerning the central "text" around which the encounters happened, I reiterate that, based on western documentation, it is assumed at the time, that this text was the metanarrative, *Heilsgeschichte* or story of the Bible. Though there may have actually been a named Bible text used on individual team visits, few interviewees mention or allude to a central text or assumed shared metanarrative, nor did I ask directly about this matter. This story or metanarrative was sometimes examined and discussed through specific text studies or theme-centered gatherings of Germans and Americans. At other times, it served only as the launching pad or umbrella for various forms of study discussions, worship events, or thematic conversations. It is also noteworthy that the majority of the German participants were active Christians, members of local congregations, and German church buildings and family homes served as the usual meeting locale. Team visits usually had 'thematic' focus, a Bible verse, the *Jahreslosung* for instance (a Moravian and German tradition of a 'watchword' verse for the year), but host congregations and the teams themselves were free to embrace or not embrace that focus.

It seems from both written and oral testimony, rather than coming together around a story from a biblical text, Berlin Fellowship participants came together *because* of a story the story of the Bible, their shared "story. " As Christians united in faith and reconciled in Christ, they also came together *because* of the story and encounter which they themselves experienced at a Berlin Fellowship gathering or event and were somehow affected by it.

Does the "story" of Berlin Fellowship, recalled and told from the eastern perspective, the side of the so-called "receiver," in any way fit a missional hermeneutic paradigm? Rather, can a recalled story like this contribute a new dimension or act as a corrective to the definition of a missional hermeneutic? Might this kind of recollection and history-giving from the perspective of the "receiving" end of a missional activity highlight an important but thus-far overlooked aspect of mission history, that is, specifically, the role of fellowship?

Conclusion

Though fellowship is a commonly labeled a hallmark of the activities of the gathered and active body of Christ, the Church, it is only recently that missiological studies have delved into it as an aspect of the mission of the Church or a characteristic of missional activity. Life together, life in communion, as a sign, Bevans and Schroeder contend, flows out of God in his deepest identity, in relationship. Alluded to and often mentioned but seldom as more than a footnote in mission history, this "sign" of the body of Christ uniquely contributes to and challenges the Church's missional self-understanding and the self-understanding of its participant members. Paul' focus is clearly Christological, and he makes clear that fellowship happens "in Christ" and in a place where he is, and as such, it is that which is experienced together, held in common, shared, participated in or acted together upon in that place, "in Christ" fellowship happens. The experience for Berlin Fellowship was one of sharing, talking and listening, and of finding and being found. As with the Church through the ages, the celebration of the sacraments, the proclamation of the word, mutually shared testimony about the present and coming kingdom, along with service and witness all contribute to the community experience, the participatory communion of *koinonia*. Focal to this "life together" is the physical and visible presence of the other, a living reminder in the other, present in the body made possible, in spite of borders or boundaries by that reconciling person and presence of God in Jesus Christ and what he has done for both participants. That reconciliation, already accomplished, is not just to be received but to be passed on. It becomes the message and the task to be shared, and in acts of recognition, conversation, and newly discovered mutuality, Christians find each other in fellowship, not strangers but partners, reconciled and united with God and with each other in various forms of cooperation and community.

Post WWII years witnessed a shift in mission and ecumenical exchange and service with a movement towards this reciprocity, mutuality, and cooperation in partnerships across boundaries and borders of all manner. Many of these ecumenical and missionary encounters and partnerships have provided the impetus for new fields of missiological research relating to border crossing, what partners can offer to and receive from each other, and the role of legitimate differences and genuine boundaries. In addition though, research points to how shared times spent together, in dialogue, in work or service, and in celebration are meaningful activities and perhaps as meaningful as the "mission acts" often extended by the wealthier or the more powerful partners (i.e. CARE packages sent by partner churches to the GDR). Recognizing the other and coming together in cooperative times of learning and getting to know one another merit deeper consideration and study, especially from the perspective of the visited or the so-called more receiving side of the partnership.

Furthermore, intercontextuality or interculturality are now clearly acknowledged as seminal components in the "mix" of ecumenical and mission encounters. With the text of the New Testament as a paradigmatic model, it can be said that this coming together of very different partners in fellowship and dialogue is indeed key to how the early church got its start. It is exactly in and through this place of coming together that Christ becomes known, and this so because this is a place where God is moving and at work. God's movement, *missio Dei*, and its relatively new definition and usage has propelled mission thinkers and doers to self-reflection and re-tooling of the definition of mission. Though not limited to the place where Christians meet and engage, God's mission is most assuredly anchored in the Church and in its activities of proclamation, worship, service, witness and fellowship. As the gathered live out of and into *missio Dei*, the movement of God's love toward all people (Bosch), they find themselves surprised by the communicative and dialogical place that mission has brought them. That place is one of contact with people and customs that are unlike their own. At the same time this is a place of contact with people with commonalities and shared faith. *Missio Dei*, the way of God, though varied in its manifestations (Bevans and Schroeder), is most certainly a place of communication, dialogue, and encounter. This encounter is very often experienced simply in the presence of the other. Dialogue is comprised of witness and proclamation, but it is, as importantly, a place of listening and learning from the other, of learning about the commonalties while recognizing the differences, and learning how Christ unites. All of this communication is a sign of transforming accompaniment and solidarity, not just to the participants but also to the watching world.

By being a place of mission and by being in mission, the church or a gathered fellowship of Christians is a distinctive community, and even in an existential manner becomes the "hermeneutic of the gospel" (Newbigin) each time it gathers. As such, that gathered body, imperfect and only partially aware of what is happening in and through it, is parabolic, pointing beyond itself, as does a parable, to the coming and very present kingdom, to Jesus Christ and his presence in their midst.

Is fellowship then a missional experience? As a hallmark of the Church, is it not also a sign, an instrument and a foretaste or like first fruits (Newbigin) of both what is and what is to come? *Koinonia* as a form of missional activity, as described and reflected upon by the other voice, that of the recipient or partner, may offer the ongoing *missio Dei* and missionality discussion serious reason to re-think the parameters of description. How does the voice of the partner in the dialogue, provide the other side of the story, a side worthy of consideration and study? Is it not time that both the voice of the "other" and the importance of *koinonia* in missional activity be paid much closer attention? These questions hopefully shall be answered in the interview analysis and findings.

Chapter Three

Berlin Fellowship: Origin, Developments and Context

In 1960, Berlin Fellowship evolves "among a small circle of interested church members concerned about and wanting to identify themselves with hard-pressed Christians in East Germany."[1] This group from the First Presbyterian Church of Hollywood then grows into an organized, multi-congregation-supported visitation program of American Presbyterians to German Christians, first inside the city of Berlin and then throughout East Germany, the German Democratic Republic, GDR (*Deutsche Demokratische Republic, DDR*).

1. Origins

Berlin Fellowship begins as a small group of church members from California who are interested participants and supporters. Its roots stem from Hollywood First Presbyterian Church's college-age "world deputation teams" in the 1950's, some of which participate in mission work trips to Berlin.[2] In Germany, Berlin Fellowship is supported by the Berlin City Youth Pastor Alfred Schroeder, Bishop Otto Dibelius and his successor, Bishop Kurt Scharf. At the invitation of the Protestant Church of Berlin-Brandenburg, handfuls of student volunteers travel to Berlin for six to eight weeks. The work there involves helping with Christian youth camps, clean-up actions, and attending youth worker and pastors' meetings in the western part of the city. After the Berlin Wall is erected in 1961, the contacts with pastors and leaders from East Berlin and the "zone" (the surrounding country of East Germany) could only be maintained by Americans traveling across the Wall into East Berlin. Soon,

[1] Personal conversation with Ralph Hamburger, Pasadena, CA May 17, 2011.
[2] James, *Tumbling Walls*, 130.

however, the visits spread beyond the city limits of East Berlin, the capitol of the GDR (*Hauptstadt der DDR*). It gradually takes on programmatic shape and form in the late 1960's. From the 1960's until the mid-1990's, Berlin Fellowship teams visit village-, small town-, and city-congregations in all regions of the GDR.[3] By 1989, more than 200 different American Christians from all parts of the United States and from many denominations participate in this visitation program

Over the course of more than twenty years, at least 100 East German congregations host twice yearly visits from Berlin Fellowship teams in their homes and parishes. Though officially recognized, supported and in great part financed by the Protestant Church of Berlin-Brandenburg in West Berlin (*Evangelische Kirche Berlin-Brandenburg, Berlin/West*)[4], Berlin Fellowship is never officially registered as an ecumenical partner to any one of church of the East German regional churches (*Landeskirchen*) of the GDR, though eastern church leadership is fully aware and informed of the ministry.

In 1950, coincident with the first deputation team being sent from the Hollywood Presbyterian congregation but long before the first Berlin Fellowship team goes to East Germany, the Politburo of the Socialist Unity Party (*Sozialistische Einheitspartei Deutschlands, SED*) creates the Ministry for State Security of the GDR (*Ministerium für Staatssicherheit der DDR, MfS, Stasi*).[5] Unbeknownst to both German and American Berlin Fellowship participants, one of their members enters the employ of the *Stasi* in the late 1960's and keeps the state security offices well-informed about all plans and activities through the late 1980's.[6] This chapter recounts the origins and developments of the Berlin Fellowship, using primarily western archival material from Berlin records and files, *MfS* archives, and supplementary materials from published research and popular literature. The chapter is divided into three eras: Berlin Fellowship's roots in the 1960's, its development and growth in the 1970's, and continued visits through the unsettling 1980's. Not unlike the varied eras

[3] As example, a 12-page report addressed to Oberkonsistorialrat Alfred Schroeder contains a request for reimbursement for team costs, detailed description of team preparation and orientation in West Berlin, a pastors' meeting in East Berlin and reports from the three team visits in Görlitz-Dresden-Eisenhüttenstadt, Wittenberg- Magdeburg- Eisenach- Plauen, and Schwerin-Rostock-Greifswald, June 15, 1969, Zinzendorf Collection.

[4] Letter from Bishop Kurt Scharf to Pastor Theodor Schapp regarding consistory reimbursement amount for Spring Berlin Fellowship group in West and East Berlin and for group trip in the GDR, May 6, 1969, Zinzendorf Collection.

[5] Jens Gieseke, *The GDR State Security, Shield and Sword of the Party*, Berlin 2006.

[6] BStU MfS, BV/Gera, Abt. XII/Archiv, AOP 1456-78, III OV-"*Rollbahn*", Bericht, May 7, 1969, 4-5. Earliest MfS Berlin Fellowship-related report.

in the development of the GDR (founded in 1949), each era of Berlin Fellowship is a bit different in self-understanding and growth as the program quietly and gradually institutes itself beyond the city limits of Berlin.

Research Data

The research material gathered for this particular chapter was initially assembled to be used in a focused study of the East German perspectives of Berlin Fellowship during the period from 1961 - 1989. Seeking the eastern perspective of program activities and of German congregational involvement, I began research with available recorded western documentation pertaining directly to Berlin Fellowship. Though limited primarily to second-hand data from American and West Berlin correspondence, reports, and finance records, this chapter goes beyond that data and provides, in broad strokes, an overview of the larger contextual setting for the interview findings and final discussion (see Chapters 4 and 5). The focus of the dissertation is the research question, "Is fellowship encounter a missional experience?" Through its narrative, this chapter presents material on the origin and development of the program, but it also provides both context and possible beginnings of answers to that research question.

From the first visits in the 1960's, it was important that the American visitors know as much as possible about the place and the people they were visiting. This is equally important for the reader of this research, and this chapter presents an overview of political, social, cultural, and religious contextual information. Most of the German personal commentary cited in this chapter is colored by the fact that almost all of it is second-hand reporting and is taken primarily from the written reports of American visitors. For these years and this chapter, the information is anecdotal a recollected recounting of how the German hosts talked about their lives *then*. It is clear that this remembering, interpreting and reporting of German experiences is biased and tempered by the sharpness of memories as well as the ability of the American visitors to articulate those memories and record this material. However, these particular written records are a unique source of one form of empirical German perspective and documentation related specifically to this visitation program. Those instances of American assessment of the situation, though limited in scope and tempered by individual personalities, are another source of data, specific to the Berlin Fellowship experience. This body of information is supplemented and confirmed by published literature, both popular and scholarly (see footnotes and Bibliography).

There do exist, of course, extensive forms of empirical archival data at the government level, and the interest and attention given this 20+ year-long activity by the *MfS* Department XX/4, the "*Stasi,*" is included. The *Stasi* files provide the government's primary documented official view and assessment of the Berlin Fellowship's various activities and its leadership. Most of this material is contained in two operative procedure files (*Operativer Vorgang, OV*) from the collection of the Federal Commissioner for the Stasi Archives (*Bundesbeauftragter für die Stasi-Unterlagen, BStU*). In this chapter, a condensation of *Stasi* activities and findings ends each era's contextual narrative. These short summaries describe the *Stasi's* relation and "work" with Berlin Fellowship for the time period. A more thorough explanation of this branch of the government and more detailed material related to this research is included in Appendix 1. Further, this research has been provided with some copies from individual participants' personal *Stasi* files, as well as copies of pastors' calendar notations,[7] German photos from Berlin Fellowship visits, copies of correspondence between eastern participants,[8] and copies of house book signatures (citizens were required by the state to have guests register their presence).[9] This combined collection of eastern data might be further supplemented by written documentation in higher level East German official church records. However, Berlin Fellowship is not an agenda item at the synod meetings for the Federation of Churches (*Bund der Evangelischen Kirchen, BEK*),[10] nor did the name or word of the program appear in any congregation publications or church display billboards, though it is noted once there are ecumenical guests in a "Sunday

---

[7] June 21, 1983, "27.6.-2.7. Gruppe von Christen aus USA zu DDR," June 22, 1984, "Ökumenische Gäste, June 17-18. Amerikaner in Zittau und Olbersdorf", personal *Amtskalendar*/office calendar, Pastor Wolfgang Müller, Olbersdorf, Saxony.

[8] January 22, 1968 note from F.-W. Merkel, Berlin-Malchow to Pfarrer Günter Mieth, Dresden, inviting him to a February 3 planning at noon, for the next *Treffen*/meeting. This will take place in the Auguststr. Hospiz. Private papers Günter Mieth, Detmold.

[9] House book for Pastor Joachim and Mrs. Monika Tutzschke shows signatures from the following Berlin Fellowship leaders and participants: Joe Mangina/Ted Schapp January 3, 1984, Bärbel Eccardt/Ted Schapp/Rachel Haney April 3, 1982; Ted Schapp/Bärbel Eccardt/Uwe Larson March 26, 1984; Bill and Bea Haitz September 7, 1987. Private holdings Pastor Joachim Tutzschke, Barnewitz.

[10] Taped interviews with Bishop Johannes Hempel, Dresden, November 22, 2005 and with Bishop Werner Krusche, Magdeburg December 27, 2005.

announcement" notebook of one pastor[11] and in another pastor's scrap-book journal about a new church construction project.[12]

Besides *MfS* records and copies of available personal records from East German participants(see above), there are archives for other offices and departments of the government and the party system of administration (*Staatsapparat*), all of which might play a role in providing further empirical data for this research. The Central Committee (*Zentralkomitee*) of the Socialist Unity Party and the politburo had a "working group for church questions" (*Arbeitsgruppe für Kirchenfragen*) whose duties and significance varied over the years. Directives and plans from the Central Committee or its working group ordered regional and local government officers and functionaries and their district, county, and city councils (*Räte der Bezirke, Räte der Kreisen, and Räte der Städte*) to carry out official state-church policy (*Kirchenpolitik*). The State Secretary for Church Questions (*Staatssekretäriat für Kirchenfragen*) is a separate national-level office, whose network of regional and district offices oversees church activities and monitors official ecumenical and international guests and programs,[13] along with its primary task of ensuring the church-state policy is being carried out properly.

The State Secretary's office had other tasks, including being abreast of what ecumenical bodies like the World Council of Churches (WCC) knew about the situation in the GDR.[14] The archives show this office also producing periodic reports on the current situation of the church in the United States (i.e. denominational statistics and key social issues,).[15] Of course, it takes note of church publications, activities, groups, and events in the GDR. The task of this office on the meta-level is a comprehensive one, including information reports dealing with plans and preparations (*Maßnahmen*) for carrying out the state's church policy, and instructions

---

[11] "*Christen aus USA*" announced in Möthlow, June 25, 1976, page 5; "*Ökumenische Gäste*" announced in Buschow, October 11, 1984, page 15; "*Ökumenische Gäste*" announced in Barnewitz, September 23, 1987, page 17. *Abkündigungsbuch*, private holdings, Pastor Joachim Tutschke, Barnewitz, Brandenburg.

[12] Excerpt from building journal of Pastor Wolfgang Müller, recorded for the building project of the parish center in Olbersdorf, October 1985, page 46, private holdings, Pastor Wolfgang Müller, Dresden.

[13] i.e. BArch DO4/1249 *Christliche Friedenkonferenz* 1964 - 1988, BArch DO4/1290 *Ökumenische Versammlung für Gerechtigkeit, Frieden und Bewahrung der Schöpfung*, 26-30 April 1989 Dresden, BArch DO4/2554 *Besuch einer ökumenische Gruppe von Christen aus der DDR in der Schweiz* 1974 .

[14] A 20-page copy of the WCC Church and Society report, The Wtiness and Service of the Evangelical Church and Christians in the Socialist Society of the German Democratic Republic(GDR), labeled PRIVATE AND CONFIDENTIAL, NOT FOR PUBLICATION IN WHOLE OR IN PART; July 30, 1973, BA Berlin, DO4/4890, 1179-1203.

[15] i.e. 1988 report on the church in the USA, BA Berlin DO/4899, 751-767.

and orders (*Anweisungen*) detailing how that job is to be accomplished. In addition, there are various kinds of reports (*Berichte*) and documentation (*Dokumentation*) about: inter-office meetings to conversations with high church officials; reports analyzing synod meetings and assessment of church life in the GDR; reports about human rights discussions in the congregations; entry applications, reports and correspondence regarding international church guests and their travels to and in the country. The extensive archive is replete with many years of such files.

At the government's administrative district (*Bezirk*) and local or county level (*Kreis*), the reports take on a more distinct analytical form, shaped to specific church districts (*Kirchenkreisen*) and even to individual pastors and congregations in those districts. These often contain ongoing assessments of the political and ideological work being done with pastors, superintendents, theologians and lay representatives to synod meetings (i.e. how "progressive" and positive they were about the socialist ideology and government). In addition, actions to be taken are outlined:

> In the long run we will only achieve progress and get our point across more effectively when we are more active on the grass-roots level in the congregations that is with church elders, pastors in the parishes [...] For the development of the progressive forces within the church there needs to be a very intensive work with the members of the synod. The makeup of the new synod must be thoroughly analyzed and a concrete way forward for differentiated work with each individual synod representative must be very quickly decided on."[16]

In a so-called *Dokumentation* from 1969, the State Secretary for Church Question's office displays a posture of suspicion, and this office assumes that the church is an instrument through which the west is seeking to influence the society. "Simply put, it is through church channels that ideological contraband is being smuggled into the GDR."[17] An earlier report in this same district level file indicates that Bonn (capitol of West Germany) has growing influence and is attempting to extend that

---

[16] Schwerin Landeshauptarchiv, BL SED Schwerin, 10.34.3 4926, Abteilung Staat, Recht und Eingaben, "Dauerhaft Fortschritte erzielen wir nur, wenn die Arbeit an der Basis, in den Kirchengemeinden—also mit den Kirchgemeinderäten, den Pfarrferständen, und den Pastoren in Kirchengemeinden---wesentlich aktiver und vom Inhalt her wirksamer gestaltet wird [...] Zur Profilierung der progressiven kirchlichen Kräfte gehört auch eine sehr intensive Arbeit mit den Synodalen. Die Zusammensetzung der neuen Synode ist nun sehr gründlich zu analysieren und sehr schnell sollten ganz konkrete Festlegungen zur differenzierten Arbeit mit jedem einzelnen Synodalen getroffen werden." February 9, 1988, 26-27.

[17] Landesarchiv Berlin CRep 104:2204, "[...] es geht einfach darum, dass über kirchliche Kanäle ideologische Kontraband in die DDR hineingeschleust wird," March 5, 1969.

by creating points of contact to pass on news, to spread their own propaganda and even to introduce public corruption.[18] In this light, one could assume Berlin Fellowship activity might potentially draw attention to itself, especially on the more local level. It does not, but insofar as some of its leading personalities from the east do indeed draw attention, American team visits are not necessarily ignored. However, the attention does not come from any of the county or even district government officials. Rather it is the *Stasi* who takes note and for years on end, as evidenced by extensive files pertaining to Berlin Fellowship. As already mentioned, individual eastern participants may read about themselves and possibly their American visitors in their own *Stasi* files.[19]

Both the State Secretary meta-level files researched and those for local, district, and regional government church activities' offices or officers (*Referat/Referent für Kirchenfragen*), provide no indication of awareness or knowledge of the Berlin Fellowship.[20] The Federal Archive (*Bundesarchiv*) files for the State Secretary for Church Questions clearly evidence that church-related individuals or groups who officially enter the GDR are either processed or noted in this office.[21] However, Berlin Fellowship American participants do not register with the State Secretary for Church Questions and do not enter the country officially in a group but rather as private individuals. They apply for visas and accommodations through the travel bureau in Berlin, staying as private guests in Interhotels and traveling in groups of three or four in private automobiles. Practically speaking, all information about plans for team visits, itineraries, parishes, hotels, and names of team members appear in the operational procedure files for the *MfS*. The main unofficial informer performs most of this reporting and information sharing.

Berlin Fellowship was primarily a "person to person" visitation program, made possible and carried out within the structure and organization of the regional Protestant Church of Berlin-Brandenburg (West) and in

---

[18] Landesarchiv Berlin CRep 104:66 Präsidium der Volkspolizei Berlin Abteilung Schutz- und Verkehrspolizei, March 7, 1966.

[19] (partial report from the county level) KD Rathenow, 8.4.1982, Sachstandbericht zur KK-Erfassung der Person Joachim Tutzschke, " Bedeutsam sind auch Kontakte des Genannten mit kirchlichen Kreisen in den USA." Personal BStU copy. (partial report from IM, 16.07.1980) "Die Gruppe der in den Nordbezirken weilenden Amerikaner wurde hier in Schwerin aus Greifswald empfangen. Das Programm für diese Amerikaner wurde durch Frau Haker vorbereitet." Personal BStU copy, Joachim Tutzschke, Barnewitz.

[20] Bundesarchiv Berlin, Landesarchiv Berlin, Land Brandenburg Archiv, Schwerin Landeshauptarchiv, Schwerin Stadtarchiv, Hauptstadtarchiv Dresden.

[21] BArch Berlin DO4/4899, Copy of a letter from Pastor Donald H. McCord (participant in Berlin Fellowship 1973) of the Austin Boulevard Christian Church, Oak Park, IL, requesting permission to bring the church choir to the GDR, February 24, 1987, 714.

unofficial cooperation with the other regional church bodies (*Landeskirchen*) in the GDR, and with the knowledge of the bishops of each regional church. Early personal contacts and acquaintanceships made in the 1950's were essential to the foundational roots of Berlin Fellowship. Some of the organization's leading figures through the years were: Reverend Walter James, Presbyterian pastor in California; Reverend Ralph Hamburger, Presbyterian pastor in California and New Jersey; Reverend Ted Schapp, American Presbyterian pastor in West Berlin, Reverend Ralph Zorn, American Lutheran pastor in West Berlin; Ms. Bärbel Eccardt, German church worker in West Berlin; Mrs. Ursula Dibbern Unterumsberger, lay person in East Berlin and Pfarrer Friedrich-Wilhelm Merkel German pastor in Malchow, East Berlin. Leading figures in West Berlin were Pfarrer Alfred Schroeder, Berlin City Youth Pastor; Bishop Otto Dibelius/Berlin (1948-1966) and his successor, Bishop Kurt Scharf /Evangelical Church of Berlin-Brandenburg-West (1966-76).

2. Development of Berlin Fellowship 1950 – 1966

Convinced that there is a great need for reconciliation and peace in a world torn apart by World War II, lay leaders and pastors of the First Presbyterian Church of Hollywood in California join with Church of the Brethren (Brethren Service Commission), efforts of the WCC, and CIMADE (Comité Inter-Mouvements Aupres des Évacués) in sending a small team of college students to six-week long work camps in France and Germany in 1950. The work is done with German, British, French, Dutch, Italian young people and varies from cleaning up war rubble to reconstructing buildings and working in soup kitchens. The purpose of the camps is to reconcile "different nationalities through the process of living, working, and worshipping together."[22] The "world deputation" movement of the First Presbyterian congregation continues until 1959, with students going to various countries in Europe, as well as to Africa, Asia, Alaska, migrant camps along the Pacific Coast, and the inner-cities of Los Angeles and New York.

The "world deputation" connection with Germany, however, is fostered and deepened by Pastor Walt James at First Presbyterian, Hollywood and a young church member and immigrant from the Netherlands, Ralph Hamburger. In the course of the 1950's, Berlin became a focus and a passion for both James and Hamburger and for this California congre-

[22] James, *Walls*, 22.

gation.[23] In consultation with denominational headquarters (The United Presbyterian Church, New York City) and with help from people like Corrie Ten Boom, Hendrik Kraemer, J.B. Phillips, and Philippe Maury, secretary-general of the World Student Christian Federation,[24] the first teams to Germany prepare themselves by studying history and current events, doing what they can to acquire some language facility, meeting regularly for team building, Bible study and prayer. Moreover, the newly installed Berlin City Youth Pastor, Alfred Schroeder, visits California several times, opening new avenues of connection between the regional church of Berlin-Brandenburg and the First Presbyterian Church in Hollywood.[25] Schroeder, a member of the confessing church movement, studied with Dietrich Bonhoeffer in Finkenwalde, and his training, convictions and skills were recognized by Bishop Otto Dibelius as essential for the task of youth work in over 250 parishes in the divided city and the surrounding "zone." Shortly after his first California visit in 1952, Schroeder invites Pastor Walt James to come and meet some of those youth pastors, "to talk with them and to learn their situation."[26]

As would be the case for the immediate future, in the years leading up to Stalin's death on March 5, 1953 and beyond, the communist party pressure on the church in East Germany and its ministry with youth and student groups is drastic and threatening, with serious consequences.[27] This greatly affects Schroeder's work in Berlin and the zone; youth meetings and pastors' gatherings then have to be held only in West Berlin. James notes, for instance, that it is not safe for East German pastors working with students to return to the east with any mimeographed materials which might call attention to the Christian student movement.[28]

> In the early 50's the East German state conducted a campaign to discredit the church. It accused the church youth groups of operating as a front for Western sabotage and espionage, and it banned them. It arrested pastors and raided church

---

[23] James, Schroeder, Hamburger correspondence, 1952-1967, Hamburger Collection.

[24] Correspondence, Hamburger Collection.

[25] "Mr. Schroeder said that he came here to strengthen the already strong links between youth groups in his area and Hollywood Presbyterian Church, which has sent 'work teams' to Berlin in past seasons and will send another this summer." Los Angeles Times article "Berlin Pastor to Give Sidelight on War", Part 1A, April 7, 1957. Docket of the Stated Meeting of the Presbytery of Los Angeles of the United Presbyterian Church in the USA, March 14-15, 1961, 3:30 p.m. Presentation of and address by the Reverend Dr. Alfred Schroeder of the German Evangelical Church of Germany, in charge of all youth work in the area of Berlin, Hamburger Collection.

[26] Schroeder letter to James, November 3, 1952, Hamburger Collection.

[27] Lepp, Claudia and Kurt Nowak (eds.), *Evangelische Kirche im geteilten Deutschland (1945-1989/90)*, Göttingen 2001, 166-67.

[28] James, *Walls*, 109.

> properties. Though it eventually backed down from these extreme measures, it continued to pressure individual Christians[...]to withdraw from the church.[29]

The government's concerted efforts and policy in the 1950's are indeed to reduce the church's public influence, to secularize the society in the east, and to replicate and replace Christian customs and traditions with socialist rites and interpretations.[30] Furthermore, Christians are rarely allowed leadership roles or important positions in their places of work. The *Volkskirche* (the established church) church tax system is privatized, and the state no longer provides that service of collection. Religious instruction in the schools is totally dismantled. Youth and children's ministry is often hindered. Arrests, as well as trials of Christian leaders and pastors, punctuate this era.[31]

Church historian Rudolf Mau labels the time period 1952 - 1961 a "totalitarian culture revolution, an assault on the peoples' church tradition."[32] It is during these years of development or the "build-up of socialism" (*Aufbau des Sozialismus*) that persecution and aggression against the church, its leaders and members is the most open and intense. This policy results in increasing emigration from all levels of the society, but even after May 1953 when Walter Ulbricht, head of state, calls for easing the manner in which people are treated, and there is some change, though the goal of the party and the state remains the "death of religion." The new primary means for fighting against the reactionary influence of the Church, however, is now to be a "strenuous, well-conceived awareness and cultural training instead of reprisal."[33]

The situation for Schroeder and for the regional church of Berlin-Brandenburg is unique because the city is politically divided, but the church boundaries encompass the *entire* city and the surrounding territory of Brandenburg. West Berlin is an island in the sea of a new state barely five years old, the GDR. The government of the GDR, with its communist ideological posture and connections to Moscow, is confronted with a geographically- and organizationally-united Protestant church in Berlin and Brandenburg. In a letter to James dated April 15, 1953, Schroeder writes in English about his youth work, noting:

---

[29] John Burgess, *The East German Church and the End of Communism*, New York 1997, 46.

[30] Dokumentation, *Ein Informationsdienst, Kirche im Sozialismus, Texte aus der DDR*, Frankfurt June 1974 (English version), 33.

[31] Op.cit., 34.

[32] Rudolf Mau, *Der Protestantismus im Osten Deutschlands: (1945-1990)*, Leipzig, 2005, chapter 2 entitled Totalitäre „Kulturrevolution. Angriff auf die volkskirchliche Tradition (1952-1961), " 45.

[33] Op. cit., 49, "[…] tüchtig durchdachte Aufklärungs- und Kulturarbeit sein statt Repressalien."

> The situation of our whole church youthwork in the eastern zone is becoming more and more difficult. The youth groups in different parishes are under hard pressure. The so called "free german youth' the only existing youth organisation in the zone has developed a special system to observe our groups. All the youth in our groups are declared as enemies of the state and in many ways they were pressed no longer to attend our evening meetings. In the highschools our boys and girls were asked to defend their faith and to declare why they are visiting the church youthgroups. And then they had to make their decision. In the case of attending furthermore our youth groups they were released from highschool [...] and they have no possibility in the future to go to another school or university [...] They are confessing with their life that they are christians. We are helping them so good as we can. In some cases in the last weeks leaders of our church youth work were put in prison and we don't know why[...]we don't know what will happen in the future.[34]

It must be added, though, that the "pressure" is somehow mitigated, for even in the 1950's, the Church (Roman Catholic and Protestant) in the entire GDR has more religious freedom than in any other east bloc country. It can hold meetings and worship services in its facilties, and though there are seasons of more tension and problems in the coming decades, the church maintains the only "free space" not controlled or under the thumb of the state authorities.[35] The church also maintains a kind of special status in the land reform and in its rights of employment and work.[36]

In this time of heightened tensions between East and West, uncertainties in the city of Berlin (i.e. the uprising of workers on June 17, 1953) and increasing state-church conflicts throughout the GDR, handfuls of young American Presbyterians, their pastor and a few other church leaders begin traveling to visit Christians and congregations in Berlin, to help in church-related work camps, to participate and even lead in Bible studies, youth rallies and city-wide meetings. In 1953, the Bishop of Berlin, Otto Dibelius requests that the First Presbyterian congregation in Hollywood send a "field worker" (longer-term helper); he and his family work in the city youth mission project at West Berlin's main train station (*Bahnhof Zoo*).[37]

Teams and small groups continued to travel from California to Berlin in the following years. James and Schroeder continued to correspond,

---

[34] Schroeder letter, April 15, 1953, Hamburger Collection.
[35] Burgess, *East German Church*, 45.
[36] Mau, *Protestantismus*, 34f.
[37] Letter from Bishop Otto Dibelius to First Presbyterian Church of Hollywood, August 31, 1953, response letter from Reverend Walt James to Pastor Alfred Schroeder, March 16, 1954, Hamburger Collection.

and in 1957 Schroeder pays his second visit to Los Angeles and the Presbyterian congregations of the area. In an interview with the *Los Angeles Times*, referring to the summer work camps which eastern youth attend in West Berlin, he says, "These spiritual adventures are of much benefit. We no longer are in special need of material assistance, but the fact that Christians are coming from all over the world to work with us in ecumenical fashion is a real testimony to the meaning of faith."[38] By 1958, however, a new difficulty arose: "Just now, we have hard difficulties with our work in the zone[...]our summer camps in the east must happen mostly in secret because only the state licensed FDJ (Free German Youth) is allowed to have summer camps."[39]

By 1959, plans are set for another "field worker," a theological student, to be sent from the Presbyterian congregation in California, and he starts a year of service and study in Berlin. That same year James and Hamburger (now a theological student in Basel) visit Berlin and attend a conference with 60 church leaders from the east. Confirming what Schroeder wrote about camps, the eastern pastors and leaders report to James that it is clear the state is clamping down further, and the goal of the state building up socialism is no longer to be solely through economic and social measures. "The Socialist Unity Party (*SED*) seeks increasingly to weaken the Christian tradition and to establish its own ideology."[40] Further, the communist youth dedication (*Jugendweihe*), the name-giving ceremony (*Namenweihe*), wedding and funeral rites as well as the "Ten Commandments of Socialist Morals" (announced at the 5th Party Congress, 1958) are all intended to infringe upon Christian traditions and norms.[41]

Increasing numbers of East German citizens leave the country, while at the same time the state program for capturing the youth proceeds. Otto Grotewohl, Minister President and Chairman of the Council of Ministers of the GDR, accuses the church of interfering with the "progressive development of our young people."[42] Hamburger's notes from a lecture held by Dr. Jürgen W. Winterhager in January 1959 further explain:

> The young East German is conscious of the mission of a total world picture in which there is room only for the collectivism of the young worker[...]the young East German is more versed in the doctrine of Marx and Lenin than many a

---

[38] *Los Angeles Times*, April 7, 1957, Hamburger Collection.
[39] Letter from Alfred Schroder to Walt James, March 27, 1958, Hamburger Collection.
[40] Ibid.
[41] Mau, *Protestantismus*, 61.
[42] James, *Walls*, 134.

> young Russian communist[...]at the age of twelve to thirteen many young East Germans feel ready to give the pledge of allegiance to the Socialist State, promising to work for and if need be, die for a better world; to work for peace; and to disbelieve any inclination that might point in the direction of a transcendental God. In 1959 85% of the East German youth took part in the *Jugendweihe*, a Communist substitution for the church practice of confirmation. The names of all who take the oath are inscribed in a book which ironically is called THE BOOK OF LIFE.[43]

Writing to the members of the United Presbyterian Church of the Synod of California, Bishop Dibelius describes the severity of the situation and the role of two recent visitors from California:

> At no other period of history has the witness to Christian unity come to be so vital as in the present days of world decision. In these times of testing, it has been a most helpful event to have the two visitors which your United Presbyterian Church sent to our island city for ten days. This city of Berlin is completely surrounded by a totalitarian system which leaves no room for living up to the Christian faith.
> The greater part of my own province happens to be in that Soviet-controlled area. The pressure exerted upon well over seventeen millions of Protestants is increasing. We are all the more grateful for the expression of your sympathy and the intercession assured to our people in all the perplexities of the present period.
> Berlin is the only sizable place on earth where Christians from East and West can still meet together for an exchange of experience and hope. It is essential that this island city should remain what it is at present in the way of fulfilling its historic mission.
> Your Church's concern for the fundamental rights of men and for Religious Liberty over here, is a reassuring fact for which we thank our Lord and Redeemer.
> Sincerely, Dr. Otto Dibelius, Joint President, World Council of Churches[44]

At a subsequent meeting which James had with Dibelius he asked, "How may we in America help you in Berlin?" The bishop replied,

> We are in the front line of the battle against Marxist atheism[...]It is important for people from other parts of the world to come to the Island City of Berlin to let the people in the East know that they are not alone; that they are not forgotten. They need to know there are Christians in other parts of the world who know about them and who do really care about them, who still claim them as part of the worldwide community of believers.[45]

---

[43] Op. cit., 134 f.
[44] Otto Dibelius letter to Synod of California, dated "fourth Sunday after Easter" 1959, Hamburger Collection.
[45] James, *Walls*, 140f.

The situation in Berlin and in the GDR is growing more tense and unclear and at the same time, the interest and awareness in California is growing as well. August 13, 1960 a group meets for Bible study, prayer and the reading of a letter from Pastor Schroeder (Berlin Fellowship mailing list in 1959 indicates 50 members)[46]. James leads the discussion at what was certainly one of the first California "Berlin Fellowship" meetings. This group has already sent Christmas packages to families in both parts of Berlin with greetings,"we are thinking of you and we intercede for you constantly."[47] In response, Schroeder writing James says, "We here are happy for all the care-parcels, so we could help people in need, especially in the east-zone. It is not so easy to bring all the cans over the border, but all have done it and without special difficulties[...]We thank you all for this help and christian facts. I wish we could do more from our side in order to show you how thankfull we are for this christian belonging together."[48]

1961, the year the Wall is built, marks a new phase in the development of Berlin Fellowship. In March, Schroeder is again invited to Los Angeles where he speaks to a Presbytery meeting (church district composed of some 40 congregations) about the situation in his city. Upon return to Berlin, his letters make the situation there sound critical, "People in the East Zone are taking the Soviet threats against Berlin seriously. In July more than 30,000 found refuge in the West, nearly twice the previous monthly average. More than 11,000 refugees arrived in West Berlin in the first six days of August."[49] Another letter invites an American "team" to come to West Berlin in October to attend an upcoming "conference." On August 12, 1961 at James' request, the Berlin Fellowship group meets to determine how they might show solidarity and support for the Germans. Though informal gatherings have already been going on for two years, those gathered agree to begin meeting regularly and to appoint ten people to go to the fall conference.

One day later, August 13, 1961, the GDR closes its border in Berlin, and the wall begins to be built. August 23, Schroeder writes, "Only a little more than one week and what for facts has happened. It was and is a turbulent time. Tragedies you could see at the border. It is impossible to describe. It is like in a war. For the moment nobody from the east will have the permit to such a conference (reference to the upcoming October

---

[46] Hamburger Collection.

[47] Berlin Fellowship letter, Dec. 16, 1959, signed by Ted Nissen, secretary Berlin Fellowship, Hamburger Collection.

[48] Alfred Schroeder letter to Walt James, Dec. 23, 1959, Hamburger Collection.

[49] James, *Walls*, 148.

conference)..."[50] Schroeder writes again September 3, "I have no permit to enter the east sector [...] so I am now separated from my coworkers in the east [...] The struggle is hard and we have to work on our program because the church there is called a non peace-loving organization." [51] However, he indicates that plans are still going forward for the fall conference.

In fall 1961 the first Berlin Fellowship team of ten Presbyterian pastors and elders, flies to Berlin and meets in the western part of the city. In a gathering with Bishop Dibelius and other church leaders, Dr. Scharf clarifies the situation,

> Since August 13, things are completely changed [...] The government is endeavoring to break the moral stamina of the population. Families are completely separated. Party members, protected by the Wall, have begun tightening control in all phases of life because no one can flee anymore[...]Listening to TV or radio from the West is illegal[...]Teachers in schools must make spies out of the children, tricking them to tell what stations their parents are listening to[...]Farmers, whose families have owned their land for centuries, are disposed and the farms nationalized (occurred in 1960) [...] Fellowship circles outside the Church have been closed down. There can be no more prayer circles in homes, meetings or Bible studies among professionals in the work place.[52]

While in Berlin, this team also meets with. Erich Andler, general superintendent of Berlin, now restricted in his activity to East Berlin. James asks his often repeated question, "What can we do to help?" Andler answers, "Keep in contact. Just love us and pray. It is good that you have come today."[53]

From 1962 through 1966, various groups and individuals related to Berlin Fellowship continue to travel to Berlin, meeting with church leaders on both sides of the Wall, and information continues to be shared via letter. In one 1962 letter Schroeder mentions that some of his eastern youth pastors, members of youth groups and some youth workers have been imprisoned.[54] During Schroeder's 1962 visit to the Hollywood church, he preaches, leads Bible studies in five neighboring Presbyterian churches, and reports personally to the Berlin Fellowship group, which finances his trip as well offering financial support for ministry needs. Not long thereafter, Schroeder is promoted to a new position as Assistant to

---

[50] Handwritten letter from Alfred Schroeder to Walt James, Aug. 23, 1961, Hamburger Collection.

[51] Letter Alfred from Schroeder to Walt James, Sept. 3, 1961, Hamburger Collection.

[52] James, *Walls*, 153f.

[53] Op. cit., 160.

[54] Letter from Alfred Schroeder to Walt James, Jan. 15, 1962, Hamburger Collection.

the Bishop for Ecumenical Affairs in the West Berlin church headquarters and ceases to do regional youth work, but the correspondence and cooperation with James and the Berlin Fellowship continue.

Through the years, Schroeder reiterates what he learned from Dietrich Bonhoeffer, often citing him. In 1958, he writes James, "Through my friend Bonhoeffer, I have learned a long time ago, as he was director for young pastors, that it is a present of the Lord, if christians can see one another face by face. You can be sure, that it is not only an idea, but a far more deeper wish and prayer, to have you here for a time."[55] In 1964, he echoes the same sentiment, "The connection with the East is growing more and more difficult. We have to find new ways of communication. The best way is the personal one, when someone from abroad with good understanding of the situation is here."[56]

In 1964 a Berlin Fellowship spring team of ten Presbyterian pastors and elders from various parts of the U.S. travel first to Presbyterian headquarters in New York, then to the World Council of Churches in Geneva, and on to Berlin, where they attend a ten-day conference in West Berlin. The conference is with western pastors, but in small groups, the Americans take day trips to homes and congregations in East Berlin. It is at this conference that two American pastors serving in Berlin, Reverend Ted Schapp and Reverend Ralph Zorn, are more formally introduced to the Berlin Fellowship. This is the first of many such encounters and cooperative ventures between Schapp, Zorn, and the Berlin Fellowship. Schapp will eventually take on leadership in West Berlin.

In spring 1966 the first women's team from various Presbyterian congregations attends a Women's Institute with pastors' wives in East Berlin. Later in the year James, Hamburger and an African-American pastor, venture beyond the city limits, visiting Wittenberg, Weimar, Eisenach, Karl-Marx-Stadt, Dresden and Eisenhüttenstadt, to explore the advisability and possibilities of future team visits to congregations outside Berlin. This venture was prepared by Scharf and Schroeder, and Schroeder explains:

> In East Berlin we have seen what an event it is when Christians from so far away as California visit. Your visits strengthen them, give them new hope, new power to live as Christians on the other side. The Christians in the GDR (Russian Zone) are even more isolated than those in E. Berlin. East German pastors say, "The material help is not the same as the spiritual help. We need the personal contact and the opportunity to pray together because we can no longer pray

[55] Letter from Alfred Schroeder to Walt James, March 27, 1958, Hamburger Collection.
[56] James, *Walls*, 171.

> alone."[...]Bishop Scharf, now bishop for just West Berlin, is very interested in seeing the visitation trips continue. "We don't want your visits to be official, connected with the church headquarters. We hope you can make contact with the individual parishes which are still quite isolated."[57]

It is this statement from Bishop Scharf which will set the tone and direction for the emerging and more regular program of visitation with unofficial status, choosing not to go to often-visited cities like Berlin and Leipzig but rather in small groups visiting lesser-known town congregations in Schwerin or Zittau, Thale or Plauen, or isolated villages like Crostau or Dittersdorf.

The situation in the GDR is indeed isolating and contradiction-ridden for many Christians and congregations, regardless of the size of their town, and these topics, among others, importantly occupy many of the conversations and discussions during these first years of Berlin Fellowship visits. Though Walter Ulbricht in 1960 declares, "Christianity and the humanistic goals of socialism are not contradictions,"[58] the hard facts of what congregations, individual Christians and the church can and can't do are clear. There may be no new churches built in new residential areas, and any remodeling done on old churches (allowed if materials could be found and financed) must be within the old foundations.[59] The state refuses to let church members make visits in the apartment complexes on the outskirts of cities.[60] Many youth who openly attend worship or church events can reckon with not being allowed to earn their *Abitur* (comparable to a high school diploma, allowing one to go on to university studies). In addition, the "choice" regarding learning a trade is often restricted for Christians. However, at the same time, church institutions provide alternative avenues for learning in a few private church schools offering a church-recognized diploma.[61] Unlike any other east bloc country, an alternative service for conscripted soldiers is possible; the "construction soldier" (*Bausoldat*, alternative military service) option is chosen by many young Christians, even though it means disadvantages like being excluded from further higher education.[62] These "options" in a land of very few options are examples of some of the contradictions and arbitrariness of daily life for practicing Christians, for pastors seeking to

---

[57] Op. cit., 180-181.
[58] Mau, *Protestantismus*, 76.
[59] James, *Walls*, 182.
[60] Op. cit., 183.
[61] Mau, *Protestantismus*, 90.
[62] Op. cit., 87.

serve and help their congregations, and for synods and bishops working to support and lead the Church in the socialist system.

From the beginning years of the establishment of this system until the chaotic final days of the period in 1989 named the "Wende," the SED is the driving force of the entire GDR government administration. The state's church policy is clear, for the SED sees itself in battle with the church. Both the Roman Catholic and the Protestant church in the GDR are seen as politically threatening. Ideologically stamped and unbending, the party is fixated on and convinced by its own rhetoric. In this conviction church policy is determined and shaped, planned and carried out.[63] The task of executing that policy is mandated by the party and performed by three bodies within the government: a church questions section of the Central Committee of the Communist Party established in the 1950's which later evolves into a working group for church questions (*Arbeitsgruppe für Kirchenfragen*); the State Secretary for Church Questions and his offices around the country; and the *MfS* Department XX/4, responsible for the state and party administrative organizaiton, block parties, churches, culture, and "political underground" (*Staatsapparat, Blockparteien, Kirchen, Kultur, "politischer Untergrund"*).

Though the first constitution of the new country is relatively liberal in its church policy, the repressions of the 50's hardly reflect a liberal position or the church's voiced wish for the "rebuilding of the German people in peace and freedom." [64] Actions are taken by the state against the church youth groups and university student parishes (under suspicion of being connected to a U.S. undercover organization). The dismantling of religious instruction in the schools, the communist youth dedication (*Jugendweihe*)as a substitute for confirmation, and the forced collectivization of farmlands are but some of the contributing factors to the growing flood of citizens moving to West Germany in the 1950's.

By the time the Berlin Wall is built, the ruling party and state church policy for all government offices and functionaries is established, but it isn't cemented, in that it swings between a "straightjacket" and a "tranquilizer" over the course of the following 40 years. That is, there is basically the same policy during the early years of repression as during the latter years of the Honecker era, when more subtle methods of control and influence are used. In the case of Berlin Fellowship, the *MfS* is the chief government representative and primary actor seeking to achieve its

[63] Rudolf Mau, *Eingebunden in den Realsozialismus? Die Evangelische Kirche als Problem der SED*, Göttingen 1994, 9-13.

[64] Op.cit., Otto Grotewahl speaks with the bishops, April 28, 1950, 188.

goals (*Ziele*) and carry out its plans (*Maßnahmen*), [65]as evidenced by the two operational procedure files conducted on the Berlin Fellowship, its key leaders and its activities.

3. Programmatic Beginnings 1967 - 1970

In 1966 teams regularly begin visiting congregations in the entire GDR, and in 1967 - 68 a new chapter of the connection between Berlin and the California group begins. Berlin Fellowship in southern California formalizes a recruitment process while the newly established planning committee, the East Committee (*Ostkomitee*)[66] meeting in East Berlin begins expressing its wishes for the "form" of future team visitations: fewer presentations, more informal discussion, time for biography sharing, wearing name tags.[67] The discussion on both sides of the ocean about choosing new themes, specific Bible passages, and shaping the orientation period in West Berlin are part of the emerging pattern for American team visits.

The key personalities for the first years of this phase are two Presbyterian pastors, Reverend Schapp in West Berlin, working with displaced persons there and Reverend Hamburger, city mission director in San Diego. In addition, one west Berliner, Frau Bärbel Eccardt, becomes assistant to Schapp in 1970 in the Zinzendorf congregation, Tempelhof district. Reverend James continues to play an important role, but by 1978, both he and Hamburger will recede from direct leadership.

In April 1967 Hamburger and three others attend a pastors' conference in East Berlin and then travel farther into the east. In October, a team of eight men and women spend five days in West Berlin and then attend a five-day conference in East Berlin, which includes Bible study, small group discussion and lectures about Luther's doctrine of justification. New congregation contacts result from networking at the Berlin conference. The American team then travesl to Wittenberg, Plauen, Dresden, and Rostock. A pattern for the "content" focus of future team visits is discussed, with all future themes be chosen and prepared for in advance by both the hosts and guests.

---

[65] Martin Georg Goerner, Die Arbeitsgruppe Kirchenfragen im ZK-Apparat der SED, in: Clemens Vollnhals, *Die Kirchenpolitik und Staatsicherheit Eine Zwischenbilanz*, Berlin 1996, 59-61.

[66] Ted Schapp note to Günter Mieth thanking him for his willingness to meet for preliminary discussion, February 3-4, 1968 in East Berlin. Schapp indicates travel and overnight expenses will be covered. December 1, 1967, private holdings, Günter Mieth, Detmold.

[67] Letter from Ted Schapp to Ralph Hamburger, Dec. 8, 1967, Zinzendorf Collection.

As is the case for the next 22 years, after ten to twelve days of visitation, the Americans return to Berlin and evaluate their experience, sharing thoughts, questions, ideas, and suggestions for future visits. Reflections by Americans reveal critical issues regarding knowing more about the German context, "I think we could have been more effective, if I had known some of the issues and questions we would be dealing with in our meetings. I think it is imperative that the team prepare itself as best as possible."[68] Perhaps in response, Hamburger prepares a six-page document of "Supplementary Data on the Life of the Church in East Germany" with facts about the current political, economic, social, educational, and church situation, including property issues, church repair and construction, and the building of new satelite cities. Mission, stewardship, Christian education, and issues about house-to-house visitation are mentioned as conversation ponts. He cites articles from the 1949 constitution of the GDR which pertain to the practice of religion.[69] Less than one year later, this constitution is amended considerably, and the "religion" section is reduced from nine articles to one article "Article 39: 1) Every citizen has the right to confess a religious faith and to practice his own religious belief. 2) Churches and other religious fellowships may order their activities/affairs and carry out their activity in accordance with the constitution and the legal requirements of the German Democratic Republic. Further details can be arranged through negotiated agreements."[70] In Article 39, phrase 2, the words "negotiated agreements" make it clear how the new constitution works and who has the final word, the state. State pressure for the Protestant church in Germany mounts, and in 1968 this church finally concedes to changing its still united governmental structure. Though the country has been divided since the end of WWII, the Protestant church has remained one body, the Evangelical Church in Germany (*Evangelische Kirche in Deutschland, EKD*) until 1968 when the Federation of Protestant Churches in the GDR is founded. This new federeation, comprised of eight eastern regional churches (*BEK, Bund*

---

[68] Evaluations and suggestions, 1967 Fall Team notes, Hamburger Collection.

[69] It is to note that the previous constitution had five Articles related to the Church and the practice of religion. Though not adhered to by the state, these articles were considerably more extensive for the practice of religion: "every citizen enjoys full freedom of conscience and religious belief"(article 41). Articles 42-44, 46 stated no discrimination against Christians in hiring for public posts, and allowed religious instruction in the schools, pastoral care in hospitals, penitentiaries and other public institutions.

[70] Artikel 39 (1) Jeder Bürger der Deutschen Demokratischen Republik hat das Recht, sich zu einem religiösen Glauben zu bekennen und religiöse Handlungen auszuüben. (2) Die Kirchen und anderen Religionsgemeinschaften ordnen ihre Angelegenheiten und üben ihre Tätigkeit aus in Übereinstimmung mit der Verfassung und den gesetzlichen Bestimmungen der Deutschen Demokratischen Republik. Näheres kann durch Vereinbarungen geregelt werden.

der Evangelischen Kirchen in der DDR) now becomes its own spokesperson and voice of Protestant Christians in the GDR.

In addition to providing many pertinent facts about life in the GDR for Christians, items from Hamburger's report illumine the daily life situation of those being visited, and he includes citations from East Germans. The following are indicative of the tenor and tone of life in the GDR as well as the eastern perspective on encounters with American visitors:

- Since the Synod in February we are facing a much more serious situation. The State is speaking an entirely different language. The State affirms the Church, but allows nothing new.
- The State permits us to exist, but not to build a career.
- It is not the government officials who govern, but the party[...]in administrative way, as quietly and unnoticed as possible, the State seeks to limit the field of endeavor and the influence of the Church[...]The pressure of the State is not convincing, but it makes one tired and skeptical.
- Relating to youth work, the youth are described as skeptical, both toward the East as well as the West, toward the State and toward the Church. We are no longer able to reach large sections of youth. [71]

There are great limitations on the church and its activities: not being able to visit registered church members in their homes, experiencing difficulties in building new churches, building and repair on existing churches with bureaucratic delays for years, consequences for active involvement in church life, educational and job limitations.[72] However, at the same time restrictions like these were enforced, the work of the diaconal arm of the church (*Diakonie*) in church-run hospitals, care homes for the elderly, homes for handicapped becomes extremely important. Berlin Fellowship team visits in congregations often include visits to such church-related institutions and conversations with the workers and residents of these homes and hospitals.

Conversations (*Gespräche*) are focal in Berlin Fellowship in such visitations and more so in the congregational visits. After one planning trip, Hamburger reports comments from his conversations in the east:

- To see some fresh troops coming renews our courage.
- Through this fellowship together we learn anew that we are not left alone.

---

[71] Supplementary notes and data, November 1967, Zinzendorf Collection.

[72] Landesarchiv Berlin, CRep 104: 2204, Kirchenfragen, Information und Anweisungen des Staatsekretariats für Kirchenfragen 1968-1977 reports in a critical note that one pastor has applied to celebrate communion in a state nursing home and is refused, June 21, 1976, Landesarchiv Berlin.

- We are tremendously impressed by the fact that you have come from so far [...] words cannot express what we feel in our hearts.
- I am so thankful that I was able to creep out of my ghetto for a change, that I was able to gain new perspective.
- The joy which you Americans bring with you, your joy is real and you are real [...] children of God we gladly welcome here [...] another thing which impresses me very much is that this is a real grass roots encounter, not something on a high ecumenical level [...] come back soon.[73]

As positive as these comments may seem, 1968 is a dark year of unrest and trouble student protests in Western Europe, race riots and the assassination of Martin Luther King in the U.S., the Viet Nam war, and the Prague Spring. Both spring and fall Berlin Fellowship teams are occupied in conversation and discussion with these difficult topics. The California group is in a learning process of developing a system of team selection, procuring funds, and it begins to adopt its own set of "disciplines" which include being an active member of a congregation and preparing for the trip in the same manner as the earlier deputation groups.[74]

In spring 1968 Bishop Scharf and Pastor Schroeder visit the Synod of Los Angeles and speak about the importance of the Berlin Fellowship visits. They also attend the Presbyterian Church's General Assembly in Minneapolis. Scharf's support and enthusiasm play no small part in the decisions being made in southern California. Though Berlin Fellowship is neither an official activity of the synod in Los Angeles nor an official church activity in East Germany, the Presbyterian Church and the church headquarters in West Berlin, along with the bishops in the GDR are supportive and encouraging. Over the coming years, financial support from the West Berlin church is regular and generous, and the ministry benefits.[75] Americans always pay transportation costs and a portion of the costs during their stay in Berlin. Berlin Fellowship in California urges contributions from its members to help with expenses, and financial matters punctuate the minutes of almost all meetings. Funding always comes through, though not without considerable prayer and regular letters of appeal.

Another matter of growing concern in California has to do with international correspondence. Requests are made for pen pals, and some

---

[73] Op. cit., November 1967, Hamburger Collection.

[74] Basic Disciplines for Involvement in Berlin Fellowship Team Projects, 2/28/68, April Tagung, 1968, Zinzendorf Collection.

[75] Estimated amount contributed by the West Berlin Konsistorium (including Eccardt and Schapp salaries) approximates 1,000,000 DM. Taped interview with Rolf Schmidt (Financial Manager for Ecumenical Affairs, Consistorium West Berlin), Berlin, April 22, 2006.

team members write those they met while in the GDR.[76] Hamburger comments, "All correspondence with the east is to be cautious and prudent. Although it is all right to express concern for American race relations, the Vietnam war, and hope for peace, it is wiser not to mention political implications with the Communists, organizations, nor any relationships with W. Berlin."[77] It is also recommended that no mention be made of Berlin Fellowship.[78] Within a year, it will be decided both in the east and in California that no letters should be written or sent through the regular mail; this is viewed as potentially dangerous to the visitation program and to German host pastors and congregations. This kind of caution, urged as well by the eastern partners, belies the atmosphere and the reality of life in the GDR these years and those that follow until 1989.[79]

The fall 1968 team visits six cities and towns, meeting with church groups in each place, eating meals in private homes, often arriving after midnight. The size of the host groups and the meetings vary some with adults, some with youth. There is always sharing about church life, personal biographies, current events, and a Bible passage or theme for the trip. Getting to know one another better depends upon language facility and the translator, but in this team, there are more German speakers, which help tremendously. The 1968 team's visit begins at a conference in Berlin with approximately 60 pastors, church workers, and lay men and women in attendance. Afterward, the team spends about 8-10 days in the east. Hamburger reports,

> Everywhere we went we found an openness among our brothers and sisters in the east, no hostility at all, except in one isolated case, and that person warmed up to us afterwards. People received us with joy and expressed again and again their astonishment that we cared and were willing to come from so far to demonstrate our oneness in Christ [...] There is a deep hunger for this type of grass roots fellowship, a need to know of each other and to adjust our understanding of what is really happening in the world and in the church.[80]

---

[76] Letter of thanks from Berlin Fellowship team participant, Ward Bjerke (East San Diego Presbyterian Church), to Günter Mieth, May 16, 1967, private holdings Günter Mieth, Detmold.
[77] Berlin Fellowship Meeting Minutes, December 1968, Zinzendorf Collection.
[78] Berlin Fellowship Meeting Minutes, March 23, 1968, Zinzendorf Collection.
[79] Beginning with the first constitution of the GDR, post and telephone surveillance was a given, and though this department didn't really begin its work until 1951, it continued through 1989. Hanna Labrenz-Weiß: Abteilung M (MfS Handbuch). Hg. BStU. Berlin 2005. http://www.nbn-resolving.org/urn:nbn:de:0292-97839421301720, 3 ff.
[80] Ralph Hamburger, "A Confidential Report on the Fall 1968 Team by Berlin and Southern East Germany," Zinzendorf Collection.

Some of the topics covered were: the upcoming U.S. elections, new GDR constitution and its limitations,[81] the Prague Spring and GDR state anger over an official Church letter of regret written to the Czech church,[82] a new wave of arrests, suggestions for "gifts" bought in inter-shops for the host families and congregations (goods otherwise not readily available or affordable in the GDR coffee, chocolate, cigarettes), pressure on school children to conform, and the consequences of church confirmation affecting further education and career choice.

Both spring and fall teams in 1969 are composed of pastors *and* lay persons, and they make thorough and thoughtful evaluations of their visits. Because the program aspect of Berlin Fellowship remains in nascent stages, there are many questions in California being asked about the amount of visiting, the nature of the content and themes, the time schedule, the difficulties of listening to hours and hours of translation, and the need for the American teams to work well together and to let everyone have a say. Minutes from the fall East Committee meeting reveal similar concerns from host pastors and congregations. In spite of the difficulties the group in southern California has in recruiting and helping to finance two teams a year, and in spite of the fact that many Americans get no more than two weeks of vacation, the easterners clearly state they want visitors, and they want this program of visitation to continue and spread.

The fall team is large enough to break into three smaller traveling groups, which before departing Berlin, participate in a conference with 70 pastors and leaders from the east. The theme is "The Future of the Church," focusing on small group work. Small group techniques are introduced and tried out at the Berlin conference as well as by the teams as they travel. Visits include congregations, church-run training centers and homes for multiple-handicapped adults. Activities during a visit are planned by the host congregation and include Bible study, small group meetings, bringing extended greetings in worship services (preaching not being allowed), being hosted for meals in private homes, and meeting with youth, young couples, and women's groups. [83]

The three-day visit in Greifswald includes time in a dairy, a clinic and a school. Surprisingly this group meets with the head of the agricultural collective as well. Such "public" coverage is not usually part of Berlin Fellowship team experiences and will not be repeated. Foreign visi-

---

[81] Mau, *Der Protestantismus*, April 6, 1968 the new constitution of the GDR is ratified, no longer containing any statement about the legal status of the church, 226.
[82] Ibid.
[83] Ted Schapp, "Report on the Visitation of the Berlin Fellowship Team, October 18 to November 4, in West Berlin, East Berlin and in the DDR" November 1969, Zinzendorf Collection.

tors, especially Americans, are seldom if ever allowed to visit schools, government offices, or factories.

At the February 1970 East Committee evaluation and planning meeting in Berlin, suggestions for the future include the following: more time for going deeper and for work in smaller groups, a wish that the Americans send a trained sociologist and a African-American person (later, some teams did include Black and Native American visitors),[84] more time for Bible discussion, more young people (efforts were made in the U.S. to find mature college-age team members to offset the retired and middle-aged team members), working through the theme completely and talking practically about concrete situations. However, the Germans also note that the planned programs are always too full. The East Committee minutes over the entire 20+ years reveal this as an ongoing tension.

In lieu of a full spring team in 1970, a small group of four, including Dr. Darrell Guder, associate pastor at the Hollywood church, and Pastor James visit key German leaders in April. Guder's comments in his "Notes on the Current Situation" (in the east) reveal his own experience and views on the similarities between the East German and the American churches, in spite of the very different ideological, social and political settings:

> We are facing rapid change in every area of life. Materialism, either capitalist or socialist is the dominant mood of the age. There is a growing polarization within the church, and there are many promising attempts being made to bridge over this gap. However, the problems are very great. The church is diminishing in size and 'public authority.' Church traditions are frequently a problem, an obstacle to renewal and change the concept of authority in the church, the role of the liturgy, the kind of language one may use, the old church buildings which must be maintained, the entrenched bureaucracy of the church [...] The church does not want to be pitied it wants to be understood in its unique situation [...] There are many groupings and directions within the Protestant Church in that country. There are more traditional forms of ministry very strongly tied to the pastor [...] there are a very few radical leftists within the church. And there are many other groups seeking to find their way somewhere between these extremes. We have contact with many of these groups, except to the extreme left. All of them seem to want our fellowship and we are persuaded that we can learn from all of them [...] One of the most pressing needs of the church there is in the area of the experience of Christian community. The heavy burden of a centuries-old tradition in which the church is more of a social and ceremonial institution than a personally experienced family is still very much present and influential[...]We have never en-

[84] Photograph of congregation with team visitors including Mr. Casper Glenn, spring 1968, parish scrapbook, Markus Gemeinde Archive, Plauen. cf. Theo Lehman, *Freiheit wird dann sein Aus Meinem Leben*, Kempten 2005, 103.

> countered despair or bitterness, in spite of hardships [...]Universally, the wish is expressed that our visits continue, that they be deepened, that these contacts are vital[...]It seems to be desirable that we devote out time and energies to personal contacts and small group meetings, rather than organized conferences.[85]

In the fall of 1970, Reverend Schapp and family moves from a refugee ministry to a new pastorate, the Zinzendorf parish (*Gemeinde*) in the Tempelhof city quarter of West Berlin. This congregation and its parish house become the "headquarters" for Berlin Fellowship for the next 26 years.[86] In the course of the next decade, sleeping accommodations, a kitchen and living room and meeting area for the teams and office space for Bärbel Eccardt will be built, with financial support from both West Berlin church headquarters and California. Until this point in time, teams have been staying and meeting for the orientation week in various church–run guest houses in West Berlin; in the 70's, the "ecumenical center" in the Zinzendorf congregation becomes home base for Berlin Fellowship.

The fall team divides into two groups, with one group led by Ralph Hamburger, now a pastor at the Arcadia Presbyterian church in the Los Angeles area. Hamburger's eight-page report fills in the future "picture" of a pattern for Berlin Fellowship in the years to come. Most teams meet at the congregational level with lay people and local church leaders, but now and again a group, like this 1970 team, may conduct more formal business, calling on church leaders for information sharing and as a courtesy. Bishop Albrecht Schönherr, of Berlin-East and Brandenburg and Werner Krusche, Bishop in the regional Church District of Saxony (*Kirchenprovinz Sachsen*) are both firm supporters of this kind of visitation.[87] In Dresden, Hamburger writes about Bishop Gottfried Noth's interest in the developments in the life of the church in America, raising perceptive questions about whether U.S. ecumenical leaders really represent the grass roots church people, and whether U.S. denominational leaders genuinely combine spiritual and administrative responsibilities in one, wondering if they could really do justice to both. Noth also comments, more personally, about Berlin Fellowship, "Every time a team comes to visit us, you leave us on higher ground. It is a spiritual bath, like an inner mission festival."[88] It should be noted again, that bishops were informed as a courtesy, and some nodded implicit approval, while

---

[85] Darrell Guder Notes on the Current Situation, May 1970, Zinzendorf Collection.
[86] Berlin Fellowship officially ends in June 1996.
[87] Letter from Ralph Hamburger to Ted Schapp, October 12, 1970, Zinzendorf Collection.
[88] Ibid.

others, like those noted here, though not sanctioning the program, did support it. This evaluation report closes by outlining a strategy and recommending Berlin Fellowship remain a grass roots movement on the congregational level. This report urges caution in the visa and entry process, restates that nothing questionable should be taken by team members across the border, and relays a request from two eastern leaders in Saxony that *no* letters should be written the Communists, the easterners say, are in the process of piecing things together. Once they see the big picture, they will clap down. Letters are nice, they say, but the priority is our visits."[89]

Schapp leads the second group, and unique to visits thus far, they take a list of questions from the West Berliner Zinzendorf congregation to the eastern congregations and upon their return to Berlin, they report their findings, news for the westerners in Berlin perhaps as much as for those from the U.S.:

1. Do Christians over there feel that they are separated from us spiritually? Answer: No! The spiritual unity remains.
2. Are Christians and private business men disadvantaged in their selection of school and professions? Answer: This cannot be generalized. The discriminatory treatment is felt by a cross-section of the population.
3. Do the young people suffer under the division of Germany? Answer: Not necessarily. Reunification is not a relevant theme any more.
4. Do people there experience difficulties or problems due to the American visits? Answer: No!
5. Are the young people won over to socialism? Answer: Socialism is on the march! But not the socialism intended by this government!
6. What do they think about the political situation in West Berlin? Answer: They are asking whether Berlin can continue to exist in this fashion for a long time.
7. How does the church react to the conflict between those who are for or against the state? Answer: There are broadly differing opinions within the church. At its best the church is seeking to gain a dynamic relationship to the state.
8. What do they think about movement towards the left in the West German government? Answer: They are hoping carefully for better relationships between east and west. "A silence filled with anticipation!"
9. What do they think about the demonstrations in the west? Answer: Some people there are buying the Eastern propaganda line: Demonstrations are the proof that the situation is bad in the West. Thinking people are of the opinion that the demonstrations are positive approaches to renewal. But they are asking whether or not demonstrations are a poor strategy. In general they are critical of our demonstrations because they often lack any general conception of what ought to be done.[90]

---

[89] Ibid.
[90] 1970, Zinzendorf Collection.

Schapp concludes, "These questions aroused anger in some of the East Germans. They felt that many of the questions indicated that there were antiquated ideas about the present East. In West Berlin people ought to be better informed, they felt. The people in the east neither want to appear as "the poor brother" nor as "heroes."[91]

The written records from following years do not always include such detailed information, and later efforts to inform the West Berliners are not always so thorough. However, there is always a de-briefing once the team is back in West Berlin, which includes Zinzendorf parish members; the "situation" in the east is neither known or necessarily understood by many West Berliners, for travel restrictions in the late 1960's and early 1970's makes it difficult for them to find out more. Throughout the next eighteen years, Ted Schapp and Bärbel Eccardt involve the members of this congregation in hosting the guest American team, but the West Berliners then need to be "oriented" as well. This group becomes a circle of interested friends who host Americans for meals, commission them in a worship service and attend the debriefing time after the team returns from the East. On occasion, they accompany or lead teams.

Berlin Fellowship has barely begun its activities and the Ministry for State Security (MfS) appoints an unofficial informer to Berlin Fellowship (*inoffizielle Mitarbeiter, IM*). This pastor begins a 20-year-long job of reporting to the *MfS*, apparently being recompensed and given honorable recognition for his service.[92] His name first appears in the Berlin Fellowship files in fall 1970 as a participant in the Fall East Committee meeting, and later he participates in the monthly East Berlin group meeting (*Berliner-Gruppe*). He is, as well, a host pastor for visiting teams. Although *MfS* records show his being recruited by the MfS in 1968, his first report for the church department XX/4 only appears in May of 1969 under the cover name (*Deckname*) of "Krause." This report details how he came into contact with the Americans (Berlin Fellowship is not named) and what he already knows about their travel and hotel plans. One month later, the IM contacts Pastor Merkel (from the East Committee) in Malchow and learns more:

> Merkel told me the contact he has is with Presbyterians from Los Angeles, USA. This is an official thing from Bishop Scharf. This group of Presbyterians are sent out and commissioned to visit Europe and to study church life. These people are

---

[91] Ted Schapp, "Report on the Visitation of the Berlin Fellowship Team, October 18 to November 4, in West Berlin, East Berlin and in the D.D.R.," Zinzendorf Collection.

[92] Clemens Vollnhals, *Die Kirchenpolitik von SED und Staatssicherheit: Eine Zwischenbilanz*, Berlin 1996, 244.

> very closely tied to C.A.R.E. (care packages). Merkel elaborated: the people fly to Europe in small groups, costing 800 dollars. They enter the country as tourists. They stay about one week in the GDR, with a kind of introduction meeting at the beginning. No big lectures are to happen, rather mostly conversation, in order to give the Americans a chance to get information. The focal point of the study is parish or congregational life in the GDR. It is clear, one cannot visit the whole country, so specific sites are chosen. For 1969 those places would be Greifswald and Plauen/Vogtland. The Americans stay in Interhotels [...] the Americans want to get to know the congregations not the church leadership and bishops. They want to have conversations with parish members [...] Merkel issued an invitation, probably for 24.10.69. The American's trip should not become a big 'ecumenical' to-do, but it should be more than previous trips, be in the local parish[...]In their home congregations, the Americans will evaluate and report on what they saw and learned[...]The conversation ended, M. shared no further information. He had to go to the cemetery, for he had a funeral. I went with him. [93]

The MfS suspect this activity to be "hostile contact policy" (*Verdacht der feindlichen Kontakt-politik*); that is, it is supposed that the enemy (American or U.S. citizens or U.S. Intelligence agents) is trying to methodically infiltrate and contact citizens of the GDR. It is interesting to note that this May, 1969 Stasi report differs little from the Berlin Fellowship July 1969 statement of purpose (see above). From this point in time on, detailed and extensive measures are outlined and carried out, though it apparently takes some months, perhaps even years for the *Stasi* to institute the planned and outlined measures. In December of 1970 an operative procedure file, *OV*, and action plan are slated to be opened. In August a year later, one of two main files, "*Rollbahn*" (meaning landing strip or runway), commences by citing Paragraph 98 of the GDR's criminal code book as grounds for opening the file, stating as well the consequences strong suspicion of intelligence gathering, preparation and attempts at such are punishable by 2-12 years.[94]

4. Berlin Fellowship in Context Patterns of Visitation 1971 – 1978

In 1971, the team divides into smaller travel groups, and one group experiences several difficulties, which shade their experience. They attend a "conference" meeting in East Berlin with invited Poles, Czechs, and Hungarians, a new but short-lived idea, for it is soon judged too risky to

---

[93] BStU, MfS, BV Gera, Abt. XX, AOP1456-78, OV "*Rollbahn*", II, Bericht, 7-8, June 26, 1969.

[94] *Strafgesetzbuch der DDR –StGB- und angrenzende Gesetze und Bestimmungen*, Berlin, Herausgegeben vom Ministerium der Justiz, Staatsverlag der DDR, 1976, 55.

use Berlin Fellowship for these wider ecumenical contacts. This same American team is then to attend a conference in Greifswald on "reconciliation," but the conference is canceled by Bishop Friedrich-Wilhelm Krummacher, who wants to avoid causing further uncertainty in the state-church relationship in his district. He views this meeting with Americans to be a particular risk, in light of participants from his regional attending a synod meeting in Denmark at the same time. Another parish cancels out for this particular team because they are having difficulties with the police. They had been building a parish house with illegal labor. Over the course of the coming years, such unforeseen matters recur now and again. Sometimes the unforeseen just happens and depending on the planning done in advance, team visits may be either "smooth" or less than "fruitful" for both the visitors and the visited. Such incidents reflect the context, the reality of life in the GDR and are integral to future programmatic development.

On a larger contextual scale, this era introduces a new development for the church in the GDR, mentioned above the Federation of Protestant Churches in the GDR (*Bund der evangelischen Kirchen in der DDR, BEK)* is founded. Since the founding of the country, the Evangelical Church of Germany has been a united body, east and west, and church-state relations have been less than ideal. In fact they have been strained most of the time; the building of the Berlin Wall contributes further to the difficulties in maintaining a united church body. The GDR authorities, not pleased with the situation, pressed for years for a separation. Shortly after the new constitution is introduced, the need for a "closer, more productive and more exacting cooperative ministry in the Protestant churches of the GDR" is voiced.[95] The burning and on-going issues for individual Christians and the church as a whole now come markedly into focus. Questions the larger church was facing were also discussed in Berlin Fellowship visits and were similar to the following: How can the church be the church in this political system? What does being faithful look like on a personal level in this time and place? What is the role of this church (including the local congregation) in serving the society, in ecumenical bodies, in relation to local and world politics and issues? It is important to remember that the church in this socialist system is the only independ-

[95] Krusche, Werner, Einführung in die Sachproblematik des Bundes der evangelischen Kirchen in der DDR und seiner Ordnung auf der außerordentlichen Synode der Kirchenprovinz Sachsen, Magdeburg, 12.April 1969, in: *Nachdenken Zum Wege des Bundes der evangelischen Kirchen in der DDR*, Ulrich Schröter and Helmut Zeddies (eds.), Hannover 1995, 133.

ent entity not under the umbrella and control of the party system and as such, continues to be a problem for the state, on all levels.[96]

This new federation and its Synod meetings address these questions and related issues in the early 70's. In 1971 at the Synod in Eisenach, Bishop Schönherr formulates a new way of thinking about being the "church in socialism" – that is, the church is "in this particularly shaped society, not beside it, not against it."[97] The church in the east had faced an identity crisis as a minority church in a state whose official church policy has been not to negotiate with it as long as it is part of the Evangelical Church in Germany (*Evangelische Kirche in Deutschland* EKD). With the 1969 formation of the Federation, a new phase of church life in the GDR begins. This not so easily understood, highly controversial and often discussed phrase "church in socialism" (*Kirche im Sozialismus*) becomes a quasi-watchword for the following decades for this new church body, at synod meetings, regional Church Days (*Kirchentage*), and district meetings in the following years. It was also a matter of discussion for the Americans and their hosts in some of the congregations visited.

As the leaders of this newly formed church body seek to define themselves, other phrases like "church for others" (reference to D. Bonhoeffer's reflections in *Letters and Papers from Prison*) or "witness and service" (*Zeugnis und Dienst*) or "learning community" (*Lerngemeinschaft*) become part of the discussions in congregational visits. In 1972, at a synod meeting in Dresden Pastor Heino Falcke, then director of the Preaching Seminary in Gnadau, delivers an address entitled, "Christ Liberates – Therefore the Church for Others" ("*Christus befreit darum Kirche für andere*")[98] which proved to be quite controversial.[99] In it he states, "In the promise of Christ, we will tirelessly remind our society of

[96] i.e. title of a file in an office for church questions at the district council level reads, "The policy of the socialist state, vis-à-vis the churches and religious communities and our duties and functions in the education of the clergy and church leaders and officers regarding socialist awareness/collective consciousness", Land Brandenburg Archiv, REP401/14584, 1975, 495.

[97] Albrecht Schönherr, *Grat Wanderung*, Leipzig 1992, 36. "In dieser so geprägten Gesellschaft, nicht neben ihr, nicht gegen sie."

[98] Heino Falcke, Christ Liberates -- Therefore, the Church for Others (1972), in: *Ecumenical Review* 40:2, 1988, 204-214.

[99] Werner Krusche, Lecture "Denkt daran, daß im Herrn eure Mühe nicht vergeblich ist" VI. Synod of the BEK(Federation of Churches in the GDR), Berlin 1991, 13, in reference to Falcke's address "The lecture was declared as not having been given, it was not allowed to be printed in the GDR."

our committed hope for a socialism that can be changed for the better."[100] This suggestion that the church would remind the state of its role is totally problematic for the state authorities and also for the church leadership.[101] This is yet another manifestation of the ongoing question in synods, parish meetings and conversations about the "church in socialism" during Berlin Fellowship visits – what does it mean to be the church, here and now?

The American teams often find themselves in intense and emotional discussions with their German hosts, as both conversation partners seek to probe and answer such questions. In many cases, the American guests are called to weather unexpected changes and challenges:

> Although planned meetings and discussion groups were always fruitful to some extent, it was often the unexpected and unplanned confrontations which proved to be most enriching and rewarding [...] Hence the name Berlin Fellowship takes on a particularly significant meaning. It is precisely for *fellowship* that the American Christians go to West Berlin and East Germany [...] To a large extent our group experienced much of this oneness in Christ at a depth we had not known before.[102]
>
> Bonhoeffer in *Life Together* (*Gemeinsames Leben*) says Christian service is expressed firstly in listening, next in readiness to help, next in bearing one another's burdens, and finally in speaking God's Word ordained for that situation. We tried to do this[...]But all of this has come about "in His name," and in this we all have cause to rejoice, that our brothers who were lost (to us) have been found (and we ourselves as well).[103]

Both of these voices, those of two young American theologians, reflect a growing awareness of the reciprocity of the Berlin Fellowship experience, a unique phenomenon of encounter and coming together, in spite of differences. The visits become a two-way street, with the Germans and the Americans giving and taking, sharing the experience. The original motivation to help and offer support which initiated the work trips of the 1950's evolves in the course of the next decades into a form of ministry of presence, fellowship, and mutual encouragement.

Beginning in 1972 it becomes apparent that sending full teams of ten to twelve people from California twice a year is not possible. From now

---

[100] Ibid., "Unter der Verheißung Christi werden wir unsere Gesellschaft nicht loslassen mit der engagierten Hoffnung eines verbesserlichen Sozialismus." in Heino Falcke, *Mit Gott Schritt Halten*, 24.

[101] Krusche, "Denkt," 13.

[102] S.T. Kimbrough (Bonn), Berlin Fellowship Report, Spring 1971, Zinzendorf Collection.

[103] Letter from Jim Edwards "To the Members of Berlin Fellowship," May 20 1971, Zinzendorf Collection.

on, the spring teams (May-June) are to be the larger groups, with fall teams (September-October) averaging two to four participants. Team composition, regardless of size is varied in personalities and persuasion and often in surprising and challenging ways, to both the teams themselves and their hosts. They are often caught off guard with pressing and hard questions. The 1972 summer team is asked repeatedly about Angela Davis,[104] the Vietnam War, and the Jesus Movement.[105] "Reactions of our team members to these three issues were so varied, one of our Christian brothers in the East complained that we should send team members who all agreed on these important matters. One of his compatriots quickly put him down and he was assured *that* would not be a true picture of America or Americans."[106] That American team members did not always agree with one another, even theologically, remained a challenge to the team leaders and a goal of the orientation week to help the Americans get to know one another and especially to accept one another, and even with differences of opinion, to work together.[107] However, teamwork on the American side was not the only issue, for the "situation" in the east was often precarious and difficult.

In fall 1972, a smaller evaluation team of three led by Dr. Guder, Berlin Fellowship Moderator, southern California, traveled to nine cities and towns, meeting en route with Bishop Gienke of Mecklenburg. The report summary identifies programmatic information but more importantly describes the church's situation in the GDR. Such contextual background becomes most helpful for future teams:

1. There is a general consensus that we should come again, but that we must be more careful and cleverer than before. The pressure is on internally as a result of the external easing of pressure. Many people are being forced to state they will not be hosts of Westerners, now that Westerners are coming in greater numbers. Tourism is going to be carefully scrutinized. We may find fewer laymen able to entertain us in some areas, although church staff members have no reservations about receiving us. Amongst themselves, our DDR friends are going to be much more discreet, with less communication, less letter writing, less telephoning.
2. This increased care must also be shown by us.
3. Everyone agrees that smaller contact groups for longer periods of time would be best

---

[104] This late 1960's, 1970's activist, known for association with the Black Panthers and the Communist Party in America, was linked to a murder of a judge. She was tried and acquitted, and some of her legal costs were underwritten by the Presbyterian Church.
[105] Christian movement in the hippie subculture of the late 1960-70's in USA.
[106] Berlin Fellowship Newsletter, August 5, 1972, Berlin Fellowship Collection.
[107] Notes from a personal conversation with Bärbel Eccardt, May 1, 2008, Berlin.

4. Our team members should make much more concerted effort to acquaint themselves with the essentials of Marxist ideology and current developments in the political world.
5. Generally, it is felt that the DDR authorities are anxious about the situation. Their political course is basically dictated in Moscow, and they (DDR) are not very happy about the general shifting of positions in Europe. Their method is to intensify the ideological molding of their people. The church is a thorn in their flesh, and they have come to the conclusion that the most dangerous Christians are the ones who are trying to find a meaningful ministry in this socialist setting. They prefer Christians now who are retreatists from the world, 'cultists', specialists in liturgy, who have no sense of mission or to service in this world. Therefore, many of those Christians who have sought to be irenic and constructive are being rebuffed now. In general, it is confusing, but we see again and again that the presence of God's Spirit in people is real and very hard for non-believers to cope with. On several occasions we were told that one of the most effective ways for Christians to deal with the situation is to be considerate, understanding and sympathetic towards the representatives of the system. They are not used to this kind of treatment, and it opens doors of communication. Nothing is gained by consigning them to the devil, and they are all people for whom Christ died.
6. As the church in the DDR continues to struggle with the necessities of internal change, it is helpful for people to come who can share about the course of change in our churches in America. Although the traditional mentality of the *Volkskirche* is still very strong, many leaders in the DDR churches are grappling with the fact that they are becoming a minority, a *diaspora* church. As paradoxical as it sounds, this means that this church is developing many similarities to the American church. We have much to share in the area of the priesthood of all believers.
7. The small group movement is beginning to catch on in the DDR.[108]

The accompanying letter from Guder closes with eastern thoughts about structure for the upcoming visits and with requests that each small delegation have someone that has been in the east before, and in fact, names of people that should return are identified. James reports another aspect to the wishes of these participating East German Christians, "We have so many impressions of America the Vietnam War, the racial struggle, that are so damaging. We want to meet Americans of a different kind [...] We have many visitors and will have more, but you are the only ones with a spiritual basis where a Christian unity is involved with the West and we must have this." [109]

In April 1973, the Berlin Fellowship Newsletter reports that it is now possible to phone East Berlin from West Berlin simply by dialing, that it is more expensive now to travel in the east, that prices are rising, and that the East seems anxious to take its place in world affairs, establishing an

[108] Darrell Guder letter to Berlin Fellowship Friends, November 28, 1972, Zinzendorf Collection.
[109] Berlin Fellowship Minutes, December 9, 1972 Zinzendorf Collection.

academy for training foreign affairs officers. Furthermore, it is illegal for East Germans to have western money or to shop in Intershops (state-run stores offering western products not otherwise available for purchase).[110] This kind of information shared in newsletters and in the minutes of meetings is a reminder that such news items, detailed, plebian or note-worthy on a political level, are not easily accessible to the Berlin Fellowship team participants. Information about daily life in the GDR in English continues to be hard to come by for the average citizen in the U.S.; this necessitates personal reflections and reports like the following being sent to California.[111] Guder, now living and working in Ludwigsburg, West Germany in 1973, writes:

> It has become clear that a socialist regime, like that in the DDR confronts a Christian Church which is clearly antagonistic to the state, one which is, in their eyes, "reactionary," "western-oriented," or "bourgeois." A church which seeks to find its meaningful role in a socialist state, which wants to be "in the world but not of the world", is very hard to cope with. Where [Christians] can support and cooperate with the state, they do so. And where they cannot, they say so. This kind of freedom and inner strength is extremely perplexing to the authorities, since it is not the kind of behavior which Marxist theory has led them to expect. It leads to repression, hardship, and confusion for the church and this is the situation in which they find themselves now.[112]

A team member and theology professor, Dr. David Willis, reports on his visit and the possible effects of *détente* in East-West relations:

> Two words summarize for me what we experienced in the north: sobering, encouraging. Sobering because what we heard about the government's precautions in the face of threatening cultural exchange which would be a by-product of the East-West détente proved to be all too true. Encouraging because the Christian congregations and individuals with whom we met are, if anything, even more determined and imaginative in their Christian witness than ever [...][113]

In his report about the various villages and congregations visited, he notes the problems and the life situation in the DDR:

---

[110] Berlin Fellowship Newsletter, April 7, 1973 Berlin Fellowship Collection.

[111] Martin Walton, fraternal Worker at the Zinzendorf parish, begins sending abridged and translated articles from the *epd Dokumentation* and *Kirche im Sozialismus*, two publications of Evangelische Pressedienst Frankfurt am Main/Berlin to supplement letters and team reports, newspaper clippings and several English books on German history and the GDR.

[112] Letter from Guder to Louise Wolstencraft, April 26, 1973, Berlin Fellowship Collection.

[113] Willis Report on Berlin Fellowship Visitation, summer 1973, Berlin Fellowship Collection.

- A visit to a church-run institution for mentally-retarded persons [...] numerically understaffed
- The pastor asking that our car be parked a block away from the manse.
- Population reduction in the villages with many moving to the urban areas. Large churches needing repair and maintenance.
- Employment issues where both husband and wife must find suitable work and the related divorce rate.
- Topic of discussion at a large youth gathering (1200): how to be a member of the FDJ (Free German Youth, communist youth organization) *and* a member of the Christian church [...] and how those affect schooling opportunities.
- Because one of the regional organizers didn't want letter or telephone contact, the team visit was rather spontaneous "He feels himself quite exposed, as indeed he is, and does not want to do anything which will jeopardize future visits, especially since no one seems to know how the State is going to handle the problem of increased exposure to outsiders as a result of the window-dressing detente."
- In Schwerin, there was an "embarrassing" (at least for us) experience of having accommodations because of our Western money and of seeing DDR citizens being turned away from the hotel (lobby) which was only for foreigners.[114]

At a synod conference in Halle, November 17, 1973, Bishop Werner Krusche's lectures entitled, "The Church of Jesus Christ on the Way to the Diaspora" further clarify the church situation.[115] This document in translated form becomes a key section of the orientation manual for American team members of Berlin Fellowship, and contains many points illumining the context of congregational life in the DDR. Divided into six chapters, the paper addresses *diaspora* and mission, the uniqueness of the *diaspora* situation, the way to *diaspora* a process of learning. Krusche states the Diaspora Church must be a Church ready to learn how to spread the gospel, a church ready to learn new forms of parish life, a church ready to learn in the area of church and society. This lecture (which the censors did not allow to be published) gives decisive impulse for the church in the 70's as it sought a new orientation as a minority-church,[116] church membership having decreased markedly in the 50's and 60's. The following selection of statements from this paper mirrors the reality of life for Christians and the church in the GDR, as seen through the eyes of one of its leading theologians:

---

[114] Op.cit.

[115] Harald Schulze, *Berichte Der Magdeburger Kirchenleitung Zu Den Tagungen Der Provinzialsynode 1946-1989*,Göttingen 2005, 301-312.

[116] Schulze, *Berichte*, 301. "Krusche gab mit diesem Referat einen entscheidenden Impuls zu der Anfang der 1970er Jahre geführten Diskussion über die Neuorientierung der kirchlichen Arbeit im Blick auf die Entwicklung der Kirche von einer Mehrheit- hin zu einer Mindersheitskirche. Aus Zensurengründen kam es in der DDR nicht zum Druck dieses Referats."

- Our situation is an ideological *diaspora*. We live in a society grounded in Marxism-Leninism. It understands itself as humanistic, serving the good of the people, which it also does in many ways. We want to stay free of a resentment complex by which we would refuse to recognize any good in the state. However, the claim of the state for total allegiance offends us especially strongly. It is clear from their side and ours that no man can serve two masters or give total allegiance to two different ideologies. The state limits our activities.
- The church has to ask itself the question what it uniquely has to offer. The answer will be: The Gospel and the church in the *diaspora* situation has the opportunity to concentrate on the decisive element (it can become a city set on a hill...as a church which is underprivileged without worldly power it can understand other minorities better [...]the members of the *diaspora* churches will experience an increasing desire to come together for fellowship. In a non-Christian world the members will need one another for comfort, intercession, thanksgiving, and sharing [...] The danger of the *diaspora* that the congregation cuts itself off from the world in order to preserve its identity can only be overcome through the living Lord, who takes away the fears and calls us into service.
- We must work through the fact of pluralism in our church [...] This pluralism must stand against the unified ideology of the state that speaks with one voice.
- Our situation, the very limited nature of our possibilities to influence the society, is like a nightmare, that tempts us to say that we can do nothing, the possibilities are so small, they are laughable...We will have to deal with this nightmare in our learning process. The idea that nothing has worth that is not a great success is one of the false goals of our time. The light of the freedom in Christ lets the promise shine even in the small things. He assures us that our apparently weak and laughable small steps [...] have a secret shine. Nothing we do in his name is without purpose.[117]

The limitations on the situation and limited possibilities Krusche refers to nonetheless do not restrict all aspects ministry, for instance, with youth. The 1974 team meets an innovative evangelist and youth pastor, Theo Lehmann and a youth group in Saxony.[118] The Americans learn from these youth how they long for solidarity, for friends in their schools and places of work, where they are often ostracized by peers and pressured by teachers. However, the same youth state there are advantages to their system health care for all being one big advantage, and they express genuine concern for their society, its rising costs of living, alcohol problems, and growing criminality. The "*diaspora*" situation of the church is re-iterated, and the shrinking number of members points to the need for the church and its congregations to learn new ways of ministry and service.

---

[117] Excerpt from lecture of Bishop Werner Krusche, Protestant Church of the Province of Saxony, Halle, November 17, 1973, Zinzendorf Collection.
[118] Lehman, *Freiheit*, 103-104.

On the 1974 fall trip, Hamburger again evaluates the situation, writes down the wishes of the eastern hosts and notes topics about which they are interested in learning: congregational life and renewal in the U.S., the American Sunday School, the charismatic movement, what Americans do with confirmation courses, marriages between Christians and non-Christians, baptismal practices and finding God-parents, ethical issues in daily life. In conversation with one of the bishops, Hamburger heard that the bishop was in complete agreement with Berlin Fellowship methods and visitation, but

> He pointed out that what we are doing is a RISK, inasmuch as we are more than tourists. He told us that the DDR has strict laws, but that the state tends to use them in a "flexible, creative" way, to its own advantage. What we are doing is known by the state, of course, he states. In fact, he is constantly amazed how much state officials know. It could be, however, that one day they will lower the boom on us. In that case, he promised to do all he can to shield us. Expulsion from the DDR would probably be the only consequence. The recent changes in the Constitution (September 27, 1974) will make the get-togethers between East and West still more difficult, he felt. For the time being, he told us, proceed, but carefully [...][119]

Hamburger continues with some personal impressions and findings:

> The relentless encroachment by the state of personal freedom and the restrictions of the church's life and functions, in spite of constitutional guarantees, continues[...]Through the registration laws and other direct checks, including attendance of state officials at church functions, the state seeks to keep an eye on everything that is happening. This, particularly in some areas, will make it more difficult for us to share in meetings where the whole congregation is invited[...]New diplomatic relations with the United Nations and the United States, instead of making life a bit easier for the church, appear to effect the very opposite. Efforts are being made to cut off contacts with people from the West even further. Exit visas for church people to attend church conferences abroad or to tend to family business, such as illness, death or a marriage, given more freely in recent years, are again much more difficult, if not impossible to obtain. Permits nowadays are given only to experts and specialists in certain fields [...] At the very time that agreements for a better flow of relationships between West and East Germany were being negotiated, the latter fortified its border areas. No Christian can be a government official, an army or police officer. Attempts are made increasingly to exclude them also from the teaching and medical/nursing professions, in fact, from all professions having to do directly with the public. A new youth law puts additional pressures on young people. Anything that is not in

[119] Ralph Hamburger Report on East German Mission, visit with Bishop Johannes Hempel, Sept. 24-October 4, 1974, 5-7, Zinzendorf Collection.

> the spirit of socialism is to be eradicated. As in Wismar the previous year, a systematic visitation of parents by state officials is being undertaken this fall in Schwerin to keep them from sending their children either to Sunday school or Confirmation class. Youth whose parents are not pastors have it harder still. If adults are not members of the party, some union, PTA or other socialist association, it is being definitely noted. The state keeps a record on every person. There is much sympathy for the church among the population, but few only are willing to pay the price. Most people live 'zweigleisig' i.e. on double tracks. Youth in school learn to give the "right" answers and write perfect socialist essays without actually believing much or any of it themselves.[120]

These remarks offer specific examples of the "politic of separation (Politik der Abgrenzung), a particular aspect life for Christians in the GDR. Hamburger notes the most recent change made in the Constitution, a change made without any notification or referendum to the citizens of the country. In this case, it is the entire citizenry which has been *abgegrenzt* or disassociated.[121] Article 1 of the 1968 constitution reads, "The German Democratic Republic is a socialistic state of the German nation." The new version reads, "The German Democratic Republic is a socialistic state of laborers and farmers." Hamburger's explanation is that this is an intentional shift indicating that though both Germanys have common historical and cultural roots, that there will be no re-unification, even on the basis of socialism. This deepening of ties with the Soviet Union causes a negative reaction among the Berlin Fellowship hosts, but Hamburger's report reiterates that continued visits are wished for:

> Everywhere we gained the impression, even confirmation, how strategic our team visitations are, particularly at this time. We are one of the most rare groups who carry on continuing in-depth Christian relationships on a congregational level. One person said, "We live off the visit long afterwards." ("*Wir zehren lang davon*")[122]

By 1975, the Federation of Protestant Churches in the GDR has about 8 ½ million members, down from 85% of the population after the war.[123] Bishop Krusche's description of the Diaspora church (see above) puts flesh on the bones of this shrinking "church in socialism," and teams

[120] Ibid.
[121] Reinhard Bickhardt (ed), *Recht Ströme wie Wasser, Christen in der DDR für Absage an Praxis und Prinzip der Abgrenzung*, Berlin 1988.
[122] Hamburger Report, citing Hempel, 1974.
[123] The Churches in the GDR, A survey of structures, developments and controversies, in: *Kirche im Sozialismus* 1974, English edition, 29f.

learn regularly from their hosts of the small and seemingly simple steps Christians take to live out their faith in the GDR.

These steps of learning, though not necessarily so articulated by the easterners, are repeatedly part of the written and oral reports, minutes from Fellowship meetings and other western documentation from the early and mid-70's: stories about individuals and their challenges, about troubles and joys in the work place, about congregational ministries to non-churched neighborhood children, about care and service in church-run nursing and children's homes, about creative public tours of churches and pastors welcoming the public to cultural events and concerts using Bible texts and stories, about the social challenges Christian youth have in their schools. All of these encounters and conversations leave deep impressions on the American visitors. In many cases, teams meet Christian professionals (physicians, engineers, social workers) and learn how they try to live out their faith in their work life. In one conversation, a pediatrician reveals his own need for western and Christian professional contacts as well as for equipment, books, journals, and supplies in his children's hospital.[124] One of the team members visiting him is a professor of urology from the University of Los Angeles, and an informal friendship is established; for many years thereafter books and other materials for his hospital manage to get delivered to this pediatrician.

Though Berlin Fellowship visits are seen as unique in that "spiritual" themes, Bible passages and church-related topics shape conversations and meetings, the social, political, and economic situation in the DDR, in the U.S., and in the world are all key elements in the conversation. In these years, the change in the GDR constitution, both German states becoming members of the United Nations (1973) and East Germany signing the Helsinki Peace Accords (1975) regularly punctuate the conversations as well. Summer 1975 themes and topics include human rights, daily life in various professions, possibilities to travel, economic struggles, confirmation class instruction, Vietnam, Nixon, race issues in the U.S., peace, and freedom.

Besides some rather hot topics, cultural background and personalities of all involved play a role in how a team visit evolves. In the case of one visit in the north, the team leader's report shares honestly that getting good conversation going in this region is often difficult. The team leader reflects that it is due, in part to the piety of the Americans clashing with the careful and analytical manner of German group discussion (*Gründlichkeit*). The team report states, "The German thoroughness was hard

---

[124] Short Report North Team, summer 1974, Zinzendorf Collection.

for the Amis to deal with and they soon grew tired of it. They are the more practical types, perhaps a little too much, but we (a German speaking) are too little!"[125] One of the Americans (a college student) on this visit reflects her side of the experience,

> I was confronted with a totally different mentality or way of studying and speaking about Christ. The emphasis seemed to be on an academic theology rather than a personal relationship with the Lord. But, I found that Christianity is not something which one culture or one group of people can set barriers around and automatically block out all other interpretations. There are many ways of expressing the faith all within the realm of Christianity speaking about it, thinking about it, and most of all living it. I didn't hear a great deal of talk about, "What Jesus means in my life," but I could see the answer in the way they lived their lives [...] I feel that the only way I was able to learn what I did was because of the people we were able to meet to spend time with them and share a small portion of their lives.[126]

This same college student concludes her report with a story that exemplifies a repeating theme, something the teams and the hosts are reminded of year after year. She writes,

> But more than anything else, as I look back on the trip, I'll remember one evening which we spent with a group of young married couples. I was speaking with a woman who was warm and completely open about her feelings. We got to talking about the value of the Berlin Fellowship and I said, "So we come and we talk and we listen. Then we go home, tell others more about your situation, and we pray for you. But what more can we do?" Her answer: "What more is there? That's all that matters, isn't it? We don't need packages or chocolates from the West. We need to see real, live people to know that they care; that we're not alone in our faith.[127]

By now the Berlin Fellowship visits are regular and expected, and the easterners voice their wishes ever more loudly. Saxony divides into two districts, and topics discussed on the fall trip include yet again what "kind" of American guests are wished for both names of previous Americans as well as specific professions are mentioned: a theologian, a student, a sociologist or psychologist, someone with industrial background, youth, and professionals from the middle generation. Bishop Johannes Hempel, bishop in Saxony, affirms and expresses gratitude for the con-

---

[125] Bärbel Eccardt, Short Report from the North Team, 1975, 29.May – 6.June, Zinzendorf Collection, "Für die Amis ist die deutsche Gründlichkeit und Tiefe schwer zu verkraften, sie werden das theoretisieren bald müde. Sie sind Praktiker, vielleicht ein bisschen zu sehr, wir zu wenig!"
[126] Heidi Van Ert, Report of 1975 Team, Zinzendorf Collection.
[127] Ibid.

tinuation of the program, reminding the Americans of the responsibility they bear with such visits, as well as describing his take on details of life in 1975:

> The situation in the GDR changes rapidly. Everything is listened to, regardless of where one is. He meant we should count on that fact in our conversations. A request: don't just go to the traditionalist, visit the reactionaries as well. Look for conversations with outsiders. It is difficult to know how to be protestant here as it is in the west. It is and remains a tight-rope walk without a net. If you are willing to take the risk and like to dream, come again and often....We are being watched with 'hungry' eyes and our being Christians can be 'read'[...]lay people are the missionaries of our time [...] There is a need for meaning, a search for truth, questions about the purpose of life in the society.[128]

1976 is an unusual year for the publicity given the entire nation. The GDR is seeking international recognition and acceptance, which membership in the United Nations has at least initiated and Honecker's signing the Helsinki Accords has furthered. However, the self-immolation of a youth pastor, Oskar Brüsewitz, in August and the SED's expulsion some months later of the protest singer, Wolf Biermann, definitely give the country a distinct form of international attention. The fall team visits Brüsewitz's grave, piquing MfS curiosity.[129]

In preparation for the 1977 team visits, Eccardt, Schapp, and the fraternal worker, Martin Walton, make a planning trip in September. Their "findings" report confirms a number of facts that now make Berlin Fellowship seem a necessary and important ministry, with details about specific topics and themes, a suggestion that the weekend visit include small-group work and include the same parish members for an entire visit. Topics covered included: Christian witness in a defined and aggressive socialist society, ministry challenges in "newly built high-rise complexes" (*Neubaugebiete*), church building maintenance and needs for new churches, and problems which pastors' children and children of active church members have with higher education opportunities, since most are barred from studies beyond 10th grade.[130]

Early in 1977, the California group adopts a statement from Darrell Guder which re-states what the BF program is about:

---

[128] Trip report from Walt and Margarit James, Dan and Rose Towler, "12-21 September.1975 in the DDR in the red VW-Bus," Zinzendorf Collection.

[129] BStU, MfS, BV Gera, Abt.XII/Archiv, AOP 1456/78, Bericht über die Reise amerikanischer Christen vom 16-25.9.76, 11-17.

[130] Reinhard Henkys, *Gottes Volk im Sozialismus, Wie Christen in der DDR leben*, Berlin 1983, 109.

> The present activity of the Fellowship continues to consist primarily of small group visitations, carefully selected, prepared, and conducted with the purpose of visiting Christians in the German Democratic Republic who otherwise have no opportunity to experience the world-wide fellowship of Christ's Church. The regular gatherings of the Fellowship in Southern California are the necessary times of prayer, consultation, study, and preparation. Every indication we have received from our brethren in the east confirms that these contacts have great significance and should continue.
>
> In light of the pressure under which our brethren live in the east, we feel it is extremely important to maintain a low profile about our visits. We go as tourists, and we are careful to avoid any encroachment upon the laws of the GDR. However, there is constant suspicion about ecumenical contacts, and they will be much harder to maintain if we publish, speak openly, or report too broadly about our experiences. In order to be able to continue our visits, and to prevent any unfortunate repercussions for our brethren in the east, we adhere stringently to the policy of careful and disciplined low profile activity in America.
>
> Now, more than ever, we need to continue our ministry, since the situation in the east, since Helsinki is particularly tense. We feel that we are an unthreatening and unthreatened form of fellowship contact, and that we have the best chance of anyone to maintain the bonds of Christian community across political boundaries.
>
> Perhaps I should add that we are not interested in being drawn into the political controversies relative to pro- or anti-socialism. The task of our brethren in the east is to be the body of Christ in the social and political situation there. Our task is to be the body of Christ in our situation. They do not need our pity, our advice, or our political theories. They do need Christian community, support, contact, and encouragement, just as we do. For this reason alone I feel that the continuing work of our Fellowship merits support and understanding.[131]

This definitive statement of the mutual need for encouragement and support, along with a gathered momentum in the east provides space for the Germans to request yet more information about social institutions in the U.S., about rehabilitation for prisoners, about environmental measures (poor air quality and other forms of pollution are noted by the visitors),[132] and the appearance of more and more "guest workers"(foreign nationals from other communist countries) continues to makes visits from minority (Black, Native American) team members important. The southeast region in Saxony voices a particular need for information, the area around Dresden being known as the "valley of the clueless" (*Tal der Ahnunglosen*). It is impossible there to receive western

---

[131] Minutes of the Berlin Fellowship Meeting, April 23, 1977, Hamburger Collection.

[132] In the late 70's and early 80's church special interest groups began forming in various regions, mostly in cities, around the country. Environment, human rights, women's issues, justice and peace groups began networking as well. These groups are problematic for the state.

television or radio. Repeated themes from previous years like general problems for Christian children in schools are counter-balanced by more pointed discussions about the specifics of parish life and programs, about how Christians try to live their faith in the work place, and about the difficulties one has in "sharing" the gospel, about the witness of Christian institutions to the DDR society (hospitals, care homes for children and the elderly). Bishop Krusche's description of the situation, not just in the southeast but in the entire country in these years sums it up, "The Church is not persecuted, but rather limited or hemmed in." [133]

March 6, 1978 is a watershed date in the history of state-church relations; it is the first official meeting since the founding of the GDR (1949) between Bishop Schönherr, Federation of Evangelical Churches, and Erich Honecker, head of state. The results are greeted by many, for it seems a loosening of the "reins" the SED state holds may be forthcoming. Concrete agreements are made regarding church building projects, radio and television broadcasts, the 1983 Luther Year 500th anniversary celebration, pastoral care in prisons, state pensions for church workers, importation of church literature, church kindergartens and retirement and nursing homes. However, the tensions regarding school military education in the use of weapons (*Wehrerziehung/Wehrkundeunterricht*) soon overshadows some of the positive results and reactions to the March 6 summit meeting. On visits in 1978, teams learn of the hard line drawn by the minister of education, Margot Honecker; socialist education methods and goals continue to be sore spots in the lives of those visited.

As this first decade of Berlin Fellowship teams visits draws to a close, so does an era of state-church relations. American team members continue to primarily learn of the developments in the GDR via orientation in Berlin, reports from previous teams, and from the conversations and the visits themselves; scholarly material in English about the changing situation for Christians in the GDR is practically non-existent. Throughout the coming decade, ongoing and greater efforts are made to inform team members about the history of the established Protestant church (*Volkskirche*), the history of the GDR, the changing situation in the east bloc, détente, and the world stage on which the cold war is playing out. Ideally, team members come informed both about the complex social and political realities in the GDR but also about those of their own nation.

One version of the East German political and social reality is found in the *Stasi* files. Berlin Fellowship's activities these first ten years are

[133] Report of the middle-team, May-June 1977, leadership Martin Walton, Zinzendorf Collection.

part of the 1900 + pages of described "reality" in reports, from the perspective of one main *Stasi* informant and his superior reporting officer. This information gathering action is at the time unknown to both the Americans and the Germans participants. Though some participants may assume such is happening, it would have been very surprising to learn that one *MfS* operative procedure file (OV "*Rollbahn*"), after approximately eight years of intelligence gathering, has been opened and closed in this decade(1972-1978). Eccardt's suspected espionage involvement cannot be confirmed. Information on Zorn, another object of the file "*Rollbahn*" is inconclusive, and Schapp, the third person under scrutiny for this file is deemed "uninteresting" in 1977. The *MfS* opened this file originally because of suspicious activity by these three West Berlin residents. The focus in these six volumes of collected reports is on team preparation, the East Committee annual meetings, the Berlin group's monthly gatherings, and Eccardt's activities; the file is replete with highly repetitious material in hundreds of *IM*-reports (progress reports, plans of action, decisions, summary reports, information reports, interim reports, final reports, etc.) and administrative recaps.

The *IM* is assigned to gain trust in the group and among its leaders, which he accomplishes. Further, he is to find out as much as possible about their real motives and their activities. Early on he learns about the purpose of the Berlin Fellowship visits to bring encouragement for the Christians in the GDR[134] and to learn about congregational life.[135] This data is repeatedly recorded in the files. However, accurate this description may be, it is dismissed or ignored after the "*Rollbahn*" file is closed. That is, two further operative procedure files are opened for at least the next six years as repositories for continuing Berlin Fellowship-related reports, and the *IM* reports through at least 1988.

The ongoing search for significant information and the *IM's* apparent uncertainty (or that of his superiors) about what the organization is doing makes for puzzling reading since this *IM* is a theologian. An example: the

---

[134] BStU MfS AOP 1456-78 Abt.XII/Archiv, The initial purpose for the program according to Zorn was that reformed Christians travel into the GDR in order to bolster up Christians in the GDR in order to keep living there. "*Die Ausgangsbasis nach Zorn war, daß Christen reformierten Glaubens in die DDR reisen, um den Christen in der DDR Mut zu machen, weiter als Christen zu leben.*" November 29, 1973.

[135] BStU MfS 1486/84 OV "*Radius*", XX/4 Band 1, April 6, 1973, "The Americans travel yearly as tourists into the GDR to get to know the GDR and the innerworkings of the church." (*Die Amerikaner einreisen jährlich in die DDR als Touristen, um die DDR und das Gemeindewesen innerhalb der Kirchen kennenzulernen.*) Names of participants at this meeting are listed and labeled as "conspirative working committee" (*Konspirativ arbeitenden Komitee*). This is taken from a progress report (*Sachstandbericht*) from OV Rollbahn, dated Nov. 11, 1970.

meaning of the word "fellowship" seems to cause considerable difficulties, though a definition is eventually determined. However, for this *IM*, the nature of the Berlin group meetings in East Berlin and the actual content of team visits seem to evade to him and his superiors, as reflected in written reports and assessments. About half of the factual information gathered is incorrect, including the spelling of the name of the organization. A typist, an officer, or the *IM* himself misspells the name, "Berlin-Fellow-Chips" being referred to until the mid-1970's.[136] Of course, it must be noted the Berlin Fellowship participants, east German and American, do take intentional and reasonable precautions in talking openly; this information is also found in the files. Precautions included not allowing pen-pals but also avoiding unnecessary writing or phoning inside the GDR; these actions are interpreted as conspiratorial. Eccardt's reported behavior involved carrying mail back and forth across the border, transferring cash donations and bringing fresh fruit and packaged foodstuffs as well as literature into the GDR; she readily talked about these actions with a few trusted friends in the east, including the *IM*. Thus, the *MfS* didn't want for information, but in fact this information is misunderstood, as are Eccardt's actions, for she is suspected of espionage and of trying to recruit agents.

It appears, as a part of the closing of the "Rollbahn" file, demoralization measures (*Zerzetzungsmassnahmen*) would be taken. In a one-time action, Eccardt is stopped at the border, interrogated, ordered to an appointment a week later, which she doesn't keep, and is to be refused entry to the country. Several individual members of the East Berlin group are to be visited by the *MfS*, with the purpose of planting mistrust and uncertainty about the leadership.[137] It is unclear, apart from the planned and executed border search and interrogation, which, if any, of these demoralization measures are ever carried out. In addition, Ursula Unterumsberger, a leader in the East Berlin group, is one of the subjects of a second operative procedure file (OV "*Radius*") and of some other demoralizing 'measures'; her apartment is searched and bugged, and she has her run-in with *Stasi* officers, but it all comes to naught. There are no further interrogations or apartment searches, and Eccardt is never stopped

---

[136] BStU MfS, BV/Gera, Abt. XII/Archiv, AOP1456/778, OV "*Rollbahn*" I, Zwischenbericht, 15.12.1974, 202-203.

[137] Lukasz Kaminski , et al (eds.), *Handbuch der kommunistischen Geheimdienste in Osteuropa 1944-1991*, Göttingen, 1991, 220. In the mid seventies a form of operative psychology was adopted by the MfS which sought to sow distrust of conflict between members of a group, seeking to loosen commitments to the church institutions or to hinder opposition forces in their actions.

from entering the GDR. Both of these actions are typical for the kind of tactics used by the *Stasi* to cause disruption, fear, and mistrust in a group. The *MfS* files also reveal telephone bugs, use of hidden tape recorders in private and group meetings, *MfS* interviews with Eccardt's neighbors from her West Berlin apartment house, handwriting samples, conspiratorial photographs, pages of "tailing" reports in East Berlin (*Stasi* officers following Schapp or Eccardt).

The *MfS* interest in Berlin Fellowship visits is initially incurred and heightened when an American team naively takes photos from a church tower in the *IM's* town. From that vantage point, a Soviet military installation can supposedly be seen, and this is all duly noted by the *IM*. Further this team meets with people in a Jena congregation, who were workers at the Zeiss plant. This congregation had scientists and academics in it (industrial espionage?). "What were these Americans looking for? We were motivated to find out!"[138]

The *MfS* interest is sustained, perhaps because they are unable to discern who is behind the Berlin Fellowship activities, where the money comes from and why Americans continue to come to the GDR. In the subsequent operative procedure file (OV, "*Radius*," 1978-1984) Eccardt and Zorn, who is by 1978 no longer involved in Berlin Fellowship, though under surveillance, are still being watched for "intentional abuse of constitutionally guaranteed freedom of belief in GDR citizens' church affiliations, use of relationships for information gathering, and for creating a negative clerical base in the GDR."[139] This file has three named persons for whom it was opened, Zorn, a former member of the Berlin Fellowship, Unterumsberger, a resident of East Berlin and member of the Berlin Fellowship, and East Berlin pastor and superintendent not involved in Berlin Fellowship.

5. The final decade 1979 – 1989

The late 70's and the 80's are punctuated on the national level with developments in the churches and in the society at large by which the state is challenged and in the end defeated. The state's church policy continues to be the same with ongoing orders and instructions from the Central Committee and the State Secretary for Church Questions to bring the

[138] Notes from personal interview with supervisory *Stasi* officer responsible for this IM and the OV "*Rollbahn*", Artur Hermann, Berlin, September 19, 2007.
[139] BStU, MfS, BV Berlin, Abt. XX, Reg.-Nr.—XVI644-73/84, Archiv-Nr. 1486/84 (5 Volumes), OV "*Radius*," Vol. III, 66.

church into conformity with the political stance of the ruling party. Conversations (*Gespräche)* are increasingly valued as the vehicle to cultivate the atmosphere for instruction of clergy and church leadership,[140] and this becomes a studied method and more intentional means of communication both at the national level (the conversation between Honecker and Schönherr on March 6, 1978) and at monthly or bi-monthly meetings held by government officials responsible for church questions at the district and local levels. In some cases, reports about local or district conversations indicate the statistics of how many of them have taken place. In the Potsdam district, for instance, in the year 1984, there were 4360 discussions and in 1985 there were (discussions between a state official responsible for church questions and a pastor, a superintendent, a synod member, a Christian educator, a parish nurse). It is then remarked that this conversation-partner system needs more attention given to choosing, training and qualifying the (state) partners.[141] These conversations were used not for mutual sharing or two-way communication but rather to instruct, convince, and evaluate.[142]

In the 80's, along with malaise and a growing dissatisfaction in the entire population, there are objections still being raised against military instruction in the schools, and the lack of freedom to travel, and the youth and young people of the country find their voices in 'blues' worship services with texts critical of the government (Zion congregation, Berlin). Environmental groups and publications critical of the GDR provoke the state authorities to react and sometimes drastically so. In addition, in 1988 and 1989 three Ecumenical Assemblies for Peace, Justice and Integrity of the Creation (WCC conciliar process launched in 1983) are convened in the GDR with both church and non-church alternative groups gathered for dialogue and earnest conversation about the need for

---

[140] Landesarchiv Berlin CRep104/541, Magistrat für Inneres, Referat für Kirchenfragen 1963-1983, Bericht über die Kirchenpolitischen Situation in der Haupstadt der DDR, "Personal conversation, the predominant method of our work, is further gaining significance." (*Die Hauptmethode unserer Arbeit, das persönliche Gespräch, gewinnt weiter an Bedeutung*), 1978, 5.

[141] Land Brandenburg Archiv Rep401/14854 Kirchenpolitische Arbeit 1972-1988, Rat des Bezirkes, Sektor Kirchenfragen, Potsdam, January 20, 1986, "*Ergebnisse der Arbeit auf dem Gebiet der Staatspolitik in Kirchenfragen im Bezirk Potsdam im Jahr 1985. "Gespräche: 1985-3506, 1984-4360. Das Gesprächspartnersystem für die Geistlichen und kirchliche Amtsträger konnte weiter ausgebaut werden. Die Auswahl geeigneter Gesprächspartner und derer Qualifizierung auf kirchenpolitischen Gebiet verlangen auch weiterhin großer Aufmerksamkeit.*" 263.

[142] Op.cit. Report January 12, 1975 entitled, "*Die Politik des sozialistischen Staates gegenüber den Kirchen und Religionsgemeinschaften und unsere Aufgaben bei der Erziehung der Geistlichen und kirchlichen Amtsträger zu einem sozialistischen Staatsbewusstsein.*" 495.

reform in the country.[143] The gatherings and resultant activity might be thought to have been just an ecumenical assembly addressing problems external to the GDR. In fact, for those on the inside and those watching closely, this assembly calling for social and political change is for the state potentially explosive but integral to what is evolving into a people‘s opposition movement in the whole country.[144]

The final decade of Berlin Fellowship visits before the Wall falls takes on a kind of regularity, while at the same time, this decade is one of growing unrest in the country. Anything but "regular" political and social happenings, like the conciliar process (see above), begin to punctuate visits and reports. Though many of the patterns for team visits have become "tradition," along with biblical themes or a watchword (*Losung*), new discussion topics related to the unrest occupy Berlin Fellowship conversation:

- The increasing numbers of applicants for emigration (*Ausreisewillige*) who are turning to the churches for counsel and help and the rise in the numbers of applicants who actually leave the GDR for example, 10,000 are allowed to leave in 1984 (application procedures have only been possible since the signing of the Helsinki Accords).
- Peace groups and the 1980 beginning of "peace decade" weeks each fall (*Friedensdekaden*) appears to both criticize and compete with the state peace initiatives. The "Swords into Ploughshares" (*Schwerde zu Pflugscharen*) action, the wearing of a cloth symbol with the biblical phrase, incites state criticism as well.[145]
- The 1980 Solidarity movement and its rise to recognition in Poland draw concern and interest of many East Germans.
- 1983 Luther Year celebrations are surprisingly acknowledged and sanctioned by the state, though primarily hosted by the Church.
- Michael Gorbachov's rise to power in the Soviet Union, his book *Perestroika* and a new posture from Moscow means many in the GDR have their hopes set on him.
- In 1989, both team visits are focused on the excitement and anxiety over recent events, like the opening of the Austria-Hungary border and the elections in the GDR May. The fall team reports reference conversations about the growing wave of demonstrations, numbers of people emigrating, reasons people are staying, and reforms needed in the country.

---

143 Stephen Brown, *Von der Unzufriedenheit zum Widerspruch: Der Konziliaren Prozess für Gerechtigkeit, Frieden und Bewahrung der Schöpfung als Wegbereiter der friedlichen Revolution in der DDR*, Frankfurt/Main 2010.

144 Heino Falcke, The Ecumenical Assembly for Justice, Peace and the Integrity of Creation, in: *The Ecumenical Review*, 56.2, 2004, 184-191.

145 Claudia Lepp and Kurt Nowak (eds.), *Evangelische Kirche im geteilten Deutschland* (1945-1989/90) Göttingen 2001, 77f.

Church-state relations wax and wane with military service issues, military education in the schools, and the state's deaf ear to the complaints of its citizens. As noted, in the second half of the 80's, peace and environmental activists openly seek and are given refuge under the "roof" of the church, the only "free space" in the society; this is greeted by some and spurned by other church members. Like it or not, the church leadership is called into action, and by 1989, congregations, particularly in the larger cities, become instrumental in the demonstrations and peaceful uprising which punctuate the weeks and months prior to the Wall being opened and the collapse of the GDR. Not all Berlin Fellowship congregations are active in this manner, but all are affected, anxious and engaged by the quickly growing movement in the fall of the 1989.

Throughout this time period, western leadership and the East Committee continue planning, evaluating and trying to expand the visitation program. All are aware that the long-standing participant congregations want return visits, but that it is important and even essential to send the Americans to new, perhaps more isolated or remote country congregations. Some Berlin staff members become close with easterners through the yearly and bi-yearly planning trips making those meetings not just times of planning but also of personal connections and intense sharing. With this awareness, the East's desire not to grow into an inner circle of regular hosts is alluded to in both the written western documentation and the eastern interviews. This might have perpetuated a mentality like that of the "*Reisekader*" (privileged GDR leaders in politics, from the sports world, universities, industry, and the church) whose status allowed them to travel to the west. In this specific regard, it must be noted this research question focuses on Berlin Fellowship and its former active eastern participants and does not include congregations and individuals not directly involved, who might have looked askew at such contacts with westerners or made such associations.

In the same time period, much proceeds regularly, in California, though a new set of "Standards and Procedures" for the Berlin Fellowship members is adopted.[146] In addition, church officials from West Berlin or from the east (i.e. Bishop Krusche in 1983 and OKR Herbert Meissner, chief ecumenical officer of the West Berlin church in 1985) come to the U.S. as guests of Berlin Fellowship and the Presbyterian Church (USA). The monthly East Berlin group (*Berliner-Gruppe*), an aspect of the Berlin Fellowship ministry known primarily to its partici-

[146] The Berlin Fellowship Standards and Procedures (approved March 1, 1980), Zinzendorf Collection.

pants as "Fellowship" (using the English word) meet, regularly as it has since the early 70's and hosts teams in East Berlin, upon leaving or returning from trip. The East Committee and the Berlin staff keep contact through regular planning trips and the annual meeting.

Though this final decade is basically a continuation of the visits, there are changes in the social and political scene in the east, in the very fabric of daily life, in the availability of goods, and in the needs that those visited might have. Teams begin to notice that what is experienced as a "hot topic" in the south may not be the case in the north, or that issues, like educational concerns for children, are not only seen differently by the various host families or pastors but actually experienced differently. The arbitrary nature of the society means that some pastors' children might not be allowed to study past grade 10 while others are allowed to get the *Abitur* (highest German high school diploma) or even go on to further studies. For the Americans, especially those who have participated on teams more than once, this means learning to interpret the "situation" in a more differentiated manner, resisting comparisons with previous visits as well as resisting generalizations about the country. The reports contain more personal stories rather than generalizations about "life in the GDR" (i.e. bad air, high rates of divorce, decrepit church buildings).

"In the GDR you can find everything, just not at the same time or everywhere." This statement or saying (*Spruch*), like many jokes, reveals much about the real world of daily life, and though it primarily refers to the availability of goods or services, it applies as well to congregational life, life in the workplace, life in the schools. Whereas one pastor may report that his confirmation pupils are bullied and mocked by their schoolmates of the Free German Youth, the state youth organization (*Freie Deutsche Jugend*, *FDJ*) and even by teachers, another pastor may report that the children who do not participate in the confirmation worship service, at least as visitors, would have to reckon with their peers as well. In one town, it is one way and at the same time, in another town or part of the country, it is another way.[147] Though hardly a revelation, the ongoing, constantly changing, relative and arbitrary nature of life for Christians in the GDR makes the communication a challenge for both guests and hosts.

In this decade some of the team members, now traveling to the east for the second or third time, have points of reference from former experiences and reflect this in their evaluations. As has been the case all along,

[147] Taped interview with Werner Krusche, Magdeburg April 24, 2008.

the American visitors return with stories, re-telling what their eastern hosts have recounted and experienced but also what their German hosts say about the experience or their lives. These reported "eastern voices," albeit second-hand, paint a limited but representative picture of life and faith for some Christians in the GDR. Besides a degenerating economic situation in the east between 1979 and 1989, ongoing pressure on school children, billboard propaganda, newspaper bias, party work groups, and political events, personal and congregational matters also stamp conversations.

Between 1979 and 1982, the team leader evaluation and eastern planning notes report efforts to "refine" the way the American teams function as well as suggestions on how the time in congregations is planned. An eastern suggestion to Berlin Fellowship California is that team members spend time in the U.S. getting to know one another better; that conversations during visits go deeper and that time be planned to allow for this (some visits are just too short); that the clear cultural as well as personal differences between Germans and Americans be talked about and acknowledged.[148] Americans are now requested by the eastern partners to be more knowledgeable and articulate about their own congregations, denominational traditions, and church history; they need to be prepared to share the negative and problematic aspects of being a Christian as well, not just talk about being a "happy Christian." Furthermore, the team members should be able to explain why they believe. For Americans to say "I have Jesus in my heart" is not enough.[149]

Throughout the 1980's issues of eastern resignation and weariness punctuate reports, along increasing degrees of questioning and uncertainty about how it can all go on. Though life on the family level is better, with fewer cares about basic material needs, the shortages of supplies, transport problems, and general lack of meaningful productivity in factories and businesses makes for depression and discouragement. Parental dismay and anger about repression, conformity, and pressures in the school system are standard themes. Nation-wide tensions reflected in the growing number of youth peace and environmental protest groups add to more cross-generational anxiety as early as 1983. Though youth were once more positive about the socialist ideology, that has changed, and the Christian youth visited are not immune to disillusion:

---

[148] Planning trip notes, Summer 1979, 26.3.79-1.4.79, Zinzendorf Collection.

[149] Lee Kliewer, Carol Primmer, B. Eccardt, T. Schapp (participant report), Key words from DDR Trip 13 -21, October 1980, Zinzendorf Collection.

> Martin is the son of a pharmacist. A Party worker came to Martin's school class and asked them to become Party members. There was no stirring among the class, so the fellow started going down the row, desk by desk, asking. He came to Martin, who was 16 at the time, and asked him why he was not standing up to join the Party. Martin said: 'Because I've seen many of my friends come forward with enthusiasm and then be disillusioned.' Today, a year later, Martin is still apparently in disfavor with the Party, and is having difficulty finding a job. Ultimately he will have to be employed, but maybe feeding pigs.[150]

Emigration applications continue to mount as do the emotions of those left behind in some cases often bitter, fearful or hopeless about possibilities for change in the socialist system with its arbitrary and dehumanizing atmosphere. There is talk of the "niche society" (*Nichegesellschaft*) in that people cope with the tension by withdrawing into their own corners or *niches*, turning to nature, friendships, music each a kind of retreat to a place of internal security.

> Three words that we heard most often were tension, loneliness, resignation....
> The church and church people live under *tension*:
> They no longer are put in jail for what they do (except in extreme cases like one pastor in the Leftist Peace movement), but they live under constant tensions. The primary one is probably the instruction the children get in the schools [...] Some children are refusing to take the military course or refusing especially to participate in the use of rifles.
> Everything that is written or published by the church must receive approval.
> Tension is caused by constant irritants and obstacles (lack of materials for building, goods appearing in a store one week and not the next, what may be said one moment is changed the next, etc.)
> *Loneliness* was heard second most often (I think the word isolation is better used here):
> Being restricted in travel is a kind of loneliness. Average church members don't necessarily travel outside the DDR.
> Parts of the country don't receive western television at all.
> Resignation is a danger: The people simply do not have a sense of commitment. We were told that many people would still agree that the church ought to exist but they will not take a stand and join the church. Life is just easier if you do not make a commitment. [151]

There is, however, another side to the story and a telling witness to the American guests themselves, one that does not go unnoticed. The American reflections and reports reveal their own learning about the context and situation:

---

[150] Stan Jones, Berlin Fellowship Report, July 1981, Zinzendorf Collection.
[151] Lee Kliewer, Berlin Fellowship trip evaluation, fall 1980, Berlin Fellowship Collection.

> Coming away, the one thought that really has stayed with me is that these people were ministering to me more than I was to them. To deal with these people, who have the courage of their Christian convictions, and the strength to see themselves through life is an honor and inspiring. They do not consider themselves special, just doing the best they can under the circumstances, which are difficult at best. They are better off than their counterparts further east, as they have better technology and access to western ideas through television. They do not ask for sympathy or praise, for our money or our advice; they simply need the contact with other Christians; brother helping brother in a Christian supportive atmosphere. They need to know that Christians elsewhere are concerned for them and that this way of life will give them what is missing in a socialist life; answers to the classic questions of 'who am I and why am I here'; a philosophy that is not based on economics, control and fear. They are prepared to live simply and poorly to support this belief. They need the contact with other Christians.[152]

Church tensions wax and wane, and the mood shifts from team to team and region to region. There is good news one visit, for example, people who have immediate relatives living in the west may now apply to travel to important family gatherings and celebrations (wedding, silver or golden anniversary, round birthdays, etc.).[153] At the same time, there is somber news with one pastor telling how eight of his confirmation boys were interrogated by their school director because they refuse to participate in a military training session for shooting pistols, automatic weapons, and using hand grenades.[154] The complaint is often that children and youth are being taught to think and act schizophrenically, talking one way in public and at school and another at home or in safe circles.

By 1986 it is almost palpable that there is a surprising kind of liberalization happening, evidenced by more exchanges with West Germany and a revival of a cultural and national self-awareness growing as village chronicles are taken up again and old folk songs and earlier traditions, once banned, are revived. At the same time church and state relations seem exceedingly fragile, with the church supporting the idea of freedom of travel and opening its doors to dissenters. It also must continue to deal with the military questions about a growing number of alternative service "building soldiers" (*Bausoldaten*) who have no affiliation with the churches. The Berlin-Brandenburg church in particular finds itself becoming a friend and a lawyer for environmental, peace and human rights groups and a conversation partner on such issues with folks from outside the church's normal circles. Church leadership at the Federation level is

---

[152] Margaret Nalbach, Report to the Session of Calvary Presbyterian Church, Berlin Fellowship Team Visitation to East Germany, June 10 to July 2 1980, Berlin Fellowship Collection.
[153] Op. cit.
[154] Planning trip notes, summer 1982, Hamburger Collection.

divided over this issue and is judged by some as too quiet about an "official" position, raising the anger and dismay of church members. Few of the Berlin Fellowship congregations are active in these last years of protest actions, but these matters, themes and topics are hot items for discussion with American visitors right up through the fall of 1989.

More East German voices

Over the years, the normal planning and team reports recount perspectives from individuals visited and their comments or questions, as recorded by the visitors. In 1981 one pastor urges caution to speak about politics in general, but he suggests something very specific and current. "Peace in and with Poland" is a very real topic, for his congregation is only kilometers from the Polish border. He contends that the whole mood in the GDR is most critical against Poland and that this attitude is being supported or even called for by the government. Another eastern voice concurred saying that pastors can think up lots to talk about in relation to the general topic of "peace," but that it would be important to address a real situation, Poland. He then notes that the Church often makes more propaganda for peace than the individual congregations are ready for.[155]

The American team reports in these years reflect upon and retell stories about daily life for East German citizens. One such report from July 1981 includes the writer's attempt at a form of verbatim reflection:

> I recall sitting in kitchen one day with his daughter, K, age 16, just the three of us. I asked her what she was going to do with her life. She said she had hoped to be a medical student, but that was impossible because she wouldn't take this Oath to the State. And that, second, she had thought of becoming a teacher at the University, because she is, according to her father, the brightest in her class. That was also impossible. Then tears came to her eyes, and she said she didn't know what she was going to do, at this point, with her life. So I said, her, "K, do you do this for your father because he is a pastor or is this from your own heart?" She looked at her father and she said, "Of course, I love my father, I'm very close to my father; but I do this from my own heart."[...] this situation in East Germany is reproducing the kind of Christian that can't play both ends against the middle.[156]

Reports also contain many citations that echo voices from the east and attempt to describe how the Americans were affected and changed by the witness of the German hosts:

---

[155] Notes from Planning Trip, Spring Team 1981, Zinzendorf Collection.
[156] Stan Jones, Berlin Fellowship Report, July 1981, Zinzendorf Collection.

> The people who impressed me most were not the outspoken and critical anti-Communists, muttering and cynical about the State and the system. They were, rather, people like Dr. , a Christ-like figure who was very tired the day we were with him. But he took us around the crowded and inadequate quarters of his hospital. They have 130 beds in that hospital, with children filling every one of them. I asked this man how the State felt about his hospital. He told me: "They like the nurses we produce. In the last 5 years we've produced 127 nurses, of which the Health Bureau has said, 'We can't get nurses like these from other schools. They not only are skilled, but they also care.' So the Dept. of Health is pleased. But the Dept. of Education is displeased, because of the news that out of a Christian hospital is coming the kind of nurses the State needs.[157]

Eastern critique and humor often go together. Slogans on ubiquitous billboards around the country are often the brunt of jokes. Slogans like, "The power of the people is for the welfare of the people" or "My workplace: My battleground for peace." One of the eastern hosts, when asked what people thought of the slogans, answered, "What slogans? If you leave anything anywhere for more than two weeks, people don't see it anymore. They ought to at least move them around so you see a different slogan now and then."

Jokes and sayings to counter the depression, skepticism, and resignation were always a welcome addition to an evening of conversation:

- A father said to his son, "We have a new, more efficient car this year. They've decided not to put a motor in it's very fuel efficient." The son asks, "But then how does it run?" The father answers, "Never mind, everything in East Germany is down-hill."
- There is the one about a man who was walking at night, who suddenly said out loud, "Crappy country!" There was a sudden hand on his shoulder, and the policeman said, "Come with me." The man protested, "Why? I didn't say WHAT country!" The policeman relented. "I guess you're right. I'll have to let you go." Five minutes later the same hand hits the man's shoulder, and the policeman says, "Come with me." The man says, "I thought we had this worked out." The policeman, however, insists, "It could only have been this country."
- The system is not producing the "social man" (*sozialistischer Mensch*) as hoped. They speak of private pigs. There's private property being created more and more as people invest more of their time in the after-hours production. They explained that a 'private pig' is when a litter comes, and there are, say, 8 little pigs in the litter. You create 'private pigs' by reporting 6.[158]

[157] Ibid.
[158] Ibid.

However, there were many Germans who did more than tell jokes to lighten the mood; there were eastern voices calling for faithfulness, affirming the Berlin Fellowship visitation as a worthy endeavor:

> We must use this opportunity of visitation to find the way to mutual understanding together. What separates us up front should be dismantled. In our meetings we need to put it all out on the table, our requirements for life [...] honestly both sides have security and insecurity, both the Amis and the Germans. Overcome the already baked prejudices and ignorance that is what we're to be doing. For this, both sides need a good dose of trust. [159]

And the expressions of both gratitude and need for support and recognition offer yet another picture of this time period:

> As you know, as a church in the GDR we are trying to walk in the way of discipleship, being faithfully obedient, under the new conditions of a socialist society. We say yes to God's planned way to be church as difficult as it is, as a minority church in a land where once the entire population belonged. For this we need the brotherly caring accompaniment of other members in other churches. Besides, we want you from non-socialist countries, to get a picture of life here, in order to understand us and to help dismantle false assumptions and a false picture.[160]

> For the many years you have made it your task to develop relationships with church parishes in our country, to expand them and to deepen them. In accordance with the possibilities at your command you have thus visibly expressed the fellowship which is given to us in the Lord Jesus Christ\, and you have made that fellowship experienceable, I am extremely grateful to you for this ministry [...] In conversations with those of you who have visited me in Eisenach I have sensed that your faith has been strengthened as we have heard the word of God together and prayed together, just as the faith of our parish members has been strengthened. This confirms our experience that it is neither our good will nor our capacity which brings about and maintains the bonds of the church of Jesus

---

[159] Reinhard Glöckner, East Committee Meeting, Feb. 21, 1983, Zinzendorf Collection, Berlin. "Wir müssen die Gelegenheit dieser Besuche nutzen, um gegenseitiges Verständnis bemüht zu sein. Die Differenzen im Vorfeld gilt es abzubauen. Bei den Begegnungen ehrlich die Voraussetzungen für das Leben auf den Tische legen welche Sicherheiten und Unsicherheiten haben beide Seiten: die Amis und die Ostdeutschen? Fertige Vorurteile und Ignoranz überwinden---darum sollte es gehen. Dafür braucht jede Seite eine gute Portion Vertrauen."

[160] Werner Krusche, Letter to Berlin Fellowship Southern California, Nov. 18, 1983, Zinzendorf Collection, "Wie Sie wissen, versuchen wir als Kirchen in der DDR den Weg des Glaubensgehorsame in der Nachfolge Christi unter den neuen Bedingungen einer sozialistischen Gesellschaft zu gehen. Wir sagen Ja zu dem uns von Gott zugedachten Weg von einer Kirche, zu der einmal fast die ganze Bevölkerung gehörte, zu einer Minderheitskirche, auch wenn das einer sehr schwieriger Weg ist. Dazu brauchen wir die brüderliche aufmerksame Begleitung durch Glieder anderer Kirchen. Andererseits liegt uns euch daran, dass Christus aus nicht-sozialischten Ländern sich selber ein Bild machen von unserem Leben, um uns zu verstehen und bestimmte falsche Vorstellungen abbauen zu helfen."

> Christ; it is rather Jesus Christ himself who is at work in our midst and who links us to each other.[161]

As is apparent, Berlin Fellowship's visitation program has been "faithfully" accompanied by attention from the MfS and its unofficial informer, the *IM*, remains a participant in the East Committee, in the Berlin group, and in hosting American teams in his congregation. Even though one file, OV "*Rollbahn*" is officially closed in 1978, OV "Radius" is opened and maintained through 1984. In addition to OV "*Radius*," the *MfS* open yet another operative procedure file, OV "*Resident*," mainly to assemble information about Zorn, not active with Berlin Fellowship but still under suspicion of espionage. This file contains reports on Zorn and Berlin Fellowship activities, the IM's personal conversations with Schapp and Eccardt, reports on Berlin group meetings, East Committee meetings, and team trip plans. This file stops quite abruptly in 1986, and there is no formal final report. It may be assumed that "*Resident*" and perhaps "*Radius*" may have been still active files in November 1989 when the opening of the Berlin wall occurs, and as with many MfS records, these files have disappeared or have been destroyed.[162]

MfS suspicions are never substantiated, even though the IM continues gathering information perhaps through 1988.[163] However insidious and overarching these files appear, the researched and available material shows no record of follow-through on many of the "action" plan items, no written evaluation of *IM* reports, no examination of problematic issues like the transfer of money or letters that were carried into the country, both of which are questionably legal activities. Though educated at the *MfS* center in Potsdam, *MfS* officers are not theologically educated which certainly contributes to confusion about information they are working with.[164] Half-true information and suppositions, suspected U.S. intelligence connections, trips both the *IM* and Eccardt take to the Soviet Union during these years all add to the "intrigue," but the end result in the case of Berlin Fellowship is nothing more than 5,000 pages of file reports.

---

[161] Werner Leich, Letter to Presbyterian Congregations (translation), May 15 1986, Berlin Fellowship Collection.

[162] Research application for this dissertation was first made to the Federal Commission for the Stasi Files in 2005 (see Bibliography and Sources). Two subsequent applications for 'new' material, in 2008 and 2012, produced nothing new.

[163] BStU Archiv der Zentralstelle, MfS Abt.X/1580, Department for International Connections/*Internationale Verbindungen*, Nr. 641-82, January 12-June 6 1988 , 232-9, labeled top secret (*streng geheim*), this series of reports on Ted Schapp and his parish activities with the Polish Reformed congregations comprise the latest dated *MfS* state records available for this research.

[164] Vollnhals, *Die Kirchenpolitik*, 84.

Apart from a few isolated comments and the demoralization measures described above, there are no "findings" that either interest the *MfS* administration or lead them to wonder further about Berlin Fellowship or its key figures. Both "*Rollbahn*" and "*Radius*" are closed for lack of concrete evidence.[165] That is, no evidence of legally punishable operations were found, and the suspicion of espionage (Strafgesetzbuch der DDR, paragraph 98) was unfounded.[166]. That a new operative procedure file for Zorn is opened in 1984 might attest to a bureaucracy perpetuating itself, or perhaps the *MfS* simply wanting to keep its finger on the pulse "just in case" something turned up.[167] Regardless, the effort seems to prove fruitless. The *IM*, who might be able to provide answers to these and many other open questions, is unavailable for this research.

Conclusion

In cooperation with the Evangelical Church of Berlin-Brandenburg, the organization known as Berlin Fellowship begins in the early 1960's, as a kind of "happening" or "movement" evolving out of "world deputation" teams from the First Presbyterian Church of Hollywood.By the early 1970's Berlin Fellowship takes on an organizational form as a kind of ecumenical program with American participants who are primarily Presbyterian lay persons and clergy and East German participants from 12-20 different congregations. In Berlin, two church workers, Pastor Schapp (American Presbyterian) and Frau Eccardt (West Berlin parish coworker), become permanent staff , and teams of Americans (between 2 and 12 people) travel to the GDR twice yearly to visit Christians and Protestant congregations in the German Democratic Republic. A group of key leaders from the various cities and regions in the GDR is formed and begins to meet yearly. Known as the East Committee, this group evaluates U.S. team visits and plans for future visits in their own and neighboring congregations. The Berlin staff conducts yearly planning trips in preparation for team visits. Berlin Fellowship also becomes identified with a small group of friends from East Berlin, labeled "Fellowship" (*die Berlinergruppe*), and this group meets monthly with the Berlin staff.

---

[165] BStU MFS 1486/84, 24-page Final Report for "*Radius*"(*Abschlußbericht*) states as reason for closing and archiving this file, lack of confirmation for suspicion of legally punishable operations (*Nichtbestätigung des Verdachts strafbarer Handlungen §98 StGB*), January 2 1984, 156-169.

[166] Cf. Chapter 3, Developmental Beginnings 1967-1970

[167] Notes from personal interview with Joachim Wiegand, former Stasi officer and director of MfS Dept. XX/4, Berlin, February 2, 2007, indicate this as a possible explanation for continuing observation, even though orginal two files, *Rollbahn* and Radius, had already been closed.

Coincident to the work in Berlin, the Berlin Fellowship group in southern California meets monthly or bi-monthly with 20-30 in attendance and 50+ on the mailing list. Minutes of the meetings are sent to Berlin regularly, and membership lists are amended yearly. Planning correspondence between Berlin and California continues, as often as twice monthly. A list of 'disciplines' is proposed and adopted,[168] and by 1980 new "standards and procedures" are adopted. The Berlin Fellowship meetings in California are times of information sharing, study, reports from returning team members, discussion about recruitment, selection for upcoming teams, and prayer for friends in the east.

As the 1970's close, Berlin Fellowship sees a kind of "regularizing" of the visitation program. The general social, economic and political issues and questions are always topics for team orientation in Berlin, and central to discussion during congregation visits. Other topics of interest include matters related to the East German Church like the communist youth dedication (*Jugendweihe*), confirmation practices which changed over the years, and alternative military service (*Bausoldaten*). Though sometimes introduced in worship services, teams usually and primarily meet with small groups in the congregations. More and more new congregations are visited, keeping some of the "old" standby congregations as yearly or bi-yearly visits, usually on the weekends of the 12-day visit in the GDR. The American team members come from all occupations, and the eastern request to have special "types" of Americans can be fulfilled on occasion. The group in southern California regularly ponders and reviews its motives and structure, financial stability, and the minutes reflect ongoing self-examination and critical reflection about motivation. From the very outset of the program, the question of motivation is also factor for the MfS, who position an IM in the center of the Berlin Fellowship eastern leadership group. The *Stasi* is active and quite thorough in its information gathering efforts from as early as 1969, and although the efforts continue for about twenty years, the two main "official" files on Berlin Fellowship are both closed, due to lack of evidence of illegal ac-

[168] Opening paragraph defines the Berlin Fellowship: The Berlin Fellowship is an informal organization of Christians who share a concern for the life and spiritual support of our Christian brethren in the churches of Berlin, the German Democratic Republic, and the Federal Republic of Germany. Under the sponsorship of the Synod of Southern California of the United Presbyterian Church in the USA, the Berlin Fellowship is open to all Christians who wish to share this basic concern. The Fellowship expresses its concern through its prayer for the German churches, through visitations at the invitation of German churches, through financial support of worthwhile objectives, through sponsorship of meaningful exchanges where possible, and through continual study of the situation of our brethren in that part of the world. A proposal, July 5, 1969, Hamburger Collection.

tivity. In an interview with one of the MfS officers responsible for the administrative oversight of the Berlin Fellowship file, I asked what the bottom line assessment of Berlin Fellowship was. The answer he gave "meaningless" (*bedeutungslos*).[169]

Over the course of two decades, Berlin Fellowship "participants" meet and plan both in Germany and in California. Teams of American Christians travel to East Germany for the purpose of visiting, encouragement and sharing in fellowship on the congregational level with brother and sister Christians in the GDR. Between 1961 and 1989, more than 100 individual East German congregations in all regions of the GDR host 45 teams of Americans. Although there are hundreds of conversations and encounters that occur over the years, the only documented material about those conversations is found in the West Berlin Zinzendorf Collection and in archived American team reports, sermons, and letters. This chapter's rehearsal of the East German voices and anecdotal reports, western data and correspondence and contextual information from the time period provides a foundation from which to listen further to the voice and perspectives of the eastern partners in the interviews.

[169] Wiegand interview notes, February 2, 2007.

Chapter Four

Eastern Participant Interview Data - Analysis and Discussion

> I remember a very moving conversation (with an American visitor). There were lots of children, and the question was asked, 'What do you know about America?' And a small young girl then spoke as she had been taught in school: "The Americans are our enemies," or prescribed phrasing in the GDR which had been taught. And I can still see right in front of me, how our guest took a deep breath, was stunned for a minute by this spontaneous answer from a small girl. And then she answered, rightly I think and asked in return, "Do you believe that I am your enemy?" And then I noticed how this little girl thought about this and then said, "No." And I think that is an explanation for the effect of the entire ministry.[1]

This story is a mini-incident and unique glimpse of a Berlin Fellowship encounter between an American guest and a group of East German children gathered for an after-school Christian education program. Though hardly as dramatic, similar episodes punctuate most of the 27 transcribed interviews of eastern participants in the Berlin Fellowship program; this chapter will compile and synthesize similar stories, recollections and other regularly occurring findings, observations, opinions, themes, and vocabulary. This short episode with a visitor and a child acts as both example and paradigm for that which the following pages will clarify, as

---

[1] Taped interview with Bernhard Stempel, Oberoderwitz, October 19, 2005, "Und da entsinn´ ich mich an ein sehr bewegendes Gespräch, und ich glaube, das war Jane Holslag, die dort angesprochen hat. Da warn viele Kinder, warn viele Kinder da und was wisst ihr von Amerika. Und da sagte ein Mädchen, so wie sie es in der Schule gelernt hatte: 'Die Amerikaner sind unsere Feinde, ' oder so eine Formel, die man versuchte, in der DDR den Kindern einzugeben. Und ich seh´ noch vor mir, wie die Jane die Luft anhielt, fassungslos war einen Augenblick ob dieser Antwort, einer spontanen Antwort eines kleinen Mädchens. Und dann richtig reagierte, denke ich, in dem sie rückfragte: 'Glaubst du, dass ich dein Feind bin?' Und dann merkte ich, wie das Mädchen überlegte und dann sagte: 'Nein.' Und ich denke, das ist, damit ist auch die ganze Arbeit erklärt, was das bewirkt hat."

the eastern "perspectives" of the Berlin Fellowship encounters and experiences emerge.

After a description of the interview process and procedures, I shall describe how the coding process evolved, from the initial code category list to the composing of this chapter. The coding process, code family groupings, and the data analysis follow. I am using a form of grounded theory analysis as the foundation for discussion throughout the chapter but especially as key to the conclusions.

There are several very clear limitations and parameters to this manner of qualitative rhetorical text analysis. Because I was both a participant in the 1980's and in leadership in the 1990's in Berlin and the east and acquainted with almost all of those interviewed, my knowledge, access to people and records, along with my own recollections (for instance the details of the above incident) undoubtedly affect this entire data analysis process. Secondly, these interviews took place 15-25 years after the events and incidents being recalled; this distance in time affected each interviewee, and they mention this more than once. In addition, I am neither a sociologist nor a historian, but after attending a short course on interviewing and oral history (OMSC, Overseas Missionary Study Center, New Haven, Connecticut) and doing reading on qualitative analysis, I conducted as thorough and as careful a series of interviews as I could. I sought to be as attentive to the process and as careful and objective with the data as possible. Lastly, the fact that I was both an American Berlin Fellowship participant and an acquaintance of many of those interviewed played no small role in both the ease of interviewing and my own assessment techniques. All of this then contributes to the subjective and qualitative nature of the research; I trust it also enhances the nature of analysis and evaluation.

However, these very interesting and often surprising findings are the central issue, and they are so revealing as to merit focused attention. Apart from my analysis for this research, these interviews constitute a contribution to the theological and missional discussion of *koinonia* and the role it played and plays in *missional* engagement, encounter, and in ecumenical exchange. As stated previously in this research, the role recipients and partners play in missional activities seems to have been generally an overlooked and under-researched matter, particularly in such intercultural or intercontextual Christian missional activities. However, the conversation partners in this visitation program played an enormous role, and their reflections offer many insights, some quite new, into the nature of fellowship, offering noteworthy information about missionality.

1. Methodology

Between March 2005 and December 2008, I conducted more than 40 interviews with former Berlin Fellowship German participants and with church officials from both West and East Berlin. All of these church officials were aware of Berlin Fellowship's activities but did not participate directly in the program. I also interviewed Bärbel Eccardt (German), Ted Schapp (USA), and Ralph Zorn (USA), the three leading personages from West Berlin. After a brief biographical statement from the interviewees, they were asked the following questions:

1. Concerning Berlin Fellowship, how did you become involved? Do you know now when you began with Fellowship?
2. How often did your parish host teams? Which years? What did your congregation do when teams came?
3. Can you recall a particular or special meeting or occasion when a team was with you? What made that encounter special or different?
4. How did Berlin Fellowship influence or affect your parish or your family?
5. Were you a member of the East Committee? When you traveled to Berlin for those meetings, what happened?
6. Did you ever have problems, with church higher-ups/officials, the STASI or anyone else? Did you ever have doubts or second thoughts about being a Berlin Fellowship participant?
7. What, in your opinion, was Berlin Fellowship? How would you describe that program today? Did you see it that same way back then?
8. As pastor or as lay person, how do you value or gauge the value of the time, the encounters, the meetings, or this kind of contact from today's perspective? Did you see it the same back then?
9. Do you have other thoughts or reflections about Berlin Fellowship you would like to express?[2]

---

[2] German version:

1. Es geht jetzt um Berlin Fellowship. Wie bist du dazu gekommen, mit Fellowship zu arbeiten? Weißt Du jetzt wenn Du angefangen hast?
2. Wie oft hat deine Gemeinde Teams gehabt? Welche Jahre? Was habt Ihr in Eurer Gemeinde mit Teams gemacht?
3. Kannst Du dich an eine besonderen Anlass oder Begegnung dich erinnern? Warum ist das Treffen besonders gewesen?
4. Wie hat BF deine Gemeinde, deine Familie, dich beeinflusst?
5. Bist Du in dem Ostkomitee gewesen? Wenn Ihr nach Berlin(zu Ostkomiteesitzung) gefahren seid, was passierte dort?
6. Hast Du je Problemen bekommen? (Stasi, Kirchenbehörde, usw.) Zweite Gedanken, Zweifel?
7. Was, Deiner Meinung nach, war Berlin Fellowship? Wie beschreibst du dieses Program heute? Hast Du das so damals auch gesehen?
8. Als Pastor/Laie, wie wertest Du diese Zeit, diese Begegnungen, diese Treffen, diese Kontakte aus? Von der heutigen Sicht? Damals?

These questions were often answered by the eastern participants before they were posed, in part because the interviewees seemed quite anxious to talk about Berlin Fellowship, and they often opened up with memories, stories, and their own opinions and perspectives on the program, its strengths and weaknesses, and their own involvement. I conducted all interviews in German, and they were transcribed by native speakers. I have translated all German interview citations in this research into English, and all participants signed releases allowing interview material to be used for research purposes. All direct quotations appear in German in footnotes. In addition, this list of questions, which is primarily a general overview and history-giving inquiry, was not designed with the current research question in mind; my initial research direction was to capture in broad terms the eastern perspective of the experience. Because the western records contain thorough program details, I was not looking for recollection of what happened as much as personal recall of how it happened, why participation was important, what resulted, and how the Berlin Fellowship program was received and critiqued then and now.

The transcribed interviews represent a "mixed" group of former participants from various locations in the former German Democratic Republic. These men and women were chosen, in part, for their availability, the length of time they were active in the program and their status as either lay (twelve persons) or clergy (fifteen persons). There were fifteen men and twelve women, ten of these 27 had participated less than five years. Five of the seven couples represented clergy (pastors - male), while one of those couples had both husband and wife as clergy. The interview process could have continued for months, for there were more people eager to be interviewed, and there were a handful of "one-timers" whose voices should have been sought out. However, the time available for research ended. Since virtually nothing substantial had been written down by the easterners, interview participants were recalling information and drawing on memories from as many as 30 years previous; furthermore, all but one or two had no journals or diaries, calendars or letters to which they might refer. In the case of a few of the pastors, there were some scant and somewhat encrypted notes in work calendars[3]; generally, however, all interviewees relied on recall. For those interviewees, who had in the meantime travelled to the USA and visited Berlin Fellowship contacts or who had since developed personal friendships with Ameri-

9. Hast Du noch Gedanken über BF oder Bemerkungen dazu?

[3] i.e. Wolfgang Müller, personal *Amstkalendar* notations: June 21, 1983, June 23, 1984, August 7, 1987, June 22, 1988, private holdings.

cans in the years since 1990, the recollections may have been shaded by those encounters and experiences.

For the actual coding and categorizing of the transcript texts, I first listened and read through the interview transcripts, coding as I went, initially using a list of key words gleaned from the second chapter of this research, which I label "prescribed" codes (See Appendix 2). Over the course of the coding period, categories or labels I didn't anticipate emerged, which I call "emergent." During the second and third rounds of selected text review, I didn't listen to the recordings again, but quotation excerpts were refined and edited and in some cases, code groups were combined, labels changed, or new code groups emerged. ATLASti.5 is the software program used for the coding and analyzing process. Although I did not use the full potential of this software, it enabled management of over 1500 quotations and provided basic data regarding groundedness. A theory emerged which illumines and illustrates the research question, providing this chapter's discussion.

2. Code Labels and Code Families

The starting point for an initial code list contained over 100 terms which might be associated either with fellowship or with mission and missionality. As interviews began to reflect certain similarities, repeated patterns of expression, word choice, and vocabulary, the number of categories narrowed to 30 code categories, which included both prescribed and emergent categories. Groundedness, the number of quotations labeled with a given code, offered a key to begin the following analysis and pointed to some initial answers regarding the research question, "Is fellowship encounter a missional experience?" (see Appendix 3)

From 27 interviews, this list provides the basis for this chapter's discussion:

CODE CATEGORY	GROUNDEDNESS
1. DDR/GDR context	266
2. essence of Berlin Fellowship	228
3. direct result of Berlin Fellowship	224
4. personal encounter	216
5. recognition	184
6. qualitative descriptionn	161
7. sharing of a personal memory	156
8. conversation	146

9.	name or specific person remembered	135
10.	information learned or corrected	133
11.	boundaries, borders	112
12.	America and American	103
13.	different contexts shared	94
14.	faith sharing	78
15.	other ecumenical/partner contact	62
16.	missional witness	60
17.	critical view of BF	59
18.	encounter with world	53
19.	thematic discussion	50
20.	hospitality	47
21.	motivation for BF participation	43
22.	celebration	42
23.	education/exposure children or youth	34
24.	Bible study	34
25.	tourist activity	32
26.	surprise	31
27.	"third bank"/Ephesian Moment	28
28.	table fellowship	21
29.	*Feindbild*-picture of the enemy	18
30.	belonging	12

The above code labels seemed to fall naturally into four code families, and these code families provide the framework for this chapter's discussion:

Context Family: 441
(the "givens" and context reference relating to the historical time period, the locale, the political, social, religious context of the Berlin Fellowship visits)

- GDR Context
- Boundaries and Borders
- America and Americans

Activities Family: 179
(programmatic and activity aspects of "being Church" mentioned or referred to, as well as activities done together with American guests)

- Thematic Discussion

- Celebration (worship, parish festivals)
- Bible Study and Discussion
- Tourist Activity
- Table Fellowship

Koinonia Family: 1036
(shared and participatory fellowship via contact, conversation, intentional exchange, time spent together, mutuality)

- Essence of Berlin Fellowship
- Personal Encounter
- Recognition
- Conversation, Qualitative Description of Encounter, Sharing of a Personal Memory, Name of Person Remembered
- Faith Sharing
- Different Contexts Shared, Other Ecumenical Partnerships
- Hospitality

Outcomes Family: 623
(happened as a result of Berlin Fellowship, change noted in understanding, outlook, action, or perspective in eastern participant's assessment or in the congregation)

- Direct Result of Berlin Fellowship
- Information Learned or Corrected, Encounter with World beyond the doorstep, Education/Exposure for youth and children, Picture of Enemy changed
- Critical View of Berlin Fellowship
- Motivation

Three of the code categories could fit in several families, but these code categories, Missional Witness, "third bank" / Ephesian Moment, and Surprises shall be addressed separately as part of the conclusion of this chapter.

The largest code families are Koinonia and Outcomes. Koinonia reflects the essence of the program, and interviews speak primarily in terms of the personal encounter, recognition, and conversation. The Outcomes family is less substantial in size though still important. Activities turn out to be only a small part of how the interviewees recall their Berlin Fellowship experience and seem to build cohesion for the encounters. The Context family provides the setting for the Berlin Fellowship encounters and the starting point for discussion and code family analysis. In the following discussion of each code family, there are redundancies, reflecting density of some code labels. This discussion will not attempt to address those; these repetitions indicate a more complex system of analysis than I was prepared to undergo.

3. Code Family Analysis

The larger setting and context for the time period covered in this research is the German Democratic Republic (founding 1949 to reunification in 1990). It was in East Germany, after the Berlin Wall was built, that 25 years of formalized Berlin Fellowship visits between and East German Christians took place (1963/4-1989). Though a member of the Warsaw Pact, East Germany was not an ordinary member of this communist alliance. It was a walled-in, fenced-off nation on the frontier border between these countries and Western Europe. This border, known as the Iron Curtain, also defined the context of life for residents and visitors. The Berlin Wall, though not built until 1961, came to be the central symbol for that "border and boundary" which determined the post WWII geographic, political, social, economic and religious frontier between east and west. Americans, as visitors to the GDR behind the Iron Curtain and the Berlin Wall, made up the third contextual aspect for this research and interview analysis. These American visitors were not fellow Europeans or comrades from other east bloc countries; they were not brother or sister West Germans, but rather they were citizens from the land of an enemy, the capitalist west. As representatives of that enemy, they were the very persons least likely expected as tourists or visitors in this country. Most importantly, they were Christians visiting Christians.

In spite of this larger setting and context, it was within this context that Christian-to-Christian contact occurred and fellowship or *koinonia* happened. This *koinonia* was experienced through personal encounter, ensuing conversation and recognition, faith sharing and witness, indeed, missional witness. It was occasioned through typical kinds of Christian activities (Bible study and table fellowship) and resulted not only in change and learning for the eastern Germans but also motivation for continued contact, active and repeated participation, and a distinct form of experiencing this missional endeavor with new self-understanding.

All of this happened and is attested to by the eastern participants, whose voices now tell their side of the story, a story thus far only represented by the western voices, western documentation and American visitors' reports. The remainder of this chapter will be shaped by the code categories and family groupings which address the research question and its key concepts of fellowship and missionality.

Context Family 441 quotations

Three codes, (1) DDR Context, (2) America and (3) Americans, Borders and Boundaries compose this code family and act as a stage setting and backdrop for the entire data gathering and analysis. Each contribute to the setting for the Berlin Fellowship visits, but the encounters themselves are most important to the research question at hand.

The larger framework, the context and conditions in East Germany under which Berlin Fellowship operated have been covered in Chapter 3 of this research. Virtually every interviewee referred in one way or another to the "situation" in the GDR, the living conditions, school matters, travel restrictions, and most often the border. At least 83 times the word wall or border occurs (*Mauer* 28, *Grenze* 55); this boundary was a fact, a part of the scenery, the reality with which East Germans lived. Related verb forms (being walled in or fenced off, insulated, cut off) also occurred regularly not as complaints but in descriptive statements of fact. This insular (*abgeschottet*) GDR as a "place of residence" with its distinct borders and boundaries was entered by America and Americans, markedly affecting the picture. Almost as a matter of fact, these foreigners, labeled by the state as particularly hostile (*feindlich*) people, were surprising visitors and at the same time welcomed as guests in the Christian homes and congregations they visited.

The border or boundary and the anti-capitalist, anti-western, anti-American propaganda colored all relationships for Berlin Fellowship from the outset, regardless of whether the border was understood to be physical, political, economic, geographic, social, religious or cultural. In fact, it was the building of the Berlin Wall and the change in travel restrictions, a physical and political assault on the city of Berlin in particular on August 13, 1961, which contributed to the first group of American Presbyterians being urged by German hosts to attend a pastors' conference in East Berlin that same autumn. The tension in the city, as well as across the entire country, added to the dramatic and initially unusual and even exotic nature of these first years' visits. The border itself and its somewhat porous nature prior to 1961 meant tens of thousands of refugees could flee to the west through Berlin, necessitating refugee camps in West Berlin and West Germany throughout the 1960's.

Looking back, interviewees articulate the undeniable factor of this wall and amazement at the fact that people from the other side crossed over it to visit them; the interviewees all refer repeatedly to the border's existence and its power to create a ghetto-like life, to wall in, to lock up, to isolate, to insulate, and to cut off news from the outside (especially in the area around Dresden). While at the same time and often in the same sentence, they also repeatedly comment on the ways in which visitors from the other part of the world afforded them a window on the world, a glance over the edge of the dinner plate (*über den Tellerand* a phrase used by several of the interviewees), a widening of the horizon. Besides just looking beyond the horizon, interviewees considered the Americans who had crossed the border as occasioning an expansion or liberation in thinking beyond the condition of being "locked in." Meeting with the visiting Americans meant the visited had contact (*Kontakt*), personal contact with the outside, with the other side, with the very persons who were labeled and judged opponents, who came specifically to visit them.

That the visitors were from America particularly seems to play a role for many of those interviewed. Many note this by tone of voice, expression and commentary. Some interviewees draw attention to the fact that these visitors paid for their own travel and time in the GDR, took their vacation days to come, while others find it noteworthy that the Ami's, as they are called, underwent less than welcoming experiences entering and leaving the country. Often, there is a remark about the Americans being "from outside," that is, not from West Germany; they were a special kind of ecumenical guests, whose "otherness" made them different. It is no surprise that the words America, American, or Ami occurred in all interviews, but that these very guests had also been labeled by the state as the "enemy of the people" (*der Klassenfeind*) contributed to this especially unusual situation.

Of course, the East Germans knew they were meeting sister and brother Christians, but the dividing line between these two peoples was not simply erased because of a shared tenet of faith. It was clear that even with these other Christians, the borders of understanding needed to be crossed, thus the border was not only a physical boundary and reality but a spiritual one as well. However, the border had not only a negative effect, for it is quite often noted by the easterners that being cut off from the outside (from the other side) somehow made "something" unique happen in a Berlin Fellowship encounter. This separating border was a physical but also an existential reality for all involved. Many of those interviewed sought to pinpoint the essence of this unique border crossing, to put their finger on just what it was that happened. This is labeled "contact" (*Kontakt*), an oft-repeated word in the interviews. These were "[…] visits from Christians from the other side of the border, over which we could never go […] contact from others to us, from others who've walked into a one-way street."[4] For this speaker, that the visitors *entered* and "crossed over" is a special aspect of the Berlin Fellowship contacts.

Preceding the time period of this research in the post-World War II 1950's and early 1960's, the early and initial contacts between Americans and Germans focused on reconciliation. Though that thematic focus was less and less central in the 1970's and 1980's, the dividing wall between these two peoples nonetheless was penetrated, crossed, perhaps broken down, affording a way for a meeting and a reconciliation. As one person remarked, "America and the GDR they were two worlds and between these two worlds, suddenly, [we had] a bridge [...]"[5] That way or that bridge was discovered most readily and not surprisingly in Christians doing what Christians do when they gather as Church, as congregations, as believers in fellowship with other believers praying, singing, worshiping. These very traditional church-related activities, common meeting ground for Christians around the globe, were, as well, the means of engagement and opening the door for initial contact and deeper conversation. It is this ensuing conversation and the happening in a personal encounter which is remembered most vividly by eastern participants; however, along with that conversation, the activities which guests and hosts engaged in provide a further contextual setting.

Activities Family 179 quotations (Bible Study, Celebration/worship-/prayer/festivals, Thematic Discussion, Table Fellowship, Tourist Activities)

Though interviewees mentioned and referred to the Activities that a host congregation would plan as part of the American visitors' program, the occurrence of these references is considerably less significant than I anticipated. This code family is the least well-grounded. However, each code merits brief examination and remark:

(1) Table Fellowship. References are mostly about meals shared with the visitors in homes or in a larger gathering. The topic is mentioned 21 times in fourteen interviews in relation to celebration, to conversation, and to tourist activities. Eating together and conversing are usually mentioned in conjunction with each other.

(2) Tourist Activities includes everything from a walk through a nearby forest to a picnic to touring a cathedral, attending a concert or traveling to

[4] Taped interview with Wolfgang Mueller, Kamenz, November 21, 2005, "Kontakte zu schaffen, Besuche von Christen über Grenzen hinweg, die wir von uns aus nicht übertreten können, wo wir nicht hinkönnen, Kontakte von anderen zu uns, die in eine Einbahnstraße hineinlaufen."

[5] Taped interview with Günter Mieth, Detmold, February 25, 2006, "Amerika und die DDR - das waren ja zwei Welten und zwischen diesen zwei Welten plötzlich eine Brücke zu haben..."

some tourist site in the area. The host congregations or host group intentionally planned such outings, and one interviewee says such trips were planned *because* they seem to naturally lead to personal conversation between the Americans and the Germans, noting that doing something together encouraged communication. There was thus a kind of joy or pride in showing the country or special sites to the foreigners. In this context, it was then puzzling to them that the Americans expressly asked to meet with people and not spend time being tourists.

(3) Bible study and thematic or topical discussions are referred to in at least 24 interviews. The Bible discussions would include focus on a theme text or the watchword for the year (*Jahreslosung*) and usually led to exchanges about faith traditions and practices, daily life, politics, congregational activities, and customs. In this regard, the Americans sometimes brought a song or a canon with them, especially composed by the music director at the Zinzendorf congregation in West Berlin. Bible discussions often went late into the night and were described as "serious and light-hearted" at the same time. Except in a few cases, Bible study isn't noted as a focal point, though three pastors found it to be foundational to the visits. Several thought the Americans knew their Bibles well, and one pastor is impressed with the fact that the visitors talked about their own personal faith understanding, while his wife liked the Bible discussion particularly, for she said it disallowed superficial chatter. At least by the 1980's, the Bible text or verse was chosen at the planning meeting of the East Committee, so the local pastors or leaders could be prepared with program ideas in advance of a team visit.

The general discussion themes covered were often tied to the political events of the time (Polish Solidarity movement, black/white relations in the U.S., the current U.S. President, stationing of missiles on both sides of the Iron Curtain), but the topics also included such things as comparison of congregational life on all levels from Sunday school to governance, the role of the church in society (how the Church functions in socialism), personal faith issues, differences in education and school systems, family life and raising children.Biographical sharing often started the times of conversation, and topics were then naturally related to the individuals gathered, their curiosities about the others and their lives.

(4) Celebration as a code label refers to shared activities like worship services, church-related musical events, parish festivals, afternoon coffees, devotionals, communion services, singing, prayer, fellowship and sometimes farewell parties. Some from the East Berlin group, which met monthly, mention sending the visiting American team into the rest of the country with a blessing and receiving them back in East Berlin with a

meal before the team would return to West Berlin. There were also farewells in the visited congregations, and one pastor recalls regular final evening group dinners and closing communion services. In some cases, the worship services were planned together, or the Americans took on leadership roles in worship, at least by bringing greetings. Several interviewees mention the music and especially singing of Black spirituals. Many East Germans were very interested in the tradition of Negro spirituals, perhaps due in part to a well-known youth pastor, Theo Lehmann and his writings. He also happened to be a very early Berlin Fellowship participant. Several teams had African-American team members, and between their presence and singing the spirituals, a deep impression was left. One jointly planned worship service is recalled, "The atmosphere was particularly special, gives me goose bumps even now to think of it, and it was just wonderful, singing and the sermon. It was a beautiful day, a day when one could breathe a little bit more freely."[6] It was a freedom foreign to the Germans in some sense and second nature to some of the Americans.

The Americans and what came to them as second nature often surprised the Germans; one pastor mentions how she was taken aback by the seemingly spontaneous habit some visitors had, to fold their hands and bow and just start praying. According to another pastor, it was because of joint celebration activities that the Germans were so accepting of the Americans; he attributed the success of the visits to being together, to the conversation and to common prayer and singing. This same pastor, in describing the whole program, notes that the American participants were people one could sing and pray with, not people who would come and hold a lecture.

The "togetherness" of these usual and common congregational Christian activities plowed the ground in a natural and somewhat disarming manner for the actual impact of the Berlin Fellowship visits. This impact is measured at first glance by the number of code categories in the Koinonia family of quotations, as I have assembled them. This code family totals a startling 1036 quotations, most of which relate to incarnational, intercontextual, intercultural encounter in personal conversation and exchange.

[6] Taped interview with Erika Lauschus, Zeuthen, September 14, 2006, "Es war aber auch eine Atmosphäre, das geht mir jetzt noch über die Haut, wenn ich daran denke, das war einfach schön, gesungen und Predigt alles auch, Heiner hatte gepredigt und es war schön, war ein schöner Tag, ein Tag wo man ja, mal wieder ein bisschen freier atmen konnte."

Koinonia Family 1036 quotations
This code family is defined as a shared and participatory activity or encounter via contact, conversation, recognition, intentional exchange, time spent together, or mutuality. For the purpose of this data analysis and discussion and in order to manage this code family (13 codes), I've divided it into three sub-groupings:

- Essence 228
- People to People (Personal encounter, Recognition and Hospitality) 428
- Communication (Conversation, Qualitative Descriptions, Personal Memories, Names, Faith Sharing, Different Contexts Shared, Comparisons with Other Ecumenical Partners) 832

Each of these Koinonia Family sub-groupings illustrate different yet integral aspects of the Berlin Fellowship experience as discussed and described by the eastern participants.

(1) Essence
"What WAS Berlin Fellowship? Looking back on it, how would you give it definition today?" This is one of the final questions asked in every interview. Essence as a code was created initially to be the repository for answers to that question and grew to become the second largest grounded code, acting as a foundational overview in broad strokes for a general and overarching German understanding and definition of the Berlin Fellowship. Almost all of the remaining Koinonia code family categories are related to or emerge from these quotations, and it actually serves to introduce the remainder of the discussion for this entire family code.

The essence of the Berlin Fellowship was described in various ways, but the interviewees focus first on the "coming" of the American visitors. Noting that travel in the opposite direction was impossible and the idea of going anywhere in a western direction wouldn't have occurred the Germans, one person interpreted the American intent to make contact (*Kontakt*), to speak with people, and to get to know them personally; simply put, "the American visitors *came* to East Germany." This phrase repeated itself again and again, and the guests met *personally* with the Germans in their homes, in their congregations and "we talked." By coming in person, engaging in conversation, spending time listening and talking, a statement was being made, if not consciously, then implicitly, or so it was understood or interpreted by many interviewees. Whether the Americans were aware of their role in this regard isn't discussed, but one person makes it very clear what happened, at least for him; Berlin Fellowship communicated to him that he and his congregation counted, were worth visiting. "We are interesting for them."[7] Coming in person spoke loudly, and points in fact to something akin to service, a kind of care-giving or pastoral action. The coming was more than tourists crossing borders, for it is labeled a *Zuwendung*, an act of care and attention, or as one bishop put it, naming it an example of diaconal power and solidarity.[8] That solidarity was named the *oikumene* (Greek, inhabited world) by some and viewed as a great chance to experience the world-wide church "live," to learn about it as the body of Christ, not just in an intellectual or theological dimension but as something tangible across country borders "they came to visit me." Berlin Fellowship is alluded to or regularly named as a live and very personal experience of ecumenism.

This "place" of solidarity and ecumenical being together was achieved rather rapidly, often happening quickly in the first hours of meeting between Germans and Americans. That is noted by almost all those interviewed and marveled at, even years after the events; a rapport and a unique kind of intimacy or trust, a kind of closeness seemed to happen. This place of meeting was created and is spoken of in personal terms, as a place where pretenses could disappear and a momentary community would be created. In that place of momentary community something unusual happened. Because personal encounter, conversation and recognition of the other became entwined, having contact, which was first seen as just meeting someone, became something more.

For many of those interviewed, these intercontextual and intercultural encounters took on a significance labeled by one person as a "sign."

> Berlin Fellowship was [...] a clear sign of readiness to help, of ecumenism over the borders. The Catholic Church talks about the world church, but what was here was also very big, that people got up and took the trouble, the expense, the energy, the time, and the heart to give a sign to others. And it was more than a letter or a broadcast and also more than a Care package it was a personal act of encounter. And it was to visit those who *couldn't* return the visit. [9]

---

[7] Taped interview with Hans-Christoph Spitzner, Plauen August 20, 2005.

[8] Taped interview with Johannes Hempel, Dresden November 22, 2005, "Aber es ist schon eine starke Kraft der der christlichen Solidarität, und zwar eben in der eigentümlichen Mischung, die mir so gefallen hat: aus spiritueller Kraft und diakonischer."

[9] Taped interview with Johanna Schmidt, Rostock April 14, 2005. "Berlin Fellowship war[...]ein deutliches Zeichen von Hilfsbereitschaft, von Ökumene über die Grenzen. Also die katholische Kirche spricht von der Weltkirche, aber das war hier auch etwas ganz Großes, dass sich hier Menschen aufmachen und Mühe, Kosten, Kraft, Zeit, Gedanken und Herz haben um anderen Christen ein Zeichen zu geben. Und zwar mehr als ein Brief und eine Sendung und auch mehr als ein Carepaket, persönlich sich zu begegnen. Und zwar solche Menschen, die das in umgekehrter Weise nicht konnten."

Others equate this "sign" (*Zeichen*) with a message; in fact there were two key messages named by several participants. One message heard was, "you are not alone," while the other was, "you won't be forgotten."

This demonstration of solidarity or interest was a live (*lebhaft*) experience of real, living people, and this is emphasized very often with the phrase "we experienced that" (*das haben wir erlebt*). Emphasis on the flesh and blood presence of the other person is underscored in at least half of the interviews, as direct and immediate (*unmittelbar),* giving intensity to what the speakers are trying to name. "I can only say this theologically, to experience the Body of Christ not only as an intellectual matter or a theological matter but as something one can touch across country borders [...] that moves me to this day."[10] These words are reminders that the encounters enabled theological or confessional truth to come alive through meeting actual people. In this regard, it is acknowledged through the decades that there was an "exotic" nature to the whole matter, for having American visitors was certainly exotic. However, it should also be noted that the immediate experience of this "other" is often described not as exotic but as material (*wesentlich*) or substantial; that is to say, this was a genuine human being speaking, talking, and eating. Furthermore, though not everyone equated this meeting with a theological truth, the interviews contain sufficient references to these personal encounters as examples of "life together" to suggest that many experienced and viewed the encounter as one occasioning mutuality and reciprocal fellowship.

Interviewees refer throughout to the effects and results of the Berlin Fellowship visits, but not just in answer to a question, for mutuality in this case is much more of an owned matter by the easterners than I anticipated. It seems the visits engendered a feeling of belonging, provided opportunities to give and receive, be connected, and to have "contact." In addition, a kind of "team spirit" grew through the East Committee, the Berlin group, and Berlin leadership planning trips.

This code entitled Essence is but the tip of an iceberg for more details and specifics in the remaining discussion of the Koinonia family group.

---

[10] Taped interview with Christian Hoeser, Güstrow, October 3, 2005, "[...] und dann kann ich das nur theologisch sagen, den Leib Christi zu erfahren —nicht nur als 'ne intellektuelle Größe, 'ne theologische Größe, sondern als anfassbar über Ländergrenzen hinweg [...] Das ja das berührt mich auch heute noch."

(2) People to People (Personal Encounter, Recognition, Hospitality)
Berlin Fellowship was first and foremost personal encounter and a distinct kind of incarnational engagement. Hospitality was extended by host families and congregations and something happened, both expected and yet surprising. Someone from another part of the world was interested enough to travel to meet East Germans *personally*, and time for getting to know one another was then spent. The interviewees emphasize the importance of this personal meeting in a number of ways. "This living presence of the other decided everything for me."[11] This other was moreover an outsider and labeled an "enemy." The repeated and recurring mention of this being a face-to-face, person-to-person meeting drives the point home.

For many, if not most Germans, this was a unique and special experience, and the recollections regularly identify this encounter by describing the getting to know one another on an intimate, trusting, personal level, and all in a direct face-to-face manner (*unmittelbar*), with emphasis on the lack of pretense. Faith experiences were exchanged, and it soon became clear that the cultural differences meant different ways of faith expression and practice. In one case, the speaker refers to his 'take" on the way the guests expressed their faith, by describing the joyful demeanor of the American and how that encouraged and strengthened him.

It was indeed the bodily presence of Christians from the "outside" that were "different" (not just as the enemy), different, in that they came in person; they were there, flesh and blood and that counted:

> There were [other] people who thought of me or the family and sent packages. Sometimes I wished: just come yourself. And for me that was the secret of Berlin Fellowship, that some people then said: We're not just going to 'pray' for you; we're not just going to send some letters and say 'we're with you! Rather, 'we are coming' [...] and are personally present. That made an impression on me.[12]

The memory of direct encounter left a deep impression, and for some interviewees this was important, for it created a "place" of confidence to share deeply, "regardless of who listens in."

---

[11] Taped interview with Constanze Schroeder, Neu-Kalиß October 3 2005, "Bei diesem Halleluja-Amen-Fest war für mich sozusagen auch wieder die leibhaftige Präsenz das alles Entscheidende."

[12] Spitzner interview, "Da gab´s irgendwelche Leute, die ich dann vielleicht nie kannte, die haben an mich gedacht oder an unsere Familie gedacht, hab´ haben Pakete geschickt. Manchmal hätt´ ich mir gewünscht: Kommt doch mal selber. Und das ist für mich das Geheimnis bei Berlin Fellowship, dass eben wirklich Leute gesagt haben: Wir beten in Anführungsstrichen nicht nur für die; wir schicken jetzt nicht nur irgendwelche Post und sagen: Wir stehen hinter euch! Sondern: Wir fahren dort hin und sind persönlich da. Das war für mich beeindruckend."

This direct contact with real live people was not just important for the participants but also for their children. The guests were tangible and present, rather normal folks, who were Christians; this recognition was important. This act of recognizing the other as a fellow human being is alluded to in many of the interviews, and as different as the Germans and Americans were, it was important to the German hosts to get to know their guests as real people, close enough to touch.

The Americans coming and being there, the getting to know the other, people from two entirely different parts of the world, and the fact that these others were real people, different but not so very different, all contributed to the phenomena of recognition taking place again and again. It even seemed to be re-discovered in the interviews with reflective amazement and a bit of bewilderment. This recognition went in both directions and was certainly accentuated because of the "enemy" status of the other. However, through this recognition, a unique or particular "place" is created where Christians experience what they are talking about, and this experience caught many off guard and caused thoughtful analysis throughout the interviews. Reflecting upon this place, there is repeated reference to a definite sense of belonging and to a surprising atmosphere of freedom.

The East Germans describe their guests as free, as looser, more casual, more relaxed, and they described them as open, even able to talk about problematic aspects in their homeland as well as in their church. The atmosphere that the guests brought contrasted starkly with their hosts' culture, but it wasn't viewed as off-putting. It was viewed rather as fascinating, transforming and freeing. One interviewee recalls, "[…] one could swim in this, open oneself […] and our folks experienced that with Berlin Fellowship visits and nowhere else and they were changed through it and that was exciting."[13]

What is further described in this act of personal encounter centers around recognition and takes place primarily through conversation which goes far beyond a handshake and the "nice to meet you" courtesy greeting. Seeing the other and being seen, acknowledging and being acknowledged, finding and being interested in and being found interesting and important as well all forms of recognition which punctuate the quotations in the Recognition code category. Again, the message "you are not forgotten" or "you are not alone" is communicated and reciprocated. As is

[13] Taped interview with Angelika Gloeckner, Greifswald December 22, 2008, "[...] von freier Spiritualität mitschwimmen konnte, sich öffnen konnte —das haben manche Menschen in diesen Gruppen erlebt und sonst nie. Aber sie sind nicht unverändert gewesen dadurch […] Und das ist was ganz Spannendes."

already apparent, the warp and weave of this fabric of the eastern perspective is growing tighter; very little about this human encounter and interaction is said that doesn't relate to fellowship. This includes the simple courtesies extended and shared on all levels. The welcome mat was out for the visitors, and though Hospitality is a less densely populated code, hospitality was practiced and is a key factor in recognition of the "other," where first-time hosts and guests may be very conscious of their roles. As such, acts of hospitality were acts of recognition, formalized a bit but nonetheless offering a defined and purposeful manner or context in which Germans and Americans could come together. Acts of hospitality set the stage for recognition.

Seventeen of the interviewees specifically mention being hosts, welcoming or caring for guests, taking time to consider their needs and wishes, planning the program to include conversation, meals with families, and tourist sites. There is also evidenced a certain degree of both pride and joy in being able to host Americans in private homes, as well as show them the sights. Having this unique chance also pushed some Germans into new territory. For some it was a first-time experience hosting international visitors and a somewhat unnerving one at that. "While some were open, there were still anxieties among us, 'What does one offer the Americans? So what do they eat?' That was a revolution in our village!" [14] For many it seemed an especially good thing, to have these guests at home and the guests would hardly be gone when it would be asked, when are they coming again?[15]

This ardor was at least held in check, however, by a certain degree of disappointment and dissatisfaction, expressed in several interviews regarding the role the hosts would have liked to have played; that the Americans were, by state law, forbidden to stay in private homes was irritating to many. Foreigners were required by law to apply for entry into the country through the official central travel bureau and stay only in certain hotels. In addition, the program developed in such a way as to have the American teams with two congregations over two weekends and with several others during the week but only for an evening. This elicited strong German critique at the time, and this point is remembered during the interviews. The critique itself, however, is indicative of a blatant posture of German ownership and participation. In spite of the critique, several interviewees draw theological conclusions, embracing the host/guest

[14] Taped interview with Wolfgang Eichhorn, Zwickau August 29, 2005, "Während die anderen offener sind, waren Ängste da: „Ja was bietet man denn Amerikanern an? Was essen die denn?" und aber hallo! Das war ja 'ne, das war 'ne Revolution auf dem auf dem Dorf!"

[15] Taped interview with Reinhard Gloeckner, Greifswald, December 22, 2008.

relationship: "It is not exaggerating to say, [we were able to] 'to discover Christ in the other', [to experience] that you were here as Christ and guest."[16]

This voice of a theologian naming an experienced truth in the encounter, long after the events of visiting Berlin Fellowship teams, is but one expression. Recognition is more often articulated in less theological terms, having to do with mutuality, acceptance, acknowledgment, affirmation, being remembered and the desire for reciprocity.

That reciprocity began at the threshold of the visit with initial encounters, in the first minutes of Americans and Germans meeting. Introductory formalities certainly composed the first steps of recognizing and being recognized. In some cases, where an American spoke German or a German English, there was a faster connection. For some Germans, their English facility was what initially drew them in, and because they were often called on to translate, their interest and knowledge of the language gave them a special feeling of acknowledgment.[17] Generally though, meeting and seeming to connect quite readily was a source of bewilderment and provocation at least for some. Speaking of a particular American guest who introduced a small group dynamics technique on one trip but referring to the collective experience over many years of teams, one church leader said, "It is as impressive now as then, that after an hour, a much stronger, personal and human penetrating relationship or connection comes into being in this way, life together."[18]

Though this so-called life together constantly faced misunderstanding because of language differences and translation needs, almost no interviewees mention it being an issue, a concern or a stumbling block. The memory of how the Americans got the conversation rolling stuck with many, however. They asked questions, direct, forthright, and perhaps too personal, but these questions made an impression and opened up the communication,

> Why do you come to this house meeting? Or why aren't you a church-goer? Or why do you attend worship service? Or why don't you attend worship?"[...] And I found this great, that someone else asked [...] and these were questions that I could have asked (pastor speaking). But suddenly they were posed quite infor-

[16] Hoeser interview, "Deswegen ist das nicht übertrieben, dieses 'Christus in dem Andern entdecken', das Ihr-seid-da-als-Gäste-Christus-gewesen."
[17] Taped interview with Ursula Unterumsberger, Berlin, September 6, 2005.
[18] Taped interview with Friedhelm Merchel, Radebeul October 17, 2005. "Es ist mir nach wie vor eindrücklich, wie[...]nach einer Stunde [...] dass also eine viel stärkere persönliche und menschliche aber auch tiefgehende Beziehung entstand—auf diese Weise gemeinsames Leben."

> mally and directly. And suddenly they [the congregants] were confronted with them.[19]

Although this manner of leaping headfirst into the exchange might well have been offensive, it is not often remembered as such and indeed seems to have opened things up for similar return questions; this is but one of the noted acts of recognition that most interviews refer to at least once.

Between question and answer rounds as well as sharing biographies, the first hours of a team visit often passed easily and seemed to establish a sense of mutuality. The eastern participants affirm this, referring to the "learning" about the other, and more specifically, correcting of misinformation. It might also be that conversation partners find out new information from the "other" about church governance or public education, raising children, public health care, GDR diaconal work or what families do on vacation.

Recognition in both directions also entails acknowledgement and affirmation of the other person, acts of acceptance, and for some, the sense of satisfaction at having one's story listened to and perhaps even made known beyond the borders. "[...] here are people with whom we can safely talk [...] they will leave and travel far away and they can then talk about how we live, the bad and the good, what catacombs and conformity mean."[20]

Which comes first the interest and desire to listen or the desire for and interest in being listened to? The interviews indicate both have equal weight. The dynamic of a Berlin Fellowship encounter unfolds in a variety of ways as described by the Germans. Each interview reveals how, in one way or another, interest, acceptance, affirmation, being remembered, feeling like an important and worthy conversation partner, all contribute not only to a sense of self-worth but to action, transformation, change on an individual or congregation level. This recognition factor is incarnated first in the visitors'' coming; then through time spent together and in conversation, a message is communicated to the eastern participants,

---

[19] Eichhorn interview, "Eine fragte „Warum kommst du eigentlich hier zum Hauskreis? Oder warum gehst du in die Kirche? Oder warum gehst du zum Gottesdienst? Oder warum geht sie nicht zum Gottesdienst?" Oh, sind die ja noch nie gefragt worden! Und ich fand das toll, dass jemand anders das macht, fragte und eigentlich waren´s Fragen, die ich hätte auch stellen können. Aber plötzlich kamen die ganz ungezwungen sehr direkt. Ja und plötzlich waren die damit konfrontiert."

[20] Schmidt interview, "[...] jetzt sind hier Leute, denen können wir das mal erzählen, die fahren noch weit weg und da können sie dann erzählen, wie wir hier leben, sowohl negativ als auch positiv, was Katakombe und was Anpassung betrifft."

"You are not alone" and, "Your life is important." A pastor thinking aloud about the recognition factor recalls:

> To experience and hear how others live their faith and to find out that someone is interested in us [...] that was important, because we were very much in a minority situation, were in a position of being on the outer fringes. If one was a practicing, conscientious Christian, well, there weren't many places [in the society] to participate, for we were hindered in many ways. Sure one could lead a reasonable life, if we look at it in a relative sense, but as Christians, we had the feeling we had been totally pushed in the corner.[21]

It was just this feeling of being excluded or pushed in the corner which was countered in a unique and unusual way by the visitors who returned year in and year out. This experience affected the direct participants' lives in a variety of ways, as will be covered in the Outcomes discussion. The after-effect of participation in a single visit or continual visits over years seems to have engendered change and in the broadest sense in that recognition opens doors, builds bridges and illumines new horizons. One pastor's wife notes that these encounters were not something most German young people were accustomed to, and she found it was very good that they were given the chance to learn to talk about faith openly.[22]

Recognition spurred on new recognition, for one village noticed that their congregation, one in which relatively few participated, had foreign guests yearly: "It was noticed by non-Christians, when the Americans came, although it was a bit secret, but it couldn't be hidden and they thought: My goodness, the *church* congregation has *those* kinds of contacts and how is it that?"[23] (Italics indicating voice emphasis). Unbeknownst to the American visitors, they acted as catalysts in this case to shift the village perception of the church congregation's "status" in some manner, according to this pastor's wife. That this is remembered and noted is important; the encounters resulted in change, a change for those

[21] Mueller interview, "[...] zu erleben und zu hören wie andere, wie andere ihren Glauben leben und ich denke, es ist für uns auch wichtig gewesen, in der DDR-Zeit als Christen zu erleben, da interessiert sich jemand für uns [...] das war wichtig, weil wir uns doch sehr stark in einer Minderheitssituation befunden haben, erlebt haben in einer Ausgrenzungssituation. Also wir konnten uns am öffentlichen Leben, wenn man bewusst Christ war, na ja, an vielen Stellen nicht so beteiligen. Man wurde behindert an vielen Stellen. Man konnte vernünftig leben, no, das also, wenn wir das jetzt alles relativ sehen, aber von, von unserem Glauben als Christenheer hatten wir doch sehr stark das Gefühl, man versucht, total in die Ecke zu treiben."

[22] Taped interview with Renate Stempel, Oberoderwitz, October 19, 2005.

[23] Ibid. "Das ist auch Nichtchristen dort aufgefallen, wenn Amerikaner kommen, obwohl da alles 'n bissel geheim war, aber das konnte man ja nicht verstecken und da haben die gedacht: Meine Güte, die Kirchgemeinde, die hat solche Kontakte und wieso gerade wir, Crostau?"

visited in this village, in how their neighbors perceived them. Parish life was also affected in some instances, with some interviewees stating there was new life in the congregation or that the Berlin Fellowship participation "infected" the congregation with a new sense of closeness and cooperation.[24]

Moreover, many of the Germans interviewed note how they were personally changed by the recognition. One young woman from the Berlin Group, whose primary contact with the Ami's was through the monthly meetings in East Berlin, remembers how one individual's personal spirituality left her with a new understanding of herself, one that meant she was accepted as she was. Naming another individual, Pastor Ted Schapp from West Berlin, she continues, "It was simply this being carried [...] I was carried [...] through Fellowship, really carried."[25] Besides this acceptance, the recognition factor left its footprints in that the conversations forced new attentiveness to the German self-perception and self-recognition. In a similar vein, it is recalled that the conversations themselves had their effect, forcing reflection about the German situation, giving new attentiveness to things not previously considered.

(3) Communication (Conversation, Qualitative Descriptions, Personal Memories, Names, Faith Sharing, Different Contexts Shared, Comparisons with other Ecumenical Partners)

Without a doubt, conversation was central in importance and in remembrance from a Berlin Fellowship visit. In fact, this was named as the focal and central "event" in a visit and is the most densely populated code in this subgroup. The other code categories that make up the Communication family subgroup (827 quotations) are all facets of this topic. Noteworthy is that most interviews contain at least one detailed description of an encounter, a personal memory of a visit, and the mentioning of specific names. Specific names occur over 135 times, and 40 different names of Americans are used.

"The main point was conversation." Whether referring directly to evenings of conversation or to tourist excursions, conversation was the highlight in the recollections of the eastern participants. Repeated use of the key words like exchange (*Austausch* 26x) or conversation (*Gespräch* 142x) suffice to underscore this. However, the conversations (*Gespräche*) were in themselves made unique by a number of factors named by the interviewees.

---

[24] Taped interview with Christine Eichhorn, Zwickau, August 29, 2005.

[25] Taped interview with Christel Langhoff, Potsdam, March 24, 2005, " Einfach dieses Getragen[...]ich war mitgetragen. Ich fühlte mich besonders durch Ted aber auch durch die anderen Freundschaften aus Fellowship wirklich getragen."

- The fact that participants met as total strangers is often mentioned.
- Having guests who were truly outsiders and guests who were so very different (cultural and political differences) also contributed to the unique nature of the conversations.
- Though topics or discussion themes are named and alluded to, they don't stand out as key memories as much as the intensity and the exciting nature of the encounter and resultant dialogue.
- The previous "knowledge" about the other is mentioned as being corrected.
- The critique of not being able to continue the conversations via letter writing is regularly voiced.

Though meeting a total stranger may not necessarily lead to a deep and personal conversation, as memory recounts it, Berlin Fellowship encounters seemed to have produced just such conversations. Of course, the unique nature of the meeting, East Germans and Americans, made for an odd and compelling engagement, one that few East Germans (or Americans) could have otherwise imagined. This is acknowledged again and again and in recollection seen even yet as astonishing. It was surprising for many to meet with strangers "from the outside," albeit Christian strangers and to connect so readily. One person attributed this immediacy to the fact that the participants were total strangers and the experience itself so new for both sides as to be disarming.

The experience was new and different, as new and as different as were the American guests, these strangers who'd come to visit. In fact, their presence and manner of conversing, asking questions and even responding caught the Germans a bit off guard. They repeatedly note how different their guests were, first of all because they were from the "other side" the opposition, the enemy.

> And it was always fascinating to hear from the opposite side [...] the intensity these meetings had because they were unusual, also for us [...] I think they were out of the ordinary in two ways [...] for the Americans who had the opportunity to see how we live, what the reality of the Iron Curtain was [...] and [we could meet] the reality of the evil capitalists, as Americans were labeled, yes, this picture of the enemy was softened by human encounter, by a person-to-person meeting.[26]

---

[26] Schroeder interview, "Und das war auch immer spannend zu hören von der Gegenseite [...] Aber die Intensität, die diese Begegnung hatte, weil sie außergewöhnlich war auch für uns...ich denke, sie war im doppelten Sinne außergewöhnlich: Sie war außergewöhnlich für Amerikaner, die die Möglichkeit hatten, zu sehen, wie wir leben, was die Realität dieses Eisernen Vorhangs, der ja also auch in Amerika teilweise sehr sehr, ne, woll'n wir nicht drüber reden [...] sehr schwierig dargestellt worden ist. Und die die Realität äh des bösen Kapitalisten, der ja [...] Amerikaner waren ja immer der Inbegriff von 'der böse Kapitalist',ne, der, ja, dieses Feindbild aufzuweichen durch menschliche Begegnungen."

However, this picture of the enemy, in both directions, is not just softened but transformed. Both the encounter and the information shared corrected false assumptions, misunderstandings and previously shaped prejudices about the "other." For the Germans to see the Americans disagree with each other was a surprise. Hearing these guests be critical of their own country or aspects of life there somehow contributed to producing a kind of free feeling and a new "place." "A movement simply happened. We were moved and caused to reflect, we were in conversation with one another and this I think liberated us. That liberated us in our thinking, in this state of being closed or locked in."[27]

Secondly, the guests posed questions that would otherwise never have been asked in German interchange, with remembered results, creating a kind of intimacy or closeness. This closeness for at least one person created a safe place for expressing doubt and question; in a similar light, others noted that personal and sometimes even quite private matters (for German standards) would be part of the interchange. Matters of faith were openly queried by the Americans and more openly discussed than might have been the case in an all-German gathering. Though thematic topics are alluded to throughout the interviews, not one interviewee specifically drew attention to a topic or did more than mention in passing those political, cultural, often church-, faith- or biography-related topics which composed at least a portionof all of the conversations in the twenty-five years of visits.

The passing acknowledgement of specific topics talked about is overshadowed by the oft-mentioned recollection of intensity regarding deep and personal sharing, people 'clicking' with one another, how spontaneous one-on-one conversations occurred, and how this surprised all those involved. One of the interviewees, a professional counselor, had given some thought to analyzing this intense sense of intimacy, and she remarks that she often has counselees who find it helpful to withdraw after deep sharing in order not to be constantly confronted with the problem. She wonders if the intensity of sharing in a Berlin Fellowship encounter wasn't likewise "released" when the visitors left. That the visitors withdrew and took the information with them afforded a safety valve. This may have been the case, but whether the intensity functioned that way is hard to tell, especially in light of the critique and dissatisfaction expressed by participants who wished for continued contact via let-

[27] Wolfgang Eichhorn interview, "Da ist einfach ´ne Bewegung passiert. Wir sind in Bewegung gekommen und sind ins Nachdenken gekommen, sind ins Gespräch gekommen miteinander, ja, und hat und hat uns, denk´ ich, auch befreit. Das hat uns äh, ja [...] Hat uns befreit in unserem Denken in äh diesem Eingeschlossensein."

ter-writing, which was forbidden by Berlin Fellowship leadership. It was a dissatisfying paradox that conversation became intimate and personal quite rapidly and then as quickly as this intimate and trusting connection was achieved, it ended and was not allowed to continue with correspondence.

The seemingly astounding instantaneous and intense encounters, emotional farewells, clearly remembered conversations, and visitor personalities contribute to the interviews being replete with vivid descriptions, reflections, and memories about people, incidents, and emotions. All further underscore how important the contact and the communication between host and guest were. In fact, those lively stories and descriptions drew my attention to such regularly recurring words as contact *(Kontakt)*, to experience *(erleben)*, important (*wichtig*), intensive *(intensiv)*; indeed these terms each point to recalled relationships and conversations of a unique sort. Having this kind of contact was judged as exceedingly important, particularly because it was other than what the East Germans were accustomed. To experience and to meet was more than to just have a connection or a passing exchange of information; all of this was wrapped up in the totality of the encounter itself and evidenced in descriptive recollections, as well as in other code categories.

The word contact/*Kontakt* (occurred in some form 233 times) highlights the value placed on both the experience as well as the memory of it.[28] Those memories often take the form of a story in the interview, and 156 personal memory stories of varying lengths are identified, many of which include remembered or partially remembered names. Quite often these are the very first Americans met by the interviewee; first encounters seem to have left deeper impressions and often very clear recollections. In 25 interviews with stories mentioning American names, the most often named were Ted Schapp, Bärbel Eccardt, and Ralph Hamburger, each of whom was remembered for different and often personal reasons. Perhaps as interesting is the fact that names of Americans, mentioned 135 times, who only visited the GDR *once* are remembered, highlighting the importance East German participants placed on such person-to-person conversations and meetings.

What made a person memorable enough for a story or to be named is hard to say, but the uniqueness of the whole experience and hosting such persons forced a realization that these American Christians came from a different context and weren't like other ecumenical contacts. Some, but not all participating congregations in the GDR had other "outside" con-

---

[28] Notes from personal conversation with Ursula Unterumsberger, January 1, 2011.

tacts. Church-to-church partnerships with congregations from West Germany and the Netherlands are mentioned most often, but other east bloc countries, Switzerland, the Scandinavian countries, Tanzania and Kazakhstan all receive note. As a point of comparison, the West German partner is often named in contrast to the Berlin Fellowship visits, which are said to have been of a very different nature.

Of course, that there would be American visitors in a church meeting, at least in part, drew participants to the gathering; how the "other" thinks, reacts, speaks about home country, profession, faith tradition are all matters which piqued curiosity. However, it is noteworthy that certain remembrances of both similarities and differences are mentioned with quite such specificity, even twenty years after the events. Commonalities mentioned include that everyone had their common human problems, family and parenting concerns, and that all Christians had certain contextual givens in which to witness. As a matter of course, the radical differences in social and political realities are also noted, but the interviewees draw attention to how faith practices also are different: prayer habits, familiarity with the Bible, parish systems and church government are most often referred to. It is often said that Germans and Americans have different mentalities and general social characteristics, in that Americans are more open and "freer spirits" while the Germans are more closed and somewhat more private or reserved in interpersonal exchange. The interviewees note how different the contextual backgrounds of Berlin Fellowship participants are, and yet also note that these differences don't seem to markedly affect faith sharing. Many of the interviews reveal how context, mentality, and life experience backgrounds are clearly contrasting. However, when it comes to the issue of talking about Christian life, sharing faith stories, or discussing the Bible, the differences no longer seem to play a role in the recollections.

In this vein, Faith Sharing, though a less dense code (78x), is usually named with Conversation as one of the focus points identifying what Berlin Fellowship was all about. There is reference made in all but one interview to the centrality of the exchange of information about faith traditions, the nature of belief, the practice of faith, personal spirituality, corporate or private worship, prayer and piety. For many eastern interviewees, Berlin Fellowship widens the horizon and the personal and spiritual knowledge of each other. It was talking about faith, but not theoretically, for it included sharing personal problems, biographies, and the specifics of the unique contexts in which the conversation partners lived. There were also questions of practical faith application and confessional distinctives. One interviewee, speaking of faith in practical terms labeled his encounter with guests as "*oikumene* alive," something unique for him: "And the difference between Berlin Fellowship and all other things that I got to know about, was that people really talked about their faith to each other face to face, and that was live *oikumene* really experienced."[29] This lived faith wasn't so much new as it was different and present in the other in a new manner, and this is mostly because the Americans described faith as integrated into daily life. Live faith encountered in the conversations and sharing at Berlin Fellowship meetings brought with it a form of liberation and a new perspective.

One of the aspects of the faith sharing which gains regular mention from the Germans is the distinct nature of faith expression or piety and the role prayer seemed to play for the American visitors. Noting these guests seemed ready to pray on the spot is a surprise to the Germans and something new. Germans describe themselves as being stiff, whereas they label the Ami's as being freer and more personal.

In spite of being touched or affected by such visits where the depth and earnestness of faith sharing did indeed bind the participants to each other, it is sometimes a bit much. One pastor's wife takes exception to the over-personal manner of the Americans, while nonetheless finding them freeing. "We were freed by these encounters with our American friends, and we took the visits as gifts and looked forward to them, even though they were somehow a bit over-enthusiastic."[30] The memories attest to not just emotional recollections and the various aspects thus far discussed but also to changes that result, changes the eastern participants note in themselves.

As mentioned, the guests' efforts, time and money to travel to Germany seem to speak loudly, but the efforts to share in the gospel were as important. "[…] but they came, to share the Gospel with us, to exchange stories about the good news […] that wasn't just a gesture, it was a diaconal act it gave expression to our union as Christians in spite of the differences in a very moving way."[31] Through the visits, some Germans say

---

[28] Berhard Stempel interview, " Und das unterschied Berlin Fellowship von allen anderen Dingen, die ich kennen gelernt hab´, dass wirklich Menschen face to face miteinander ins Gespräch kamen in, über ihren Glauben sprechen konnten wirklich und ja, das war eine Ökumene, die wirklich angekommen ist."

[30] Taped interview with Gretel Mieth, Detmold, February 26, 2005. "Und das, das machte uns auch frei im Umgang mit unseren amerikanischen Freunden und ja, und wir nahmen diese Begegnungen wirklich als Geschenke an und freuten uns über, ja, auch die Zuversicht und die sie ausstrahlten, wenn sie mir auch manchmal ein bisschen sehr schwärmerisch vorkamen."

[31] Günter Mieth interview, " [...] sondern sie kommen, um mit dem Evangelium uns […] sich über das Evangelium auszutauschen und das Evangelium und seinen Lauf zu fördern. Und das fand ich, finde ich einfach eine großartige nicht nur Geste sondern das ist ein Dienst gewesen, eine Diakonie, die hier über politische Unterschiede der entsprechenden Regionen hinweg unsere

they learned to talk about their faith, grew closer within the congregation, were encouraged and strengthened, and they were changed. After a visit, one woman describes the Germans, saying the participants "would go home and be astounded about themselves 'Yes, What happened to me? What did I let go of? What have I dared to do/say?' And that happens in a protected place that is a one-time thing [which] can't be produced again so easily."[32] Whether or not it can be reproduced may not be the question though. The next question might rather be, is the change resultant from the shared witness? Has God's spirit worked in and through the "other" to effect that change, and what is the next step for each involved, both host and guest? Could this learning outcome or this change be understood to result from a form of missional witness in and between these German and American Christians?

Outcomes Family 683 quotations (Direct Result of Berlin Fellowship, Information Learned or Corrected, Encounter with World Beyond, Education for Children/Youth, Critical View of Berlin Fellowship, Motivation, Belonging)

These code categories in this family overlap with each other and duplicate many previously discussed findings. However, both in response to interview questions and in the context of musings and recollections, the interviews reveal clear patterns of results or outcomes that the interviewees regularly note because of Berlin Fellowship involvement. This network of outcomes is woven together primarily by the recognition offered and received in the visitation program and through the personal encounters and conversation.

As previously discussed, participants generally say their "horizons were widened" or the "window to the world" was opened, and an expanded picture of life elsewhere was brought through the visit. One example is that the picture of the enemy (*das Feindbild*) is transformed or even erased, and the import of this for children is reiterated. Meeting with these foreign visitors means the occasion for new behavior and self-understanding among the youth as well, allowing them to talk about faith, something not so common for German young people at the time. Of course, the process of learning new information extends beyond the chil-

---

Verbundenheit als Christen zum Ausdruck gebracht hat und das in einer sehr, sehr bewegenden Weise."

[32] Angelika Glöckner interview, " [...] gehen die Menschen nach Hause, staunen über sich selbst: Ja, was steckt da in mir? Was hab ich rausgelassen? Was hab ich mich getraut? Und das geht in diesem geschützten Raum. Der ebenso einmalig ist. Den kann man nicht jederzeit herstellen."

dren and youth, and often results from sharing biographies and asking questions of one another, German to American and vice versa.

"The Americans were very interested in the question: How can one live as a Christian here? [...] One lived naturally [though] not in such a public manner. We didn't have a public life as such [...] we lived with a certain degree of conformity."[33] Besides the sharing about church, faith matters, and tradition background differences, there was information exchanged and corrected through discussions about parenting, politics, the arms race, education, environment, geography, small group dynamics, holidays and other celebrations, family and relatives, and race relations. Getting to know the individuals during a team visit helped dismantle some assumptions in both directions. For both Germans and Americans, the learning came not just from information but also from exposure to the different mentality of the other. As time went on, for instance, in a weekend visit or after several years of team visits, the differences, though not ignored, seemed to be less marked.

Through information exchange and the presence of the other, that world outside then entered into the lives and life realm of the visited, if only for a few hours, affecting real and noted change in the Germans themselves, motivating ongoing participation in Berlin Fellowship and the local congregation. This is often expressed in terms of receiving a new perspective in what ecumenism or being church meant. Astonishingly, simple expressions belie learning about the larger church. Recalling what happened 20 or more years previous, one person says, "I really discovered probably for the very first time that faith can unite, over and beyond borders."[34] Interviewees recalled that people-to-people relationships inside the host congregation actually changed and were affected positively because of Berlin Fellowship. Phrases like "we got to know one another better" or "this built our congregation up" or "new and lasting friendships were formed" all point to change *inside* the German setting because of a team visit or repeated years of participation. In several congregations, pastors note that the Berlin Fellowship host congregation members emerged as a new small group in the parish or became leaders

---

[33] Schmidt interview, " Die Amerikaner waren ja sehr interessiert an der Frage: Wie kann man hier Christ sein? Und wir haben das immer etwas überspitzt ausgedrückt, sie kommen hierher und denken, entweder sind wir alle Opportunisten oder wir leben in Katakomben. Und wir haben zu ihrer Beruhigung festgestellt, dass weder das eine noch das andere zutraf. Man lebte natürlich, was die Katakomben betrifft, nicht so öffentlich. Die Öffentlichkeit hatten wir ja nicht, [...] natürlich lebten wir auch in gewisser Weise angepasst."

[34] Spitzner inteview, "Dass ich da wahrscheinlich zum ersten Mal so richtig entdeckt hab′, Glaube kann verbinden, über Grenzen hinweg."

in church activities. There are repeated references to "impetus to action" (*Impulse*) resulting from the contact with the outsiders.

This stimulation from "outside" made not just for congregational growth; it motivated participation and influenced how individuals viewed the benefits or results of their own personal engagement with the visitors. The walls in people's heads were broken down, says one pastor, while another mentions that his co-workers finally heard and heeded the American visitors saying things he himself had said but which they had previously not seemed to have understood. New news or old news? he was glad for the learning regardless. On a more personal note, an interviewee said, "One opens oneself up completely differently, than when one is with one's peers or one's own kind, in a GDR group for instance."[35] In response to the question about Berlin Fellowship's influence on individuals, another mentioned that her abilities to speak openly and boldly with the state officials were strengthened. In both instances, the speakers pointed to the conversations and encounters with the guests being the source for their own personal growth, change, and encouragement.

There is a degree of excitement and enthusiasm around this aspect of personal growth in the interviews, and those interviewed concede that the 'exotic' nature of the visitors and the visits might well be a contributing factor. However, this is viewed as limited in its long-term influence. Moreover, this whole realm of "outside" stimulation and growth is clearly perceived to have been resultant from more than a one-time exotic get-together. The very presence of visitors becomes a motivating factor, for it offered a widening of the GDR feeling of being penned in, providing access to first-hand non-state-controlled information and personal exposure to an inaccessible world. Moreover, it wasn't one-way exposure, for eastern hosts understood the Berlin Fellowship encounter as a substantial and mutually upbuilding faith experience for all and described it as enrichment (*Bereicherung*).

Indeed, mutuality emerges and is expressed in many ways in the interviews, though only minimally noted in the smallest code category, Belonging. However, in almost all interviews, a sense of belonging is evidenced in the rhetoric, in expressions of shared ownership. This belonging is also apparent in statements about being a "member of Berlin Fellowship" and in reference to program planning by the East Committee. Belonging is, as well, manifest in the criticism voiced in a few inter-

---

[35] Langhoff interview,"Man öffnet sich ganz anders, als wenn man nur unter seinesgleichen, also in DDR-Gruppen oder so was..."

views, where comments are lodged openly at what isn't liked or agreed upon at the time nor yet seen as fair or right.

Critical evaluation and comment are also part of the yearly eastern planning meetings, which become a key gathering for the regional leaders and representatives of participating congregations to plan for upcoming teams and to assure a team visits their congregation. In some cases, the critique is a reflection upon limitations, foibles, shortcomings of personalities, while in other cases, there are more substantive concerns. The easterners are clear in a number of critiques: the visits are too short; there is often jealousy between congregations about length of stays; writing is understandably not allowed, but this is difficult to accept; the Americans are too polite and are not probing enough on a political level; always needing translation is frustrating; East Committee meetings are often a bit chaotic and planning is challenging; saying good-bye is always hard, and it is sad not knowing if you will ever see these people again; there never seems to be enough time. Several interviewees mention they would like certain types of Americans, minority representatives or doctors or educators, and they remember those wishes don't always get fulfilled. Twenty of the twenty-seven interviews contained a comment or two taking a critical stand on some issue; though made in the context of excitement, affirmation, and a degree of enthusiasm, these critical comments reveal a sense of responsibility and *belonging* regarding the whole enterprise and the speaker's remembered desire to see it improve and change.

Both Belonging and Critical View emerged as unanticipated code categories, coming late in the coding process. Both, however, are indications of commitment and conviction about the worth of the program for the participants. There were certain drawbacks to the manner of visitation, especially in the first years when too many congregations were visited. Over the years, changes were made to extend the time spent with a smaller number of congregations. Regular efforts were exerted by the East Committee to work cooperatively and democratically in planning and evaluating the visits. All of these actions contributed to the German participants' sense of mutuality and expressed feeling of not just being "part of" but actually being Berlin Fellowship; interview rhetoric confirms this strong sense of committed ownership and membership.

At this point, I want to say I was caught off-guard and pleasantly so, by the findings related to Belonging and Critical View mostly because both categories were unexpected. This was only one of a number of surprises I experienced in the interviews themselves and in the process of coding, analyzing and writing. As a participant myself in Berlin Fellowship in the 1980's, I had certainly formulated my own picture of what I thought it was. Through the research process and even after, that picture turned out to be rather one-dimensional and quite limited, colored primarily by my own memories and recollections. In the midst of the coding analysis and particular surprises, I created a new code category, named Surprises. In addition, during the process of theory building and writing this chapter, two code categories, Missional Witness and Ephesian Moment, both seem ill-placed in any one code family. This chapter concludes with a discussion of these three "outlier" categories, which in fact are not outliers at all but each unique and integral to the findings discussion and to the research question.

Outlier Codes Surprises, Missional Witness, and "third bank" or the Ephesian Moment

(1) Surprises

The Berlin Fellowship experience and encounter often goes deeper than anticipated and wider in scope than some participants were prepared for, and that is often expressed in words of surprise and wonder. This category includes matters which catch the interviewees off guard as well as matters which surprised me, both during the interviews and throughout the period of coding and text analysis. This category is not densely populated, but some notes made throughout the coding process add to the following discussion.

There are a number of surprises for the German interviewees as they reflect on the experience, as well as during the interview, though only a few of these statements occur more than once or twice. One German is quite taken that the Americans seem to know so much about the GDR. Another is surprised that the Americans are as self-critical as he remembers them to be and openly disagree with each other. In the 1960's and early 1970's, the organizing Germans are startled at the fact that the Americans aren't apparently interested in doing much tourism but would rather meet with people. At the time of the interviews, no small number still express amazement that the Americans actually *come* to the GDR, take the time, money and energy to visit and seem to come with no apparent ulterior motives.[36] It is often noted with a surprised tone, "I got to speak with a real American Americans were in our worship service." One pastor notes his surprise that the Americans seemed to have a good knowledge of the Bible, for that was not the case so much in his own parish. That Christians, but total strangers, could meet and yet talk about

[36] Hempel interview.

problems with each other, listen and share with one another about faith matters somehow catches a few off balance. In a few cases, the Germans remember particular conversations or individuals with whom they personally "clicked" in spite of the language barrier; sometimes it seems there is no need for translation for it is like "we are on the same wave length." In the 1970's, the "small group dynamic" method is mentioned by most of the interviewees who participated that year. Though the Germans found the visitors' manner of asking rather pointed and unusual, this was viewed mostly positively. A few, however, see this as too abrupt and off-putting. Furthermore, to talk about one's own personal faith with complete strangers is a shock to one woman but not solely in a negative light, for it seems to be both startling and yet a kind of learning experience. One interviewee recalls, the joy the small group of Germans experience among themselves each time they host Americans, and she likens the time spent with them to a party.

As surprises happen in the course of the interviews with those I am speaking with, I find myself quite regularly taken aback as well. At the end of one interview, I asked one pastor what more he would like to say about Berlin Fellowship, and without missing a beat, he answered that the whole enterprise should never have stopped. I query as to why he thought this, and he answered that we always need this kind of sharing and contact with others from outside our own "circles." In another interview, when questioned, "*What* was Berlin Fellowship?" a long-standing member answered readily, "America!" I am embarrassed and totally speechless. She goes on to explain what she means, referring to much of what has shaped her picture of this enemy from the capitalist west and her joy at meeting Christians and real people from that place. I expected some categories to receive more attention the discussion topics and themes or comments about difficulties in understanding and communication. Likewise, I didn't expect comments about how the ministry is regarded in a spirit of genuine ownership and responsibility, but it becomes clearer through the text analysis and coding that this was indeed a shared and common posture. Equally so, I knew there were points of dissatisfaction, but the fact that they are so clearly articulated in many interviews is a surprise and thus further reinforces the host's high sense of mutuality and co-ownership.

After concluding the coding and analysis, I have added the following "surprising" observations:

- The majority of "key quotations" in almost all code categories are contributed by pastors' wives and other women. Their insights, critique and thoughts are substantial and often incisive.
- The importance of the visitor who physically "came" to the GDR and to the hosts' homes and congregations caught me up short. I did not expect so much value to be placed upon this action.
- For the first time, I learn about perceived and recalled "change" and "results" in individuals and in congregations, attributed to Berlin Fellowship participation.
- It remains impressive how much weight these interviewees give to the role of conversation, in spite of translation and potential misunderstanding issues. Conversation remains a key factor years after the last actual Berlin Fellowship team visit.
- It is also surprising and inspiring that many of the interviewees were not only thoughtful and perceptive in their responses, but had given much consideration to just what Berlin Fellowship actually was. The question elicited a considerable list of "facts" about what happened, but the theological reflections and questioning, pondering and trying to articulate the essence of the encounters were equally impressive and indeed provocatively surprising. That so many of the interviewees had given considerable time, thought and effort to this issue reinforces my supposition that fellowship is indeed a meritorious subject for research, that it truly might be missional, and all of that can take place in the actual, lived world of *koinonia*, a "place" of encounter and meeting.

(2) Missional Witness

Perhaps not surprisingly, the interviews mirror how missional witness takes place as an encounter with God in the very place of encounter with the "other," in that place where fellowship happens. In and through that meeting place, one is reminded that God *is* is at work, is present, is active in ways not often or usually expected, and in ways and persons not always recognized at first glance all via mutual and shared witness, imperfect as it may be.[37] A missional encounter or activity results, at the very least, in the participant being affected or changed. First "something" happens to bring about learning and receiving; perhaps then, that "something" is passed on. That something which happens is manifest in the act and action of fellowship, participation, sharing giving and receiving and giving back and receiving back (Volf's discussion of embrace). It is this interchange which is described in various ways in the interviews.

The rhythm of the interchange in the meetings can hardly be standardized, but certain features of the whole ministry seem to give shape to a common response and evaluation by the German participants. These features are consistently attested to. In the early years the Americans were perceived as having a goal to bring a sign of Christ to the situation, and in those years, the theme of reconciliation was foremost. However, the

[37] Bevans and Schroeder, *Constants*, 357.

general effect as more years went by was that of encouragement, comfort, strengthening, and a "window to the world." *Being with* Christians from the "other" side was the place this all happened. Some Germans labeled this as a form of genuine diaconal service an act of personally visiting and conversing. Whether the Americans were aware of this is not mentioned, but it was noted they sought to be well-informed and to come with a posture of listeners and learners.

It is noted several times the Berlin Fellowship experience leads the Germans to think in new ways and express themselves in new ways when talking about faith. The ideas and the nature of the American questions, as already discussed, force impetus for changed ways of conversing among the Germans, and in some cases provides impetus for change in other areas as well. Change is most often referred to, in that the Germans respond to their guests' questions questions they would not normally either think about or at least not verbalize out loud. Some interviewees mention that this aspect of change later affects the manner of congregational life. Some also note as a result, that they think about themselves differently. There is also a form of attitudinal change and internal, even personal growth, not just in the dismantling of the picture of the enemy, but also in a bolder and more decided public presence. Another change mentioned is that Berlin Fellowship has caused some participants to look further east, to look differently at their own neighboring countries and the needs of others. Thus, on many counts, a missional action and the extended hand of fellowship from some American visitors seems to encourage or give impetus (*Anstoss*) to the Germans visited. The presence, the questions, the very coming of the visitors to the GDR made for this impetus, and it results in further action and response. The visitors are seen as having modeled something and testified to something. Experiencing the body of Christ in the Berlin Fellowship gatherings is articulated in many ways, but at its simplest descriptive level, the visitors' action is received by the visited and then further lived out, testified to in response first in answer to those visitors and then to their own Christian and local community.

What is it about the presence of the "other" that seems to affect such response and in some manner, such change and such memories? At the time of the visits and even in the years afterwards, participants from both sides continue to question and ponder what Berlin Fellowship was. The importance and benefits of reverse trips to the U.S. by East German teams in the early 1990's, and the final farewell three-day gathering and celebration entitled "Hallelujah-AMEN!" in Berlin 1996 to close the ministry are both mentioned throughout the interviews. Both seem to reinforce impressions about Berlin Fellowship and its effects. Though the question "What was Berlin Fellowship?" elicits varied answers, even the most articulate of interviewees often stumble in trying to pinpoint the actual "happening" in so many words.

(3) "third bank" or Ephesian Moment

A code category emerged to address this issue of a "happening." I first named this category "third bank" referring to an image in the novel *Love in the Time of Cholera*, the "third bank" being a unique place of meeting for two passengers on a boat in this intriguing love story. As identified by Hans de Wit,[38] this "third bank," was neither the bank (background and life history) from which one passenger came, nor that of the other (different background and life history). It was a new location altogether a boat, a new place of meeting for both passengers, a "third bank." It was on this bank, which is, in the boat in the story, that the two parties finally met, really met. This image's somewhat limited metaphorical value was replaced in my thinking by the "Ephesian Moment," taken from the title of an article of the same name by Andrew Walls. The reference is to a place where God lives, in the midst of Christian community and the temporal and spatial dimension of the body of Christ. Walls refers to the 1st century coming together of two very diverse cultures, those of the Jewish Christians and the Gentile Christians. In that coming together, these two groups meet in a place where Christ becomes known.[39] Walls labels that place and time the "Ephesian Moment." This label seems closer to the actual descriptions offered by the interviewees as they try to put their finger on identifying what happens in a Berlin Fellowship encounter *what* the presence of the other means. In both of these metaphors, "third bank" and Ephesian Moment, the two participants, in spite of their differences, have one thing in common, the "place" where they meet. In the Marquez novel it is love between a man and a woman, and in the Ephesian Moment metaphor it is Jesus Christ.

In one interview the speaker refers to the fact that the "walls had fallen" because of or through Berlin Fellowship, and he concludes with reference to a time and a place. "The wall in Berlin stood as before. The border was as always. But through this [meeting], I believe that the walls in peoples' heads were considerably reduced in size. And that one can even have contact over deep trenches and high borders [in a place and

[38] Hans de Wit, *"My God," she said, "ships make me so crazy." Reflections on Empirical Hermeneutics, Interculturality, and Holy Scripture*, Amsterdam 2008, 11.

[39] Andrew F. Walls, *The Cross-Cultural Process in Christian History*, Maryknoll, N.Y. 2002, 78.

point in time] where people find one another."[40] This spatial and temporal "finding" or coming together is only alluded to in a few of the interviews, though many of the quotations throughout the coding analysis contain hints of this not easily named aspect of the Berlin Fellowship encounters. Like an embrace, there is giving and taking, reaching out, hanging on and letting go, reckoning with the unknown in the other and yet risking being changed or affected by the experience itself; this is a distinct and unique occurrence in time and space. This occurrence itself creates a place for an encounter to happen, or is the encounter itself happening. The experience and the presence of the other bring change or transformation, a widening of the horizon, and in spite of the obvious and noted differences between visitors and hosts, there is a mutual sense of belonging to one another (*Zusammengehörigkeitsgefühl*). Paradoxically, this was a place that *happened*, that was somehow *like* the "third bank" or the Ephesian moment. For the East Germans, it was a place of surprise at the belonging together in fellowship as Christians and at the same time being freed or liberated and changed by that very act of togetherness.

"You have to have visitors; otherwise there is no chance or possibility to get out of this place."[41] Geographically speaking, the place referred to here is the GDR, but the getting out happened through the visitor coming to the "other" entering in, being received and hosted, and the resultant "life together" for a few hours or a few days. Is this a new place the visitors bring with them or is it rather a new place created and experienced by both conversation partners, a place in between? Only one interview speaks so provocatively of a *new* place created by the encounter and several other interviews hint at reminders of the liminal nature of the meeting, in-betweenness not directly expressed. In some interviews this place is described as a sudden bridge between two worlds and also as a *way* to bring more openness or forthrightness in, a way to be with the other, ready for something new.[42] This unique place of meeting and engaged communication is pondered by a few other interviewees, who name its center Jesus and call it a mystery, "There was a line [of communication or connection] that made this ministry then and now unexplaina-

---

[40] Spitzner interview, "Die Mauer in Berlin, die stand nach wie vor. Die Grenze war nach wie vor. Aber dass durch diese... ich glaub' ja schon, dass in den Köpfen die Mauer ein ganzes Stück niedergerissen worden ist. Und dass man eben auch Kontakt haben kann über tiefe Gräben und hohe Grenzen hinweg [...] wo Menschen zueinander finden."

[41] Schroeder interview, "Du musst Besuch bekommen, sonst has du keine Möglichkeit, diesen Ort zu verlassen."

[42] Christine Eichhorn interview, "Dass das also auch so'n Weg war, da auch 'n Stückchen mehr Offenheit hineinzubringen. Du bist so mehr auf Neues und auf andre auch mal einlassen können."

ble. Simply, I'd say an encounter that was somehow mysterious."[43] The world from which the visitors came and even their manner of conversation didn't fit at all,[44] but somehow the people fit and then the questions and interchange did as well. Because there was a temporal and unique, albeit temporary, spatial fit, a form of human "life together" happened, in an extraordinary manner, and "one could speak differently with one another."[45] This being together is referred to in spiritual terms but also as a person-to-person phenomenon, an encounter between strangers.

None of the interviewed denies that the conversation partners are indeed strangers to each other, but this strangeness offers something special, allowing for a kind of openness from the Germans, to which they themselves aren't accustomed. A member of the Berlin Group attributes this experience of a new place of *trust* with a stranger, in part, to the unique context behind the Iron Curtain, and in part to the fact that faith matters are directly and openly spoken about in connection with everyday existential questions.[46]

Though it is perhaps a safe place, this place of trust isn't always necessarily comfortable and is indeed a liminal setting, a place "in between," fascinating and alarming at the same time.[47] However, what makes it fascinating and alarming yet safe at the same time, is what one person identifies as the work of God in the midst of the fellowship experience, there on the spot: "...it has an effect not just because it was nice for him or for me, but because it was God's doing, because the Holy Spirit found a place in the midst of our lives and in this fellowship."[48]

Conclusion

Indeed, "in some way" that place or something in that place happened. This place was created by the Berlin Fellowship encounter and though it

[43] Wolfgang Eichhorn interview, "Und da war ´n ´n Draht da... ja für mich das einfach ist nach wie vor nicht erklärbar, diese Arbeit. Ich sag´ einfach: ´ne Begegnung, die, ja, etwas Geheimnisvolles an sich hat."

[44] Mueller interview, " [...] die gleichen Ansätze, die von euch gekommen sind und die so überhaupt nicht zusammenpassen mit unserer Wirklichkeit, aber die ihre Berechtigung haben und wo ich sofort sagen würde, eigentlich müsste es genau so sein."

[45] Angelika Glöckner interview, "Diese Treffen waren so einmalig, das waren so herausgenommene Situationen und schon alleine dieses, da konnte man anders miteinander reden."

[46] Unterumsberger interview.

[47] Christine Eichhorn interview, "Und das hat manchmal Erschrecken mit sich gebracht und dann auch wieder auch 'ne Faszination. Das war immer so 'ne Balance zwischen beidem."

[48] Hoeser interview, "...es wirkt sich nicht nur aus, weil ich denke, es wär´ gerade nett für ihn oder für mich, sondern weil es Wirken Gottes ist, weil Heiliger Geist ´n Raum bekommt in dem jeweiligen Leben und in dieser Gemeinschaft. Und wo das ist, dort genau passiert es. Und das bricht an manchen Stellen sich Bahnen..."

often seemed to exceed expectations, it was certainly liminal or in-between. Yet the encounter was described as engaging, compelling, transforming, and somehow welcoming a place of coming together, of personal meeting, of being recognized and recognizing, of conversing, and of changing.

These twenty-seven interviews quite readily yield testimony to the import and impact of the Berlin Fellowship program for East German participants, who might have been thought, at the outset of this research, to have been but "recipients" of a mission or ecumenical action but who most assuredly considered themselves full partners and co-members in the ministry. Their witness and recollections affirm the missional nature of *koinonia* happening, as East German Christians hosted American Christians in their homes and congregations.

The German Democratic Republic defines the context and conditions of its citizens' reality, replete with a wall in Berlin and an Iron Curtain for its western border, the external metaphors for internal real life. In spite of this formidable boundary line, the border is penetrable; Christian visitors come from the United States and in their coming offer recognition and *Kontakte* (contacts) with a world the visited assume they would never see or experience. The hosts and the guests spend time together, talking, touring, and learning about one another, and getting to know each other. In fact, as Christians are wont to do, they worship, pray and sing, eat together and celebrate, read and discuss the Bible, their lives, the Church and their worlds. As acts of hospitality these activities, however, are but window dressing for what the host Germans name as the core of the person-to-person encounters a core with many layers: the visitors' coming, the meeting, the conversation, faith sharing and the ensuing results or effects.

As described in the interviews, Berlin Fellowship is, in essence, American visitors coming to East Germany to speak with people and share in the Gospel, a form of ecumenical engagement. However, the impact of the visits has much more to do with the personal effort and presence of these visitors and with what happens in the meetings and the message conveyed. "You are not alone" "You aren't forgotten" you have been recognized, acknowledged. In order for such a meeting to happen, the guests must journey, but the hosts must take their role seriously, which they do. In spite of the visitors being known "enemies" and in spite of obvious cultural, political, and linguistic background differences, a meeting place is found, a unexpected place of understanding and lively interchange. Real people from both "sides" recognize, meet and encounter one another in an experience that is for the Germans both endearing and binding as well as liberating and surprising.

Perhaps most central to the mutual acts of recognition that took place in a Berlin Fellowship team visit was the weight of importance given to the role of conversation and interpersonal exchange, which included *talking* about faith matters. The life context for Christians in the GDR was definitely on the borders of that society. Walled in by the political borders and walled out by the inner-societal boundaries, the East German Christians note that the American visits contradicted and counterbalanced their situation. The visitors came, were interested and asked questions, affirmed the hosts, and moreover, they shared themselves, the time, the place of meeting through their interest and presence.

The personal coming speaks, but in the recollection of the interviewees the conversational interchange speaks as loudly. The impact of conversations and the recalled personal nature of those conversations are revealed in the detailed character and event descriptions, in the many names mentioned, in amazement that total strangers communicate with each other so readily, and in recalling next to nothing about discussion topics but exhibiting enthusiasm recalling the exchange itself and memories of it. The conversations and faith sharing are intense and personal, in spite of various differences, and in spite of the Germans labeling themselves more reserved or stiff and the Americans more casual or free. Much to the surprise of some hosts, the effects of forthright questions from the visitors means the Germans break with their stereotypical natures and engage in open and trusting communication. Especially when it comes to talking about matters of faith, the Americans' references to practical faith application provoke German responses and in recollection, the interviewees remember this as a liberating new perspective and experience. The results of these encounters are often named as what might be labeled missional change, an infectious form of transformation, and that which the interviewees call a new awareness a broader and deeper understanding of faith, of the world Church, and of themselves. Most interestingly, it is also called a form of liberation. The resultant list of outcomes from participation in Berlin Fellowship influences self-understanding and awareness engendering change in some manner:

- horizons are widened
- the picture of the enemy is dismantled
- talking to outsiders about faith and context is important
- getting a realistic and up-close picture of the "other" corrected misinformation and encouraged introspection
- learning that faith can unite made a theological truth real

- personal lives are changed

However, two further and equally important and surprising outcomes stand out. Mutuality (belonging) emerges and is expressed throughout the interviews through phrases of shared ownership and in rhetoric that assumes German co-participation and membership. This posture of partnership results in sharp and voiced critiques of Berlin Fellowship. The posture of partnership reveals not only clearly defined engagement, commitment and a shared sense of responsibility but also a very important aspect of how fellowship and missionality are most certainly related and interact.

That the research findings produce these insights is surprising to me. However, the surprise goes beyond the hosts' feeling of belonging as partners and their taking a critical view of the ministry. Rather it is surprising for me to learn how, over the decades, that the easterners had given considerable thought and effort to planning and evaluation. The interviewees' efforts at describing this are most enlightening and act as helpful indicators for concluding the interview findings discussion. The final thoughts about the effects of missional witness and its significance are represented by a smaller code category, "third bank" or Ephesian Moment.

The gathered and participating community is the place where missional witness reciprocally happens, where Lesslie Newbigin contends the congregation itself is the "hermeneutic of the gospel." As these interview findings make clear in any number of ways, Berlin Fellowship team visits are an example of that gathered community. The participants are not left unchanged, and the interviews attest to this. The conversation and time spent together brings not only the "outside world" in but also offers encouragement and new perspective, new ways of talking about faith, new self-reflective insights into the East German situation, and impetus for new ways and means of being the local congregation. In some cases, the new ways and means are named, but in many interviews, the response to this place of encounter is primarily alluded to as an impulse or impetus (*Impuls*) for further action.

In part, continued participation in Berlin Fellowship is a reaction that leaves footprints in the lives of participants. It is more precisely a missional response to an encounter which happens in a place very much like the Ephesian Moment or that "third bank." A very real existential, intercontextual and intercultural Christian community is created time and time again. Year in and year out, these two very different groups of people meet and talk, and in so doing, are met by the "other" but moreover, are engaged and drawn into the community and presence of Jesus Christ. There, in fellowship with the other and in and through this experience, Jesus Christ made himself known, to the surprise and amazement of all. In spite of being strangers to one another and in spite of distinct boundaries which indeed separated host and guest, these conversation partners find each other as they simultaneously find themselves in communion and community with Christ.

Chapter Five

Fellowship as a Missional Experience

Is a fellowship encounter a missional experience? This research question has been answered in the affirmative by the interview findings, as attested to by Berlin Fellowship German participants. "Missionality" is defined and illustrated by the gathered Christian community participating in *missio Dei*, God's healing and transforming mission and movement of love to the world. Missionality is the church being church in essence *and* action, in word *and* deed, in and through *all* of its activities worship, service, witness, proclamation *and* fellowship. Berlin Fellowship encounter as the gathered body of believers, the body of Christ, the church in essence and action was the "hermeneutic of the gospel" (Newbigin). Constituted by what God has accomplished in Christ, this body as a gathered community was "church" and participated in its being church by active sharing and engagement. The activities and gatherings were varied, but at their very least, the meetings involved coming to and receiving from, recognizing and being recognized, listening and talking, learning and changing, or being changed. These things happened in personal encounters between strangers but not solely because of the people involved, though their role is not to be minimized. Rather the *koinonia* experience was foundationally acknowledged and shaped by that person around whom the gathering took place, namely Jesus Christ. Testimony from interviewed Berlin Fellowship participants repeatedly affirms this, along with the regular and sometimes extended stories of other characteristics of *koinonia*, illustrating belonging, signs of solidarity, and diaconal presence.

The church is being itself then, as a missional community, in fellowship. That gathering is a living reminder of God's presence to this world and to itself as well. This research, in its particular scope, its specificity in time, and its contextual parameters, attests to the role *koinonia* can and does play in or *as* missional endeavor.

Dietrich Bonhoeffer puts it another way in *Life Together*, stating that community or fellowship (engaged sharing/participation) is essential, central to the faith and to the church: "Christianity means community through and in Jesus Christ [...] whether it be a brief, single encounter or the daily fellowship of years, Christian community is only this. We belong to one another only through and in Jesus Christ."[1] Bonhoeffer goes on to make it clear that this *Gemeinschaft*/community is a gift, is not to be taken for granted and is a physical sign of the "gracious presence of the triune God." Both visitor and visited recognize Christ who is present in the body, Christ who is the unity, allowing the two to be one. [2] Testimonies and recollections of Berlin Fellowship participants repeatedly affirm this. Especially as they reflect upon the borders and the differences, there are surprising lessons and affirmations recognition in both directions, the importance of having a real person visit, and the amazement at how in a limited and liminal setting and period of time, communication and bonding can take place.

However, *koinonia* seems to be one of the most overlooked and underrated aspects of both traditional mission definition and more recent discussion about missional congregational engagement and self-understanding, especially in short-term mission endeavors. In-depth consideration of *koinonia* is also missing in recent missiological research. Granted, more than 50 years of shifting focus in this area have widened and deepened the awareness, discussion, and understanding of mission (*missio Dei*). The vocabulary has even changed, and there is the emerging new paradigm of *missionality* or *missional* perspectives. Yet, there remains a gap or a hole some kind of unmapped territory in the field of mission and missiological research that I believe has been overlooked and warrants notice. What has been overlooked is the role which *koinonia* definitively plays as an instrument or means in missional encounter, that is, its role as one of the very *places* where transformation occurs. This research attests to the role that fellowship encounters play in missional endeavor.

It would also seem there is a gap and equally unmapped territory when it comes to the voices of the partners, labeled earlier in this research mistakenly as only "recipients." In spite of the anecdotal and biographical evidence from mission history, the researched and documented

---

[1] Bonhoeffer, *Life*, 21. "Christliche Gemeinschaft heißt Gemeinschaft durch Jesus Christus und in Jesus Christus. Es gibt keine christliche Gemeinschaft, die mehr, und keine, die weniger wäre als dieses. Von der kurzen einmaligen Begegnung bis zur langjährigen täglichen Gemeinschaft ist christliche Gemeinschaft nur dieses. Wir gehören einander allen durch und in Jesus Christus."
[2] Op. cit., 20.

voices of the partners in many mission and missional encounters are yet but a faint whisper. Though but one example, Berlin Fellowship eastern voices testify in answer to the research questions throughout this dissertation. While these voices and thoughts clearly add to the understanding of the relationship of fellowship and missionality, such voices seem hard to locate in mission history and missiological reflection and research. Why? I am not sure if it is because they haven't been asked, having been traditionally viewed as only recipients, or because they are often too busy just making it through until tomorrow, or because the initiators of missional and ecumenical actions are often more eager to tell the story from their own perspective, documenting and researching primarily their actions, learnings, and enthusiasm. Of course, those initiators of mission or missional endeavors certainly experience transformation and do indeed have a story to tell, but is it not too often their stories alone which have dictated the terms, the vocabulary, the memories, and the shape of the mission story and mission history?

Granted, this research has been conducted by one of those very doers, an American, who traveled to the GDR in the 1980's and then lived as a mission worker in eastern Germany after reunification. It would have been better conducted by an East German, but that didn't happen. Instead it has been my desire in this research to listen for and to voices and memories, reflections and learning and to allow *those* voices then to speak, inform, teach, correct, and illumine. What they say is testimony to God's work in and through fellowship encounters that is, *koinonia* is a locale of missional experience and action, that very place where those who dare to gather in his name and call Jesus Lord, meet with the "other" and are met by the "other," and may be met, as well, by Jesus Christ.

This "meeting," over the course of the Berlin Fellowship years, it must be conceded, was a unique, illuminating illustration of *koinonia* as one-time encounter but even so, as missional activity. However, whether this collection of memories serves as a paradigmatic model for what Bonhoeffer and others identify as the "daily fellowship of years" the usual ways and means for God's people to be in community, is another question.

1. Fellowship is Missional

In the Berlin Fellowship encounters, the church, being and doing "church," participates in a missional activity as the gathered body, a fellowship, or an existential community, and testifies in word and deed to the gospel. In so doing, this particular gathered body of Christ, joins together in worship, service, witness, proclamation, and as a fellowship serves as a hermeneutic of the gospel for itself and to the world, albeit quietly and in a specific and limited sense. Such a mission community or gathering as in this case, solely for fellowship, reminds itself of who it is in Christ and in so doing, in a parabolic sense, points beyond itself to Christ. At the same time, it may remind others in word and deed, of *missio Dei*, the movement of God's love to all. It may do so intentionally or unconsciously; it may do so willingly or hesitantly; it may do so loudly or in a quiet, hardly noticeable manner. Rarely does it do so perfectly.[3] In the case of Berlin Fellowship, this missional encounter of shared participation, this *coming* together, this being a 'sign' to the other talking and listening, asking and answering questions, this meeting and dialoguing even prophetically, this embracing and risking and letting go all create a place of mutuality and communion for the partners, for a time. It is a place of meeting and being met, an incarnational encounter with one another as bearers of the Word of Christ.[4] In this place made possible by what Christ has done for both, the boundaries are not erased but nonetheless crossed by both partners, and they meet on a "third bank" or in a moment where they find themselves being built and bound together, belonging, yet freed and made "into a dwelling place for God."(Eph. 2:14).

2. A Few Rhetorical and Not-So-Rhetorical Questions

Throughout this research there have been a number of rhetorical questions related to fellowship and missional experience. The following are thoughts to some of the questions posed throughout the research. They are formulated and only answered in part, hopefully to provoke further discussion and dialogue, perhaps prophetic in the community of missiological and missional research and reflection.

1. *Was Berlin Fellowship a missional endeavor or mission, in a pre-Bosch sense? How was it received and perceived?*

Berlin Fellowship had its roots in the pre-Bosch, "pre-missional" era and as such started out as a mission in the 1950's a gospel team with the goal of taking the "message of Christ's redeeming, forgiving love to the war-

[3] Bevans and Schroeder, *Constants*, 357.
[4] Bonhoeffer, *Life*, 18 f.

weary students of Europe."[5] However, the early world deputation teams were challenged by Corrie Ten Boom (friend of Ralph Hamburger), to take caution before leaping into such a project:

> I wonder whether or not many of the students would ask why you Americans came to Europe to evangelize? Why you did not stay at home witnessing to Jesus Christ to the youth of your own country?[...]the people of Europe do need to see the love and forgiveness of Christ. But the gospel team idea won't work. You have not suffered as the people in Europe have suffered, so what right have you to speak? If you want to make a vital witness to the power of your faith, go to a city destroyed by American bombs. Identify with the people. Work with them. Eat what they eat. Sleep where they sleep. Maybe if you do it well enough and long enough, without compensation, they will hear what you have to say [...] You must earn the right to be heard.[6]

This admonition turned the tables, and the deputation teams chose to join work groups. They decided to prepare for such work trips by meeting regularly to study the Bible, to learn about Europe and its peoples, and to learn German. Secondly, they embraced a discipline of prayer and enlisted in inner-city "field work" to practice.[7] By the 1960's, the California teams were engaging in "ecumenical endeavors," responding to the repeated invitations from the Germans, whom they clearly identified as their brothers and sisters in faith. Berlin Fellowship visits began in the early 1960's with this foundation. These teams and groups were, per their reports, well-received.

2. *Berlin Fellowship was an activity in and on the borderland, a kind of intercontextual or intercultural crossing of borders. Does one have to cross borders to have fellowship? What role do boundaries play in this activity? Was this boundary-breaking or more likely boundary-crossing? How does Christian fellowship overcome such borders or does it simply allow for borders and boundaries to be crossed?*

Our world and our individual lives are certainly defined and often confined by borders and boundaries; fallen and broken without and within, the human being is trapped. The interviewees' repeated reference to the "coming" of some Americans to visit some Germans through Berlin Fellowship is but a metaphoric reminder of the breach that was crossed by God coming to his creation in Jesus Christ. Fellowship in Christ is a gift

---

[5] James, *Tumbling Walls*, 22.
[6] Op. cit., 23.
[7] Op. cit., 24.

given by God overcoming the boundaries, allowing or enabling a "crossing" of the border to the place of meeting. The surprise for the participants in the Berlin Fellowship endeavor was that the borders remained, and fellowship still happened. Moreover, fellowship did happen and was a gift because those borders *were* crossed by all participants and because of what God in Christ had done for and in the people, in and through the meeting place, the dialogue and the encounter itself. This usually transpired in conversation and dialogue, in time spent touring and picnicking, in worship services and Bible discussions people got to know one another, and through the intercontextual potpourri of meeting they found they were equal partners in dialogue and yet partners who were very different. They were partners in spite of the border from opposite sides of the boundary line, partners whose mentalities and national characteristics were certainly different and whose cultures, church traditions, and languages were also different. They were nonetheless partners who were surprisingly interested and interesting, who were willing to risk, who were Christians and perhaps because of that, whose posture of openness and listening was welcoming and inviting.

This is no overcoming of a boundary; it is being overcome by the truth of the Gospel in the face and person and presence of the "other" recognized and welcomed and embraced. This is what makes Christian fellowship different than friendship or mutual agreement or people who just like each other and get along. It may not always happen, but when it does, it can't be ignored. It may not always be noticed, but when it is, it is compelling and transformative and invites response.

3. *Is Christian fellowship to be realized in a one-time encounter, a conversation between strangers? Can the place where God lives through his Spirit be the place where he becomes known more completely, in spite of fragmented knowledge and understanding or incorrect perceptions?*

The interviewees' answers to direct questions about what Berlin Fellowship was and their ponderings throughout the interviews about the phenomena itself point to the encounters as transforming, and they are labeled as spiritual. These visits, one-time encounters, brought strangers together in a way or ways neither expected. Even after years of teams visiting, the experience seemed again and again to hold surprises and give new insight and encouragement, engendering a kind of enthusiasm. Had the above questions been posed in the interviews, I can imagine receiving affirmative answers, though I don't know that many, myself included, would have been able to pinpoint the reasons.

4. *Was Berlin Fellowship really so different than any ecumenical or partnership meeting? What made interviewees draw this comparison? Are the memories not exaggerated or remembered too positively?*

Some of the German interviewees quite readily compared Berlin Fellowship to the *oikumene,* reflecting the vocabulary of the time and the speaker's life experience. The encounters were, as well, compared to other established ecumenical partnerships, though Berlin Fellowship encounters were labeled as more spiritual, for they are remembered as engaging the participants on a personal level. The Berlin Fellowship team wasn't "official" ecumenism; that is, it wasn't a delegation from Geneva or West Germany. It was, however, understood as Christians who wanted to encourage and share in the Gospel and, and they did so primarily by coming in person, acknowledging and recognizing the hosts in various ways, for many years. The encounters left deep impressions on both host and guest, but not necessarily in ways expected by either. While these memories are perhaps glorified, personal experience tells me every team encounter was not wonderful; some were mundane and rather ordinary, formalities being obliged. This aspect was not, however, explored or considered at the time of the interviews, nor was it spontaneously mentioned.

5. *Is the Berlin Fellowship experience as "a brief, single encounter" in some way paradigmatic for koinonia as "the daily fellowship of years" or was it but a blip on the radar screen in mission history? Does fellowship, realistically created only by God's Spirit, have boundaries put on it by time or place, culture or context, language, Christian tradition, gender, age, etc.? If fellowship encounter is missional, what does this mean for the "missional" church movement, for short-term mission trips, for ecumenical exchange at the grassroots level across borders of all manner, for congregation-to-congregation partnerships?*

These questions lie at the heart of this research. It is not presumptuous to assert such queries merit genuine attention. They point to the nature of what happens in the fellowship moment, be it in a one-time meeting or in a community over decades. The fellowship moment is, at its simplest, an invasion, a happening, the creation of a "place" where God dwells. Because of God, the dialogue becomes prophetic, and the listening and sharing result in learning and change. The events and the engagement become memorable, with outcomes that are not just amazement or new information but something else action, new self-awareness, transformation, change, and in the case of Berlin Fellowship, an enthusiasm and commitment to continued participation.

A number of Berlin Fellowship participants, both Germans and Americans, were drawn to participate again and again. However, they were not drawn back solely to specific personal contacts, though friendships grew out of these encounters. They were not drawn back to a "high" or some "exotic glow" often experienced during the first visit. The next visit was usually completely different, and some team visits were less than overwhelming. They were not drawn back to that warm and wonderful recognition, affirmation and confirmation and reciprocal activity of good times spent together. Though each of these aspects do play a role, it would rather seem participants were drawn back to that "place" where God dwells, a place Bonhoeffer describes as "not an ideal which we must realize [...] rather a reality created by God in Christ in which we may participate."[8] Although not articulated in any of the interviews, what happens in this place is not a glowing or uplifting "aha" experience but rather an encounter of a sort few interviewees could describe or name. It is a realization that "we" belong together and are bound to each other by faith not even by the experience or the very encounter that provided us with this realization but by faith in Christ.[9] This place of life together, for a moment or a day or longer, is the locale of this new understanding made to be that locale by Jesus Christ, made by what he has done and is doing for those gathered, made in them and through them in the fellowship in his name, shared but for the moment *or* over time.

It would seem all kinds of boundaries and reasons exist as reasons for this kind of encounter not to work. At the same time, it would also seem that the boundaries are crossed even unwittingly, when *koinonia* is a reason, a goal or stated purpose for the meeting, trip, or visit. The question was often posed to the Americans upon their return to the U.S., "What did you do?" The answer was usually quite puzzling to the inquirer, "We talked and listened, ate and worshipped, spent time with families and in Bible studies, took long walks, and saw a few sights." Perhaps the North Americans and their partners in the short-term mission craze of recent years, bent on work and helping projects, would benefit from re-thinking what one can really "do" in ten days.

---

[8] Bonhoeffer, *Life*, 30.
[9] Op. cit., 39.

6. *Was there a central text which brought Berlin Fellowship into being, around which it gathered? Or was the Berlin Fellowship encounter itself in some way the locale for the mutually embraced text of the gospel, assumed by all who gathered, though certainly understood and practiced differently? What happens after an encounter and who tells the story afterwards? Whose voices are necessary? What makes for a missional hermeneutic in any kind of similar encounter?*

As discussed briefly in Chapter 2 of this research, James Brownson asserts that everyone needs to hear the gospel from someone who is deeply "other," from someone not like us.[10] The gospel was indeed assumed by both the host and the guest to be the central text occasioning the Berlin Fellowship gathering. However, over the course of years the stories and memories of previous encounters and persons met, the learning, the feelings, the spiritual food provided through the experience itself, all became a kind of "incarnated" text as well. Though no two visits were the same, some "encounters" became almost like liturgical events for hosts and guests alike. For example, in the 1980's, at one family's home, often the last village visited in the GDR, all three traveling groups would meet for a day of debriefing. After the hard work of critical reflection and sharing experiences, there was a party, held by the hosts for the guests. Provided by the host pastor and his family, the final meal and party consisted of a celebration of Christmas, Easter, the 4th of July, any number of other holidays, and of course, everyone's birthday. It was a time of hilarity and great fun.

Because of context, circumstances and caution during these years, participant stories like this and others scattered throughout the interviews have never been widely shared, and little ever written down, even by the Americans. Until this modest research project, the voices of the visited, the host-partners for Berlin Fellowship, have not been heard. They are ultimately necessary for mission history and for future missional and missiological research. These voices don't just fill in the gaps; they tell their side of the story. They tell the East German story of Berlin Fellowship.

---

[10] Brownson, A Response.

3. A State-Sponsored hermeneutic?

On a final note, it should be repeated that I initially thought the Ministry for State Security (*MfS*) files on Berlin Fellowship would lend another East German perspective to the contextual background, providing an outsider's take or hermeneutic on two decades of American-German encounter. That was hardly the case. As it turned out, the known and understood purpose of Berlin Fellowship, recorded first in 1969, included that the visitors were,

> Presbyterians from Los Angeles, U.S.A. [...] sent out and commissioned to visit Europe and to study church life...they enter the country as tourists. They stay about one week in the GDR, with a kind of introduction meeting at the beginning. No big lectures are to happen, rather mostly conversation [...] The focal point of the study is parish or congregational life in the GDR. The Americans want to get to know the congregations [...] to have conversations with parish members.[11]

Later reports nuance this somewhat, but basically, the Stasi got the main idea from day one. The immediate and ongoing suspicion was that the Americans were doing intelligence work, and a file was opened. In spite of the fact that the unofficial informer (*IM*) was a pastor and a trained theologian, there was confusion about the name of the organization, who was in charge, and among other things, the source of funding. It is impossible to determine from the files alone whether that stemmed from the IM's silence on the matter (reporting just the facts), his lack of English knowledge, or a particular theological training or lack thereof (by the officers or the IM). Regardless, Berlin Fellowship's activities and key personalities were scrutinized thoroughly, and though the Berlin Fellowship's purpose is clearly stated in the first pages of the files, it was doubted, disbelieved, or ignored for years. Moreover, misinformation and misunderstanding repeatedly contributed to Stasi "hermeneutical" errors on a regular basis. The following story, a paradigm for the MfS "read" on Berlin Fellowship, illustrates how my initial expectations for MfS files could hardly be fulfilled.

The Berlin Fellowship IM written file reports most often record facts and only observable information about activities (who, what, when, where). When there is a form of interpretation of actual speech, the files sometimes catch a bit of the "meaning" but often misconstrue intent or context. Dated 1975, the following statement is very good example of

---

[11] Rollbahn, I, 7-8.

this kind of misreading: "Ferner hat er ausgeführt, dass die Finanzen in Westberlin im schrumpfen sind, dass man sich aber keine Sorgen machen brauche, der *Herr* wird Geld schaffen, er hat aber nicht gesagt, welcher *Herr*.[12] "Further he elaborated that the finances in West Berlin were shrinking but there was no reason to worry for the Man/the Lord will provide the money, but he didn't say which Man/Lord." *Herr* in German is the word for man but is also used in reference to God, the Lord. It would appear the IM is confused about vocabulary and context. The statement sounds like typical American Christian speech, and the speaker, one of the founders of Berlin Fellowship, would have been very likely to have said just this. Why the IM, a trained theologian and pastor, already active with Berlin Fellowship for five years, would not grasp the intended meaning or choose not to understand or communicate the meaning remains an open question.

4. No Place Like Home

Berlin Fellowship took place under the roof of the Church and was a signpost of the church's essence and action. The "missional" nature of the fellowship encounters attests loudly to the paradox which this "place" of encounter and *koinonia* really is. Christians reconciled and united in Christ, who were at the same time Christians from the "enemy camps," came together for brief encounters. They knew what brought them to that common place of meeting the gospel of Jesus Christ, shared confession, and the shared biblical metanarrative. At the same time, in that coming together, they were confronted with what might well separate them their diversity, intercultural and intercontextual boundaries (i.e. language, culture, nationality, social status, political/economic categories, and economic inequality). These were real boundaries, which they embodied and encountered in one another, in spite of their jointly embraced unity in Christ.

Long before the discussion of mission grew to its current volume, a small group of North American Christians and a small group of German Christians launched an intentional and open "praxis of mutual recognition and cross-cultural conversation."[13] "The gospel imperative is always an imperative for a permanent openness to the other, the stranger, the

[12] Rollbahn IV, 189.

[13] Christopher Duraisingh, Contextual and Catholic: Conditions for Cross-Cultural Hermeneutices, in *Anglican Theological Review*, 82.4, 2000, 685.

alien. Hospitality to strangers and mutuality of recognition of "the other" are intrinsic to the Christian story of God's love in Jesus Christ."[14] Living out of and into this imperative, Berlin Fellowship happened in one form or another from the early 60's until the mid-1990's.

Through and in short-lived snippets of time between 1961 and 1989, limited by language facility and riddled with good reason for skepticism and misunderstanding, a form of joint missional witness and community happened, almost unwittingly and without bureaucratic efforts or programmatic, ecclesial direction. Participants, both German and American, spent time together, and in a missional sense, witnessed to the broken world they lived in and carried within and among themselves. In that time together, they witnessed to the love of God in Jesus Christ, testifying to each other of God's love and reconciling plan for all creation.

The message of reconciliation, recognition, and encouragement embraced by both conversation partners but also delivered in both directions, was enfleshed in the person of the dialogue partner, the "other." Differences in faith understanding, language, culture, and church background offered an excuse to see the differences as divisive, as boundaries and as borders of separation. For reasons described in this research but certainly in the phenomena itself and recollections thereof, one stranger met another stranger and in that encounter, they found themselves on neither's territory, for they met in a kind of *Sperrgebiet*, a border-land, a land in-between.

However, it was *that* border-land which became the place of genuine engagement and meeting. It was there, in a place *between* strangers who had never met before and would probably never meet again "in the gap" that Berlin Fellowship was at home.[15] This place of between-ness or in-betweenness became a place of missional encounter and coming together, of listening and being listened to, of nurture and encouragement, of solidarity and dialogue of fellowship. In the midst of differences and in spite of what even at the time spoke against it, because of the short-lived nature of the encounters, this "place" became *oikos* (home) in the *oikumene (*world*)*, not as an abstract universality but as a lived experience and encounter.

---

14 Op. cit., 683.

15 Op. cit., 683 citing Philip Potter.

Summary

"Is fellowship encounter a missional experience?" In order to answer, this research examines the recollections of eastern 'recipient partners' who were participants in a twice yearly visitation program of American Presbyterians to East Germans between 1961 and 1989. Although there were many church-to-church partnerships between East and West German congregations and between Dutch and East Germans in these years, this was a unique form of ecumenical exchange that wasn't a partnership, yet an ongoing activity and encounter. There is scant missiological scholarship pertaining either East Germany or Eastern Europe for the years 1961 - 1989. There is also neglible research done from the perspective of eastern recipients or partners in various mission or ecumenical actions in that part of the world. Moreover, little seems to have been examined from the point of view of the "others," those engaged in joint missional or ecumenical ventures by virtue of being visited, ministered to, evangelized, or given various forms of aid and support. This is particularly true of central and Eastern Europe and the former Soviet Union, but there would also seem to be a void in research regarding partners' voices elsewhere in the world. In addition, though more recent developments in missional studies and in missiology regularly mention fellowship as a means of mission action or activity, it is most often noted only in passing, usually after a long list of other more "mission-like" activities preaching, teaching, evangelizing, offering acts of service and aid.

Since fellowship is mentioned as a signpost of the Church, and it has been said "the Church *is* mission," I have chosen to examine the relationship between missionality *and* fellowship. Though missional discussion was launched in the mid-20th century, the years since 1980 reflect heightened scholarly interest, research and popular writing. David Bosch's voice in *Transforming Mission*, along with other scholars and missiologists like Lesslie Newbigin, Andrew Walls, Christopher Wright, Stephen Bevans and Roger Schroeder, have lent fervor and varying tones to the discussion. Besides examining these resources as well as looking at select biblical and historical aspects of fellowship, this research listens to interviews of one sample group of East German recipient-partners in a mission-like ecumenical activity, entitled Berlin Fellowship. Their perspectives and impressions, recollections and critiques are a decided support to the research question being answered in the affirmative.

Berlin Fellowship was foundationally an ecumenical endeavor, Christians visiting Christians under the umbrella of the Church. It developed over the years with the thematic emphasis shifting from a ministry of reconciliation to one of encouragement and presence. East German mutuality and ownership was essential to this endeavor's success.

Because the terminology used in this research is central to the discussion, after an introductory chapter (research, resources, methodology, structure), the foundational concepts, relating to the key terms and vocabulary, are examined. Paul is the primary source for the biblical definition of *koinonia* communion, participation, sharing. Though fellowship takes on many forms in the New Testament and is focal to Trinitarian discussion, in this research, fellowship centers "in Christ" and "in the Gospel," in sharing the good news and in a significantly concrete manner, through personal encounter and experience (cf. 1 John 1:1-3). Moreover, *koinonia* is described as having an effect, causing change in the gathered body. In the early Church this effect was a community which shared time together in teaching and fellowship, meals, sacrament and prayers, as well as sharing property and goods with those in need.

Since the 1980's the World Council of Churches has focused fellowship as central to the Christian unity and the Church's self-understanding. Three documents attest to the importance of boundaries and recognition in spite of those boundaries and the role fellowship plays in the mix. These discussions emphasize that fellowship begins with God's act of recognition and crossing the border by entering into and becoming a present and active part of the fallen creation through the incarnation in Jesus Christ. It is in Christ that life in community can be experienced.

In Dietrich Bonhoeffer's *Life Together* Christian community or fellowship is defined by the physical presence of the sister or brother in faith. This community is a call, a blessing, a gift, a joy, a place of belonging and a sign of the physical presence of the triune God. The bodily presence and words of the other remind those in fellowship of who they are and whose they are bringers of the message of salvation to one another. Bonhoeffer acknowledges the hard reality of life together, which is not an illusory hermetic existence. He says that they may recognize each other, in whatever shape or form, as "signs" of the bodily presence of

Christ. Bonhoeffer's Christocentric focus is complimented by the more recent emphasis on relational communication within the Trinity. Both of these perspectives afford a launching pad for further consideration of what binds and brings together recognition, reconciliation and partnership.

Reconciled to God through Christ, the believer has new eyes with which to see and recognize those others, once regarded as strangers or enemies. The believer can then respond, reach out and embrace those others and in turn, be embraced. All of this is based on God's model for doing just that, in and through Christ. The boundary was clear, the breach obvious, and in the gracious coming, sacrificial and reconciling death and resurrection of Jesus Christ, the boundary of separation is repaired. Miroslav Volf's metaphoric "drama of embrace" affords an engaging metaphor for what this looks like in human fellowship and relationships. It might seem that Volf's embrace, if just practiced enough, is the answer. In reality, the complexity of intercultural and intercontextual partnerships reveals how easy it is to miss the mark and how hard it is to understand why. Several studies in which the voice of the "other" is at least in part heard affirm this dilemma. Yet in each case, the reports of the others are hardly above a whisper. However, the partners' voices in this research clearly refer to coming together, to conversation, to relationships that developed and grew to friendships, and to the transformation or change, which ensued.

Encounter on the edges of culture and context is complex, but it is exactly in this place where the study's participants are forced to reckon with the paradoxes of difference and particularity, at the same time they are finding themselves *in* community. In union with Christ, partners are built into to a new place where God dwells through his Spirit (Ephesians 2: 22), a place where he is at work. The Church has long thought itself to be that locale and its job to send out missionaries on God's behalf. David Bosch reconfigures the definition of mission from an activity of the church to an attribute and action of God, his mission at work for the transformation of the world. However, God, already in mission for his creation, does not disconnect mission from the church's essence (the church is mission). Moreover, God's movement in and for the whole world is as well in and for the whole Church, as evidenced in missional engagements like Berlin Fellowship.

Proposing mission to be "prophetic dialogue," Stephen Bevans and Roger Schroeder describe the church as a community serving the world, while *learning* from its involvement and participating with the triune God in a multi-dimensional manner, with witness, proclamation, inculturation, and reconciliation among the component activities. Living as community, albeit imperfectly, in the light of faith and as a ministry of presence in the GDR, the East German Church and its members testified (witness and proclamation) to those who visited from abroad, to those who lived alongside as neighbors, and even to itself. This testimony was not just of an idea, but it was to the person and work of Jesus Christ. Dialogue with the visitors ensued because of reconciliation in Christ, and a new place of coming together was created. Mission was then lived out as a sign of the reign of God to the outside world but also to those who gathered.

The recent missional church movement has contributed to missional understanding from a different perspective, reminding the churches and particularly local congregations, that they are no longer at home in "Christendom." This movement's proponents suggest a conversion of the church's self-understanding in relation to mission, urging the congregation to point beyond itself to God, doing so under the umbrella of the biblical metanarrative. With insights from James Brownson and George Hunsberger, it becomes clear that the actual intercultural encounter is exactly the *place* where the Gospel may be proclaimed or shared, in word and deed and with those who are quite different.

Brownson's assertion is that this place of encounter is the center of a missional hermeneutic and is not about an idea but about Christ. Because it is about Christ, it allows for those differences in the midst of shared and embraced common identity, unifying and reconciling strangers. In the case of this study, the missional hermeneutic reflects the posture, perspective and voice of the other the receiver, the host, the partner.

Berlin Fellowship was primarily a person-to-person visitation ministry, loosely housed under the umbrella of the Presbyterian Church in southern California and the Evangelical Church of Berlin-Brandenburg. Its roots began in the 1950's with the college deputation program of the 1st Presbyterian Church of Hollywood participating in work trips after WWII. Developing in the 1960's into a specific ministry of visitation and encouragement to Christians in East Germany, Berlin Fellowship then continued to organize and refine this ministry through the 1970's and 1980's.

In this researched and documented historical review of Berlin Fellowship and East Germany in the 1960's, 1970's and 1980's, I have sought to let the voices and perspectives of the German partners speak for themselves, complementing the picture of the changing context in the German Democratic Republic between 1961 and 1989. Composed of 10-12 members primarily from Presbyterian congregations, teams traveled twice yearly to congregations throughout the country. Beginning in 1970 Reverend Ted Schapp and Ms. Bärbel Eccardt at the Zinzendorf congregation in West Berlin took on important leadership roles, maintaining communication and contact with those in the east, with the group in southern California, with West Berlin church headquarters, and with eastern regional church offices. This information is documented in western archives.

Coincident to these early developments, in 1968 and continuing through at least 1986, the Ministry for State Security (*MfS*) focused its interest on activities of Berlin Fellowship, planting an unofficial informer in a key position of trust. Although 5500 + pages of *MfS* documentation might have offered insight or another eastern perspective on the ministry and its participants, in the end, the findings were unspectacular and no more than an indication of thorough "information gathering."

It is then the actual interview data which provides the clearest, most interesting and revealing picture of what the voice of the eastern partner has to say. A subjective and qualitative coding and analysis process helped categorize and consolidate hours of interview transcripts. After 40 individual interviews, 27 interviews were transcribed and analyzed, via a rhetorical and qualitative coding process, relying on density for order. The final 30 codes were then divided into four major code families and three remaining smaller outlier categories. The family groupings (Context, Activities, *Koinonia*, and Outcomes) and three outlier categories (Surprise, Missional witness, and so-labeled "third bank"/Ephesian moment) gather the hundreds of quotations into groups. The Context and Activities families afford perspective on the general setting and conditions for Berlin Fellowship encounters and for what happened during a typical visit. As such, the GDR had definite boundaries geographic, geopolitical and for certain sectors of the society, personal. For Christians there were even more boundaries, and these boundaries played no small role. The Activities family gives sufficient testimony to memories of and reference to the types of shared activities, providing the contextual setting for the *Koinonia* code family and its three key subgroups: essence, people-to-people, and communication.

The *essence* of Berlin Fellowship was identified as the coming of American visitors personally (not sending a package or a post card) for conversation and encouragement, in the name of Jesus Christ. This was experienced as a literal act of ecumenical and diaconal solidarity and a kind of "place" where pretenses could disappear and a momentary community might be created. The encounter provided contact, opportunities to give and receive, and engendered a feeling of belonging. The emphasis upon the *people-to-people* nature of the program is repeatedly noted, and many draw attention to how the participants differed. In fact it is noted with surprise, that the differences and the place created by the encounter brought a kind of freedom, in part because of mutual recognition. This act of recognition, which began with simple courtesies extended in both directions, initiated the encounter, with hosts offering hospitality and sharing their surroundings and their homes with joy and pride. Besides commenting about planning the visits as hosts, the interviewees also noted their dissatisfaction with some of the contextual restrictions place on their role. An embraced posture of recognition, reciprocity and ownership meant the hosts were changed, and the interviews indicate transforming effects of the encounters.

When the guests arrived, *conversation* was central to the encounters and gatherings, and is named by many as "the event" in Berlin Fellowship. Specifics of themes or topics discussed are not recalled, but the intensity of the interchange is and resulted in knowledge about the "other" being corrected or increased. Further, it is surprising that visitors are definitely not "like us," but nonetheless, communication easily happens. The American guests asked questions, pursuing conversation in a way uncommon to the Germans. Though this manner of talking so personally was unusual for the hosts, it engendered an openness which they note with surprise. Many of the interviews then relate mini-narratives about an encounter or conversation, identifying the guests by name, noting similarities but also differences, especially the differences in talking about faith. The Americans talked in a manner clearly *other* than the Germans, and this is noted again and again.

Besides new information being learned or misinformation corrected, the visit was an encounter with the world beyond, benefitting both children and youth, and the easterners assumed active ownership of the program. All of this is part of the recognition factor recognition offered and received. Through information exchange and the presence of the other, participants gained a new perspective on the "enemy," on the world inside or outside the GDR, and on the Church worldwide. Labeled as "enriching," this new perspective was reciprocal and contributed to the deepening of faith understanding. In fact, the Outcomes family clearly points to transformation, recognition, ownership, and belonging.

This transformational aspect, especially as it related to the German sense of ownership and belonging led me to name a new code "missional witness" and then to grapple with the "surprises" and the "third bank/Ephesian moment" categories. For both the interviewees and for me, there were surprises during the interviews, in coding and analysis.

For example, two simple "facts" of Berlin Fellowship which took the hosts by surprise and pleasantly so, were that the visitors came at all and had a very different way of conversing. Just as surprising to me were the Eastern German sense of responsibility and "say" in the program, along with critiques of various aspects. Lastly, personal or corporate change occurred in some manner and is remembered years later. I found this a confirmation of my inkled assumptions that fellowship might be a factor of missional action and transformation.

The interviews reveal that "missional witness" can happen in that "place" in the midst of the gathered community, in fellowship. It happens among and between those gathered, and it results in an engaged and interactive encounter. This mutual and shared witness can have lasting effects, serving as encouragement, comfort, and motivation beyond the time of meeting. It may result from or be an attribute of recognition given and received in the shared encounter. "Something" happens to cause change. Exactly what happened was difficult for these interviewees to identify, but it has to do with the presence of the very different other, as much as with what happens or is said. I label this happening with two metaphors. In both, the place of meeting is liminal, in-between, and yet this place acts as a bridge to connect two very different worlds. Describing how these worlds differed, one interviewee says the world from which the visitors came and even their manner of conversation didn't fit at all, but somehow the people fit and then mysteriously the questions and interchange did as well. It was as if a new path was forged, and a new place was entered by both host and guest. The fit, I contend, was "in Christ," Christ making this encounter a unique place, albeit temporary. This was a new form of "life together" which happened in an extraordinary manner in Berlin Fellowship meetings over the course of more than 25 years.

The transcribed interviews point decisively to the owned and embraced sense of belonging for eastern participants. They point to the Berlin Fellowship encounter as a place of *koinonia* though a place of boundaries, boundaries of culture and context, it was yet a place contained "in Christ." It was a place filled with meeting and being met, recognizing and being recognized, giving and receiving. It was a place of encounter in conversation, of transformation, a place where a message "you are not alone" was heard, where the ever-present context of the GDR was somehow counterbalanced by the fleeting but very real presence of some visitors from outside. Through and in that temporary meeting, reciprocal witness became a momentary "hermeneutic of the gospel." Participants were not just engaged with and by each other but also with and by the presence of the living Christ, and they, all of them together, found themselves both host and guest at once.

In conclusion, in the case of this research, fellowship encounter is a missional experience one of many in which the church lives out its call in word and deed. As in worship, service, witness, and proclamation, so in fellowship, the gathered community testifies to the world and to itself of its reason for being. In fellowship, as in other ecclesial "hallmarks," the gathered community reminds itself and the 'others' of the living Lord Jesus Christ. As a missional activity, fellowship can and does act in a parabolic sense to point beyond itself. As an incarnational encounter for all participants, this place of meeting becomes a place of liberation and freedom, while at the same time a place of belonging and of home, a "dwelling place for God."

Though some attention has been given to this topic by theologians and missiologists, *koinonia* has largely been overlooked as a means of missional activity. This research examines one small corner of a potentially large complex of subjects and does so, in a specific and modest manner. Convinced of the merit in such study I close by commending some further thoughts and findings.

With its roots in a mission movement of a local congregation in southern California, Berlin Fellowship began as an ecumenical visitation. In today's parlance it should be also viewed as a missional activity as testified by the German voices studied in this research. Borders and boundaries (i.e. the Iron Curtain and the enemy status of the others) both play a key role in the story, but neither have the last word; the gift of fellowship allowed for borders to be crossed. In spite of boundaries and as followers of Christ, the participants were able to embrace one another, reconciled not just in principle but in fact, able to experience that reconciliation in the act of fellowship and sharing, encouragement and presence. Though one-time encounters might be discounted, a one-time, short-term meeting is attested to in this study as valid, as much as the fellowship of years. Lastly, the central text under which the Berlin Fellowship met was that of the gospel of Jesus Christ, assumed, embraced, and believed. Yet, the German story of these encounters represents an important part of the hermeneutical umbrella for communicating and understanding the missional role fellowship plays. It is time to listen to this story and to these voices.

Koinonia is a missional reality not to be underestimated. It is, I believe, a yet-to-be understood treasure of wisdom and witness, hope and learning for those seeking ways to "do" something in mission for the kingdom. Just being with and for the other as host or as guest *is* integral to "doing" mission or missional endeavors. As for the story of Berlin Fellowship and its eastern partners' recollections, the point seems clear. There was only one thing really that could be "done" in that context and that was spend time together, listen, learn and in so doing testify together to the love of God shared and experienced, over a meal, on a walk in the forest or in a Bible discussion in fellowship. The borders and boundaries of culture and language, context and politics were not erased but retreated to the shadows for an hour or two, a day or two. An often surprising encounter happened and a place was created in spite of what might have seemed improbable and certainly unlikely.

Samenvatting

“Is gemeenschap een missionaire (“missional”[1]) ervaring?” Om deze vraag te beantwoorden richt het onderzoek zich op herinneringen van ‘ontvangende partners’ bij bezoeken van Amerikaanse Presbyterianen aan Oost Duitsland tussen 1961 en 1989 onder de naam van Berlin Fellowship. Hoewel er in die jaren tussen Oost en West Duitse gemeenten en tussen Nederlanders en Oost Duitsters vele kerkelijke partnerschappen waren, was Berlin Fellowship een unieke vorm van oecumenische uitwisseling die geen partnerschap was, maarl een doorgaande activiteit en ontmoeting. In wetenschappelijk onderzoek over missiologie in de periode 1961 – 1989 is zeer weinig vanuit een westers perspectief te vinden met betrekking tot Oost Duitsland of Oost Europa. Ook is er nauwelijks onderzoek naar het perspectief van ontvangers of partners in Oost Europa, de ‘anderen’ die betrokken waren in gezamenlijke missionaire of oecumenische ondernemingen doordat zij bezocht of met het evangelie in contact gebracht werden, ofwel bijstand of een vorm van hulpverlening of ondersteuning ontvingen. Dat geldt in het bijzonder voor Midden en Oost Europa en voor de voormalige Sovjet Unie. Eveneens blijkt dat er een lacune bestaat met betrekking tot de stem van partners elders in de wereld. Hoewel in recentere missionaire studies en missiologie gemeenschap als een middel van missionaire activiteit wordt genoemd, is dat meestal slechts in het voorbijgaan en dan na een lange lijst van andere, meer ‘missie-achtige’ activiteiten, zoals prediking, onderricht, evangelisatie, dienstverlening en ondersteuning.

Omdat gemeenschap meestal als kenmerk (nota) van de kerk wordt genoemd en men tegelijk gesteld heeft dat de kerk missie is, heb ik ervoor gekozen om de relatie tussen het missionaire (‘missionality’) en gemeenschap nader te onderzoeken. Hoewel de discussie over het missionaire karakter van de kerk reeds halverwege de twintigste eeuw op gang

[1] Waar de term ‘missionary’ in het Engels naar een activiteit van de kerk verwijst, wordt de term ‘missional’ gebruikt om naar een kwaliteit of wezenskenmerk van de kerk aan te duiden. In het Nederlands, dat alleen de vertaling ‘missionaire’ kent, gaat het onderscheid verloren. De Nederlandse lezer dient het onderscheid voor ogen te houden.

kwam, zien we in de jaren na 1980 een verhoogde mate van missiologisch onderzoek en missiologische studies, met name door de impact van het boek *Transforming Mission* van David Bosch. Zijn stem, samen met die van andere wetenschappers en missiologen, zoals Lesslie Newbigin, Andrew Walls, Christopher Wright, Stephen Bevans en Roger Schroeder, hebben de discussie intensiteit en een variatie aan toonzettingen verleend. Naast het nader verkennen van die bronnen en het bespreken van geselecteerde Bijbelse en historische aspecten van gemeenschap en gemeenschapsvorming, luistert deze studie nauwkeurig naar interviews van een voorbeeldgroep van ontvangende partners uit Oost Duistland, die tussen 1960 en 1989 aan een missie-achtig oecumenisch programma deelnamen: Berlin Fellowship. Hun perspectieven en indrukken, herinneringen en kritische opmerkingen zijn een beslissende ondersteuning bij het bieden van een positief antwoord op de onderzoeksvraag.

Berlin Fellowship was in fundamentele zin een oecumenische onderneming van christenen die christenen bezochten, broeders en zusters die onder de paraplu van de kerk elkaar in gemeenschap ontmoetten. Door de jaren heen verschoof de nadruk van een 'dienst van verzoening' naar een 'dienst van bemoediging en presentie'. De wederkerigheid en het mede-eigenaarschap van de Oost Duitse partners waren essentieel voor het welslagen van de onderneming.

Omdat de terminologie die in deze studie gebruikt wordt in de discussie centraal staat, worde - na inleidende opmerkingen over het onderzoek en de methodologie – de fundamentele concepten en termen besproken met een focus op de sleutelbegrippen 'gemeenschap' en 'missionair' ('missional'). Paulus dient als primaire bron voor een Bijbelstheologische definitie van *koinonia*: communio, participatie, delen. Hoewel gemeenschap in het Nieuwe Testament vele vormen aanneemt en in trinitarische discussies een centrale rol spelen, wordt in dit onderzoek gemeenschap "in Christus" en "in het evangelie" gecentreerd, in het delen van de goede boodschap op een concrete manier en door persoonlijke ontmoeting en ervaring (vgl. 1 Johannes 1:1-3). Bovendien wordt aan *koinonia* het effect toegeschreven van het veroorzaken van verandering in het bijeengekomen lichaam. In de vroege kerk was het effect van *koinonia* het scheppen van een gemeente die tijd voor onderricht en gemeenschap, voor maaltijden, sacramenten en gebeden met elkaar deelde, naast het delen van eigendom en goederen met behoeftigen.

Als een basale leerstelling van christelijke eenheid en van het zelfverstaan van de kerk, heeft de term gemeenschap vanaf 1980 een sleutelrol in discussies van de Wereldraad van Kerken gespeeld. Drie documenten belijden het belang van grenzen tussen kerken én van erkenning ondanks de grenzen, om vervolgens de rol die 'gemeenschap' speelt in het geheel te onderstrepen. De discussies benadrukken dat gemeenschap begint met Gods acte van erkennen en overschrijden van een grens. In de incarnatie treedt de Zoon van God in de vervallen schepping binnen om er een aanwezig en actief deel van te worden. Het is in Christus dat leven in gemeenschap ervaren kan worden.

In *Leven met elkander* van Dietrich Bonhoeffer wordt christelijke gemeenschap gedefinieerd door de fysieke aanwezigheid van een zuster of broeder in het geloof. De gemeenschap wordt verstaan als een roeping, een zegen, een gave, een vreugde, een plek van saamhorigheid en een teken van de fysieke aanwezigheid van de drie-enige God. De lichamelijke aanwezigheid van de ander en zijn of haar woorden herinnert hen die in gemeenschap bijeen zijn aan wie zij zijn en aan wie zij toebehoren, als dragers van de boodschap van het heil voor elkaar. Bonhoeffer erkent de harde werkelijkheid van het leven met elkaar dat geen illusoir, hermetisch bestaan is. Hij herinnert de gelovigen eraan dat zij elkaar kunnen erkennen, in welke vorm dan ook, als 'tekenen' van de lichamelijke aanwezigheid van Christus. De christocentrische focus van Bonhoeffer wordt gecomplementeerd door de nadruk die recenter op relationele communicatie binnen de triniteit wordt gelegd. Die perspectieven bieden een vertrekpunt voor een verdere overweging van wat bindt en samen brengt: erkenning, verzoening en partnerschap.

Verzoend met God in Christus heeft de gelovige nieuwe ogen om anderen te zien en te erkennen, anderen die misschien eerst als vreemdelingen of zelfs vijanden werden gezien. De gelovige kan zo op een ander reageren, zich naar een ander uitstrekken, een ander omarmen en omgekeerd door een ander omarmd worden. Dat alles is gebaseerd op het model waarin God in en door Christus hetzelfde heeft gedaan. Er was een heldere grens en een duidelijke breuk. In het genadig komen van Jezus Christus, in zijn offerende en verzoenende dood en in zijn opstanding is in de scheidende grens een bres geslagen. Een metafoor van Miroslav Volf, de "drama van de omarming", biedt een helder en aansprekend beeld van hoe dat in menselijke relaties en in een gemeenschap eruit kan zien. Het beeld van omarming, mits voldoende beoefend, lijkt misschien een afdoende antwoord te bieden. De complexiteit van interculturele en inter-contextuele partnerschappen laat tegelijk zien hoe gemakkelijk het is om het doel voorbij te schieten en hoe moeilijk het is om te begrijpen waarom. Vele studies waarin de stem van de "ander" in ieder geval gedeeltelijk gehoord wordt bevestigen dit dilemma. In alle gevallen stijgen de rapportages vanuit de stem van de ander echter nauwelijks boven een fluistertoon uit. In dit onderzoek wijzen de stemmen van de partners duidelijk naar elementen van samenkomen, gesprekken, relaties die zich ontwikkelen, vriendschappen die ontstonden en de transformatie die volgde.

Een ontmoeting op de grens van cultuur en context is een ingewikkelde zaak, maar ook een mogelijkheid voor deelnemers om met de paradoxen van verschil en particulariteit te rekenen, terwijl zij zich tegelijkertijd *in* gemeenschap vinden. In de verbintenis met Christus, worden partners samen opgebouwd tot een nieuwe plaats waar God woont door zijn Geest (Efeziërs 2:22). Als dat daadwerkelijk een woonplaats van God is, dan is dat ook een plaats waar God aan het werk is. Hoewel de kerk meestal als die plaats wordt verstaan, vormt David Bosch de definitie van missie om van een activiteit van de kerk naar een eigenschap van God, Gods eigen missie met het oog op de transformatie van de wereld. De beweging van God naar de wereld neemt echter niet weg dat missie tot het fundament van de kerk hoort: de kerk is missie. Gods beweging in en voor de hele wereld is tegelijk in en voor de hele kerk, waartoe oecumenische en gemeenschappelijke projecten als Berlin Fellowship getuigen.

Stephen Bevans and Roger Schroeder verstaan missie als "profetische dialoog" (die het innerlijk leven van de Triniteit weerspiegelt). Van daaruit beschrijven zij de kerk als een gemeenschap die de wereld dient en van haar betrokkenheid leert door op multi-dimensionele wijze met de drie-enige God aan missie deel te nemen. De activiteiten van getuigenis, verkondiging, inculturatie en verzoening maken daar deel van uit. Door in het licht van het geloof als gemeenschap te leven (hoezeer onvolkomen) en als een dienst van aanwezigheid in de DDR, legde de Oost Duitse kerk aan buitenlands bezoekers, naasten maar ook aan zich zelf getuigenis af. Die getuigenis had niet slechts op een idee betrekking, maar op de persoon en werk van Jezus Christus. Dialoog volgde uit de verzoening in Christus en een nieuwe plaats van samenkomen werd geschapen. Voor de buitenwereld maar ook voor de gemeenschap zelf werd missie geleefd als een teken van het regeren van God.

De recente "missional church movement" heeft bijgedragen aan een missionair verstaan vanuit een ander perspectief door kerken en gemeenten eraan te herinneren dat zij niet meer thuis kunnen zijn in het 'christendom'. De voorstanders van de beweging stellen een omkering in het zelfverstaan van de kerk in relatie tot missie voor, door de gemeenten aan te sporen voorbij zichzelf naar God te wijzen. Daarbij wordt naar het overkoepelend verhaal ("meta-narrative") van de Bijbel verwezen. Met inzichten van James Brownson en Geoerge Hunsberger wordt duidelijk gemaakt dat de actuele, interculturele ontmoeting precies de *plaats* is waar het evangelie (als 'meta-narrative') in woord en daad verkondigd en gedeeld kan worden, met hen die zeer anders zijn.

Brownson stelt dat de ontmoeting de kern van een missionaire hermeneutiek vormt en betrekking heeft niet op een idee maar op Christus zelf. Omdat het om Christus gaat, is er ruimte voor verschillen te midden van een gedeelde en omarmde identiteit die vreemdelingen verzoent en één maakt. In het geval van deze studie weerspiegelt de missionaire hermeneutiek de houding, het perspectief en de stem van de ontvanger, de ander, de gastheer/-vrouw en de partner.

Berlin Fellowship was vooral een dienst van bezoeken en ontmoetingen van mens tot mens, die losjes onder de paraplu van de Presbyteriaanse Kerk in het zuiden van California en van de Evangelische kerk in Berlin-Brandenburg onderdak vond. De wortels reiken terug naar de jaren vijftig van de vorige eeuw met de uitzending van studenten van First Presbyterian Church of Hollywood voor deelname aan werkreizen na de tweede wereldoorlog. In de jaren zestig ontwikkelde zich Berlin Fellowship specifiek in de richting van een dienst van bezoeken aan en bemoediging van christenen in Oost Duitsland. In de jaren zeventig en tachtig werd de organisatie voortgezet en verfijnd.

In een historisch en gedocumenteerd overzicht van Berlin Fellowship en Oost Duitsland tussen 1961 en 1989 heb ik geprobeerd om de stemmen en perspectieven van de Duitse deelnemers zo veel mogelijk voor zichzelf te laten spreken, als aanvulling op het beeld van de veranderende context van de Duitse Democratische Republiek in die periode. Met 10 tot 12 deelnemers uit voornamelijk Presbyteriaanse gemeenten reisden groepen ('teams') twee keer per jaar naar gemeenten in de hele DDR. Van 1970 namen ds. Ted Schapp en mevrouw Bärbel Eccardt van de Zinzendorf gemeente in West Berlijn een leidende rol in het onderhouden van de communicatie en de contacten met de betrokkenen in Oost Duitsland en met de groep in zuidelijk California, met het kerkelijk hoofdbureau in West Berlijn en met de regionale kerkelijke bureau's in Oost Duitsland. Deze informatie vindt men in westerse archieven gedocumenteerd.

Tegelijk met deze vroege ontwikkelingen richtte de Staatsveiligheid Dienst (MfS) vanaf 1968 en in ieder geval tot en met 1986 zijn aandacht op de activiteiten van Berlin Fellowship en positioneerde een inofficiële informant in een centrale vertrouwenspositie. Hoewel de meer dan 5500 bladzijden van MfS documentatie over Berlin Fellowship inzicht in, of een ander oost perspectief op, de onderneming en haar deelnemers had kunnen bieden, bleek de opbrengst uiteindelijk mager en niet meer dan een indicatie van het nauwgezet verzamelen van informatie.

Het zijn de data uit interviews met deelnemers die het meest heldere, interessante en openhartige beeld geven van wat de stem van de partner te zeggen heeft. Een proces met subjectieve en kwalitatieve codering en analyse hielp om vele uren interviewmateriaal in de vorm van transcripten te categoriseren en consolideren. Na het houden van 40 individuele interviews werden 27 ervan getranscribeerd en geanalyseerd door middel van retorische en kwalitatieve coderingsprocessen, waarbij dichtheid als ordeningsprincipe diende. De laatste 30 codes werden vervolgens in vier hoofdfamilies ingedeeld, plus drie kleinere, randcategorieën. De families (context, activiteiten, *koinonia*, en resultaten) en de drie randcategorieën (verrassing, missionaire getuigenis en de zogenaamde "third bank/Ephesian moment") brengen honderden van citaten samen in groepen. De families 'context' en 'activiteiten' bieden een perspectief op de algemene setting en voorwaarden voor ontmoetingen in Berlin Fellowship en voor wat er gebeurde in typische bezoeken. De DDR had duidelijke grenzen, geografisch, geopolitiek en – in bepaalde maatschappelijke sectoren – ook persoonlijk. Voor christenen waren er nog meer grenzen en die grenzen speelden een niet geringe rol. De codefamilie 'activiteiten' biedt in de vorm van herinneringen en verwijzingen voldoende getuigenis van de soorten gedeelde activiteiten die plaatsvonden. Die boden een context voor de codefamilie '*koinonia*' met drie belangrijke subgroepen: essentie, het intermenselijke ("people-to-people") en communicatie.

De essentie van Berlin Fellowship werd gezien als het komen en persoonlijk aanwezig zijn van de Amerikaanse bezoekers (in tegenstelling tot een pakje of kaartje sturen) voor gesprek en bemoediging in de naam van Jezus Christus. De bezoeken werden als een letterlijke daad van oecumenische en diaconale solidariteit ervaren, een soort "plaats" waar schijn en pretentie konden verdwijnen en een tijdelijke gemeenschap gevormd werd. Het programma bood contact en gelegenheid voor geven en ontvangen en het schiep een gevoel van saamhorigheid. De nadruk op het intermenselijke karakter van het programma werd herhaaldelijk opgemerkt en vele geïnterviewden wezen erop hoe de deelnemers van elkaar verschilden. Met verbazing werd opgemerkt dat de verschillen, in samenhang met de "plaats" die door de ontmoeting geschapen werd, een soort vrijheid met zich meebrachten, in niet onbelangrijke mate vanwege de wederkerige erkenning. Die acte van erkenning, die telkens met kleine beleefdheden begon, maakte het hen mogelijk om te geven en om gastvrijheid te bieden, om met vreugde en trots hun woningen en omgevingen te delen. Naast het nemen van verantwoordelijkheid als gastheer en -vrouw voor het plannen van de bezoeken, noemden de geïnterviewden ook hun ontevredenheid over de beperkingen in hun rol die de context met zich meebracht. Een omarmende houding van erkenning, wederkerigheid en eigenaarschap betekende een verandering, en de geïnterviewden wezen naar de transformerende effecten als gevolg van de ontmoetingen.

Als de gasten arriveerden stond het gesprek centraal in de ontmoetingen en bijeenkomsten. Velen noemen het gesprek de gebeurtenis ("the event") van Berlin Fellowship. Specifieke thema's of onderwerpen herinnert men zich niet, maar wel de intensiteit van de uitwisseling, met als gevolg een bijstelling of toename in kennis van de "ander". Verder vond men het verrassend dat de bezoekers bepaald niet waren "zoals wij zijn", maar dat men gemakkelijk met hen kon communiceren. De Amerikaanse gasten stelden vragen en converseerden op een manier die voor de Duitsers ongewoon was. Hoewel de persoonlijke manier van praten voor de gastheren en -vrouwen ongewoon was, stimuleerde het een openheid die zij met verbazing opmerkten. Velen van de geïnterviewden vertelden dan kleine verhalen over een ontmoeting of gesprek, waarbij zij de gesprekspartner bij naam noemden en overeenkomsten en verschillen vermeldden, in het bijzonder verschillen in het spreken over eigen geloof. De Amerikanen spraken op een manier die duidelijk *anders* was dan die van de Duitsers. Keer op keer werd dat opgemerkt.

Behalve een gelegenheid voor het horen van nieuwe informatie of het bijstellen van verkeerde informatie was een bezoek een ontmoeting met een wereld ver weg, hetgeen ook kinderen en jongeren ten goede kwam. De Oost Duitse deelnemers beschouweden zich als mede-eigenaar van het programma. Dat alles had te maken met het geven en ontvangen van erkenning. Door de uitwisseling van informatie en door de aanwezigheid van de ander kregen deelnemers een nieuw perspectief op de "vijand", op de wereld binnen en buiten de DDR en op de wereldwijde kerk. Dat nieuwe perspectief vond men "verrijkend". Het was wederkerig en droeg bij tot een verdieping van het geloofsverstaan. De codefamilie 'resultaten' wijst naar transformatie, erkenning, eigenaarschap en saamhorigheid.

Het transformerend aspect, vooral in zijn relatie tot het Duitse gevoel van mede-eigenaarschap en saamhorigheid, leidde ertoe dat ik een nieuwe codenaam formuleerde, namelijk, 'missionaire getuigenis' ("missional witness") om vervolgens ook met de categorieën 'verrassingen' en 'Third bank/Ephesian moment' te werken. Zowel de geïnterviewden als ik werden verrast, tijdens de interviews en in de codering en analyse. Bijvoorbeeld, eenvoudige gegevenheden van Berlin Fellowship, die de gastheren en -vrouwen op aangename wijze verrasten, waren het feit *dat* de bezoekers kwamen en dat hun wijze van converseren zo anders was. Een verrassing voor mij was het besef van verantwoordelijkheid en de inbreng in het programma van Oost Duitse kant, samen met kritiek op bepaalde onderdelen. Misschien het meest verrassend was dat persoonlijke of gemeenschappelijke verandering op een of andere manier daadwerkelijk plaatsvond en jaren later herinnerd werd. Dat dient als bevestiging van mijn aanname dat gemeenschap een factor in missionair handelen en missionaire transformatie kan zijn.

De interviews laten zien dat missionaire getuigenis ("missional witness") zich op een dergelijke "plaats" kan voltrekken, te midden van een samengekomen gemeente, in gemeenschap. Het voltrekt zich onder en tussen hen die bijeen zijn. Het resultaat is een betrokken en interactieve ontmoeting. Die wederkerige en gedeelde

getuigenis kan blijvende effecten hebben en als bemoediging, troost en bekrachtiging dienen, die verder reiken dan het moment van de ontmoeting. Het is wellicht een resultaat of eigenschap van de erkenning die in de gedeelde ontmoeting gegeven en ontvangen wordt. "Iets" gebeurt dat verandering veroorzaakt. Wat precies gebeurde was voor de geïnterviewden moeilijk om te identificeren, maar het had net zo veel te maken met de aanwezigheid van de ander die anders was als met wat gebeurde of gezegd werd. Ik benoem dit gebeuren met behulp van twee metaforen. In beide is de plaats van ontmoeting liminaal, een tussenin, die tegelijk als brug dient om twee zeer verschillende werelden te verbinden. In het beschrijven van hoe de werelden verschilden, zei een geïnterviewde dat de wereld waar de bezoekers vandaan kwamen en hun manier van converseren niet pasten, maar dat op een of andere manier de mensen bij elkaar pasten. Het was alsof een nieuwe weg gebaand werd en een nieuwe plaats werd betreden door zowel gastheer/-vrouw als gast. Het passen, wil ik betogen, geschiedde "in Christus". Christus maakte de ontmoeting tot een unieke plaats, al was het tijdelijk. Het was een nieuwe vorm van "leven met elkander" dat geschiedde op een uitzonderlijke wijze in Berlin Fellowship bijeenkomsten over een periode van meer dan 25 jaar.

De getranscribeerde interviews toonden resoluut een besef van saamhorigheid, toegeëigend en omarmd door de Oost Duitse deelnemers. Zij wezen naar de ontmoetingen in Berlin Fellowship als een plaats van *koinonia* – een plaats met grenzen van cultuur en context die tegelijk "in Christus" omvat werd. Het was een plaats gevuld met ontmoeten en ontmoet worden, erkennen en erkend worden, geven en ontvangen. Het was een plaats van ontmoeting in gesprek, in transformatie, een plaats waar een boodschap "Je bent niet alleen" gehoord werd. De sterk aanwezige context van de DDR vond op een of ander manier een tegenwicht in de vluchtige maar tegelijk werkelijke aanwezigheid van bezoekers van buiten. Door en in die tijdelijke ontmoeting werd wederkerige getuigenis tot een momentane "hermeneutiek van het evangelie". De deelnemers ontdekten in hun betrokkenheid met en op elkaar, in en door de aanwezigheid van de levende Christus, dat zij gastheer/-vrouw en gast tegelijk waren.

Een conclusie van het onderzoek is dat de ervaring van gemeenschap een missionaire ervaring kan zijn – een van vele waarin de kerk haar roeping in woord en daad aan de dag legt. Net als in haar eredienst, dienstbetoon, getuigenis en verkondiging legt de vergaderde gemeente ook in haar gestalte als gemeenschap getuigenis af aan de wereld en aan zich zelf van haar reden van bestaan. In gemeenschap, net als in de andere kenmerken van de kerk, herinnert de vergaderde gemeente zich zelf en anderen aan de levende Heer Jezus Christus. Als een missionaire activiteit werkt gemeenschap als een gelijkenis en wijst voorbij zichzelf. Als een incarnerend gebeuren voor alle deelnemers wordt de plaats van ontmoeting een plaats van bevrijding en tegelijk een plaats van saamhorigheid als een thuis, een "woonplaats voor God".

Hoewel er onder theologen en missiologen enige aandacht voor het onderwerp aanwezig is, heeft men doorgaans *koinonia* als een middel van missionaire activiteit over het hoofd gezien. Dit onderzoek richt zich op specifieke en bescheiden wijze op een klein hoekje van wat in potentieel een groot complex van subjecten behelst. Tegelijk ligt daarin een verdienste van het onderzoek. Ik sluit af met nog een paar gedachten en uitkomsten.

De wortels van Berlin Fellowship lagen in missionaire activiteiten van een plaatselijke gemeente in zuidelijk California. In huidige termen kan het als missionaire ("missional") activiteit beschouwd worden, in overeenstemming met het getuigenis van de Duitse stemmen die onderzocht werden. Grenzen (van het ijzeren gordijn en van de status als vijanden van elkaar) speelden een sleutelrol in de geschiedenis van Berlin Fellowship, maar zij hadden niet het laatste woord. De gave van gemeenschap maakte het mogelijk om grenzen te overschrijden. Ondanks de grenzen waren de deelnemers als volgelingen van Christus in staat om elkaar te omarmen, verzoend als zij waren, niet alleen principieel maar daadwerkelijk, en in staat om de verzoening als een acte van gemeenschap en delen met elkaar, van bemoediging en presentie te ervaren. Hoewel eenmalige ontmoetingen gemakkelijk afgeschreven zouden kunnen worden, blijkt uit dit onderzoek dat een eenmalige, kortdurende ontmoeting net zo geldig kan zijn als een contact over vele jaren. Ten slotte, de centrale tekst waaronder Berlin Fellowship zich afspeelde was die van het evangelie van Jesus Christus, aangenomen, omarmd en geloofd. Tegelijk dient het Oost Duitse verhaal van de ontmoetingen ook zelf als een belangrijke hermeneutische paraplu voor het verstaan en het communiceren van de missionaire rol die gemeenschap speelt. Het wordt tijd om naar dat verhaal en naar die stemmen te luisteren.

Koinonia is een missionaire werkelijkheid die niet onderschat moet worden. Het is mijn overtuiging dat *koinonia* een schat van wijsheid en getuigenis, van hoop en leren omvat, die nog ontsloten moet worden voor hen die manieren zoeken om met het oog op het koninkrijk iets in missie te "doen". Eenvoudigweg het met en voor een ander zijn als gastheer/-vrouw of gast maakt integraal deel uit van wat er te "doen" valt in missie en in missionaire ondernemingen. Met betrekking tot het verhaal van Berlin Fellowship en de herinneringen van de Oost Duitse partners ervan lijkt het punt duidelijk. Er was maar een ding dat men echt kon "doen" in die context en dat was tijd met elkaar doorbrengen, tijd om te luisteren en leren en op die wijze samen getuigen van de liefde van God die men deelde en ervoer. Dat gebeurde bij een maaltijd, tijdens een boswandeling of in een gesprek over de Bijbel, kortom, in gemeenschap. De grenzen van cultuur en taal, van de context en de politiek, werden niet uitgewist, maar zij trokken zich terug in de schaduwen voor een uur of twee of een dag of twee. Vaak voltrok zich een verrassende ontmoeting en werd, hoe onwaarschijnlijk het ook leek, een "plaats" geschapen.

Vertaling: Elisabeth Posthumus Meyjes & Martin Walton

Zusammenfassung

„Sind Gemeinschaftsreffen (fellowship encounter) missionale Erfahrungen?“ Um diese Frage zu beantworten, untersucht die vorliegende Forschungsarbeit die Erinnerungen ostdeutscher „empfangender Partner“, die an einem Besuchsprogramm durch amerikanische presbyterianische Christen teilnahmen, die zwischen 1961 und 1989 zweimal jährlich zu Besuchen in Ostdeutschland waren. Es gab in jenen Jahren viele Partnerschaften zwischen ost- und westdeutschen Kirchengemeinden und ebenso Partnerschaften zwischen Niederländern und Ostdeutschen, doch war das Fellowship-Programm keine Partnerschaft, sondern eine einzigartige Form ökumenischen Austausches – fortgehende Aktivität und Begegnung. Es gibt bisher nur spärliche missionswissenschaftliche Untersuchungen, die sich mit Ostdeutschland oder Osteuropa in den Jahren 1961-1989 beschäftigen. Auch wurde nur geringfügige und damit zu vernachlässigende Forschungsarbeit aus der Perspektive östlicher Empfänger oder Partner bei verschiedenen missionarischen oder ökumenischen Aktionen in jenem Teil der Welt geleistet. Darüber hinaus scheint nur wenig aus der Sicht der „Anderen“ untersucht worden zu sein, jener ‚die an den gemeinsamen missionarischen oder ökumenischen Unternehmungen beteiligt waren, sei es dadurch, dass sie besucht und seelsorgerlich begleitet wurden, sie an Evangelisationen beteiligt waren oder ihnen verschiede Formen von Hilfe und Unterstützung zuteilwurden. Dies gilt besonders für Mittel- und Osteuropa sowie die ehemalige Sowjetunion, doch scheint es auch in der Forschung zu den Stimmen der Partner anderswo in der Welt in dieser Hinsicht eine Lücke zu geben. Außerdem, obwohl die jüngeren Entwicklungen in Missionsstudien und in der Missionswissenschaft Gemeinschaft (fellowship) regelmäßig als Form missionarischer Arbeit und Aktivität nennen, wird selbige doch meist nur nebenbei erwähnt, normalerweise nach einer langen Liste anderer eher „missionsartiger“ Aktivitäten – Predigt, Lehre, Evangelisation, Dienst und Hilfe.

Da Gemeinschaft normalerweise als ein Charakteristikum der Kirche angesehen wird und da gesagt wird „Die Kirche *ist* Mission“, habe ich mich entschlossen, die Beziehung zwischen Missionalität *und* Gemeinschaft zu untersuchen. Obwohl die missionale Diskussion in der Mitte des 20. Jahrhunderts begann, reflektieren die Jahre seit 1980 verstärkt missionswissenschaftliche Forschung und allgemeine Publikationen. Gemeinsam mit anderen Gelehrten und Missionswissenschaftlern wie Lesslie Newbigin, Andrew Walls, Christopher Wright, Stephen Bevans und Roger Schroeder verleiht David Boschs Stimme in „*Transforming Mission*" der Diskussion Leidenschaft und unterschiedliche Färbung. Neben der Untersuchung dieser Quellen und der Betrachtung ausgewählter biblischer und historischer Aspekte von Gemeinschaft konzentriert sich diese Arbeit auf Interviews mit einer Stichprobengruppe ostdeutscher Partner auf der Empfängerseite bei einer missionsähnlichen ökumenischen Aktivität – genannt Berlin Fellowship. Ihre Ansichten und Eindrücke, Erinnerungen und Kritiken sind entscheidend dafür, dass die Forschungsfrage positiv beantwortet wird.

Berlin Fellowship war im Wesentlichen eine ökumenische Unternehmung, Christen besuchten Christen unter dem Dach der Kirche. Sie entwickelte sich über die Jahre weiter, wobei sich der thematische Schwerpunkt von einem Dienst zur Versöhnung hin zu Ermutigung und Präsenz verlagerte. Ostdeutsche Haltung von Gegenseitigkeit und Mitverantwortung waren essenziell für den Erfolg dieser Unternehmung.

Da die in dieser Arbeit verwendete Terminologie für die Diskussion wesentlich ist, werden nach einem Einleitungskapitel (Forschungsstand, Quellen, Methodologie und Struktur) grundlegende Konzepte bezogen auf das Vokabular und Schlüsselbegriffe untersucht. Paulus ist die Primärquelle für die biblische Definition von *koinonia* – Gemeinschaft, Teilhabe, Teilen. Obwohl Gemeinschaft im Neuen Testament viele Formen annimmt und im Brennpunkt der Trinitäts-Diskussion steht, ist Gemeinschaft in dieser Arbeit zentriert auf „in Christus" und „im Evangelium", zentriert darauf, die Botschaft des Evangeliums in einer signifikanten konkreten Art durch persönliche Begegnung und Erfahrung miteinander zu teilen (vgl. 1. Joh. 1,1-3). Zudem wird *koinonia* so beschrieben, dass sie Auswirkungen hat, die in der versammelten Gemeinde Veränderungen bewirken. In der frühen Kirche bedeutete dies, dass sich eine Gemeinde bildete, die Zeit miteinander verbrachte, sich zu Unterricht und Gemeinschaft, Mahlzeiten, Sakrament und Gebeten versammelte, auch ihr Eigentum gemeinschaftlich nutzte und Güter an Bedürftige verteilte.

Seit den 1980er Jahren hat der Ökumenische Rat der Kirchen (World Council of Churches) mehr und mehr den Fokus darauf gelegt, Gemeinschaft als zentral für die christlichen Einheit und das kirchliche Selbstverständnis zu betrachten. Drei Dokumente attestieren die Bedeutung von Beschränkungen oder Grenzen und von Anerkennung trotz dieser Grenzen, sowie die Rolle, die Gemeinschaft in dieser Mischung spielt *(Baptism, Eucharist, and Ministry, 1982*; *On the Way to Fuller Koinonia, 1994*; *The Nature and the Mission of the Church, A Stage on the Way to a Common Statement, 2005)*. Diese Diskussionen betonen, dass Gemeinschaft mit Gottes Tat der Zuwendung zu uns Menschen und einer Grenzüberschreitung beginnt, dadurch dass sein Sohn durch die Menschwerdung die gefallene Schöpfung betritt und ein präsenter und aktiver Teil von ihr wird. In Christus kann Leben in Gemeinschaft erfahren werden.

In Dietrich Bonhoeffers „*Gemeinsames Leben*" ist christliche Gemeinde oder Gemeinschaft definiert durch die physische Gegenwart einer Schwester oder eines Bruders im Glauben. Diese Gemeinschaft ist eine Berufung, ein Segen, ein Geschenk, eine Freude, eine Stelle, an die man gehört und ein Zeichen der physischen Gegenwart des dreieinigen Gottes. Die körperliche Gegenwart und die hörbaren Worte des anderen erinnern all jene in Gemeinschaft daran, wer sie sind und wessen sie sind – gegenseitige Überbringer der Botschaft von der Erlösung. Bonhoeffer erkennt die harte Realität dieses gemeinschaftlichen Lebens, das gerade keine illusorische hermetisch abgeschlossene Existenz bedeutet. Er sagt, dass glaubende Menschen einander – in welcher Form auch immer – als „Zeichen" der körperlichen Gegenwart Christi erkennen können. Bonhoeffers Christus-zentrierter Fokus wird heute durch die neuere Betonung der gegenseitigen Kommunikation innerhalb der Dreieinigkeit ergänzt. Beide dieser Perspektiven bieten einen Ausgangspunkt für weitere Betrachtungen darüber, was verbindet und zusammenbringt – Anerkennung, Versöhnung und Partnerschaft.

Durch Christus mit Gott versöhnt, hat der Glaubende neue Augen mit denen er andere sieht und erkennt, die er zuvor als Fremde, sogar als Feinde ansah. Der Glaubende kann dann auf jene Anderen eingehen, ihnen die Hand ausstrecken und sie umarmen und selbst umarmt werden. All dies basiert darauf, dass Gott genau dies tut, und zwar in und durch Christus. Die Trennung zwischen Gott und Menschen war klar, der Bruch zwischen ihnen offensichtlich, doch im barmherzigen Kommen, dem versöhnenden Opfertod und der Auferstehung Jesu Christi ist diese Trennung überwunden. Miroslav Volfs metaphorisches „Drama der Umarmung" bietet eine eindrückliche Metapher dafür, wie dies in menschlicher Gemeinschaft und Beziehung aussieht. Es könnte so scheinen, als biete Volfs Umarmung – würde sie nur ausreichend ausgeübt – die Antwort. In Wahrheit zeigt die Komplexität interkultureller und interkontextueller Partnerschaften, wie leicht es ist, am Ziel vorbeizuschießen und wie schwer es ist, zu verstehen warum. Verschiedene Studien in denen die Stimme des „Anderen“ zumindest zum Teil vernommen wird, bestätigen dieses Dilemma. Doch sind die Berichte über die Anderen in jedem dieser Fälle kaum lauter als ein Flüstern. In dieser Untersuchung jedoch verweisen die Stimmen der Partner klar auf Zusammenkommen, auf Gespräche, auf Beziehungen, die sich entwickeln und zu Freundschaften werden und auf die Transformation oder Veränderung, die sich daraus ergab.

Ein Zusammentreffen an den Rändern von Kultur und Kontext ist eine komplexe Angelegenheit, doch gerade diese Stelle ist es, wo die Teilnehmenden der Untersuchung dazu gezwungen sind, mit den Paradoxen von Verschiedenheit und Besonderheit zu rechnen, während sie sich gleichzeitig *in* Gemeinschaft befinden. In der Einheit mit Christus werden die Partner zu einem neuen Ort geformt, an dem Gott durch seinen Geist wohnt und wirkt (Eph. 2,22). Lange Zeit hat die Kirche geglaubt, dieser Ort zu sein und ihre Aufgabe darin gesehen, Missionare in Gottes Auftrag auszusenden. David Bosch konfiguriert die Definition von Mission von einer Aktivität der Kirche hin zu einer Eigenschaft und einem Handeln Gottes, seiner Mission für die Veränderung der Welt. Jedoch entbindet Gott, der so für seine Schöpfung bereits missionarisch handelt, die Kirche nicht davon, Mission als essentiell für ihr Wesen zu betrachten (Kirche ist Mission). Vielmehr geschieht Gottes Wirken in der Welt und für die ganze Welt ebenso auch in und für die gesamte Kirche, wie es bezeugt wird im missionalen Engagement wie Berlin Fellowship.

Indem sie anregen, Mission als „prophetischen Dialog“ anzusehen, beschreiben Stephen Bevans und Roger Schroeder die Kirche als eine Gemeinschaft, die der Welt dient mit Handlungen wie Bekenntnis, Verkündigung, Inkulturation und Versöhnung, während sie dabei aus ihrem Engagement lernt und dabei mit dem dreieinigen Gott auf multidimensionale Weise verbunden ist. Als lebendige Gemeinschaft – wenn auch nicht perfekt – im Licht des Glaubens und durch den Dienst ihrer Gegenwart in der DDR (Bekenntnis und Verkündigung) legten die Ostdeutsche Kirche und ihre Glieder Zeugnis ab vor ihren Besuchern aus dem Ausland, vor ihren Nachbarn und auch untereinander. Dieses Bekenntnis betraf nicht nur eine Idee sondern bezeugte die Person und das Wirken Jesu Christi. Aus der Versöhnung in Christus ergaben sich Dialoge, und ein neuer Ort zur Begegnung wurde geschaffen. Mission wurde so als Zeichen der Königsherrschaft Gottes nach außen und innen gelebt.

Die gegenwärtige missionale Kirchenbewegung (missional church movement) hat aus anderer Perspektive zum missionalen Verständnis beigetragen, indem sie die Kirchen und insbesondere örtliche Gemeinden daran erinnert, dass sie nicht mehr im „Christentum" zu Hause sind. Die Vertreter dieser Bewegung fordern eine Umkehr des kirchlichen Selbstverständnisses in Bezug auf Mission und drängen die Gemeinde, über sich selbst hinaus auf Gott zu weisen, und zwar unter dem Dach der biblischen Metaerzählung. Nach dem Verständnis von James Brownson und George Hunsberger ist die eigentliche interkulturelle Begegnung genau der Ort, an dem das Evangelium verkündigt oder miteinander geteilt werden kann, in Wort und Tat – und mit denen, die durchaus andersartig sind.

Brownsons behauptet, dass dieser Ort der Begegnung das Zentrum einer missionalen Hermeneutik darstellt und dabei geht es nicht um eine Idee sondern um Christus. Weil Christus im Fokus steht, darf es diese Unterschiede inmitten einer umfassenden allgemeinen Identität geben und so werden Fremde vereint und versöhnt. Im Fall dieser Studie reflektiert die missionale Hermeneutik die Haltung, Sichtweise und Stimme des Anderen– des Empfangenden, des Gastgebers, des Partners.

Berlin Fellowship war in erster Linie ein Besuchsdienst von Mensch-zu-Mensch, der lose unter der Schirmherrschaft der Presbyterianischen Kirche in Südkalifornien sowie der evangelischen Kirche Berlin-Brandenburg stand. Ihre Wurzeln reichen zurück in die 1950er Jahre, als die Erste Presbyterianische Kirche von Hollywood ein College-Deputationsprogramm entwickelte, in dem Studenten an Arbeitseinsätzen im In- und Ausland teilnahmen. In den 1960er Jahren entwickelte sich Berlin Fellowship dann zu einem spezifischen Besuchs- und Ermutigungsdienst für Christen in Ostdeutschland und organisierte und verfeinerte in den 1970er und 1980er Jahren kontinuierlich diesen Dienst.

In dieser recherchierten und dokumentierten historischen Übersicht zu Berlin Fellowship und Ostdeutschland in den 1960er, 1970er und 1980er Jahren habe ich versucht, die Stimmen und Perspektiven der deutschen Partner für sich selbst sprechen zu lassen, wobei das Bild des sich verändernden Kontextes in der Deutschen Demokratischen Republik zwischen 1961 und 1989 vervollständigt wurde. Zweimal im Jahr reisten Teams, meist aus Presbyterianischen Gemeinden, mit 10-12 Teilnehmenden zu Gemeinden durch das Land. Ab 1970 übernahmen Pfarrer Ted Schapp und Frau Bärbel Eccardt aus der Zinzendorf Gemeinde in West-Berlin wichtige Leitungsfunktionen, indem sie Kommunikation und Verbindung mit den östlichen Partnern, der Gruppe in Süd-Kalifornien sowie mit der West-Berliner Kirchenleitung und regionalen Büros von Kirchen im Osten aufrechterhielten. Diese Informationen sind in westlichen Archiven dokumentiert.

Zeitgleich mit diesen frühen Entwicklungen richtete ab 1968 bis mindestens 1986 das Ministerium für Staatssicherheit (MfS) sein Interesse auf Aktivitäten von Berlin Fellowship und schleuste einen informellen Mitarbeiter in eine wichtige Vertrauensposition ein. Obwohl über 5500 Seiten der MfS-Dokumentation einen Einblick in und vielleicht sogar eine differenzierte östliche Perspektive auf den Dienst und die Teilnehmenden hätten ermöglichen können, waren die Resultate letztendlich unspektakulär und nicht mehr als ein Zeichen gründlicher „Informationssammlung".

Daher sind es die Daten aus den eigentlichen Interviews, die das klarste, interessanteste und aufschlussreichste Bild davon zeichnen, was die Stimme der östlichen Partner zu sagen hatte. Ein subjektiver und qualitativer Codierungs- und Analyseprozess half dabei, Transkriptionen von vielen Stunden Interviews zu kategorisieren und zu verdichten. Von 40 individuellen Interviews ließ ich 27 Interviews transkribieren und analysierte sie nach einem rhetorischen und qualitativen Codierungssystem, das auf der Häufigkeit der verwendeten Worte basiert. Die 30 endgültigen Codes wurden danach in vier Hauptgruppen (family groupings) und drei verbleibende kleinere Randgruppen aufgeteilt. Hunderte von Zitaten aus den Interviews konnten so den Hauptgruppen Kontext, Aktivitäten, *Koinonia* und Ergebnisse sowie den drei zusätzlichen Randgruppen Überraschendes, missionales Zeugnis und die als „Drittes Ufer" bzw. „Ephesermoment" bezeichnete Gruppe zugeordnet werden. Die Gruppen Kontext und Aktivitäten ermöglichen einen Einblick in das allgemeine Umfeld und die Rahmenbedingungen der Berlin Fellowship-Treffen und zeigen, was während eines typischen Besuches passierte. So existierten in der DDR feste Grenzen – geografische, geopolitische und in bestimmten Bereichen der Gesellschaft auch persönliche. Für Christen gab es dazu noch mehr Einschränkungen, und diese spielten keine geringe Rolle. Die Gruppe Aktivitäten führt hinreichende Beweise für Erinnerungen an gemeinsame Aktivitäten an und gibt Auskunft über die verschiedenen Arten gemeinsamer Unternehmungen, und liefert so den Kontext für die Gruppe *Koinonia* und deren drei wichtigste Untergruppen: Wesenskern, Mensch-zu-Mensch und Kommunikation.

Zum *Wesenskern* von Berlin Fellowship gehörte, dass die amerikanischen Besucher im Namen Jesu Christi persönlich zu Gesprächen und Ermutigung kamen (nicht Pakete oder Postkarten schickten). Dies wurde als buchstäblicher Akt ökumenischer und diakonischer Solidarität erlebt, und als eine Art „Ort", an dem Masken verschwinden und für den Augenblick eine Gemeinschaft entstehen konnte. Die Begegnung stellte Kontakte her, bot Möglichkeiten zu geben und zu empfangen, und erzeugte ein Gefühl der Zugehörigkeit. Wiederholt wurde die Mensch-zu-Mensch-Natur des Programms betont, und viele lenkten die Aufmerksamkeit darauf, wie unterschiedlich die Teilnehmenden doch waren. In der Tat wurde mit Überraschung festgestellt, dass die Unterschiede und der Ort, der durch diese Zusammenkünfte geschaffen wurde, eine Art Freiheit mit sich brachte, zum Teil aufgrund gegenseitiger Anerkennung. Diese Anerkennung, die mit dem Austausch einfacher Höflichkeiten in beiden Richtungen begann, setzte Begegnung in Gang, erlaubte es, Gastfreundschaft zu üben und das Umfeld und Zuhause mit Freude und Stolz zu teilen. Neben kritischer Kommentierung darüber, wie sie als Gastgeber bei der Besuchsplanung einbezogen waren, äußerten die Interviewten auch Ihre Unzufriedenheit mit einigen kontextbezogenen Einschränkungen, die ihnen in ihrer Rolle auferlegt wurden. Eine positive Haltung von Anerkennung, Gegenseitigkeit und Mitsprache bedeutete eine Veränderung der Gastgeber, und die Interviews zeigen deutlich anhaltende Verwandlungseffekte durch die Begegnungen.

Wenn die Gäste eintrafen, stand das *Gespräch* im Mittelpunkt der Zusammenkünfte und Treffen und wird von vielen als „das Ereignis" von Berlin Fellowship bezeichnet. Die Erinnerung bezieht sich nicht auf spezifische Gesprächsthemen oder Inhalte, sondern auf die Intensität des Austauschs, durch den das Wissen über den „anderen" korrigiert oder erweitert wurde. Weiterhin ist es überraschend, dass die Gäste definitiv nicht „wie wir" sind, und trotzdem kam Kommunikation leicht zustande. Obwohl die amerikanische, sehr persönliche Art der Unterhaltung für die Gastgeber ungewohnt war, wurde die Offenheit, die sie zur Folge hatte, mit Erstaunen hervorgehoben. Viele der Interviews enthalten daher kleine Geschichten über eine Begegnung oder ein Gespräch, wobei die Gesprächspartner namentlich genannt werden. Sie berichten von Übereinstimmungen aber ebenso von Unterschieden, besonders beim Reden über den eigenen Glauben. Die Amerikaner sprachen in einer deutlich *anderen* Art und Weise als die Deutschen, und dies wird wieder und wieder betont.

Neben der Tatsache, neue Informationen zu erhalten oder Falschinformationen zu korrigieren, war jeder Besuch ein Treffen mit der Welt außerhalb, wovon auch Kinder und Jugendliche profitierten, und die Ostdeutschen machten sich das Programm aktiv zu Eigen. All dies ist mit dem Faktor Anerkennung verbunden – die sowohl gegeben als auch empfangen wurde. Durch Informationsaustausch und die Gegenwart der anderen, gewannen die Teilnehmenden eine neue Sicht auf den „Feind", auf die Welt innerhalb und außerhalb der DDR, auf die weltweite Kirche. Diese neue Sicht wurde als „bereichernd" bezeichnet, beruhte auf Gegenseitigkeit und trug zur Vertiefung des Glaubensverständnisses bei. So weist die Gruppe Ergebnisse in der Tat klar auf Veränderung, Anerkennung, Mitsprache und Zugehörigkeit hin.

Dieser Veränderungsaspekt, insbesondere verbunden mit dem Sinn der Deutschen für Mitsprache und Zugehörigkeit, führte mich dazu, einen neuen Code/eine neue Gruppe zu benennen – „missionales Zeugnis" – und mich dann nochmals mit den Gruppen „Überraschendes" und „Ephesermoment" auseinander zu setzen. Für beide, die Interviewten und auch für mich, gab es Überraschendes, sowohl während der Interviews als auch beim Kodieren und der Analyse. Als Beispiel dafür seien zwei einfache „Fakten" der Berlin Fellowship genannt, die die Gastgeber mit Überraschung und Freude erfüllten, nämlich dass die Besucher überhaupt kamen und dass sie auf deutlich andere Art Gespräche führten. Genauso überraschend für mich waren der Sinn der Ostdeutschen für Verantwortung und Mitsprache im Programm sowie ihre Kritik an verschiedenen Aspekten. Noch Jahre später wurden in gewisser Weise persönliche oder gemeinsam erfahrene Veränderungen im Gedächtnis behalten. Ich betrachte dies als eine Bestätigung meiner Annahme, dass Gemeinschaft möglicherweise ein Faktor missionalen Handelns und Veränderung sein könnte.

Die Interviews zeigten, dass „missionales Zeugnis" an jenem „Ort"– inmitten einer versammelten Gemeinde, im Erleben von Gemeinschaft geschehen kann. Es geschieht unter und zwischen den Versammelten und resultiert in einer engagierten und interaktiven Begegnung. Dieses wechselseitige und miteinander geteilte Zeugnis kann langanhaltende Auswirkungen haben und als Ermutigung, Trost und Motivation über die Zeit des Treffens hinaus wirken. Dies mag ein Ergebnis oder ein Attribut der Anerkennung sein, die während solch einer Begegnung gegeben und empfangen wurde. „Irgendetwas" geschieht und bewirkt Veränderung. Was genau geschah, konnten die Interviewten nur schwer in Worte fassen, doch es hatte zu tun mit der Gegenwart des so deutlich „Anderen" und gleichermaßen mit dem, was geschah oder gesagt wurde. Ich bezeichne dieses Geschehen mit zwei Metaphern. In beiden ist der Ort der Begegnung ein Grenzraum, zwischen den Welten, und dennoch fungiert gerade dieser Ort als eine Brücke, die zwei sehr verschiedene Welten verbindet. Bei der Beschreibung, wie sich diese Welten voneinander unterschieden, sagte ein Interviewter, dass die Welt, aus der die Besucher kamen und sogar ihre Art der Konversation überhaupt nicht passten, und doch irgendwie passten die Menschen und dann passten auf mysteriöse Weise die Fragen und der Austausch auch. Es war, als ob ein neuer Weg erfunden und ein neuer Ort von beiden, den Gästen und den Gastgebern, betreten wurde. Das „Passen", behaupte ich, geschah „in Christus". Christus machte die Begegnungen zu einem einzigartigen Ort, wenn auch nur zeitweilig. Dies war eine neue Form von „gemeinsamen Leben" das sich über einen Zeitraum von mehr als 25 Jahren auf außergewöhnliche Weise bei den Berlin Fellowship-Treffen ereignete.

Die transkribierten Interviews verweisen entschieden auf das beanspruchte und aufgenommene Gefühl der Zugehörigkeit für östliche Teilnehmende. Sie deuten die Berlin-Fellowship-Treffen als einen Ort der *koinonia* - wenn auch ein Ort der Grenzen, Grenzen von Kultur und Kontext, so doch ein Ort geborgen „ in Christus". Es war ein Ort, erfüllt von gegenseitigem Begegnen, von Anerkennen und Anerkannt werden, von Geben und Empfangen. Es war ein Ort von Begegnung im Gespräch, von Veränderung, ein Ort, an dem eine Botschaft gehört wurde, die hieß „Du bist nicht allein", ein Ort, an dem der allgegenwärtige Kontext der DDR durch die kurzzeitige aber doch sehr reale Gegenwart einiger Besucher von außen irgendwie aufgewogen wurde. Durch und während jener vorübergehenden Treffen wurde das gegenseitige Zeugnis zu einer momentanen „Hermeneutik des Evangeliums". Die Teilnehmenden waren nicht nur engagiert, sondern darüber hinaus auch verbunden mit und durch die Präsenz des lebendigen Christus, und sie alle fanden sich als Gastgeber und Gäste zugleich wieder.

Die Schlussfolgerung im Falle dieser Untersuchung besagt, dass Gemeinschaft eine missionale Erfahrung ist und sein kann - eine von vielen, in denen die Kirche ihren Ruf in Wort und Tat auslebt. Wie in Anbetung, Dienst, Bekenntnis und Verkündigung so auch in Gemeinschaft bezeugt die versammelte Gemeinde vor der Welt und vor sich selbst den Grund ihrer Existenz. In Gemeinschaft wie auch in anderen kirchlichen „Merkmalen" erinnert sie sich selbst und „die Anderen" an den lebendigen Herrn Jesus Christus. Als missionale Aktivität wirkt Gemeinschaft in gewissem Sinn parabolisch und richtet den Fokus über sich selbst hinaus. Als Begegnung mit Christus wird ein solches Treffen für alle Teilnehmenden ein Ort der Befreiung und Freiheit und gleichzeitig ein Ort der Zugehörigkeit und ein Zuhause, eine „Wohnung Gottes im Geist" (s. Eph. 2,22).

Koinonia ist bisher als eine Form der Mission weitestgehend übersehen worden, obwohl einige Theologen und Missionswissenschaftler ihr Augenmerk auch auf diesen Aspekt gerichtet haben. Diese Arbeit untersucht nur einen kleinen Teil eines potentiell großen Komplexes von Themen und zwar auf spezifische und bescheidene Weise. Ich bin jedoch vom Wert einer solchen Studie überzeugt und schließe mit der Erwähnung weiterer Gedanken und Ergebnisse.

Berlin Fellowship hat ihre Wurzeln in der Missionsbewegung einer lokalen Gemeinde in Südkalifornien und begann als ökumenische Besuchsreise. Unter heutiger Terminologie sollte sie aber auch als missionale Aktivität betrachtet werden - wie durch die deutschen Stimmen bestätigt wird, die in dieser Arbeit untersucht und ausgewertet wurden. Grenzen und Einschränkungen (z. B. der Eiserne Vorhang und der Feindesstatus der Anderen) spielen beide eine Schlüsselrolle in der Geschichte der Berlin Fellowship, aber sie haben nicht das letzte Wort; das Geschenk der Gemeinschaft erlaubte die Überwindung derartiger Grenzen. Trotz Einschränkungen und als Nachfolger Christi konnten die Teilnehmenden einander umarmen, versöhnt, nicht nur prinzipiell sondern tatsächlich. Sie waren fähig, diese Versöhnung durch Gemeinschaft und Beteiligung, Ermutigung und physische Gegenwart zu erfahren. Obwohl einmalige Begegnungen gering geschätzt werden mögen, zeigte sich - zumindest als Ergebnis dieser Untersuchung - dass eine einmalige kurzzeitige Begegnung ebenso viel gelten kann wie Gemeinschaft über Jahre. Letzten Endes war der zentrale Text, unter dem Berlin Fellowship zusammen kam, das Evangelium von Jesus Christus, das angenommen, verinnerlicht und geglaubt wurde. Doch die deutschen Berichte dieser Begegnungen repräsentieren einen bedeutenden Teil der hermeneutischen Dimension für die Vermittlung und das Verständnis der missionalen Rolle von Gemeinschaft. Es ist an der Zeit, diese Geschichte und diese Stimmen zu hören.

Koinonia ist eine missionale Realität, die man nicht unterschätzen sollte. Ich bin der Meinung, sie ist ein noch unerkannter und zu hebender Schatz an Weisheit und Zeugnis, Hoffnung und Erkenntnis für jene, die Wege suchen, in der Mission für das Reich Gottes etwas zu „tun". Einfach als Gast oder Gastgeber bei dem Anderen zu sein und für den Anderen da zu sein, *ist* wesentlich für Mission oder Missionsvorhaben. Was die Geschichte der Berlin Fellowship und die Erinnerungen ihrer östlichen Partner betrifft, ist die Schlussfolgerung ganz klar. Es gab nur eine Sache, die wirklich im damaligen Kontext „getan" werden konnte, nämlich, Zeit miteinander zu verbringen, zuzuhören, zu lernen und dadurch einander Gottes Liebe zu bezeugen, die man erfahren und geteilt hatte, während eines Essens, bei einem Spaziergang im Wald oder in einem Bibelgespräch - in gelebter Gemeinschaft. Die Grenzen und Beschränkungen durch Kultur und Sprache, durch Kontext und Politik wurden nicht ausradiert sondern traten für ein oder zwei Stunden, für ein oder zwei Tage in den Hintergrund. So kam es zu oft überraschender Begegnung und ein Ort war geschaffen - obwohl dies unwahrscheinlich, ja sogar unmöglich schien. *Übers.: U. Unterumsberger und B. Völker*

APPENDIX 1

The Ministry for State Security of the GDR
(Das Ministerium für Staatssicherheit der DDR / MfS)
Background Information

1. MfS History and Background

"In order to be secure, one must know everything." This quotation is attributed to Erich Mielke, head of the Ministry for State Security (*Ministerium für Staatssicherheit, MfS*) from 1957 to 1989. It might serve as a title for this brief overview of the MfS and the decades-long surveillance and intelligence gathering done by the "*Stasi*," the State Security Service (*Staatssicherheitsdienst*) of the German Democratic Republic (*GDR*). When the Berlin wall began to crumble in 1989, Erich Mielke's intelligence service (espionage, surveillance, and society-wide information gathering) employed around 189,000 unofficial informers (*inoffizielle Mitarbeiter IM)*[1] and 91,000 core employees *(Hauptmitarbeiter)*.[2] However, the work of this arm of the ruling party, the Socialist Unity Party or SED (*Sozialistische Einheitspartei Deutschland*) had much humbler beginnings. Erich Mielke, whose name was practically synonymous with the Stasi, was politically active establishing the new East German state in the early post-war years and was appointed the first "Permanent Secretary for State Security," though at the outset, he hardly had a staff. The earliest records from these first years show 1100 MfS employees for all

[1] Helmut Müller-Enbergs (ed.), *Die inoffiziellen Mitarbeiter (MfS-Handbuch)*. BStU. Berlin 2008. http://www.nbn-resolving.org/urn:nbn:de:0292-97839421302647, 3.
[2] Jens Gieseke (ed.), *Die hauptamtlichen Mitarbeiter des Ministeriums für Staatssicherheit(MfS-Handbuch),* BStU, Berlin 1996. http://www.nbn-resolving.org/urn:nbn:de:0292-97839421302572. 3.

areas of surveillance, though by the end of 1952, this number had increased to 8800.[3]

From the 1950's, the MfS called itself the "Shield and Sword of the Party." Mielke, along with help from the Soviets and other communist party leaders, was instrumental in shaping, directing, and establishing this arm of the *SED*. Initially designed to serve as an internal secret police force to deal with opponents and threats to the regime, the *MfS* was also an intelligence gathering instrument and in time became an immense bureaucratic and administrative operation, overseeing matters as diverse as passport controls, weapons trade, body guard training, surveillance of visiting politicians and guests of the state, along with surveillance of religious institutions, cultural events, international contacts and connections at every level of the society.

All churches Roman Catholic, Protestant, independent churches and such sects as the Mormons and Jehovah's Witnesses were included in the surveillance; church administrative offices at the national, district and local level were under observation, and by many branches of the state administration (*Staatsapparat*). The neighborhood congregation was, of course, included. By 1954 a "Working Group for Church Questions" was established by the Central Committee of the *SED* to address the church's political involvement (*kirchenpolitische Fragen*). Simultaneously, the *MfS* opened their own department for church matters, to be known as Department XX/4 "Churches and Religious Communities" (*XX/4, Abteilung 4:Kirchen und Religionsgemeinschaften* was one of nine subdepartments of HA XX/Main Department XX, state apparatus, block parties, church, art, culture, political underground (*Hauptabteilung XX Staatsapparat, Blockparteien, Kirche, Kunst, Kultur, "politischer Untergrund"*). In 1957, the government Office of the State Secretary for Church Questions was established.[4] This office operated "independently" from the MfS and served as the "official" bridge between state and church. These three branches of the state apparatus the *SED*/communist party, the Secretary for Church Questions, and Department XX/4 of the Ministry for State Security, were the dictating voices for the political stance of the state in regard to the church, church involvements and activities, though the MfS was unofficial organizing arm of the 'measures' (Maßnahmen) for state policy.[5]

---

[3] Hans Giesecke, *The GDR State Security, Shield and Sword of the Party*, Berlin 2006, 19.
[4] Clemens Vollnhals, Die Kirchenpolitische Abteilung des Ministeriums für Staatssicherheit, *Die Kirchenpolitik von SED und Staatssicherheit, Eine Zwischenbilanz*, Berlin 1996, 79.
[5] Op. cit., 81.

For purposes of this discussion regarding church activity, it is helpful to consider the political system in the *GDR* as a two-track system, though the two tracks were very tightly knit together. One track was the party and the government with its official "church policy or politic"(*Kirchenpolitik*). Contact between church and state took place through the government's Office of the State Secretary for Church Questions (*Staatssekretariat für Kirchenfragen*) and through the local and district level officials responsible for church matters. The second track was the more conspiratorial branch, the Ministry for State Security, with its own organized and specific work, its own regional and district offices, its own recruiting and training programs, ranks of officers and a multi-level system of gathering information.

The ideology, strategy, activities, plans, focus of the political system policy varied only slightly over four decades. The early 1950's were especially repressive; after Stalin's death in 1953 the situation relaxed somewhat. The following decades had ebbs and flows of "state security" activity and government regulations. Reasons for the flux might have been, for example, that relations with West Germany (*Ost-Politik*) were changing at the time or that world events were affecting the *GDR's* reputation and status (Helsinki Peace Accords in 1975). Often because of the political situation in or with Moscow, matters of security tightened or loosened in church policy, as well as in other areas. Other matters like the stationing of missiles by the USSR and the USA on German soil or the establishment of interest and protest groups in the 80's also affected how the *MfS* and government handled matters of security. All of these and other issues affected what was deemed by the *MfS* to warrant intelligence gathering in various corners of the society, including the church. In addition, as the *MfS* methods of listening, observing, following, reporting were made easier by technological advancements, and as the number of full-time employees increased, the detail and amount of information gathered changed and increased as well.

In this context, the Protestant church, its historical role and its relative independence from the state apparatus meant both the government and the *MfS* paid close attention to it, though in the early *MfS* years, the number of employees working in church matters was hardly noteworthy. In 1957, the total number of *MfS* employees assigned to church affairs for the entire country was 95 full-time workers (*hauptamtliche Mitarbeiter*). At the same time, the whole Ministry had in its employ 14,440.[6] By 1970, Department XX/4 department in Berlin, had only 218 employees

[6] Op. cit., 85.

(total *MfS* employees 43,300) and by 1982, there were but 400 church-related workers (total *MfS* employees were 81,500). [7]

Regardless of the numbers of *MfS* workers and the fluctuation in the state's church policy, the purpose and goal of the *SED* and its relation to the churches remained steady.[8] The Church, both Roman Catholic and Protestant, as an independent entity within the east German society "ideologically co-existing" with Marxism-Leninism was indeed a total contradiction. This can be illustrated: In October 1949 the *GDR* was founded upon a constitution that in principle formally recognized the separation of church and state. However, by 1952, key functions of the church, like the university fellowship (*Studentengemeinde*) and the youth congregation (*Jungegemeinde*) were declared illegal. Such things as religious instruction in the schools (*Religionsunterricht*) and the government service of collecting of church taxes ceased entirely. The persecution and arrests of pastors and church workers in this period revealed how the church was clearly viewed by the state as a competitor, which could not be tolerated. [9] By 1956, east/west church contacts inside Berlin city limits were named criminal acts, and objections from the side of the church against the hardening government front were rebuffed and labeled as subversive behavior (*Staatsfeindlichkeit*). Over the course of the next 30 years, though the official and public government tactic" concerning the church fluctuated, the state and party's suspicious posture remained constant until November 9, 1989 when the wall opened. In 1984, in a not-for-publication text, Mielke's second-in-command made the following statement, "Religion is and remains a form of bourgeois ideology and does not belong within the Marxist-Leninist system."[10]

2. Berlin Fellowship and the MfS

Between August 1961 and 1989, all aspects of East German life and its system of government were cemented in by the building of the Berlin Wall on August 13, 1961, a clear statement further punctuating the division of post-war Germany, already defined by a highly guarded border, the 731 km long "Iron Curtain." In this dramatic and not uncomplicated historical and political context and era, the visitation program known as

---

[7] Op. cit., 93.
[8] Robert F. Goeckel, Thesen zu Kontinuität und Wandel in der Kirchenpolitik der SED, in Vollnhals *Die Kirchenpolitik*, 35.
[9] Rudolf Mau, *Der Protestantismus*), 40-41.
[10] Vollnhals, *Die Kirchenpolitik*, 80.

Berlin Fellowship pursued its modest ministry of visitation. As a church-related activity and viewed as hostile influence and unfriendly to the state (*feindliche Negative*), twice yearly visits from Americans did capture MfS attention. The monthly meeting of the 'Fellowship' group in East Berlin was equally as noteworthy. However, it was actually the Berlin Fellowship leaders from West Berlin, two pastors (Schapp and Zorn) and a church worker (Eccardt) and their more regular visits in the East, which aroused initial MfS suspicion, and occasioned twenty years of surveillance measures.

3. The MfS at work: OV's, IM's and the MfS officers

The inner-workings and structure of the entire MfS need not be detailed, for much has already been written. However, MfS specifics relating to the Berlin Fellowship and its key leaders comprise at least 5500 pages of accessible files and materials, and these pages serve to paint a picture of how the MfS functioned in information gathering.

The primary document, which illustrates information gathering, planning, methods, evaluation, and analysis, is the file known as an OV, Operative Procedure file (*operativer Vorgang*). In the case of Berlin Fellowship per se, no OV exists. OV's were only opened or established because a person or several persons roused suspicion, were viewed as a threat or potential threat to the population or to the government, or were suspected to be in counter-intelligence having either already done something illegal or evidenced intention of illegal activity in the GDR. When an OV was opened, the highest level of interest and attention had already been reached. In both of the major OV's examined for this research, "*Rollbahn*" (runway) and "*Radius*" (radius), five of six persons named as objects or foci of investigation were directly related to Berlin Fellowship: Bärbel Eccardt, then a church worker and resident of West Berlin; Ted Schapp, an American Presbyterian pastor living and working in West Berlin; Ralph Zorn, an American Lutheran pastor living and working in West Berlin; Ursula Unterumsberger, a young East German woman in her late 20s living in East Berlin, a participant in Berlin Fellowship; Friedrich-Wilhelm Merkel, an pastor from Malchow, a suburb of East Berlin, active participant in the first decade of Berlin Fellowship. Both OV's are replete with personal, biographical, and descriptive information about these individuals, as well as many kinds of "reports" about personal and telephone conversations, planned meetings, encounters and all forms of Berlin Fellowship gatherings.

The main job of the MfS was to know everything and to gather information for that purpose. The quota of material to be worked on (*bearbeitet*) was established monthly or even weekly.[11] The Berlin Fellowship-related material was comprised of IM reports, administrative reports and other kinds of surveillance findings: findings from apartments searches, post and mail confiscation; border crossing records as well as body search reports; interrogations at border crossings; tracing reports/ observation reports; hidden microphone manuscripts from meetings, telephone calls, and a private family apartment search. Furthermore, some photos of the OV-related individuals are included in the files as are copies of passport and identification papers.

However, the two main OV files contain primarily IM reports. At peak periods, this amounted to 15 IM reports a month. The primary Berlin Fellowship IM dictated hundreds of reports, and these were received and analyzed by the MfS officers who were responsible for directing the IM's activities, for meeting with and supporting him, for overseeing the files and for determining when the OVs should be closed. These officers were all ideologically committed to the party line and the system, and they, in turn, were responsible for dozens of further evaluative and administrative reports. In two cases, MfS officers named in the OV's rose to the top ranks of responsibility, and in 1989, they were administrators in MfS central headquarters in Berlin in the Department XX/4, "Church and Religious Communities."

Though the MfS records for the entire period covered in this research (1961-1989) are far from complete, it is clear that as early as 1965[12] and until as late as 1988,[13] the MfS had its eyes and ears on the key leaders of Berlin Fellowship in West Berlin as well as in the east. The files contain exact plans and information about American Berlin Fellowship teams, in-depth reports on monthly meetings of the East Berlin group (*Berliner-Gruppe*), and reports on yearly meetings of the East Committee (*Ostkomitee*) and on many other Berlin Fellowship-related appointments, meetings, phone calls, encounters, and personal conversations.

---

[11] Ibid.
[12] BStU MfS, BE54 20954/92, June 28, 1965, 259-261.
[13] BStU MfS Abt. X/1580, BStU Nr. 641/82, June 21, 1988, 238-239.

4. Berlin Fellowship's Files/Strategic Operational Files (OV's)

There are two primary OV's researched for this project, each divided into volumes or *Bände*:

- OV "*Rollbahn*," administrated in Gera/Thuringia has 6 chapters, 1902 pages, and was officially opened in August, 1971 and officially closed and archived in 1978. It is the primary source for comments in chapter 2 of this research.
- OV "*Radius*," administrated in Berlin, comprises five chapters, 1495 pages, was opened in March 1973, closed once in 1978 and again closed and archived in 1984.

In OV "*Rollbahn*," there are reports, pre-dating the official opening of the file, which quite clearly identify and articulate the purpose and goals of the BF visitation program.[14] These goals and the purpose of Berlin Fellowship activities are repeatedly doubted and questioned over the years and suspected by the MfS to be a "cover" for intelligence gathering. Again it must be noted, the official reason for opening the file was "immediate suspicion of intensive intelligence and information gathering according to §98."[15]

Both "*Rollbahn*" and "*Radius*" contain hundreds of pages of IM reports delivered in person by the IM to his officers or dictated into a recorder, then later typed, filed, and signed by a case-related officer. In 1974 the decision was made to "coordinate" the files between Berlin and Gera (Thuringia), and IM reports "delivered" for Gera("*Rollbahn*") were copied and sent to Berlin ("*Radius*") or vice versa. These duplications add considerably to the length of both OVs.

MfS officers' reports constitute another large portion of the OV's. These notes or administrative reports included the following:

- progress reports (*Sachstandberichte*)
- decision, resolution, rulings (*Beschlüsse*)
- planned measures/plan of action (*Maßnahmeplan*)
- summary reports (*Zusammenfassender Berichte*)
- information or disclosure reports (*Auskunftsberichte*)
- conception or design (*Konzeption*)

---

[14] BStU MfS 1486/84 OV Radius, XX/4 Band 1, April 6, 1973, "The Americans travel yearly as tourists into the GDR to get to know the GDR and the innerworkings of the church." (*Die Amerikaner einreisen jährlich in die DDR als Touristen, um die DDR und das Gemeindewesen innerhalb der Kirchen kennezulernen.*) Names of participants at this meeting are listed and labeled as "conspirative working committee" (*Konspirativ arbeitenden Komitee*). This is taken from a progress report (*Sachstandbericht*) from OV Rollbahn, dated Nov. 11, 1970.

[15] BStU MfS, BV/Gera, Abt. XII, AOP 1456-78, OV "Rollbahn" Band I, Beschluss für das Anlegen eines Operativ-Vorgangs, August 12, 1971, 7.

- notes for the file (*Aktenvermerke*)
- results, findings, conclusions (*Ergebnisse*)
- interim reports (*Zwischenberichte*)
- declaration-determination of results (*Feststellungsergebnisse*)
- final report, termination reports (*Aschlußberichte*)
- consultation (*Beratung*)
- intelligence/information reports (*Informationsberichte*)
- appraisal/ investigation/evaluation reports(*Ermittlungsberichte*)

6. Files on Individual Persons

In some cases a file would be opened to determine just what an individual was doing and why or to keep them under observation and control, even though they may not be viewed as 'negative' from the MfS perspective.

This is the case in one Berlin Fellowship-related file. Focused on Bärbel Eccardt, this particular file serves to reveal the MfS suspicion, her supposed intelligence gathering role, her relation to Berlin Fellowship and to the Protestant Church in West Berlin, her official relation to the enemy (West Germany, the USA), and possible breaking of GDR laws. However, Bärbel Eccardt's personal documentation revolves almost exclusively around Berlin Fellowship activities and meetings, duplicating numerous reports from "*Rollbahn*" or "*Radius*." Her file contains reports dated both prior to and simultaneous to the OV "*Rollbahn*," as well as a number of different kinds of reports and documentation, periodically indicating that several IM's having been at work:

- orders for an apartment search and findings
- photocopies of papers/photos found in purse during a border crossing
- notes from an interrogation, a signed interrogation report
- passport photo copies
- observation reports and tracing/following/tailing reports by agents who followed the person (time, activity, date, dress, etc.)
- manuscripts of conversations from planted microphones

Eccardt's two personal files (542 pages) date from 1965 through 1985 and are given no code name; all material was archived (*Archivmaterial Allgemeine Personenablage*).

Another individual file of archived materials is for Reverend Ralph Zorn. His OV, named "*Resident*," was first opened in 1984, right after "*Radius*" was officially closed. In the April 1984 opening report which calls for a "renewed political operative treatment (*Bearbeitung*) of

Zorn,"[16] he is identified as someone needing to be "*erarbeitet*" or worked on further. His activities and continued friendship and contact with the IM over the years enable MfS efforts; Zorn is suspected of intelligence activity or of being used (by whom is unclear) for intelligence purposes through his church connections.[17] Zorn's personal file contains three separate volumes totaling 716 pages. After 1976, Ralph Zorn had very limited and irregular contact with the Berlin Fellowship activities, but it appears that the IM's friendship with Zorn and the IM's ongoing participation in Berlin Fellowship meant that "*Resident*" became the repository for reports on Berlin Fellowship activity through 1986.

1,258 pages of Zorn and Eccardt material later, it is clear that Berlin Fellowship and these two personalities were kept in the vizier of the MfS at least through 1986 and perhaps even until the last days of the GDR. The latest-dated identifiable Berlin Fellowship-related MfS pages (September 1986) appear to be a report from two meetings in East Berlin. Evaluation of the 1985 team trip and plans for 1986 is included.[18] However, there are other MfS materials related to individuals dating from as late as 1988.[19]

Finally, Reverend Ted Schapp, one of the OV persons in "*Rollbahn*," was evidently not suspicious enough for the MfS to find him of much interest. His name appears seldom. Indeed, in March 1977 an administrative report notes, "Investigation in other MfS files reveal no operative interesting connections with hostile offices[…]to date there is no proof of illegal activity[...]further work for this file will concentrate on Zorn and Eccardt."[20] Schapp fades from focus and the MfS story regarding Berlin Fellowship from that point. However, a 1988 non-file report indicates that Schapp is tailed by HA VI (Main Department VI, Passport control and tourism), noted to have connections with Poland, and kept under observation while he is in East Berlin. He is not found guilty of any criminal activities. It is further noted that he officially retired from ministry on April 17, 1988 and is moving soon to California.

---

[16] BStU MfS, BV/Berlin, Abt. XX/4, AKG0342, OV "Resident", May 15, 1984, 8.
[17] Op. cit., 9.
[18] BStU MfS HA XX ZMA 3970, "Resident", 11. Includes remarks about an employee of the West Berlin consistory, Bishop Johannes Hempel and General Superintendent Günter Krusche of East Berlin affirming continuing the visitation program and further, state offices in the GDR have voiced wishes for the Berlin Fellowship to continue.
[19] BStU Archiv der Zentralstelle, MfS Abt.X/1580 Department for international connections/*Internationale Verbindungen*, Nr. 641-82, January 12-June 6, 1988 , 232-9.
[20] BStU MfS, BV/Gera, Abt.XII, AOP1456-78, OV "Rollbahn" I, March 30, 1977, 282.

6. Berlin Fellowship's IM?

The key source of basic intelligence information gathered by the MfS comes from the unofficial informer (IM) assigned, who had two cover names (*Deckname*), "*Krause*" and "*Tomachewsky.*" He befriended all three persons focused on in "*Rollbahn*" (Eccardt, Schapp, and Zorn) and was a regular member and participant of Berlin Fellowship. In reports about Berlin Fellowship meetings and events, phone conversations and private meetings, the IM provided the files long and detailed accounts with "information. " He commented on such things as the food eaten, what happened first, second, third, how much things cost, how much money he was given, what was said by whom to whom about what, and who was in attendance.

Besides gathering such information, an IM was schooled in psychological tactics. At the top of the list for the MfS was the goal of causing disruption, uncertainty, and using repressive measures of demoralization (*Zersetzungmaßnahmen*). Rumors or falsehoods should be spread, in order to denounce or "mob" a person or to disrupt effective work in the group. Spreading mistrust or suspicion was a usual method of disruption.[21] It is highly likely this IM received such training.

Among members of the Berlin Fellowship group, which met in East Berlin, and among those in the East Committee, a high level of trust existed. In keeping with the Stasi methods, the IM managed to be unquestionably included in both of these circles of trust. That allowed him a position of power and left him free to spread distrust, to plant doubt, and to contribute further to what were already marked personality differences in the East Committee. It should be added here that this IM was never suspected or questioned by any member of any of the groupings in Berlin Fellowship.

Berlin Fellowship's various activities from the 1960's through 1989 were faithfully and regularly reported on, and in spite of the IM being a leading voice in the eastern side of the organization and a close friend of the West Berlin leaders, the MfS findings and reports are repetitive, often appear inconclusive, are sometimes contradictory and often seem to belie a poor or even disinterested grasp of the actual activities. Based on repeated evidence that no aspect of Berlin Fellowship nor the key figures' involvement warranted further observation or constituted criminal activity, the two main OV's were officially closed in 1978; however, the IM was assigned a third OV, "*Resident*,"(reports from 1974-1986). A former

[21] Ibid.

officer explained MfS persistence as that which was done "just in case" something would turn up.[22]

No substantial evidence for illegal activity was found, but this one IM continued to be the primary source for all information about the personages and activities from 1969 to 1986 and thus the primary source for most if not all MfS understanding of Berlin Fellowship. His longstanding commitment and regular reporting to his commanding Stasi officer, the chronological unfolding of the reports, plans for subverting Berlin Fellowship's activities, and evaluations of MfS successes, all constitute the bulk of the files. Besides the file on Pastor Ralph Zorn, three other personal files accessed for this research, all containing many copies of reports from the two main operative procedure files.

This curious saga recounted by available MfS files begins with three copies of registration cards for the main IM recruited for service in February of 1968.[23] According to a former MfS officer, this IM could not have volunteered, for no one was ever accepted if he/she volunteered, this aroused too much suspicion.[24]

The exact nature of motivation for this IM remains unknown, but it seems he worked with the MfS out of conviction.[25] No personal file on him was available for this research. However, reference in print in *Die Kirchenpolitik von SED und Staatssicherheit, Eine Zwischenbilanz* by Clemens Vollnhals(ed.) mentions there having been an IM intelligence information report/personal file (*Auskunftsbericht*) on microfilm. [26] That microfilmed report reveals that this IM initiated efforts to infiltrate an "enemy" group (not identified, but I surmise Berlin Fellowship). Also, he was awarded an NVA (National People's Army)bronze, silver and gold service medals for his efforts. In the 90's when this information became known, the IM arranged with his report officer to have his name disassociated with the files.[27] This documented reference to this specific IM is cited from a chapter in Vollnhals' book, which discusses, among other themes, the problem of identifying and working with former unofficial informers. Walter Schilling, author of the chapter and former pastor in Thuringia, notes that as of 1996 the IM in question, refused to acknowledge anything to his regional church leaders. After repeated at-

---

[22] Wiegand interview.

[23] BStU MfS, Abt.XX/4 photocopy of one registration card and two other cards dated February 26, 1968 noting changes made in rank of IM.

[24] Notes from personal interview with former Stasi officer Artur Hermann, former associate director of department XX/4, September 19, Berlin 2007

[25] Vollnhals, Die *Kirchenpolitik*, 244

[26] Ibid.

[27] Ibid.

tempts, I have been unable to gain access to the microfilm data. Furthermore, there are no contemporary remarks in this research from the IM, for he is not available for comment. In addition, there is, to date, also no official "*Klarname*" for this IM (a cover name officially decoded by the Federal Commission for the Stasi Archives). The IM has refused all efforts at contact from Berlin Fellowship members and from colleagues in his own regional church.[28]

7. Conclusion? A few thousand pages and more than twenty years later...

Thus, from as early as 1965 to as late as 1988, the MfS was aware of the activities and of the key persons of the OV "*Rollbahn*." Individuals and their relation to Berlin Fellowship were more or less observed. They and the Berlin Fellowship program in the GDR were viewed as a cover for intelligence-related activities (cf. Chapter 2, Developmental Beginnings). OV "*Radius*" echoes this suspicion. Though not directly interested in Berlin Fellowship, OV "*Resident*" became the collection site for a small number of periodic Berlin Fellowship IM reports through 1986. The bulk of MfS Berlin Fellowship-related material dates from the 1970's, with scattered reports from the 1960's and from the 1980's.

Why there is so little information on Berlin Fellowship in the 1980's may be attributed to that information being kept in active files, which were possibly destroyed in the fall of 1989. It is assumed that the files at hand were most likely the first destroyed in the MfS offices all over the country beginning in late summer. "*Rollbahn*" was already archived, but that doesn't seem to be the case with "*Radius*" or "*Resident.*" One could also reasonably conclude that Berlin Fellowship had ceased to be of interest, was too predictable, too small, or not political enough. As the 80's proceeded, besides those applying to leave and being permitted to exit the country, there were ever-growing opposition groups developing in the GDR, in the church and under its protection. This citizens' movement drew MfS attention away from what may have been judged as '*harmlos*' or '*bedeutungslos*,' (harmless, meaningless....both words affixed to the BF activities by a former MfS officer).[29]

---

[28] Conversation notes, Pfr. i.R. Walter Schilling, September 30, 2006, Guthmannhausen/Thuringia.
[29] Notes from interview with former Stasi officer and director of MfS Dept. XX/4, Joachim Wiegand February 2, 2007.

APPENDIX 2

Potential Code Labels for Fellowship and Mission Interview Manuscript Analysis

Using Chapter 2 of this research and recollection from the interviews, I listed all of the words, concepts, topics, themes related to fellowship or to mission/missionality which might possibly afford this analysis labels for code categories: words related to fellowship, to missionality. This list was the starting point and deductive or prescriptive tool with which I began the coding process:

a window to the west
accompaniment
acknowledgement of other and other as Christian
being noticed, not forgotten, thought of, prayed for
being present to the other
Bible studies
bond
borders
boundaries
breaking of bread
burden
cared for, cared about
caring for the other
celebrating together
changed vision/understanding
close to one another
common meals
common mission witnessing God's grace
common suffering
communion
community
community gains new understanding of self
concern
confession of faith
contacts more important than…
contextual, intercontextual, intercultural
conversation
crossing geographical frontiers
cultural diversity
curiosity about the other's life, society,
faith
desire to just be together
dialogue
different expectations
different views of what "happened" in a meeting
different voice from the dialogue partner noticing how different the contexts are
difficulties with language or communication
dignity, worth, being acknowledged
discovery
dismantling of the picture of the enemy

distance traveled to come
dividing wall broken, hostility dismantled
dwelling place for God
ecumenical
encounter
encouragement
event pointing to the kingdom of God
exchange of ideas
family, household for God
fellowship
fragmented understanding
friendly
friendship
genuine critical accompaniment
gift and reception
gift of koinonia
having goodwill for all
helping the other
hope
human barriers broken
human interaction
identity and openness to the other
in midst of world and as enemy
incarnation
intercession
kingdom of God
learning
learning from the encounter
life together
message shared
mission
missional self-awareness
Mittragen, bearing one another, letting oneself be born
momentary fellowship experience
more than words
mutual acceptance
mutual encouragement
mutual support, mutual responsibility
mutual understanding
nature of the Church
niche
not understanding the other
noting needs
one-time meeting, repeated meetings
open
other brings the message
overcoming differences
participation
partnering
persecuted
personal conversations about faith and pesonal cares
place where God is at work
prayer
presence (ministry of presence)
presence of God
proclamation of faith to one another
reciprocity
recognition of need
recognition of the other
relationship
reminder
revelation
sacrament
share in suffering
share in wealth
shared gospel experience
shared metanarrative
shared theological, spiritual insights
sharing of self
sharing sorrow and joy
sign of solidarity

significance of plurality in the others
solidarity
space shared…making space in oneself
spending time togetherspontaneous nature of the happening
strangers, strangers no more
strengthening of faith
telling and listening to Scripture, the story
telling and listening, sharing message
testimony to Christ, to faith
text or story as focal point
time spent together
trusting
unity
visible fellowship, physical presence of the other
voice of experience from the other
willing acts of kindness, witness and service
worship

APPENDIX 3

Code Category Labels Definitions and Number of Quotations

Codes listed in order of groundedness (number of quotations):

1. DDR context / 266

Direct or indirect mention or reference to the "situation" for the population in the DDR, political, religious, social, educational, etc. In some cases, the DDR context refers to the caution regarding talking about Berlin Fellowship in public, writing letters to the Americans, telephone contact. In other cases, the DDR context for instance, demanded certain behavior, i.e. Americans staying in inter-hotels.

This category acts as the super-context for the entire project. In fact, if the GDR hadn't been the context, things would have been entirely different.

2. Essence of Berlin Fellowship / 228

This category contains phrases, sentences, and replies to the question "What was Berlin Fellowship?" It is perhaps more reflective and theological, though the answers often at first glance seem only to be descriptive of the activity engaged in.

3. Direct result of Berlin Fellowship / 224

Several code categories were melded together in the course of the coding process to compose this code label. Some respondents mentioned that a new *self-understanding* resulted. In other cases, quotations reflect *changes* inside the parish or in the person as a result of the Berlin Fellowship encounter. *After-effects* of the BF experience on parish life in general, the life of the individual speaking, their faith understanding, perspective of the world, the larger Church are also all represented.

4. Personal encounter / 216

People meeting people the fact that a "person" in the flesh is present plays an important role. The issue is either alluded to or directly referred to. Time spent with one another and the getting to know one another intentionally arranged directed conversations, Bible studies, thematic discussions, question/answer sessions are contributing factors to giving the encounter "room" to happen.

5. Recognition / 184

Recognition comprises seeing the "other" or being seen, acknowledging or being acknowledged, considered important, being remembered. This is either directly or indirectly referred to by the eastern German interviewee. In some cases this recognition is in the mouth of the speaker referring to *being* recognized, and in other cases, it refers to them recognizing the "other," the American. *This is a two-way street.* It is the encounter but goes beyond it to the getting to know the other in some way and having a new picture of "them" or realizing something new about them and finding oneself and one's world therefore changed. One interview refers to the Berliner-Gruppe affording this to itself. This was a gathering where evidently everyone could be who they were, doubting Thomases or otherwise and this group was then a great forum for recognition, acceptance and affirmation.

6. Qualitative description of encounter / 161

Adjectives or descriptive phrases, emphasis or repeated terms all reflecting the speaker's evaluation and often emotional descriptive memory of an encounter or of Berlin Fellowship meeting. Virtually all interviewees use adjectives, adjectival phrases and lapse into personal memories or use examples of personal memories to make a point. A few of these stand as "models" for what *happened* in a BF visit.

7. Sharing of a personal memory / 156

Story was often the vehicle for an interviewee to talk about someone or to make a point. These stories are biographical or related to some aspect of the Berlin Fellowship experience that was particularly meaningful. In some cases, they are germane to this research topic, while in others, they seem less so.

8. Conversation / 146

Simple interchange or extended discussion or getting to know one another through introduction rounds or discussions about themes or topics. These conversations (*Gespräche)* are key to the whole Berlin Fellowship experience, and they are mentioned specifically in all but two of the interviews.

9. Name or specific person remembered / 135

Specific U.S. or Berlin Fellowship West Berlin participants are mentioned in the context of the general responses to questions. No questions were asked regarding individuals per se. Their names simply occur.

In 25 of the 27 interviews transcribed, specific names of Americans were used repeatedly. Named most often were Ted Schapp(70x), Bärbel Eccardt(86x) and Ralph Hamburger(40x). 45 other individual names were mentioned . Though not always easily remembered by the interviewee, if I could supply a possible name, usually that 'fit' and was affirmed. Since most of these Americans didn't participate more than once, that any names were remembered is pretty amazing I think.

10. Information learned, corrected / 133

It seems that this code and "different contexts shared" code overlap. In many cases information learned was a correction on the accuracy about the other's national character or the other's country, and this correction was made by both partners in the conversations. This "learning" happened through the encounter because of differences, through the happening itself and because of intentional question and answer sessions.

11. Boundaries, borders / 112

This can refer to the geographic, social, cultural, political boundaries that separate people. It may also refer to the inner-boundaries and borders we carry within us.

Regardless of the context being discussion, the border between the GDR and the visitor is referred to. The visitor, someone from the west represents his/her own country but also the "outside," the rest of the world. This border reality is not complained about or necessarily a topic of conversation. *It is.* This is evidenced by reference to the boundaries and borders and lines of separation in all but two of the interviews.

In recapping these quotes, it seems quite clear that the whole enterprise was clearly affected by the border, the wall and the east/west divide. It also seems clear that this border was also that which affected how the "fellowship" happened in some very unique way.

12. America and Americans / 103

26 of 29 interviewees used the word in some form, and though not coded as such, the word form occurs 380+ times in all interviews. In contrast, the name DDR is mentioned 100 times and reference to Germany (east or west) occurred also approximately 100 times.

13. Different contexts shared / 94

Berlin Fellowship participants from the U.S.A. and the GDR meet and find out how different from each other they are either through casual conversation, guided dialogue or group discussion. Much of the intention on the part of the leadership was to encourage sharing about each side's home and home church, family, school, profession, social situation. The interviews indicate as the participants got to know and trust each other, the differences and the similarities became more apparent.

14. Faith sharing / 78

Direct reference to speech or activity that related to the faith traditions of both Germans and Americans. Often the conversations centered on talk about what it means to be Christian in one's personal context; this was then as well an exchange ideas regarding Christian faith walk. This may also be a direct statement about spirituality or a spiritual moment which occurred during an encounter, or it may be a recollection of an aspect of the sharing and exchange which took place.

15. Other ecumenical/partner contacts / 62

This meant a reference to other ecumenical contacts, partnerships OR comparison of Berlin Fellowship with such. The early years of Berlin Fellowship included visitors from Hungary, Poland, and CSSR (Czechoslovakian Soviet Socialist Republic). 24 interviewees mentioned other foreign or ecumenical contacts. In addition, if there were comparisons made between the West Germans or those the congregation had with "foreigners" like the Dutch, both partnerships and with the Berlin Fellowship experience, which was *not* a partnership. This difference is only seldom commented on and then not always negatively; it seems these recollections all fell into a similar memory slot for many interviewees.

16. Missional witness / 60

One pastor's wife's comment indicates she is very much aware of what the Berlin Fellowship visits said to the larger community..."about the nature of OUR church congregation." In another interview, the interviewee talks about how the openness of the talking about spiritual matters might have rubbed off on the Germans.

Bevans and Schroeder discuss mission being in two directions, one to the world and the other to the church itself, based on a 3-fold structure of word(kerygma), action or service(*diakonia*) and being(koinonia or *martyria*). This synthesis is in many ways what the East Germans attest to. Berlin Fellowship seems to have been a catalyst for the congregations growing internally, though only a few people mention that in so many words. If I had been looking for this category, I may have seen more instances of this.

17. Critical view of BF / 59

Something to do with Berlin Fellowship, its manner, assumptions, *modus operendi* is viewed critically. This is not necessarily negative, though it may be. It may be a reflection upon limitations, shortcomings, foibles of individuals or the whole experience, either because of the Americans, the shortness of the visits, the cultural differences and expectations.

--In some cases, this is a comment regarding the precaution taken which disallowed contact after a visit and thus many names, specifics are lost today to memory....due to communication having been forbidden.

--In some cases, it is a critical view of what kind of people were on teams....

--In some cases, it is a 'learning' from the experience or a carry-over from other ecumenical contacts that makes the speaker critical of the way the program was conducted.

--Finally, several interviews indicate that there were people in some of the parishes, who when they found out about Berlin Fellowship, chose to keep their distance, for whatever reason. It was, for certain professions, unwise or forbidden to have contact with foreigners.

18. Encounter with world beyond the doorstep / 53

Hearing about LIFE somewhere other than what the listener knows or is familiar with. Though this category originally had more quotations, it was pared down, since many of the quotes related more completely to *information learned or corrected* or *different contexts shared* or *borders*. Though the word "world" was often used, the context of many of these quotes refers mostly to the American setting or to Americans. Americans represented the *world* outside?

19. Thematic discussion topics / 50

Reference to topics or themes that were discussed during a Berlin Fellowship visit.

20. Hospitality / 47

This is seldom referred to directly as such, but there are many instances where homes are shared, "guests" are referred to, intentional hospitable actions and emotions described. 17 interviews speak of hospitality in a recognizable manner.

21. Motivation for BF participation / 43

Interviewees give stated reason or reasons for being a regular participant in the Berlin Fellowship program, usually in answer to an interview question.

22. Celebration / 42

Reference primarily to worship, music, prayer, communion giving witness to faith in some form, be it testimony, comments in a Berlin Fellowship meeting, a message or greetings brought to a congregation.

23. Education/exposure for children, youth / 34

These answers often came in answer to one interview question. Children in a family or in the parish are considered by the speaker, or comments reflect the effect on children or youth. This is often in reference to the family of the interviewee but also to the effect on youth in general or on younger people, the youth groups in the GDR being up to age 25 or so.

Several interviewees mention it was important for their parish (or for them personally) to show the children that there were other people, who lived in far-away America, who were flesh and blood, and with whom one could talk to dismantle the "picture of the enemy" and to give the children a glance over the border and outside that condition of being sealed off.

24. Bible study / 34

Reference to either Bible study or discussion or Bible text (*Jahreslosung* or watchword for the year) or thematic group discussion was specifically mentioned in 17 interviews.

The discussions would include exchanges about faith as well as daily life, congregational life in both contexts, and often the American brought a canon (a short round) from Berlin set to the Jahreslosung. Bible discussions were serious and light-hearted at the same time and often went late into the night. Except in a few cases, Bible study is not noted as a center point, though several pastors seemed to think the Amis were particularly good students of the Bible. For several of the pastors this aspect of the visit was central and key. That the Amis talked personally about their faith in this context impressed one interviewee. One person recalled Ted Schapp leading a group, loosening them up and then launching into a very direct conversation with the text. This recollection remains a distinct memory; the speaker says it was something he had not experienced before.

25. Tourist activities / 32

Touristik (tourist activities) included everything from a walk and a picnic to touring a cathedral, to a concert, to a walk to a neighboring congregation, to a graveyard or to see a local monument. Plans often included tourist activities which allowed for individual conversations or time to talk with one or two people instead of in a larger group. In fact one interviewee says conversation was the reason for going on a field trip. There was also a certain and justified degree of pride and joy in showing off the scenery, the churches, the cities, diaconal institutions, going for a walk, and going to concerts doing things which could be shared.

26. Surprise / 31

These comments are either paradoxical or somewhat revealing, self-revealing of the speaker and perhaps not what I, as researcher, necessarily expected. They may also refer to something the speaker seems genuinely surprised about at the time of the interview or was surprised about and is now reflecting on.

27. "Third bank"/ Ephesian moment / 28

cf. Hans de Wit...meeting in between, where both people are no longer at "home" but find themselves and each other in a new "place." One has to give and receive, to let go and hang on, to reckon with the unknown in the other and risk ... and then be changed by the encounter.

In order to truly "meet" there had to be a give and a take, a readiness to step outside the norm, to trust and to go past the limits of standing alone. Both de Wit's "third bank" and M. Volf's concept of "embrace" make for a unique code. In several interviews, the interviewees repeatedly try to put their finger on just what happened when the Berlin Fellowship visit took place. One of those saw this as a place where people find each other ("wo Menschen zueinander finden"). Cf. Andrew Walls' "Ephesian moment". See Chapter 2.

28. Table fellowship / 21

The shared table is seminal in the biblical description of fellowship, and since meals were often shared in the Berlin Fellowship experience, this code is direct reference to shared meals (or to the Lord's Supper, which is also sparsely referred to). This topic is mentioned 21 times in 14 interviews. It is mentioned 7x in relation to celebration, 6x in relation to conversation, 2 times in relation to tourist activity.

29. Picture of the enemy / 18

This refers to the picture of the enemy that either the Germans had of Americans or vice versa. In the case of these interviews the "enemy" was America or Americans, and this was a *given* in the GDR context. This picture is quickly dismantled by the personal encounter, the conversation (and information learned) with recognition taking place in both directions.

30. Belonging / 12

This is an essential element of fellowship and sharing and partnership. One interviewee, when talking about Berlin Fellowship, said his parish "belonged" to the BF program/ministry. This seems to imply mutuality or perceived mutuality, responsibility, and ownership. This code category emerged late, and I think there would be more quotes if I had recognized the category earlier in the coding process.

APPENDIX 4

Biographical Information

Bärbel Eccardt was born in Potsdam, Germany in 1923. In the 1933, the family with five children moved to Berlin, where her father was a judge for the Superior Court of Justice. She studied School and Church Music and German language and literature, but was very ill for years and unable to work. Only in the 60's studied did she study again, this time to be a church parish worker in Berlin. She served in this role, working with Reverend Ted Schapp in the parish and for Berlin Fellowship in the Zinzendorf Congregation from 1970 - 1988. After retiring, Ms. Eccardt continued to be active in building relationships between east and west. She died in 2008.

Ralph Hamburger was born in Hamburg, Germany, in 1923. Escaping Hitler, the family moved to the Netherlands, where he finished high school and endured five years of German occupation. In 1947 he emigrated to the United States and studied at Los Angeles State College and Princeton Theological Seminary. Ordained in 1960, he served two Presbyterian congregations. Hamburger's passion for reconciliation led him back to Germany in the1950's and to encourage Berlin Fellowship in the 1960's and following. From 1975 - 1990, Ralph worked with World Vision International in a wide-reaching ecumenical ministry behind the Iron Curtain. He and his wife Mary live in Pasadena, California.

Ted Schapp was born in 1926 in California. During WWII he served eighteen months in the Philippines as a conscientious objector, studied at University of California, Berkeley and at San Anselmo Theological Seminary, California. After pastorates for eleven years in Presbyterian congregations in California, he and his family moved to Germany in 1963 where he worked in refugee camps in Berlin. From 1970 - 88 he was the pastor of the Zinzendorf Congregation and leader for Berlin Fellowship. Upon retirement, he and his wife returned to California.

Ralph Zorn was born in 1926 in a suburb of Boston, Massachusetts. Though he enlisted in the Navy, illness prevented him serving during WWII. After studying at Washington University, he went to Berlin as a Lutheran vicar. There he met his wife and they married in 1953. Returning to the U.S., where four of their children were born, the Zorn's served in several congregations until 1962 when they returned to Berlin. Ralph Zorn's first connection with Berlin Fellowship was in 1953 with a deputation team from the 1st Presbyterian Church of Hollywood. In the late 1960's and early 1970's he was a team translator and driver. Ralph lives in Berlin.

BIBLIOGRAPHY

Aagaard, Johannes, Trends in Missiological Thinking During the Sixties, in *International Review of Mission*, 62.245, 1973, 8-25.

Ahrberg, Edda, Roger Engelmann, Wilhelm Fricke, *Die Akten und die Wahrheit: Fünf Jahre Stasi-Unterlagen-Gesetz: Vorträge einer Fachkonferenz*, Sankt Augustin 1997.

Auerbach, Thomas, *Hauptabteilung XX : Staatsapparat, Blockparteien, Kirchen, Kultur, politischer Untergrund*, Berlin 2008.

Bakker, Janet Kragt, *Encountering the Church in the Global South: Sister Church Relationships and Their Impact in Select Washington, D.C. Area Churches*, Doctoral Dissertation, Washington, D.C. 2004.

Balbier, Uta A., and Christiane Rösch, *Umworbener Klassenfeind: das Verhältnis der DDR zu den U.S.A.*, Berlin 2006.

Barker, Peter, *The GDR and Its History: Rückblick und Revision : Die DDR im Spiegel der Enquête-Kommissionen*, Amsterdam 2000.

Barnes-Davies, Chen, Nan-Jou; Klagba, Charles; Niles, Damayanti, Toward the Fullness of Life: Intercontextual Relationships in Mission: Report from a Missiology Consultation, London, England 14-19 April, 2002, in: *International Review of Mission* 91.363, 2002, 589-603.

Barram, Michael D., The Bible, Mission, and Social Location: Toward a Missional Hermeneutic, in *Interpretation* 61.1, 2007, 42-58.

——, Located Questions for a Missional Hermeneutic | the Gospel and Our Culture Network, *Gospel and Our Culture Network*, http://-www.gocn.org/resources/articles/located-questions-missional-hermeneutic, accessed September 9, 2009.

——, A Response at AAR to Hunsberger's "Proposals..." Essay| the Gospel and Our Culture Network, http://www.gocn.org/resources-/articles/response-aar-hunsberger-s-proposals-essay, accessed May 4, 2010.

Barth, Karl, *Church Dogmatics, Part IV.3*, Edinburgh 2004.

Barth, Karl, and Johannes Hamel, *How to Serve God in a Marxist Land*, New York 1959.

Bauckham, Richard, *Bible and Mission: Christian Witness in a Postmodern World*, Grand Rapids, Michigan 2003.

Bauerochse, Lothar, *Miteinander leben lernen: Zwischenkirchliche Partnerschaften als ökumenische Lerngemeinschaften*, Erlangen 1996.

Baum, Gregory, *The Church for Others: Protestant Theology in Communist East Germany*, Grand Rapids, Michigan 1996.

Benedict XVI, Pope, Culture, Identity and Church Unity, in: *Ecumenical Review*, 57.3, 2005 358-360.

Berg, Stefan, *Das lange Leben der DDR: Ostdeutsche zwischen Emanzipation und Nationalismus*, Berlin 1995.

Ernst-Bertram, Bettina and Jens Planer-Friedrich, *Pfarrerkinder in der DDR*, Berlin, 2008.

Besier, Gerhard, and Stephan Wolf (Hg.), *Pfarrer, Christen, und Katholiken, Band 1, Das Ministerium for Staatssicherheit der ehemaligen DDR und die Kirchen*, Neukirchen-Vluyn 1991.

Besier, Gerhard, Die Rolle des MfS bei der Durchsetzung der Kirchenpolitik der SED in: *Aktenlage: die Bedeutung der Unterlagen des Staatssicherheitsdienstes für die Zeitgeschichtsforschung* / hrsg. von Klaus-Dietmar Henke und Roger Engelmann, Berlin 1995, 98-117.

Best Thomas and Günther Gassman, *On the Way to Fuller Koinonia: Official Report of the Fifth World Conference on Faith and Order*, Geneva 1994.

Betts, Paul, *Within Walls: Private Life in the German Democratic Republic*, Oxford 2010.

Bevans, Stephen B., *Models of Contextual Theology*, Maryknoll, N.Y. 2002.

——, God Inside Out: Toward a Missionary Theology of the Holy Spirit, in: *International Bulletin of Missionary Research* 22.3, 1998, 102-105.

Bevans, Stephen B., and Roger Schroeder, *Constants in Context: A Theology of Mission for Today*, Maryknoll, N.Y. 2004.

——, *Prophetic Dialogue, Reflections on Christian Mission Today*, Maryknoll, N.Y. 2011.

Bevans, Stephen, Doidge, Eleanor, and Robert J. Schreiter, *The Healing Circle: Essays in Cross-cultural Mission Presented to the Rev. Dr. Claude Marie Barbour*, Chicago, Illinois 2000.

Bickhardt, Stephan (ed), *Recht Ströme wie Wasser: Christen in der DDR für Absage an Praxis und Prinzip der Abgrenzung. Ein Arbeitsbuch*, Berlin 1988.

Blomjous, Joseph, Development in Mission Thinking and Practice 1959 - 1980: Inculturation and Interculturation, in: *Afer* 22.6, 1980, 393-398.

Bonhoeffer, Dietrich, *Life Together*, San Francisco 1954.

——, *Gemeinsames Leben*, München 1982.

——, *Sanctorum Communio, A Theological Study of the Sociology of the Church*, Minneapolis 2009.

Bosch, David Jacobus, *Transforming Mission: Paradigm Shifts in Theology of Mission*, Maryknoll, New York 1992.

——, Bosch, David Jacobus, A *Spirituality of the Road*, Eugene, Oregon 2000.

Brockmeier, Jens, Remembering and Forgetting: Narrative as Cultural Memory, in: *Culture & Psychology,* March 2002, vol. 8, 1, 15-43, http:// cap.sagepub.com, accessed October 13, 2009.

Brown, Colin., *New International Dictionary of New Testament Theology*, Grand Rapids, Michigan 1999.

Brown, Raymond Edward, *The Epistles of John*, Garden City, New York 1982.

Brown, John P., Some Questions on International Relationships in Mission, in: *International Review of Mission*, 86.343, 1997, 411-416.

Brown, John, International Relationships in Mission: A Study Project, in: *International Review of Mission*, 86.342, 1997, 207-273.

Brown, Stephen, *Von der Unzufriedenheit zum Widerspruch: Der Konziliare Prozess für Gerechtigkeit, Frieden und Bewahrung der Schöpfung als Wegbereiter der friedlichen Revolution in der DDR*, 1. Auflage, Wil, 2010.

——, "Introduction to Heino Falcke," in: *Ecumenical Review,* 56.2, 2004, 160–165.

——, Angepasste Kirchenleitungen und aufmüpfige Basis? Die Kirchen im Spiegel der Enquete-Kommission, in: *The GDR and Its History: Rückblick Und Revision : Die DDR im Spiegel der Enquête-Kommissionen*, Peter Barker, Amsterdam 2000, 113-125.

Brownson, James V., Speaking the Truth in Love: Element of a Missional Hermeneutic, in: *International Review of Mission*, 83.330, 1994, 479-504.

Burgess, John P, *The East German Church and the End of Communism*, New York, 1997.

——, Christian Options in East Germany, in: *Christian Century* 103.3, 1986, 72-73.

Callam, Neville, The Mission of the Church in the Perspective of the World Council of Churches' Text on the Nature and Purpose of the Church, in: *International Review of Mission*, 90.358, 2001, 237-242.

Castro, Emilio, A Christocentric Trinitarian Understanding of Mission, in *International Review of Mission*, 89.355, 2000, 584-591.

Childs, David and Richard J. Popplewell, The *Stasi: The East German Intelligence and Security Service*, New York 1996.

Crow, Paul A., Ecumenics as Reflections on Models of Christian Unity, in *Ecumenical Review*, 39.4, 1987, 389-403.

Dähn, Horst, *Die Rolle der Kirchen in der DDR, Eine erste Bilanz*, München 1993.

Dähn, Horst, and Joachim Heise (eds.), *Staat und Kirchen in der DDR: Zum Stand der zeithistorischen und sozialwissenschaftlichen Forschung* 1, Aufl., Frankfurt 2003.

——, *Die Diktatur Der SED - Geschichte und Folgen*, Bornheim, 1994.

De Graaf, Beatrice, *Über die Mauer : Die DDR, die niederländischen Kirchen und die Friedensbewegung*, Münster 2007.

De Gruchy, John W., Faith and Witness on the Boundaries: Bonhoeffer's Enduring Challenge, in: *Journal of Theology for Southern Africa*, 127, 2007, 6-21.

Demke, Christoph, Manfred Falkenau, and Helmut Zeddies, *Zwischen Anpassung und Verweigerung: Dokumente aus der Arbeit des Bundes der evangelischen Kirche in der DDR*, Leipzig 1994.

Deutscher Bundestag (eds.), *Materialien Der Enquete-Kommission Aufarbeitung von Geschichte und Folgen der SED-Diktatur in Deutschland" (12. Wahlperiode Des Deutschen Bundestags). Band VI. Kirchen in Der SED-Diktatur. Teilband 1*, Baden-Baden 1995.

Dulles, Avery, *Models of the Church*, Garden City, New York 1978.

Duraisingh, Christopher, Contextual and Catholic: Conditions for Cross-cultural Hermeneutics, in: *Anglican Theological Review*, 82.4, 2000, 679-701.

——, Mission Towards Reconciled and Intercontextual Communities, in: *International Review of Mission*, 91.363, 2002, 483-499.

Engelsviken, Tormod, Missio Dei: The Understanding and Misunderstanding of a Theological Concept in European Churches and Missiology, in: *International Review of Mission*, 92.367, 2003, 481-497.

Eppelmann, Rainer, Bernd Faulenbach, and Ulrich Mählert, *Bilanz und Perspektiven der DDR-Forschung*, Paderborn 2003.

Falcke, Heino, Christ Liberates -- Therefore, the Church for Others (1972), in Ecumenical *Review* 40:2, 1988, 204-214.

——, The Ecumenical Assembly for Justice, Peace and the Integrity of Creation, in: *Ecumenical Review*, 56.2, 2004, 184-191.

——, *Mit Gott Schritt halten: Reden und Aufsätze eines Theologen in der DDR aus Zwanzig Jahren*, Berlin 1986.

——, The Challenge of the 'New Thinking' in Eastern Europe, in: *Ecumenical Review* 40.2, 1988, 204–214.

——, *Vom Gebot Christi, dass die Kirche uns die Waffen aus der Hand nimmt und den Krieg verbietet: Zum konziliaren Weg des Friedens: Ein Beitrag aus der DDR*, Stuttgart 1986.

——, Was hatte die Barmer Theologische Erklärung den Kirchen in der DDR zu sagen?, http://www.uek-online.de/download/OeRundschau, 28-37.pdf.

——, *Wo bleibt die Freiheit?: Christ sein in Zeiten der Wende*, Freiburg 2009.

Findeis, Hagen, and Detlef Pollack, *Selbstbewahrung oder Selbstverlust. Bischöfe und Repräsentanten der evangelischen Kirchen über ihr Leben in der DDR*, 1. Aufl. Berlin 1999.

——, *Freikirchen im Spannungsfeld von Sammlung und Sendung*, Münster 2000.

Franks, Anne and John Meteyard, Liminality: The Transforming Grace of In-between Places, in: *Journal of Pastoral Care & Counseling*, 61.3, 2007, 215-222.

Frederiks, Martha, Meinderts Dijkstra, and Anton Houtepen (eds.), Towards *an Intercultural Theology: Essays in Honour of Jan A. B. Jongeneel*, Zoetermeer 2003.

Fulbrook, Mary, *Anatomy of a Dictatorship: Inside the GDR, 1949-1989*, New York 1995.

——, *The People's State: East German Society from Hitler to Honecker*, New Haven 2005.

Funkschmidt, Kai, New Models Mission Relationship and Partnership, in: *International Review of Mission*, 91.363, 2002, 558-576.

——, Partnership Between Unequals--mission Impossible? Mission Structures Revisited, in: *International Review of Mission*, 91.362, 2002, 395-413.

García, Alberto L, The Church for Others: Protestant Theology in Communist East Germany, in: *Concordia Journal* 26.3, 2000, 280–282.

Gauck, Joachim, *Die Stasi-Akten : Das unheimliche Erbe der DDR*, Hamburg 1991.

Gibaldi, Joseph and Walter S. Achtert, *MLA Handbook for Writers of Research Papers 7th edition*, New York 1988.

Giesecke, Jens, *Handbuch Der Kommunistischen Geheimdienste in Osteuropa 1944-1991*, Göttingen 2008.

——, Die *Hauptamtlichen Mitarbeiter der Staatssicherheit: Personalstruktur und Lebenswelt 1950-1989/90*, Berlin 2000.

——, *Staatssicherheit und Gesellschaft: Studien zum Herrschaftsalltag in der DDR*, Göttingen 2007.

Gieseke, Jens and Doris Hubert, *The GDR State Security: Shield and Sword of the Party*, Berlin 2002.

Gieseke, Jens, and Hermann Wentker, *Die Geschichte der SED: Eine Bestandsaufnahme*, Berlin 2011.

Gill, David, and Ulrich Schröter, *Das Ministerium für Staatssicherheit: Anatomie des Mielke-Imperiums*, Berlin 1991.

Gill, Theodore A., "Heino Falcke and 'the Church for Others', in: *Ecumenical Review* 56.2, 2004, 157–198

Goeckel, Robert F., *Die Evangelische Kirche und die DDR, Konflikte, Gespräche, Vereinbarungen unter Ulbricht und Honecker*, Leipzig 1995.

——, Die Beziehungen zwischen Staat und Kirche in der DDR: Zehn Jahre angloamerikanischen Studien, in: *Staat und Kirchen in der DDR Zum Stand der zeithistorischen und sozialwissenschaftlichen Forschung*, Horst Dähn and Joachim Heise (eds.), Frankfurt am Main 2003, 203-218.

Goheen, Michael W., As the Father Has Sent Me, I Am Sending You: Lesslie Newbigin's Missionary Ecclesiology, in *International Review of Mission*, 91.362, 2002, 354-369.

——, Notes Toward a Framework for a Missional Hermeneutic | the Gospel and Our Culture Network, http://www.gocn.org/resources-/articles/notes-toward-framework-missional-hermeneutic, accessed January 2010.

——, The Future of Mission in the World Council of Churches, in: *Mission Studies*, 21.1, 2004, 97-111.

Green, Clifford, *Bonhoeffer, A Theology of Sociality*, Grand Rapids, Michigan 1999.

Guder, Darrell L., and Lois Barrett, *Missional Church : A Vision for the Sending of the Church in North America*, Grand Rapids, Michigan 1998.

Guder, Darrell L., Missional Theology for a Missionary Church, in: *Journal for Preachers*, 22.1, 1998, 3-11.

——, Ambassadors for Christ, a Bible study , 2 Corinthians 5:17-21, taken from Clay Jar Christians, Louisville, Kentucky, http://oga.-pcusa.org/perspectives/jun02/bible-study.pdf, accessed January 2010.

——, *The Continuing Conversion of the Church*, Grand Rapids, Michigan 2000.

——, From Mission and Theology to Missional Theology, in: *The Princeton Seminary Bulletin* 24.1, 2003, 36–54.,

——, Missional Church, Forschungsbericht über eine missiologische Debatte in den USA, in: *Theologische Zeitschrift*, 2-66, 2010, 185-198.

——, Walking Worthily, in: *The Princeton Seminary Bulletin*, 28.3, 2008, 251-291.

——, Worthy Living: Work and Witness from the Perspective of Missional Church Theology," in: *Word & World* 25.4, 2005, 424-432.

Hahn, Udo, and Johannes Hempel, *Annehmen und frei bleiben*, Hannover 1999.

Hallesby, Norheim and Bård Eirik, From Ghetto to Communitas: Post-Soviet Youth Ministry and Leadership on a Pilgrimage to Emmaus, in *Journal of Youth and Theology*, 5.1, 2006, 67-84.

Hartweg, Frédéric, and Horst Dohle, *SED und Kirche: Eine Dokumentation ihrer Beziehungen. Bd. 2, 1968-1989*, Neukirchen-Vluyn 1995.

Heise, Joachim, Johannes Gruhn, and Horst Dähn, *Schwierige Gratwanderung: Nach-Denken über die Rolle der evangelischen Kirche in der DDR: 20 Jahre nach der friedlichen Revolution*, Berlin 2010.

Hempel, Johannes, and Udo Hahn, *Erfahrungen und Bewahrungen: ein biographischer Rückblick im Gespräch mit Udo Hahn*, Leipzig 2004.

Henke, Klaus-Dietmar and Roger Engelmann, *Aktenlage: Der Unterlagen des Staatssicherheitsdienstes für die Zeitgeschichtsforschung*, Berlin 1995.

Henker, Martin, and Evangelisch-Lutherischer Kirchenbezirk Leipzig, *Erinnern- Danken- Fragen: 20 Jahre Friedliche Revolution und die Kirchen in Sachsen*, Leipzig 2009.

Henkys, Reinhard, *Die evangelischen Kirchen in der DDR: Beiträge zu einer Bestandsaufnahme*, München 1982.

——, *Gottes Volk im Sozialismus*, Berlin 1983.

Hertzsch, Klaus-Peter, *Laß uns vorwärts in die Weite sehn, Texte zu meiner Biographie*, Stuttgart 2004.

Heydemann, Günther, and Lothar Kettenacker, *Kirchen in Der Diktatur: Drittes Reich Und SED-staat*, Göttingen 1993.

Haukanes, Haldis, Telling Lives. Autobiography and History after Socialism, in *Anthropology of East Europe Review* 23.1, 2005, http://scholarworks.iu.edu/journals/index.php/aeer/article/view/243/320, accessed May 2010.

Hazle, Dave, Practical Theology Today and the Implications for Mission, in: *International Review of Mission*, 92.366, 2003, 345-355.

Hollander, Jet den, Ecclesiology and Mission: A Reformed Perspective, in: *International Review of Mission*, 90.358, 2001, 253-259.

Hollenbach, Michael, Die Rolle der Kirche im Sozialismus - Der Weg der Protestanten bis zur friedlichen Revolution, Deutschlandradio Kultur, *dradio.de*, November 28 2009.

Hunsberger, George R. and Craig Van Gelder, *The Church Between Gospel and Culture: The Emerging Mission in North America*, Grand Rapids, Michigan 1996.

Ives, Edward D., *The Tape-Recorded Interview, A Manual for Fieldworkers in Folklore and Oral History*, Knoxville, Tennessee 1995.

Jacob, Günter, and Francis X. Quinn, The Situation of the Evangelical Church in East Germany, in: *Cross Currents* 7.4, 1957, 327–336.

James, Walter E., *Tumbling Walls*, La Jolla, California, 1990.

——, *Wenn Mauern fallen*, Berli, 1993.

Jansen, Mechteld, God on the Border: Missiology as Critical Theological Guidance for Crossing Borders?, in: *Mission Revisited Between Mission History and Intercultural Theology*, Volker Küster (ed.), Münster 2010, 45-62.

Jarausch, Konrad Hugo, *Dictatorship as Experience: Towards a Socio-cultural History of the GDR*, New York 1999.

Jüngel Eberhard, To Tell the World About God : The Task for the Mission of the Church on the Threshold of the Third Millennium, in: *International Review of Mission,* 89.353, 2000, 203–215.

Käbisch, Edmund, and David Käbisch, *Akteure der friedlichen Revolution: Didaktische Impulse und Materialien für den Geschichts-, Ethik- und Religionsunterricht aus der Region Zwickau*, La Colombe 2010.

Kahl, Werner, Intercultural Hermeneutics--Contextual Exegesis: A Model for 21st-CenturyExegesis, in: *International Review of Mission*, 89.354, 2000, 421-433.

Kamínski, Łukasz, Krzysztof Persak, and Jens Gieseke, *Handbuch der kommunistischen Geheimdienste in Osteuropa 1944-1991*, Göttingen 2009.

Katzorke, Georg, and Klaus Görig, Wolfgang Lindenberg, Ingrid Kaden, *Stückwerke, Partnerschaften zwischen, den evangelischen Kirchengemeinden Elias-Berlin(Ost) und Iserlohn(Westfalen) im politischen Spannungsfeld der Jahre, 1978-1989*, Iserlohn 2002.

Kim, Kirsteen, Missiology as Global Conversation of (contextual) Theologies, in: *Mission Studies*, 21.1, 2004, 39-53.

——, Post-Modern Mission: A Paradigm Shift in David Bosch's Theology of Mission?, in: *International Review of Mission*, 89.353, 2000, 172-179.

——, The Potential of Pneumatology for Mission in Contemporary Europe, in: *International Review of Mission*, 95.378-379, 2006, 334-340.

Kirche im Sozialismus, Dokumentation, Evangelischer Pressedienst, English edition, June 1974.

Kittel, Gerhard and Gerhard Friedrichs, *Theological Dictionary of the New Testament, Abridged in One Volume by Geoffrey Bromiley*, Grand Rapids, Michigan 2003.

Klein, Christoph, Turning to God for Renewal in Mission in Central and Eastern Europe, in: *International Review of Mission*, 87.347, 1998, 473-479.

Kleßmann, Christoph, *Kinder der Opposition. Berichte aus Pfarrhäusern in der DDR*, Gütersloh 1996.

Kool, Anne-Marie, Post-Communist Europe: From 'Intercultural Theology' to Missiology, in *Towards an Intercultural Theology: Essays in Honor of Jan A.B. Jongeneel*, Zoetermeer 2003, 181-196.

——, Trends and Challenges in Mission and Missiology in 'post-Communist' Europe, in: *Mission Studies*, 25.1, 2008, 21-36.

Koschorke, Klaus, Falling *Walls: The Year 1989/90 as a Turning Point in the History of World Christianity*, Wiesbaden 2009.

Koyama, Kōsuke, Extend Hospitality to Strangers: A Missiology of Theologia Crucis, in: *International Review of Mission*, 82.327, 1993, 283-295.

Kraemer, Hendrik, *Religion and the Christian Faith*, Cambridge 1956.

Krötke, Wolf, http://wolf-krötke.de/links.html.

Krusche, Günter, Das ökumenische Engagement des Bundes der evangelischen Kirchen in der DDR, in: *Herbergen der Christenheit 1996. Jahrbuch für deutsche Kirchengeschichte*, Günther Wartenberg, Leipzig 1997, 145-168.

Krusche, Hans-Martin, *Pfarrer in der DDR*, Berlin 2002.

Krusche, Werner, Denkt daran, daß im Herrn eure Mühe nicht vergeblich ist, Synodalvortrag auf der 3. Tagung der VI. Synode des Bundes der Evangelischen Kirchen, 22.-24. Februar 1991, Zinzendorf Collection.

——, Summary of the Lecture of Bishop Krusche, Protestant Church of the Province of Saxony, 3. Conference, VII Synod, Halle, November 17, 1973, Zinzendorf Collection.

Kühn, Ulrich, Credibility of Christian Witness in the German Democratic Republic, in: *International Review of Mission*, 67.266, 1978, 137-140.

Kunter, Katharina, *Erfüllte Hoffnungen und zerbrochene Träume: evangelische Kirchen in Deutschland im Spannungsfeld von Demokratie und Sozialismus (1980-1993)*, Göttingen 2006.

——, The End of the "Kirche im Sozialismus" 1989/90 as a Turning Point for Protestant Churches and Christians in the German Democratic Republic (GDR), in: *Falling Walls The Year 1989/90 as a Turning Point in the History of World Christianity*, Klaus Koschorke (ed.), Wiesbaden 2009.

——, Ein Stück Westen im Osten: Ökumenische Begegnungen zwischen niederländischen und ostdeutschen Christen in den siebziger und achtziger Jahren, in: *Jahrbuch des Instituts für Niederlande-Studien*, 13/2002, Münster 2003, 67-83.

Kunter, Katharina, and Jens Holger Schjørring, *Die Kirchen und das Erbe des Kommunismus: die Zeit nach 1989 - Zäsur, Vergangenheitsbewältigung und Neubeginn; Fallstudien aus Mittel- und Osteuropa und Bestandsaufnahme aus der Ökumene*, Erlangen 2007.

——, *Erfüllte Hoffnungen und zerbrochene Träume: evangelische Kirchen in Deutschland im Spannungsfeld von Demokratie und Sozialismus (1980-1993)*, Göttingen 2006.

Labrenz-Weiß, Hanna, *Abteilung M (MfS Handbuch)*. Hg. BStU, Berlin, 2005, http://www.nbn-resolving.org/urn:nbn:de:0292-9783942130-1720

Langmead, Ross, Transformed Relationships: Reconciliation as the Central Model for Mission, in: *Mission Studies*, 25.1, 2008, 5-20.

Lehmann, Paul L., Contextual Theology, in: *Theology Today*, 29.1, 1972, 3-8.

Lehmann, Theo, *Freiheit wird dann sein: Aus meinem Leben*, Neukirchen-Vluyn 2005.

Lenhartz, Christoph, and Gerhard Besier, *Evangelische Kirche, Demokratie, Stasi-Aufarbeitung*, Editions La Colombe 1997.

——, Die evangelische Kirchen in der DDR im Focus der Forschung. Darstellungen und Quellensammlungen zu Einzelthemen (1990-2009) Teil 1, in: *Theologische Rundschau* 74, 3, 2009, 309-353.

Lepp, Claudia. *Tabu der Einheit?: Die Ost-West-Gemeinschaft der evangelischen Christen und die deutsche Teilung(1945-1969)*, Göttingen 2005.

Lepp, Claudia, and Kurt Nowak. *Evangelische Kirche im geteilten Deutschland (1945-1989/90)*, Göttingen 2001.

Lindenberger, Thomas, SED-Herrschaft als soziale Praxis, Herrschaft und Eigen-Sinn: Problemstellung und Begriffe, in: *Staatssicherheit und Gesellschaft: Studien zum Herrschaftsalltag in der DDR*, Jens Giesecke, Göttingen 2007, 23-47.

Linn, Gerhard, Clarity in Ambiguity : the Witness of the Church in East Germany, in: *Ecumenical Review* 43.3, 1991, 356–363.

Lossky, Nicholas, Jose Miguez Bonino, John Pobee, Tom Stransky, Geoffrey Wainwright, Pauline Webb (eds.), *Dictionary of the Ecumenical Movement*, Geneva 2003.

Madarász, Jeannette Z., *Conflict and Compromise in East Germany, 1971-1989: A Precarious Stability*, New York 2003.

Marsh, Colin, Partnership in Mission: To Send or to Share?, in: *International Review of Mission*, 92.366, 2003, 370-381.

Marshall, Donald G, Memory, History, Forgetting, in: *Christianity and Literature*, 56.2, 2007, 373-376.

Maser, Peter, SED und Kirche, in: *Die Diktatur der SED–Geschichte und Folgen*, Konrad- Adenauer Stiftung, 1994, 29-41.

——, Beitrag zur Klärung der Grundfragen christlicher Existenz? Zur Rolle der Ost-CDU an den theologischen Fakultäten/Sektionen der DDR, in: *Diktaturen in Europa im 20. Jahrhundert-der Fall DDR*, Heiner Timmermann, Berlin 1996.411-420.

Matthey, Jacques, God's Mission Today: Summary and Conclusions, in: *International Review of Mission*, 92.367, 2003, 579–587.

Mau, Rudolf, *Der Protestantismus im Osten Deutschlands:(1945-1990)*, Leipzig 2005.

——, Die evangelische Kirche in der DDR. Zur Forschung seit 1989/90, in: *Staat und Kirchen in der DDR zum Stand der zeithistorischen und sozialwissenschaftlichen Forschung*, Horst Dähn and Joachim Heise (eds), Frankfurt am Main 2003, 141-149.

——, *Eingebunden in Den Realsozialismus: Die Evangelische Kirche als Problem der SED*, Göttingen 1994.

McCloud, Sean, Liminal Subjectivities and Religious Change: Circumscribing Giddens for the Study of Contemporary American Religion," in: *Journal of Contemporary Religion*, 22.3, 2007, 295-309.

Mendt, Dietrich, Christen in Ost und West, Partnerschaften im geteilten und in vereignigten Deutschland, in *Zeichen der Zeit*, 2.96, 62-63.

Menge, Marlies, Kirche in der DDR: Hoffen auf einen besseren Sozialismus, in: *Die Zeit,* 20, 1989.

Middleton, Darren J. N., Between Now and Not-now: On Being Church in Liminal Time, in: *Encounter*, 70.3, 2009, 63-69.

Mission and Evangelism in Unity Today (WCC), in: *International Review of Mission* 88, 348-349, 1999, 109-127.

Moses, John A., The Church Policy of the SED Regime in East Germany, 1949–89: The Fateful Dilemma, in: *Journal of Religious History,* 20.2, 1996, 228–246.

Muhle, Susanne, Hedwig Richter, and Juliane Schütterle, *Die DDR im Blick: ein zeithistorisches Lesebuch*, Berlin 2008.

Neubert, Ehrhart, *Geschichte der Opposition in der DDR 1949-1989*, Berlin 1998.

Newbigin, Lesslie and Paul Weston, *Lesslie Newbigin: Missionary Theologian: A Reader*, Grand Rapids, Michigan 2006.

Newbigin, Lesslie, *Foolishness to the Greeks, the Gospel and Western Culture*, Grand Rapids, Michigan 1986.

——, *The Gospel in a Pluralist Society*, Grand Rapids, Michigan 1989.

——, *Mission in Christ's Way*, Bible Studies, Geneva 1987.

——, *The Open Secret*, Grand Rapids, Michigan 1978.

Niethammer, Lutz, and Alexander von Plato, Dorothee Wierling, *Die volkseigene Erfahrung, Eine Archäologie des Lebens in der Industrieprovinz der DDR*, Berlin 1991.

Niethammer, Lutz, Where were you on July 17?, in: *International Yearbook of Oral History and Life Stories: Volume I: Memory and Totalitarianism*, Luisa Passerini (ed.), U.S.A. 1993, 45-71.

Niles, D. Preman, Toward the Fullness of Life: Intercontextual Relationships in Mission, in: *International Review of Mission*, 91.363, 2002, 471-482.

Nissen, Johannes, Testament in Mission: The Use of the New Methodological and Hermeneutical Reflections, in: *Mission Studies*, 21.2, 2004, 167-199.

Noack, Axel, Die Phasen der Kirchenpolitik der SED und die sich darauf beziehenden Grundlagenbeschlüsse der Partei- und Staatsführung in der Zeit von 1972 bis 1989 in: *Materialien der Enquete-Kommission »Aufarbeitung von Geschichte und Folgen der SED-Diktatur in Deutschland« Band VI,2* / Deutscher Bundestag (12. Wahlperiode), Baden-Baden 1995, 1048-1133.

On Intercultural Hermeneutics: Report of a WCC Consultation, Jerusalem, 5-12 December 1995, in: *International Review of Mission*, 85.337, 1996, 241-252.

Pachuau, Lalsangkima, Engaging the 'Other' in a Pluralistic World: Toward a Subaltern Hermeneutics of Christian Mission, in: *Studies in World Christianity*, 8.1, 2002, 63-80.

——, Missiology in a Pluralistic World: The Place of Mission Study in Theological Education, in: *International Review of Mission*, 89.355, 2000, 539-555.

Plantinga, Cornelius, The Threeness/oneness Problem of the Trinity, in: *Calvin Theological Journal*, 23.1, 1988, 37-53.

Pobee, John S., Mission from Below, in *Mission Studies*, 10.1-2, 1993, 148-170.

Pohl, Christine D., *Making Room, Recovering Hospitality as a Christian Tradition*, Grand Rapids, Michigan 1999.

Pollack, Detlef, *Kirche in der Organisationsgesellschaft : Zum Wandel der gesellschaftlichen Lage der evangelischen Kirchen in der DDR*, Stuttgart 1994.

——, Die friedliche Revolution: Strukturelle und ereignisgeschichtliche Bedingungen des Umbruchs 1989 in der DDR, in: *Jahre des Umbruchs: Friedliche Revolution in der DDR und Transition in Ostmitteleuropa*, Clemens Vollnhals (ed), Göttingen, 2011, 119-139.

——, Die politische und soziale Rolle der evangelischen Kirchen in der DDR aus sozialwissenschaftlicher Sicht, in: *Staat und Kirchen in der DDR Zum Stand der zeithistorischen und sozialwissenschaftlichen Forschung*, Horst Dähn and Joachim Heise (eds), Frankfurt am Main 2003, 69-89.

——, Der Weg in die Anpassung: Stationen der theologischen Entwicklung in den evangelischen Kirchen der DDR, in: *Herbergen der Christenheit*, 20, 1996, 9-25.

——, Von der Mehrheits- zur Minderheitskirche: Das Schicksal der evangelischen Kirchen in der DDR, in: *Die DDR im Rückblick: Politik, Wirtschaft, Gesellschaft, Kultur*, Helga Schultz and Hans-Jürgen Wagener (eds.), Berlin 2007, 49-78.

Porter, Harry Boone, Liminal Mysteries: Some Writings by Victor Turner, in: *Missiology*, 3.4, 1975, 519-524.

Presler, Titus. Mission is Ministry in the Dimension of Difference: A Definition for the Twenty-First Century, in: *International Bulletin of Missionary Research,* 34.4, 2010, 195-204.

The Protestant churches in the German Democratic Republic: partners in mission, in: *Mission Studies* 4.1, 1987, 86-98.

Rapley, Tim, *Doing Conversation, Discourse, and Document Analysis*, Los Angeles 2007.

Reeves, Samuel Broomfield, Jr., *Congregation-to-congregation Relationship: A Case Study of the Partnership Between a Liberian Church and a North American Church*, Dallas 2004.

Richebächer, Wilhelm, MISSIO DEI: The Basis of Mission Theology or a Wrong Path? in: *International Review of Mission*, 92.367, 2003, 588–605.

Richter, Hedwig, *Pietismus im Sozialismus: Die Herrnhuter Brüdergemeine in der DDR,* Göttingen 2009.

——, Wir spürten den Herzschlag brüderlicher Liebe, Vom transnationalen Austausch der Herrnhuter Brüdergemeine im Kalten Krieg, in: *Umworbener Klassenfeind: das Verhältnis der DDR zu den U.S.A.*, Berlin, 2006, Uta A. Balbier and Christiane Rösch (eds), Berlin 2006.

——, Rechtsunsicherheit als Prinzip. Die Herrnhuter Brüdergemeine und wie der SED-Staat seine Untertanen in Schach hielt, in: *Die DDR im Blick: ein zeithistorisches Lesebuch*, Susanne Mühle, Hedwig Richter, and Juliane Schütterle, Berlin 2008, 77-85.

Ritchie, Donald A., *Doing Oral History, a Practical Guide*, Oxford 2003.

Rittberger-Klas, Karoline, *Kirchenpartnerschaften im geteilten Deutschland. Am Beispiel der Landeskirchen Württemberg und Thüringen*, Göttingen 2006.

Robert, Dana, Cross-Cultural Friendship in the Creation of Twentieth-Century World Christianity, in *International Bulletin of Missionary Research*, 35.2, 2011, 100-107.

Ross, Kenneth R., Beyond Religious Tourism: Twinning as a Missionary Method, http://www.rethinkingmission.org.uk/article_ross08.html, accessed May 2009.

Rubin, Herbert J. and Irene S. Rubin, *Qualitative Interviewing: The Art of Hearing Data*, Thousand Oaks, California 2005.

Rueschemeyer, Marilyn, *The Quality of Life in the German Democratic Republic: Changes and Developments in a State Socialist Society*, Armonk, New York 1989.

Sabrow, Martin (ed.), *Erinnerungsorte der DDR*, München 2009.

Salvation in a Socialist Society: A Report from the German Democratic Republic, in: *International Review of Mission*, 61.241, 1972, 73-78.

Scandrett-Leatherman, Craig, "Ritual and Resistance: Communal Connectivity in a Church Retreat, in: *Missiology*, 27.3, 1999, 311-331.

Scherer, James A., Missiology as a Discipline and What It Includes, in: *Missiology*, 15.4, 1987, 507-528.

Schilling, Walter, and Rainer Volz, *Akteneinsicht: Staatssicherheit von Innen: Eine Dokumentation aus dem Alltag des Mielke-Ministeriums*, Bochum 1993.

Schneider, Horst, *Unter dem Dach der Kirche: "Bürgerrechtler" in der DDR*, Berlin, 2010.

Schönherr, D. Albrecht, The Evangelical Church as a Learning Community in a Changing World, in *Religious Education*, 78.3, 1983, 398-412.

——, *Gesprochen zur Zeit und zur Unzeit. Reden, Aufsätze, Predigten 1937-1994*. Berlin 1998.

——, *Gratwanderung*, Leipzig 1992.

Schröter, Ulrich, and Helmut Zeddies, *Nach-Denken: zum Weg des Bundes der evangelischen Kirchen in der DDR : im Auftrag des Kirchenamtes der EKD für die Arbeitsgemeinschaft zur Aufarbeitung der Vergangenheit*, Frankfurt am Main 1995.

Schottstädt, Bruno, Experience in the German Democratic Republic, in: *Mennonite Quarterly Review*, 55.3, 1981, 198-201.

Schreiter, Robert J., Cutting-Edge Issues in Theology and Their Bearing on Mission Studies, in: *Missiology*, 24.1, 1996, 83-92.

——, *Mission in the Third Millennium*, Maryknoll, New York 2001.

——, Reconciliation and Healing as a Paradigm for Mission, in: *International Review of Mission*, 94.372, 2005, 74-83.

Scholz, Johannes, Staatssekretär für Kirchenfragen, in: *Freikirchen Forschung 2000. Freikirchen im Spannungsfeld von Sammlung und Sendung*, Verein der Förderung freikirchlicher Geschichte und Theologie an der Universität Münster e.V. 2000, 259-291.

Schultz, Helga, and Hans-Jürgen Wagener, *Die DDR im Rückblick Politik, Wirtschaft, Gesellschaft, Kultur*, Berlin 2007.

Sebastian, J.Jayakiran, Interrogating *missio Dei*: From the mission of God towards appreciating our mission to God in India today, www.edinburgh.2010.org.

Seidel, Thomas (ed), *Gottlose Jahre? Rückblicke auf die Kirche im Sozialismus der DDR*, Leipzig 2002.

Schulze, Harald, *Berichte Der Magdeburger Kirchenleitung Zu Den Tagungen Der Provinzialsynode 1946-1989*, Göttingen 2005.

Shenk, Wilbert R., Christian Mission and the Coming 'Clash of Civilizations', in: *Missiology* 28.3, 2000, 291-304.

——, Leslie Newbigin's Contribution to Mission Theology, in: *International Bulletin of Missionary Research*, 24.2, 2000, 59-60.

Silomon, Anke, Harry Oelke, and Siegfried Hermle, *Anspruch und Wirklichkeit der »besonderen Gemeinschaft«*, Göttingen 2006.

Silverman, David, *Doing Qualitative Research: A Practical Handbook*, London 2006.

Spindler, Marc and John Pobee, Hermeneutics of Mission, in: *Missiology*, 7.1, 1979, 81-85.

Stackhouse, Max L., *Apologia : Contextualization, Globalization, and Mission in Theological Education*, Grand Rapids, Michigan 1988.

——, Contextualization and Theological Education, in: *Theological Education*, 23.1, 1986, 67-84.

Starkloff, Carl F., Church as Structure and Communitas: Victor Turner and Ecclesiology, in: *Theological Studies*, 58.4, 1997, 643-668.

Stasi-Aufarbeitung in der Thüringer Landeskirche, Dokumentation einer Tagung in der Evangelischen Akademie Thüringen, Gutmannshausen 29. September bis 1. Oktober, 2006, epd Dokumentation, Nr. 16, 17 April 1, 2007.

Strafgestzbuch der DDR, StGB, und angrenzende Gesetze und Bestimmungen, Herausgegeben vom Ministerium der Justiz, Staatsverlag der DDR, Berlin 1976.

Stein, Detlef W., and William Totok, *Die Kirchen in Osteuropa im Kommunismus*, Berlin 2008.

Steinhoff, Anthony J, Pietismus im Sozialismus: Der Herrnhutter Brüdergemeine in der DDR, in: *Journal of Moravian History*, 10, 2011, 121–123.

Suckut, Siegfried, *Das Wörterbuch der Staatssicherheit : Definitionen zur "politisch-operativen Arbeit*," Berlin 2001.

——, (ed.), *Die DDR im Blick der Stasi 1976: Die geheimen Berichte an die SED-Führung*, Göttingen 2009.

Suckut Siegfried, Ehrhart Neubert, Walter Süß, Roger Engelmann, Bernd Eisenfeld, Jens Gieseke, *Anatomie der Staatssicherheit, Geschichte, Struktur und Methoden/MfS-Handbuch*, Berlin 1995.

Sundermeier, Theo, *Den Fremden wahrnehmen: Bausteine für eine Xenologie*, Gütersloh 1992.

——, Missio Dei Today: On the Identity of Christian Mission, in *International Review of Mission*, 92.367, 2003, 560-578.

——, Understanding the Stranger: Aspects of Interreligious Hermeneutics, in *Currents in Theology and Mission*, 29.3, 2002, 181-188.

Taylor, Charles and Amy Gutmann, *Multiculturalism: Examining the Politics of Recognition*, Princeton, New Jersey 1994.

Timmermann, Heiner, *Diktaturen in Europa im 20. Jahrhundert - der Fall DDR*, Berlin 1996.

Van Gelder, Craig, *The Missional Church in Context: Helping Congregations Develop Contextual Ministry*, Grand Rapids, Michigan 2007.

Vansina, Jan, trans. H.M. Wright, *Oral Tradition, a Study in Historical Methodology*, New Brunswick 2006.

Volf, Miroslav, *After Our Likeness: The Church as the Image of the Trinity*, Grand Rapids, Michigan 1998.

——, *Exclusion and Embrace: a theological exploration of identity, otherness, and reconciliation*, Nashville 1996.

——, *The End of Memory, Remembering Rightly in a Violent World*, Grand Rapids, Michigan 2006.

——, The Trinity Is Our Social Program: The Doctrine of the Trinity and the Shape of Social Engagement, in: *Modern Theology*, 14.3, 1998, 403-423.

Vollnhals, Clemens, *Die Kirchenpolitik von SED und Staatssicherheit: Eine Zwischenbilanz,* Berlin 1996.

——, *Jahre Des Umbruchs: Friedliche Revolution in der DDR und Transition in Ostmitteleuropa*, 1. Auflage, Göttingen 2012.

Vollnhals, Clemens, and Jürgen Weber, *Der Schein der Normalität : Alltag Und Herrschaft in Der SED-Diktatur,* München 2002.

Vosloo, Robert, Reconciliation as the Embodiment of Memory and Hope, in: *Journal of Theology for Southern Africa*, 109, 2001, 25-40.

Walls, Andrew F., *The Cross-cultural Process in Christian History: Studies in the Transmission and Appropriation of Faith*, Maryknoll, N.Y. 2002.

——, The Ephesian Moment, in *The Cross-Cultural Process in Christian History*, Maryknoll, N.Y. 2002, 72-81.

Wartenberg, Günther, *Herbergen der Christenheit 1996. Jahrbuch für Deutsche Kirchengeschichte*, Leipzig 1997.

Weber, Jürgen, *Der SED-Staat : Neues über eine vergangene Diktatur,* München, 1994.

West, Charles C, Josef Hromádka and the Witness of the Church in the East and West Today, in *Communio Viatorum*, 32.4, 1989, 231-243.

Weston, Paul, *Lesslie Newbigin, Missionary Theologian, a reader*, Grand Rapids, Michigan 2006.

Wijsen, Frans J S., Intercultural Theology and the Mission of the Church, in: *Exchange*, 30.3, 2001, 218-228.

Winter, Friedrick, *Die Evangelische Kirche der Union und die Deutsche Demokratische Republik. Beziehungen und Wirkungen*, Bielefeld 2001.

——, Zeitgeschichtliche Arbeit zur Evangelische Kirche in SBZ und DDR (1945 – 1989), in: *Herbergen der Christenheit 1996. Jahrbuch für Deutsche Kirchengeschichte*, Günther Wartenberg, Leipzig 1997, 59-76.

Wit, Hans de, trans. H. Jansen, *My God, she said, ships make me so crazy, Reflections on Empirical Hermeneutics, Interculturality, and Holy Scripture*, Amsterdam 2008.

Wolle, Stefan, *Die heile Welt der Diktatur: Alltag und Herrschaft in der DDR:1971-1989*, Berlin 1998.

Wright, Christopher. *The Mission of God: Unlocking the Bible's Grand Narrative*. Downers Grove, Illinois 2006.

Wrogemann, Henning, Der Fremde in der Systematik Jürgen Moltmanns, in *Studien zum Verstehen fremder Religionen, Band 5, Den Fremden Wahrnehmen*, Gütersloh 1992, 212-223.

Yong, Amos, As the Spirit Gives Utterance: Pentecost, intra-Christian Ecumenism and the Wider Oikoumene, in: *International Review of Mission*, 92.366, 2003, 299-314.

Yow, Valerie Raleigh, *Recording Oral History*, Thousand Oaks, California 1994.

Zeitreise DDR, Elf Beiträge zur DDR-Geschichte, Leipzig 2009.

Zizoulas, Johannes von Pergamon. Gr.-orth. Metropolit), The Church as Communion: A Presentation on the Conference Theme, in: *EPD Dokumentation*, 41/93, 63-72.

Digital Resources

Bevans, Stephen, The Mission Has A Church, Perspectives of a Roman Catholic Theologian, www.edinburgh2010.org (accessed November 2011).

Brownson, James V., "A Response at SBL to Hunsberger's "Proposals..." Essay, http://www.gocn.org/resources/articles/response-sbl-hunsbergers-proposals-essay (accessed July 2011).

Gieseke, Jens (ed.), *Die hauptamtlichen Mitarbeiter des Ministeriums für Staatssicherheit(MfS-Handbuch),* BStU, Berlin 1996. http://www.-nbn-resolving.org/urn:nbn:de:0292-97839421302572. 3.

Gospel and Our Culture Network, GOCN, http://www.gocn.org/ (accessed August, 2005).

Hunsberger, George, Proposals for a Missional Hermeneutic: Mapping the Conversation | the Gospel and Our Culture Network, http://www.gocn.org/resources/articles/proposals-missional-hermeneutic-mapping-conversation (accessed June 2009).

——, Notes Toward a Framework for a Missional Hermeneutic, The Gospel and Our Culture Network, http://www.gocn.org/resources-/articles/notes-toward-framework-missional-hermeneutic (accessed June 2010).

Krötke, Wolf, http://www.wolf-kroetke.de/links.html (accessed July 2012).

Müller-Enbergs, Helmut (ed.), *Die inoffiziellen Mitarbeiter (MfS-Handbuch)*. BStU. Berlin 2008. http://www.nbn-resolving.org-/urn:nbn:de:0292-97839421302647 (accessed July 2012)

Sebastian, J. Jayakiran, Interrogating *missio Dei*: From the mission of God towards appreciating our mission to God in India today, www.edinburgh.2010.org (accessed May 2011).

Suckgut, Siegfried, *Die DDR im Blick der Stasi 1976: Die geheimen Berichte an die SED-Führung,* BStU: http://www.bstu.bund.de-/DE/Wissen/MfS-Dokumente/DDR-Blick-Stasi/_node.html. (accessed July 2012).

United Church of Christ, http://globalministries.org/get-involved/church-to-church-partnerships/GLobal-Church-Partnerships.pdf (accessed February 2013).

World Council of Churches:

Baptism, Eucharist and Ministry,12th ed., Geneva, 1982, http://www.-oikoumene.org/en/resources/documents/wcc-commissions/faith-and-order-commission/i-unity-the-church-and-its-mission/baptism-eucharist-and-ministry-faith-and-order-paper-no-111-the-lima-text.html?b2lrb=322586, (accessed May 2010).

Called to be the One Church (as adopted by the Assembly) An invitation to the churches to renew their commitment to the search for unity and to deepen their dialogue, 2006, http://www.oikoumene.org/en-/resources/documents/assembly/porto-alegre-2006/1-statements-documents-adopted/christian-unity-and-message-to-the-churches-/called-to-be-the-one-church-as-adopted.html, (accessed January 2010).

Mission and Evangelism in Unity Today, Geneva 2005, http://www.-oikoumene.org/en/resources/documents/wcc-commissions/mission-and-evangelism/cwme-world-conference-athens-2005/preparatory-paper-n-1-mission-and-evangelism-in-unity-today.html (accessed August 2009).

Mission as Ministry of Reconciliation, Geneva, 2005, http://www.-oikoumene.org/resources/documents/wcc-commissions/mission-and-evangelism/cwme-world-conference-athens-2005/preparatory-paper-n-10-mission-as-ministry-of-reconciliation.html (accessed November 2010).

Mission and Evangelism in Unity Today, CWME Preparatory Paper, Geneva, 2000, A9, http://www.oikoumene.org/en/resources/documents/wcc-commissions/mission-and-evangelism/cwme-world-conference-athens-2005/preparatory-paper-n-1-mission-and-evangelism-in-unity-today.html (accessed August 2009).

The Nature and Mission of the Church: A Stage on the Way to a Common Statement, Faith and Order Paper 198, Geneva, 2005, AII 29, http://www.oikoumene.org/en/resources/documents/wcc-commissions/faith-and-order-commission/i-unity-the-church-and-its-mission/the-nature-and-mission-of-the-church-a-stage-on-the-way-to-a-common-statement.html (accessed November 2009).

On the Way to Fuller Koinonia, Message of the World Conference, Message of the World Conference, Geneva, 1993, http://www.oikoumene.org (accessed May 2009).

The Unity of the Church: Gift and Calling – The Canberra Statement, February 2, 1991, http://www. oikoumene.org (accessed March 2012).

The Unity of the Church: Gift and Calling—The Canberra Statement, Geneva, 1991, http://www.oikoumene.org/en/resources/documents/wcc-commissions/faith-and-order-commission/i-unity-the-church-and-its-mission/the-unity-of-the-church-gift-and-calling-the-canberra-statement.htmln (accessed January 2010).

ARCHIVAL COLLECTIONS

I. Bundesarchiv, Berlin
II. Hauptstadt Archiv Dresden
III. Landeshauptarchiv Schwerin
IV. Schwerin Stadtarchiv
V. Land Brandenburg Archiv, Potsdam
VI. Landesarchiv Berlin
VII. Archiv für Christlich-Demokratische Politik, Konrad-Adenauer-Stiftung e.V., Sankt. Augustin
VIII. Evangelisches Zentralarchiv, Berlin
IX. Missionsarchiv, Konsistorium der EKBO
X. Archived materials in the United States
Hamburger Collection, Fuller Theological Seminary Archive, Pasadena
Berlin Fellowship Collection, Presbyterian Historical Society, Philadelphia
XI. Private collections
Zinzendorf Collection, Berlin (private holdings)
Private holdings: Gerlinde Haker (Schwerin), Günter Mieth (Detmold) Wolfgang Müller (Dresden), Joachim Tutzschke (Barnewitz), and photographs from Markus Gemeinde and the Vödisch Family (Plauen)
XII. Ministry for State Security Files, Federal Commission for the Stasi Files, Berlin

The so-named *Stasi* files are cited with their OV file names (OV/Operative Procedure): "*Rollbahn*," "*Radius*" or "*Resident*," volume and page number. The BStU or Federal Commissioner for the State Security Archives (*Bundesbeauftragte für die Unterlagen des Staatssicherheitsdienstes der ehemaligen Deutschen Demokratischen Republik*) cataloging numbers are as follows:

BStU, MfS, BV Gera, Abt. XX, Reg.-Nr.—X547/71, Archiv-Nr. 1456-78 (6 Volumes)
OV-"*Rollbahn*" (Ted Schapp, Bärbel Eccardt, Ralph Zorn).

BStU, MfS, BV Berlin, Abt. XX, Reg.-Nr.—XVI644-73/84, Archiv-Nr. 1486/84 (5 Volumes) OV-"*Radius*" (Ursula Unterumsberger, Friedrich Wilhelm Merckel and a Superintendent in Weissensee).

BStU, MfS, BV Berlin, Abt. XX, Reg.-Nr.— X/476/84. Personal copies of OV-"*Resident*" for Ralph Zorn. MfS AKG0342.

BStU, MfS, BV Berlin, Abt. XX, Reg.-Nr.— 20954/92. Personal copies of portions of an individual's file for Bärbel Eccardt, Band 54 labeled BE54, from 1965-1979.

BStU, MfS, BV Berlin, Abt. XX, Reg.-Nr.— 20955/92. Personal copies of portions of an individual's file for Bärbel Eccardt, Band 55 labeled BE55 from 1973-1978.

BStU, MfS, BV Berlin, Abt. XX, Reg.-Nr.— XV 1644/73, Archiv Nr. 1486/84, Band I-V "*Radius*" for Ursula Unterumsberger

Curriculum Vitae

Jane Holslag was born in 1948 in Denver, Colorado and graduated from the University of Colorado at Boulder in 1970 with a Bachelor of Arts in English. After three years of junior high school teaching, she joined the ministry staff of the First Presbyterian Church in Colorado Springs, serving first as a youth intern, then as Director of Junior High Ministries, and finally as Director of Youth. Upon graduating from Princeton Theological Seminary in 1982, she was ordained and served as Associate Pastor at Irvine Presbyterian Church and as an active presbyter in Los Ranchos Presbytery in southern California. In 1990, she entered into global mission service with the Presbyterian Church (U.S.A.), serving as Coordinator for Ecumenical Relationships in Central and Eastern Europe. Her mission service, based in Berlin and coordinated with the Evangelical Church of Berlin-Brandenburg, afforded her contact primarily with Reformed congregations in the eastern portion of Germany and in the Czech and Slovak Republics, Hungary, Romania, Poland and Lithuania. Seconded by the Presbyterian Church (U.S.A.), to teach at LCC International University in 1997, she moved to Lithuania, where she has served as Chair of both English and Theology departments and also as Academic Council Chairperson.

Mechteld Jansen
Inter Related Stories
Intercultural Pastoral Theology
This study seeks to clarify the *inter* in the word ''intercultural'', especially when it comes to the interaction of people from different cultural backgrounds coming together in a pastoral situation. As critical reflection on intercultural pastoral care, intercultural pastoral theology is relevant for immigrant congregations as well as for non-immigrants' churches and parishes that are increasingly being confronted with questions of intercultural relationships in public and private life. The study starts with the intimation of God's presence in the inter-space of awe and responsibility that occur between people truly sharing their life stories.
ContactZone – Explorations in Intercultural Theology, vol. 11, 2011, 248 pp., 24,90 €, br., ISBN-CH 978-3-643-90193-4

Bendangjungshi
Confessing Christ in the Naga Context
Towards a Liberating Ecclesiology
ContactZone
Explorations in Intercultural Theology
LIT

Mi-Rang Kang
Interpretative Identity and Hermeneutical Community
A Biblical Hermeneutics for Women's Group Bible Study in the Korean Context
In this study Mi-Rang Kang (*1969 in Seoul) investigates the role of women in Korean church life and society and shows possibilities for their empowerment. By transposing Paul Ricoeurs hermeneutics into her own context, she wants to contribute to the formation of Korean Christian women's identity. Along the lines of the book of Ruth she develops a Bible didactical theory for her own church. At the same time the book will also give Western readers an insight into one of the major Presbyterian denominations in Korea, little known so far.
ContactZone – Explorations in Intercultural Theology, vol. 7, 2011, 256 pp., 24,90 €, br., ISBN 978-3-643-10313-0

LIT Verlag Berlin – Münster – Wien – Zürich – London
Auslieferung Deutschland / Österreich / Schweiz: siehe Impressumsseite